HIGH-LEVEL CONSUMPTION

Its Behavior; Its Consequences

BY
WILLIAM H. LOUGH
President, Trade-Ways, Inc.

WITH THE ASSISTANCE OF
MARTIN R. GAINSBRUGH

McGRAW-HILL BOOK COMPANY, Inc.
NEW YORK AND LONDON
1935

THE MAPLE PRESS COMPANY, YORK, PA

PREFACE

This book is addressed, in the first instance, to business men. It offers measurements and forecasts of national consumption which should help us to steer clear of some of the worst blunders of the 1920's.

Commercial research and promotional organizations, advertising agencies, sales departments, and merchants will find data on which to base more sensible appraisals of potential markets.

Financial counselors, banking houses, and all types of investors may derive from the data some additional light on the relative stability and expansibility of various lines of trade and industry.

The responsible executives of business enterprises may get usable suggestions on sound strategy and planning under present-day conditions.

The book is addressed, also, to a wider audience. Statistical studies of consumption have been for the most part fragmentary. Many doubtful assumptions and conclusions have followed. More important, the changed character of consumption when it advances beyond the subsistence level and the unsettling effects of high-level consumption have been generally neglected.

Those who are interested in economic and social questions will discover in the following pages considerable fresh material bearing on consumers' savings, family borrowings and spendings, costs of distribution of consumption goods, American habits of living, validity of cost-of-living indexes, main sources of instability of consumption, and the feasibility of achieving a workable balance between consumers' demands and productive capacity.

Those who are concerned primarily with national policies will perhaps see more plainly the unsolved difficulties inherent in attempted control by government of production and investment, a control which implies either foreknowledge or regulation of consumers' demands.

Consumption is the chief x-factor in many of our vital problems. Well-grounded estimates of consumers' outgo, if correctly analyzed and interpreted, have much to contribute, I believe, to a clearer understanding of depression and recovery.

Unfortunately, the estimates here submitted are not at all points well-grounded, because essential data are lacking. But they will have to serve provisionally. More intensive work in this field by many hands is an urgent need.

* * * *

Just as this study, the product of a four-year investigation, was completed in manuscript, the Brookings Institution published "America's Capacity to Consume."[1] Included in the publication are estimates of the consumption expenditures and the savings of the American people in 1929—estimates using a different method and derived from different sources than were employed in forming the corresponding estimates to be presented herein. In part the two sets of estimates substantially agree; in part they diverge widely. An explanatory comparison is called for. Rather than intersperse scattered notes, it seems better to bring all my comments together in Appendix G.

* * * *

Much of this book is devoted to statistical tabulations. The necessarily detailed explanations which accompany them make hard going for readers whose taste for statistics is not highly cultivated. May I suggest to them that they can skip the most arid passages and get the gist of the matter by reading the Introduction, the chapter on "Findings," the summary of Part Two near the end of Chapter IX, and Parts Three and Four.

Full credit is due to my associate in preparing the book, Martin R. Gainsbrugh, for his unstinted and intelligent labor in compiling and organizing the statistical data here reported.

WILLIAM H. LOUGH.

NEW YORK CITY,
    January, 1935.

[1] By Maurice Leven, Harold G. Moulton, and Clark Warburton, Brookings, Washington, 1934.

240

HIGH-LEVEL CONSUMPTION

CONTENTS

PART ONE
MEASUREMENT
CHAPTER I

CHAPTER II

CHAPTER III

PART TWO
ANALYSIS
CHAPTER IV

CHAPTER XI

CHAPTER XII

PART FOUR

DEDUCTION

CHAPTER XIII

CHAPTER XIV

APPENDIXES

APPENDIX A

APPENDIX B

PAGE

APPENDIX C

APPENDIX D

APPENDIX E

APPENDIX F

APPENDIX G

LIST OF TABLES

INTRODUCTION

HIGH-LEVEL CONSUMPTION IN RELATION TO BALANCE AND RECOVERY

"Consumption," wrote Adam Smith, "is the sole end and purpose of all production; and the interest of the producer ought to be attended to only so far as it may be necessary for promoting that of the consumer. The maxim is so perfectly self-evident that it would be absurd to attempt to prove it."

The maxim has been universally accepted. But it has had only lip service, particularly on the part of economists. The facts about consumption, its trends, its effects on the development of the productive system—all have been almost completely ignored. Economic texts, evidently influenced by a feeling that something has to be said about consumption, usually offer some outdated generalities and a few irrelevant homilies on thrift and prudence in buying goods, and thereupon move hastily to more fruitful subjects.

The general neglect of consumption as a field of study is partly explainable by the scarcity of data. To measure consumers' takings is a difficult undertaking—how difficult will be amply illustrated in this book. The more fundamental reason, however, is that almost until our own generation the subject seemed hardly worth investigating. Consumption was practically a predetermined, constant factor in the economic scheme—a simple process of grasping for whatever food, clothing and shelter could be produced and making them last as long as possible. The process went on decade after decade without substantial change. No wonder economists found little to say about it.

Simon N. Patten was perhaps the first to bring out prominently the altered role of consumption in a surplus economy—an economy in which the output of goods is considerably more than enough to provide for the prime needs of the population. He foresaw the day when consumption would rise far above its former level of bare subsistence for the many plus some gewgaws for the wealthy few. That day has since arrived; and has set in motion new forces which neither Patten nor anyone else could foresee.

HIGH-LEVEL CONSUMPTION, STILL AN ENIGMA

In the seven years 1923–1929 consumption in this country was on a far higher level than any large number of men had ever before experienced. More than three-fifths of American families, according to competent estimates, after covering their subsistence requirements had money to spare for comforts and luxuries. Gewgaws, no longer restricted to the few, were mainly for the many. Widespread prosperity was acclaimed—quite properly—as a remarkable achievement. But no one stopped to inquire seriously into its consequences.

Even now when some of the damaging consequences are plainly visible their source is not commonly recognized. The essentially different character acquired by consumption when it climbs well above the subsistence level is only vaguely understood. The new problems it creates for industry and trade have not even been defined—not to speak of their being solved. High-level consumption is still an enigma; and that will remain its status until it has been patiently measured and analyzed.

One plain characteristic of high-level, in contrast with low-level, consumption is its fickleness. Offerings to consumers, if they are to hold their markets, must be continually remodeled —always with a risk that the supposed improvements will fail to "click." Popular demands are apt to shift suddenly, undermining whole industries.

An associated characteristic is unpredictability. True, we may foresee with practical certainty, as this book will endeavor to demonstrate, the broad lines of consumption at any given level of spending power; but this is quite different from foreknowing the precise objects which future consumers will accept.

Fickle, unpredictable consumption supplies only treacherous guidance for business foresight and planning. It bedevils the markets for consumers' goods, once so orderly and dependable. On top of that, it starts waves of disturbance that spread from one end to the other of the economic system. Wherever its influence reaches, it upsets delicately balanced adjustments between production and consumption and leaves wreckage behind. It is a major cause of losses, of unemployment, of dislocations, and of that general state of unbalance which we customarily refer to as depression.

If these statements appear exaggerated, I trust that judgment on them will be suspended until the facts have been submitted. This book aims, first of all, to set forth the essential facts about consumption in recent years in the United States—facts which have been left too long unstudied. It aims, second, to make such analyses and forecasts as the facts can support. It seeks, finally, a factual, rational answer to the life-or-death riddle which is posed to our generation: how to attain a lasting, workable balance between expanding productive capacity, on one side, and a high-level—that is, a fickle and unpredictable—consumption, on the other side.

Consumption Shares Its Power with Investment

The stress which has just been given to the dominating power of consumption in the economic system is not intended as an endorsement of the feather-headed fallacies of the spend-and-grow-rich school. Its members make a hurried leap from the indisputable axiom that consumption is the end-all of production to a conclusion that consumption is at all times the sole master of the economic mechanism. And from this dogma sprouts the delusion that giving people more money to spend is the sovereign remedy for economic ills. Repeatedly it is asserted in effect that high wages or large doles or redistribution of income would increase consumption and thereby automatically restore an active, prosperous economy.

Unfortunately the general neglect to study consumption— particularly, the failure to examine carefully the actual incidence on the productive system of increments to spending power—has left straight-thinking economists poorly supplied with factual ammunition. I trust some of the material in this book will be found useful. The remarks which follow are designed merely to clarify the issue.

A distinction should be drawn between the immediate effects of consumers' demands and their long-range effects. The prospective volume of consumption at an acceptable price governs the current output of most kinds of consumers' goods. Some items, on the other hand, are so inflexibly controlled by fixities of production—as is true of farm products and many intangible goods—that the output cannot be either enlarged or curtailed on short notice. The control exercised by consumers' demands over current output, therefore, is extensive but not complete. A more important point is that consumers' partial control of *current* output does not in itself determine productive capacity. It is in essence an ephemeral influence.

The truly vital relationship is on a different plane; it is the relationship between (*a*) present expectations of consumers' *future* demands and (*b*) *projected* alterations in productive capacity. The great mass of economic activity as now carried on is not to be quickly improvised; it requires long periods of preparation and a large investment of capital. Those types of production, therefore, which will eventuate in new or altered capacity *respond in the first instance not to consumption but to investment*. The investment, to be sure, if it is well thought out, is grounded in estimates of future consumption; but it is affected also by availability of capital funds, by confidence in social institutions and by expectations of profits as well as of sales.

Consumption, then, is a powerful force but not the absolute monarch of the economic realm. Current consumption does indeed directly control output; and prospective consumption indirectly controls productive capacity. In the latter field, however, it shares its power with investment. Increased consumption alone may stimulate one sector of output; but unless consumption and investment work together, the economic system cannot enjoy a healthy development.

With this preliminary statement of viewpoint in mind, it may be helpful to sketch rapidly the ground to be covered in the present study and to indicate its bearing on the problem of recovery.

FIRST, GET THE FACTS

Curiously enough, the enthusiasts for the doctrine that enlarged purchasing power is the key to prosperity have never put forth the slightest effort to ascertain the facts about the actual demands of consumers. In order to get the facts it is necessary to build up new estimates on the basis of census data and other source material.

These estimates are designed to cover the entire range of consumers' outgo in the United States for the nine censual years in the 23-year period 1909–1931. Statistics for later years are not available at this writing; and they are not necessary for our prime purpose, which is to learn more about the behavior of high-level consumption. The estimates are summarized in Part One;

they are detailed and their construction explained in Appendixes A to E.   It will be made plain that the results are far from exact; but they are submitted as fairly reliable and as conforming to customary standards of tolerance for estimates of this general character.

The findings presented in Part One have many possible uses, as for example:

Correcting false or exaggerated views about actual sales of specific lines
Revealing changes in consumers' habits of living and spending
Yielding data of value in devising methods of taxation
Ascertaining the changing proportions of tangible goods (commodities) and of intangibles in consumption
Determining the approximate proportions of consumers' annual income withheld from spendings for current consumption and used for taxes and for savings
Examining the special characteristics of American habits of living and spending in contrast with British and German habits.

In short, the findings, in spite of their unavoidable inexactness, permit a much closer approach to *comprehensive measurements* of the outgo of American consumers than has hitherto been possible.   They replace numberless loose assertions of personal opinions by definite statements of facts—in some instances confirming or only slightly modifying the assertions and in other instances disproving them.   "When you can measure what you are speaking about and express it in numbers," wrote Lord Kelvin, "you know something about it, but when you cannot measure it, when you cannot express it in numbers, your knowledge is of a meagre and unsatisfactory kind."

MOTIVES AND TRENDS

Once having the figures, what useful information can we extract from them as to the factors that determine consumers' demands? This is the question to be answered in Part Two.   The answer is sought mainly through various reclassifications of the items measured in Part One—that is to say, through statistical analysis.   The estimates listed in the base tabulation (Appendix A) are broken down into 249 items, or minor groups, arranged in 57 sub-classes which are placed under 12 major classes.   This is as fine a breakdown as it is feasible to derive from census data. A great variety of possibly useful reclassifications, additional to those included in the present study, might be made.   The analyses in Part Two utilize only the major classes and main subclasses of the base tabulation.

An initial difficulty must first be overcome. The estimates reported in Part One and appendixes are stated in current dollars; and during the 23-year period 1909–1931 the purchasing capacity of dollars fluctuated over a wide range. The estimates are restated, therefore, in terms of dollars of 1913 (that is, dollars with the same purchasing capacity as dollars of 1913); and this is the unit employed throughout Parts Two and Three.

Starting from this base, Part Two attempts to discover by statistical analysis the motivations affecting consumption and the behavior of consumption under the conditions prevailing in the 23-year period studied. I have no disposition to put forward the results as conclusive. Yet they shed a certain glimmering light, I believe, on some interesting and important questions:

Persistent trends of outgo which indicate expansion or retraction of consumers' demands for certain classes of objects

Proportions of various classes of outgo required for subsistence in accordance with American standards

The relative influence at various levels of outgo of five basic human wants

Stabilizing factors in consumption; their relative strength and the proportions of outgo under their sway in pre-war and in post-war years

Sources of instabilities in consumption and their effects on major classes of spendings

Responsiveness of broad classes of consumers' demands to (a) price changes, (b) changes in average family spending power and (c) temporal changes in the social-economic environment

The effects of the numberless offerings of closely similar competitive or substitute goods in enhancing the instabilities of consumption.

The general conclusion is that consumption appears to be more and more characterized by instability, the hazards of which are intensified by massing of consumers' demands. Fluctuations are almost certainly becoming steeper and deeper; hence, more and more dangerous to the body economic.

What Lies Ahead?

So long as the American people were rapidly gaining numbers and at the same time maintaining their zest for productive effort, forecasts of consumers' demands were scarcely needed. Markets for customary types of consumers' goods were constantly expanding. With ordinary business judgment, disastrous mistakes in gauging future demands were unlikely.

Since the war the situation has been radically altered. Consumption has grown much more volatile. Enterprises catering to long-established demands may at any moment discover that they are resting on quicksands. Unceasing watchfulness for signs of shifts in consumers' tastes and buying habits is essential. In order to interpret the signs intelligently it is necessary to be guided by forecasts of the broad movements of consumption.

To supply such forecasts is the function of Part Three. The forecasts are rooted in the measurements and analyses reported in Parts One and Two; plainly they are subject to the limitations and uncertainties referred to above and more fully discussed in the text. Moreover, forecasts can be made only for assumed conditions which may or may not be realized. Hence, the forecasts in Part Three emphatically are not offered as unqualified predictions. They are in the nature of projections of trends which now seem likely to persist. They are designed to be used with great caution and to be frequently checked and modified.

As one means of getting a line on the probable behavior of consumption when the national average family outgo reaches a higher level than has as yet been experienced, our calculated spendings at various levels of average family total outgo for food, clothing, home maintenance and "all other" objects are brought into comparison with *recorded* expenditures of groups of families on about the same levels; and our projected lines indicating probable spendings at higher levels are compared with recorded expenditures at those levels. The comparisons in general tend to confirm the reasonableness of the projections and thus supply a limited independent support of the forecasts.

Practical forecasts, however, cannot be made solely on the strength of mathematical projections. Some weight must be allowed for the influence of observed factors which seem likely to govern the output of offerings of consumers' goods and to condition consumers' reactions to anticipated offerings. A rapid survey of the social-economic scene endeavors to appraise the force and trends of the chief factors.

Projected spendings and withholdings for the 12 major classes of objects are then correlated; they constitute our forecasts of distribution of outgo at higher levels of average family spending power. In order to give more definiteness to the forecasts, they are associated with a projected rise of average family spending power to the $2,500 level (1913 dollars) in some year in the latter half of the 1940's. However, the forecasts must be understood as referring primarily to higher spending power whenever it may be attained. The greatest relative gains, as here forecast, are in outgo for home maintenance, particularly housing and household services, for savings and taxes (combined), for alcoholic beverages, for personal appearance and for recreation.

SOME USEFUL BY-PRODUCTS OF THE STUDY

Statistical computations and analyses of consumers' outgo, as previously observed, have been strangely neglected. For that reason the present study throws light on a number of questions not mentioned above because they lie somewhat outside the main line of inquiry.

The proportion of consumers' commodities in the grand total of commodities entering into commercial transactions; and the proportion of total productive effort devoted to movable goods which centers in the final stages of producing consumers' commodities.

Costs of distribution figured as a ratio of total payments for consumers' commodities, a ratio that shows a surprising tendency toward uniformity throughout the 23-year period studied; its steadiness is partially explained by a supporting calculation of the amount of retail sales to consumers per person engaged in mercantile pursuits.

The ratio of mercantile debts (open accounts and installment accounts) incurred for purchase of consumers' commodities to the totals of such purchases, a ratio which is also surprisingly steady; the big increase in the load of family debt, as shown by a supplementary inquiry, has come in personal finance loans, not in mercantile accounts.

New indexes of the price levels (a) of all consumers' purchases and (b) of all consumers' purchases and acquisitions of assets; the indexes are made up by applying specific price indexes to the spendings and withholdings of the national body of consumers.

A tentative revision of Engel's Four Laws of Consumption designed to adapt them to modern conditions and to the entire body of American consumers.

Certain deductions as to the practicability of national planning and as to the type of business management called for in order to cope with the increased hazards created by volatile consumption.

The first five of the subjects just listed are more or less incidental features of Parts One, Two and Three, and they need not be further treated at this point. The last one, however, bears so directly on the vital problem of maintaining a lasting, workable balance that it is discussed at some length in Part Four.

AN ANSWER TO THE RIDDLE

The life-or-death riddle of our times—how to achieve equilibrium between high-powered productive capacity and high-level consumption—is enormously complicated by the element stressed in this study, to which insufficient attention has been given, namely: the undependability of high-level consumption—its weakly motivated, feeble resistance to forces of depression; its slow, uncertain resilience in the early stages of recovery. Because of this factor, in conjunction with other factors named in the text, our present-day economy is continually agitated and liable to quick deterioration under any severe strain. If we are to maintain a working balance between *future* productive capacity and *future* consumption, which is the crux of the problem, it is necessary to develop, as was pointed out some years ago by the Committee on Recent Economic Changes, "a new technique of balance."

The only two solutions which offer themselves are considered in Part Four. The one solution now most loudly advocated, the installation of a planned economy, is there rejected on the ground that long-distance planning is impracticable without far more exact and reliable forecasts of consumption than are attainable. The other solution—namely, the evolution of more flexible forms of business enterprise directed by more alert, better-informed brains—is accepted as practicable, partly on the ground that even the rudimentary forecasts now available supply useful guidance for resourceful management. Essentials to the success of the second solution are improvements in business practice and revised conceptions of business ability which are defined in Part Four. Given these improvements, private business can successfully adapt itself to the more explosive economy which is in prospect; and by adapting itself it can save society from dangers which now seem overwhelming.

Regaining a High-Level Balance

The conclusions just summarized have a direct bearing on the nearby outlook for recovery from the depression. Recovery is essentially a process of regaining balance—not, to reiterate, merely a superficial balance between output and consumers' takings but a deep-seated all-pervading balance between the capacity of the economic system to turn out an immense variety of goods, on one side, and the potential, effective demands of consumers, on the other side.

From this conception of balance it follows that recovery cannot possibly be achieved by tinkering with current output, either to restrict it or to force its expansion—still less by handing money to people and urging them to spend. A little sputter of activity may ensue but will infallibly die down shortly, because it does not generate a dependable demand for capital equipment, for construction, and for products which require a lengthy period of gestation. Thus a quarter to a half of the economic system is left dormant—a condition obviously incompatible with economic balance and good health.

In a capitalistic society the impetus to recovery is normally given by the hopes and plans of men who are willing to risk capital in undertakings that will not come to fruition in the immediate future; this is investment. If consumption at the same time expands, as it will whenever liberal investment feeds the spending power of wage-earners and other consumers, a working balance is gradually established in both hemispheres—that is, (a) between consumption and consumers' goods and (b) between investment and capital goods. Day by day the circle of activity spreads—more funds are offered, more enterprises are started, more wages and salaries are paid out, more profits are gained and reinvested. A healthful, self-sustaining recovery thus gets under way.

All this is simply restatement of orthodox theory. The theory has been generally ignored in the last few years and sometimes ridiculed; but in spite of all the vaporings from Washington, it has not to my knowledge been annulled. One increasingly suspects that the theory, even though orthodox, may be right.

If it is right, foresight is the mother of recovery. Correct foresight supplies well-grounded hopes of profitable enterprises and practical plans for realizing the hopes. Foresight of economic developments for any considerable distance ahead implies some kind of forecasts of consumers' demands; for to these demands the whole economic system must adjust itself in the long run. No enterprise is powerful enough to override them; no enterprise is small enough to slip out from under their domination.

We come back, then, to renewed emphasis on the necessity of more accurate knowledge of the trends of consumers' spendings and withholdings, looking particularly toward forecasts of consumers' expansible demands. So long as consumption was restricted by productive capacity to a level little above bare subsistence, forecasts were so easy and certain as to have little practical importance; but when consumption, actual or potential, climbs to a high level, forecasts become difficult and at the same time essential.

It is a clearer understanding of the behavior of high-level consumption that is sought in this study. Insofar as the effort proves successful, it will provide a sounder basis for farsighted investment and business management; and thereby for a realistic program of recovery to a high-level balance.

PART ONE
MEASUREMENT

CHAPTER I

DEFINITIONS

Part One undertakes to show approximately how the American people use their incomes. At first glance the problem looks simple—a bit tedious perhaps to solve, but plain enough in principle. As one digs into it, however, he quickly encounters puzzling questions of logic; and, what is worse, irreconcilable disparities between the demands of logic and the niggardly supply of data.

Most of these difficulties can be set aside until we reach the particular problems to which they pertain. The fundamental concepts governing the entire inquiry, however, need to be defined at the outset; unless they are clearly grasped, the findings may easily be misconstrued.

To begin with, the term "consumers" is far from self-defining. Frequently, it is stretched to include all final takers of specified goods, even when the goods are to be converted or combined with some kind of service and resold. Thus, fully 5% of the output of finished articles of food is sold to hotels and public institutions, and such sales have been at times considered part of consumption. This may be proper when the aim is to ascertain total takings of foods, but it involves duplication when the aim is to ascertain total outgo of consumers; for that term includes under another head consumers' spendings at hotels for food, as well as for services, and their payments of taxes which provide the wherewithal for food purchases by public institutions. This is but one example of the ever-present danger of counting the same transactions two or three times. A partial safeguard is to confine the term "consumers" strictly to *natural persons*, excluding corporate entities, societies and institutions.

However, many natural persons—49 million of them, according to the 1930 Census—function not only as consumers but also as gainfully employed producers. Acting in their producer capacity, they purchase numerous articles—for instance, paint, farm implements, typewriters and automobiles for business use—which cannot properly be classed among the objects of consumers' spendings. Furthermore, they often indulge themselves in the practice, most reprehensible and annoying to the earnest-minded statistician, of making one purchase serve two ends: their pleasure in consumption, and their efficiency in production. Obviously, no one can tell with certainty just where to draw the line between natural persons acting as producers and the same persons acting as consumers. Yet the distinction must be kept in full view and applied so far as is humanly practicable. In point of fact, the distinction creates serious doubts in only a few of our estimates, the most prominent of which are purchases of automobiles and acquisitions of income-producing property.

The third element in our definition of "consumers" is particularly essential to a correct understanding of the measurements to be reported. The inquiry is concerned with *national* estimates of consumers' outgo. This implies that consumers are to be envisaged *as a national body*, not as an aggregate of individuals. Our estimates refer to transactions between the whole body of consumers, on one side, and business, professional and institutional individuals or organizations, on the other side. Transactions between one individual and another, when neither one is acting in his customary income-producing capacity, are eliminated, even when such transactions are cleared through commercial channels; for they are in effect nothing more than transfers from one consumer to another. Examples are: personal loans from individuals to individuals; trade-ins by individuals of used cars and other second-hand articles which are resold by dealers at substantially equal prices to other individuals; incidental services, outside the circle of customary money-making activities, rendered by one individual to another. Sound thinking and estimating demand that this principle be clearly grasped and applied as rigorously as the data will permit. Otherwise, we soon find ourselves lost in a mass of non-commercial transfers which are practically endless and meaningless.

Combining these three elements, we arrive at a definition for the purposes of this study which readers should bear in mind: *Consumers, as the term is here used, are (a) natural persons (b) acting in their consumer-capacity only and (c) treated as a national unit, not as an aggregate of individuals.*

OTHER DEFINITIONS AND LIMITATIONS

For the sake of clarity, it is necessary to introduce some additional definitions of terms which will be employed in a somewhat specialized sense.

Consumers' goods include all items of consumption, both tangible and intangible, which are ready-for-purchase by consumers: that is, items which do not require further distribution or processing except, in some instances, at the hands of consumers themselves. Note that the definition expressly excludes many semi-finished articles, especially of food and clothing, which are often loosely called "consumers' goods." Tangibles will be here referred to as *commodities*. Services, rentals, contributions and the like will be grouped under the heading *intangibles*.

Consumers' outgo comprehends all money disbursements by consumers from the national income. These disbursements include both *spendings* for consumers' goods and *withholdings* from spendings.

Consumers' spendings cover not only disbursements of money for consumers' goods but also uses of goods owned by the consumer *when such uses have recognized commercial value*. Accordingly, consumption of home-grown food products and rentals ascribable to owned homes are taken into account as consumers' spendings; but the pleasures derived from possession by consumers of automobiles, furniture and other durable consumers' goods are excluded on the ground that they are psychological values not measurable in monetary terms. The distinction requires cutting out, when comparisons with national incomes are to be made, a large portion, though not all, of what King calls "imputed income."[1]

Consumers' withholdings are the amounts withheld from spendings and used either (*a*) for taxes directly paid by individuals or (*b*) for savings. *Consumers' savings* are the net amounts of current income devoted to the acquisition of potential income-producing assets; for example, life insurance policies, bank deposits, securities and other ownership interests in business enterprises, and real estate. Periodic increases in these assets will be referred to as *consumers' acquisitions*.

Consumers' intake (or *takings*) is a coined term to designate the real value of goods and acquisitions purchased by consumers in a given period. *Real value* in an absolute sense cannot of course be measured; but changes in consumers'

[1] See "The National Income and Its Purchasing Power" by Willford Isbell King, National Bureau of Economic Research, New York, 1930, p. 73. For the reason indicated in the text, it would seem that in measurements of national income a distinction might well be made between imputed psychological and imputed monetary values. It is of some interest to note that an English statistician takes a similar position. "For the purpose of this investigation, whenever the 'durable consumption goods' (*e.g.*, private motor cars) pass into the hands of the consumer, consumption is considered to take place then and there. But an arbitrary line is drawn at dwelling-houses, which represent the largest item in 'consumers' capital'; they are reckoned as capital goods in this investigation." "The National Income, 1924–1931" by Colin Clark, Macmillan, London, 1932, p. 3.

takings of equivalent units, starting from a selected base (*e.g.*, takings in 1913), may be approximated.

Statistical estimates of consumers' outgo· or intake, like statistical estimates of income, are practicable only for lawful products and activities. Payments to bootleggers, dealers in narcotics, prostitutes, professional gamblers, hold-up men, racketeers and kidnapers, for instance, are left out of the reckoning. An apparent exception is made by including a portion of the estimated payments for alcoholic beverages during the years when they were legally banned; this is done because a considerable fraction of these payments were not for bootleggers' services but for such commodities as alcohol, labels and bottles, and to that extent the payments passed into legal trade channels.[2]

Consumers' spending power, as the term is here used, is synonomous with consumers' total outgo. It plainly connotes disbursement of money, which is the first subject of study. In order to avoid unnecessary hair-splitting, the same term is retained when we get into an analysis (Parts Two and Three) of consumers' intake, though *consumers' purchasing power* would be a shade more precise.

From the foregoing definitions are derived two important limitations of the estimates to be presented. First, they do not include all monetary transactions in which consumers take a hand; both inter-consumer dealings and most illegal purchases are ruled out. Second, they do not show total sales of the various commodities, intangibles and acquisitions of property to be itemized *but only sales to consumers;* sales to business, professional and institutional individuals and organizations are ruled out. These limitations should be kept in mind whenever the present estimates are compared with other estimates or are adapted to any other purpose than the one here in view. The limitations are deliberately imposed in order to approach as near as possible to accurate measurements of the sums expended by the national body of consumers.

METHOD OF MEASUREMENT

Only two practicable methods of measuring consumers' outgo are open: (*a*) to collect records of family expenditures and accept them as samples from which to compute the national figures; (*b*) to start with census and other records of output and by a

---

[2] The sums involved are far from negligible. Warburton arrives at an estimate of total payments to bootleggers in 1929 of over $4,000,000,000 ("The Economic Results of Prohibition" by Clark Warburton, Columbia University Press, New York, 1932, pp. 165ff.) and Lynch believes that the annual cost of racketeering is more than $7,000,000,000 ("Criminals and Politicians" by Dennis Tilden Lynch, Macmillan, New York, 1932).

series of steps derive from them estimates of purchases by consumers.

The first method has the great advantage of being relatively easy. It has been adopted by some competent authorities[3] and is used in this study (Chapter X) as a rough check on estimates formed by the second method. But it suffers from very serious, not to say fatal, defects.

1. The samples are inadequate in size and number.

2. They are of uneven merit, and some are highly questionable.

3. For the most part the available records are several years old; they do not properly represent later habits of living.

4. Few of them classify expenditures in any detail; and these few follow no standard classification or terminology. Hence, they provide usable information only on broad, self-defining classes of objects.

5. By far the greater number cover the outgo of carefully selected low-income families judged to be capable of keeping accurate accounts. At any rate, those are the families which in the end do their part well and contribute most of the published records. The selection obviously creates a strong bias toward representing the more settled and thrifty families rather than the run of the population.

In spite of these drawbacks, the family expenditure records yield rather surprisingly consistent and trustworthy national estimates for food and clothing. They give some help in figuring trends of outgo for home maintenance. Beyond that, they are of little use for the present purpose.

The second method has difficulties and defects of its own, but on the whole is far preferable. It will be so fully presented in later chapters that it need not be discussed here.

By any method, accurate measurements, in a literal sense, of consumers' outgo are unattainable. The facts do not march out in orderly array from census tomes or from any other records. On the contrary, they are scattered and hidden here and there over the whole socio-economic terrain. And after the fugitive facts have been ferreted out and assembled, they must pass through a laborious process of interpretation and regimentation before they are fit to be presented as usable data. All the figures in this book—without exception, I think—are built-up estimates; and like all other estimates they are quite properly subject to

[3] See "Economics of Consumption" by Paul H. Nystrom, Ronald, New York, 1929; "The Consumption of Wealth" by Elizabeth Ellis Hoyt, Macmillan, New York, 1928; and the recent publication "America's Capacity to Consume" by Maurice Leven, Harold G. Moulton and Clark Warburton, Brookings, Washington, 1934. The findings of the last-named study are examined in Appendix G.

question and revision.   It is not to be expected that all of them, ranging as they do over wide, unexplored areas, and extending through a 23-year period (1909–1931), will prove free from error.

ESTIMATES OF OUTGO SHOULD BE COMPREHENSIVE

The estimates are designed to be comprehensive.   Such items as have been entirely omitted are believed to be negligible. Comprehensiveness is indispensable in order to observe the authentic trends of consumers' spendings.   Nearly all items for which separate estimates can be made—for example, specific articles of food or clothing—are closely associated with other items; and their relations are apt to be so fluid and interactive that a study of the one item alone may be definitely misleading.

A second reason of practical importance is that comprehensive estimates can be compared with authoritative figures independently compiled.   A comparison with estimates of national income appears in the next chapter.   Another comparison of especial value can be made between our findings of total spendings for commodities and the findings of the Census of Distribution, taken in 1930, covering sales at wholesale and at retail for the year 1929; it will be found in Appendix B.   The results for 1929 obtained by the two distinct methods are close enough to establish a presumption that the formulae employed in our computations for 1929 may properly be applied, with slight modifications, in earlier years and in 1931.   Numerous other checks, some of which are referred to in later chapters, have been made against independent estimates of sales of items or groups of items.

More significant is internal evidence of the general consistency of the comprehensive estimates to be reported.   If they were widely divergent from actualities, it is probable that somewhere in the series errors would have synchronized or accumulated and would thus have produced incredible results.   No such malformation appears on the surface; nor has anything of the kind been brought to light by the varied lines of analysis in Part Two.

On the whole, though our estimates are obviously rough and in some spots, discussed in the appendixes, are highly uncertain, it seems unlikely that they can be so far from the truth as to invalidate the broad findings which are now to be summarized.

Chapter II

FINDINGS

This chapter summarizes some of the chief results of our statistical study of consumers' outgo. For the most part, it merely presents facts, leaving interpretation to later chapters.

Explanations and details omitted from this chapter will be found in Appendixes A, B, C, D and E. Those who care to do so are requested to examine the explanations critically, to judge their reasonableness for themselves and to propose whatever corrections are called for.

All measurements in Part One, with one minor exception, are computed *in current dollars*. They must be used cautiously, therefore, in making year-to-year comparisons. Partly for that reason, some of the estimates are restated in terms of percentages of total outgo, which gives a clearer view of changes in their relationships. In Parts Two and Three, however, the current dollar estimates are translated into comparable figures by applying price indexes. Judgments as to long-term trends should be suspended until the corrections for variations in price levels have been presented.

Twelve Major Classes of Outgo

Inasmuch as the main source of data is the Census of Manufactures, complete estimates of consumers' outgo can be prepared only for the censual years, as shown in Table 1. Prior to 1919, the interval between censuses of manufactures was five years; since 1919, two years. Because of the uncertainty of some of the estimates (based on non-census data) for two pre-war years, 1909 and 1914, and also because neither one of these years alone is a satisfactory representative of pre-war spending power and living habits, we have adopted a "pre-war average year" (an arithmetical average of the figures for 1909 and 1914) as a base from which to measure changes in the post-war era.

The classification shown in Table 1 conforms as closely as practicable to the customary groupings of expenditures in family budget studies. Some of the headings may not be entirely self-explanatory.

Transportation consists mainly of purchases and upkeep of automobiles and includes also local bus and street railway fares; but railroad travel, or rather that portion not treated as business expense, is assigned to the recreational group.

TABLE 1.—SUMMARY OF OUTGO BY 12 MAJOR CLASSES, 1909–1931[1]

(In billions of current dollars)

Major Classes	1909	1914	Pre-war Average	1919	1921	1923	1925	1927	1929	1931
Total Outgo...........	29.2	33.6	31.4	65.9	59.1	70.2	79.3	83.4	89.4	63.7
Food and Soft Drinks..	7.4	8.9	8.2	18.5	13.9	16.1	17.9	18.3	19.6	13.5
Alcoholic Beverages (payments to legal industries only)......	1.8	2.0	1.9	2.0	1.4	1.5	1.7	1.8	2.0	1.3
Tobacco..............	0.6	0.7	0.7	1.4	1.5	1.5	1.5	1.6	1.7	1.4
Clothing.............	3.6	4.0	3.8	8.1	8.0	9.4	9.2	9.7	9.9	7.1
Transportation........	1.1	1.7	1.4	4.1	4.3	6.2	7.7	7.3	8.5	5.6
Home Maintenance.....	7.4	8.3	7.8	12.1	13.4	16.5	18.3	20.5	22.9	18.9
Sickness and Death....	0.9	0.9	0.9	2.1	2.0	2.4	2.6	2.8	3.2	2.6
Personal Appearance...	0.4	0.5	0.5	1.0	1.0	1.3	1.4	1.5	1.7	1.2
Recreation............	1.2	1.5	1.3	2.3	2.6	3.1	3.5	4.0	4.7	3.1
Social-Cultural Activities.................	1.9	2.1	2.0	3.6	3.7	3.7	4.1	4.4	4.8	3.9
Taxes (directly paid by individuals).........	....	....	....	1.4	0.8	0.8	0.9	1.0	1.2	1.0
Savings..............	2.8	3.0	2.9	9.4	6.5	7.8	10.6	10.4	9.3	4.1

[1] Derived from Appendix A.

Home Maintenance covers furnishings, household supplies, fuel, rentals, domestic servants, commercial and public utility services pertaining directly to households—in fact, all expenditures for shelter in a broad sense.

The greater part of *Sickness and Death* is made up of payments for medicines, physicians' fees, hospital expense and the like; funeral expense, also, is placed under this head.

Social-Cultural Activities comprise a miscellany of spendings for books, instruction, fraternal dues and the like, as well as contributions to churches and charities.

The items included in each of the 12 groups, as listed in Appendix A, constitute working definitions of their make-up.

SUMMARY OF CONSUMERS' OUTGO BY MAJOR CLASSES
(In Billions of Current Dollars,   Based on Table 1)
Ratio Scale

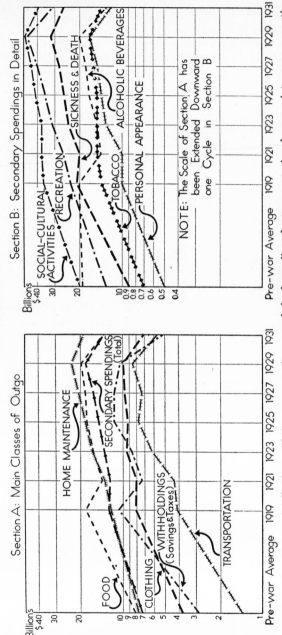

Section A: Main Classes of Outgo

Section B: Secondary Spendings in Detail

CHART A.—Note especially the rapid rise, as prosperity expanded, of spendings for transportation, home maintenance, recreation and personal appearance; and the relative steadiness of clothing, food and tobacco. As a rule, the declines in 1929–1931 were more or less correlated with the speed of the preceding advances; but withholdings, in spite of preceding sluggishness, fell off most sharply of all.

The movements of the 12 classes of outgo become clearer when we examine Chart A. Section A graphs the four largest classes of spendings, namely: food, clothing, home maintenance and transportation. To make the showing complete, it represents also (a) withholdings from spendings, which are taxes and savings, and (b) secondary spendings—that is, spendings for the six smaller classes of outgo. The feature of chief interest is the relative rate of expansion from the post-war low of 1921 to the height of 1929. As might have been expected, transportation went up most rapidly, followed in order by home maintenance, withholdings, food, secondary spendings and clothing. In the 1929–1931 decline, transportation and withholdings suffered the greatest relative losses, followed by food, home maintenance, clothing and secondary spendings. But when price changes are taken into account, the showing will be considerably modified.

Section B of Chart A graphs the movements of the six smaller classes. Their striking features are: the rapidity of the rise from 1921 to 1929 of spendings for recreation, personal appearance, and sickness and death; the slower rise of alcoholic beverages and social-cultural activities; and the steadiness of tobacco. In the slump the heaviest relative losses fell to the lot of recreation, alcoholic beverages and personal appearance, while spendings for tobacco, sickness and death and social-cultural activities receded only moderately.

There is nothing surprising in these movements—unless it be that they were not more violent both in the upswing of the 1920's and in the downswing of the first two years of depression. Much of the loose talk in both periods about alleged sweeping changes in modes of living quite obviously was exaggerated. The extent of the exaggeration will be more apparent when spendings are reduced, in Part Two, to a common base. Consumers' wants and habits, as shown by the distribution of their outgo among classes of objects, are stubbornly resistant to change.

FLUCTUATIONS IN SUB-CLASSES OF OUTGO

However, the foregoing generalization applies only to the 12 broad groups listed in Table 1. Within these groups, even the most stable of them, fluctuations were much greater. An item-by-item examination of the base tabulation in Appendix A brings to light numerous examples which cannot be discussed without entering into excessive detail. Table 2 below presents a few outstanding instances of extraordinary gains.

TABLE 2.—NOTABLE GAINS IN SUB-CLASSES OF OUTGO[1]

From Average Pre-war Year to 1929

A. Increased more than 400%, measured in current dollars

Flavoring Extracts	Washing Machines
Cigarettes	Perfumes and Cosmetics
Fancy Goods and Small Wares	Sporting Goods
Automobiles	Cereals
Gasoline and Oil	Non-alcoholic Beverages
Automobile Parts and Accessories	House Furnishings
Lamp Shades	Linoleum
Household Electrical Equipment	

B. Increased more than 300%, measured in current dollars

Canned Fruits	Women's Clothing
Cocoa	Toys
Condensed Milk	Stationery
Oleomargarine	Pens and Pencils
Confectionery and Chewing Gum	

[1] Derived from Appendix A.

Further treatment of instabilities of consumption can best be deferred to Part Two. We shall find their true sources not so much in consumers' wants and habits as in the characteristics of the goods offered to them.

THREE MAIN CATEGORIES OF OUTGO

A different classification is required in order to present clearly the sources of data and the manner in which the itemized estimates in Appendix A have been built up. The best grouping for this purpose is under three heads: (a) commodities (tangible goods); (b) intangibles (mainly services); (c) withholdings (savings and taxes).

Table 3 on page 28 summarizes our findings under these three main categories. The table takes in not only the odd-numbered years of the post-war period, shown in Table 1, but also the even-numbered years. The commodity figures for the odd-numbered years are derived, as previously explained, mainly from the biennial censuses of manufactures; for the even-numbered years, they are merely straight-line interpolations of commodity totals adjusted by the Bureau of Labor Statistics retail price index. The figures for intangibles and for withholdings, however, are derived from other sources and have about an equal degree of validity for all years. Explanations of the methods used are supplied in the appendixes. The summary estimates are graphed in Chart B, Section A. Observe that the gain in total outgo has gone mainly to intangibles.

To give a clearer picture of the trends of the three categories, Section B of Chart B represents the percentages of total outgo devoted to each category. The declining proportion of commodities and the steeply rising proportion of intangibles as here depicted are truly startling. If these trends go on, they will bring about an even greater shifting than we have already experienced of capital and personnel toward the service industries and occupations.

The proportion of withholdings has fluctuated between 8% and 16%. When taxes are separated, the range of savings is found to be from 6% to 14% with a general downward trend.

Consumers' National Outgo Compared with National Income

In principle, consumers' outgo and consumers' income should be equal. If we were able to measure spendings and withholdings accurately, therefore, their total would measure the national income. This procedure has in fact been applied by Clark in order to check estimates of British income obtained by other methods.[1]

The best American national income estimates for the years 1909–1925 as yet published are King's. They are estimates of *realized incomes of individuals* and do not include the gross incomes of business enterprises, business savings, or gains and losses of investors.[2] For the years 1926–1929 King's original estimates have been revised as explained in the notes to Table 4. For 1930 and 1931 we use unadjusted estimates on a somewhat different base recently issued by the United States Department

[1] "The National Income and the Theory of Production" by Colin Clark, *Economic Journal*, June, 1933.

[2] "The National Income and Its Purchasing Power" by Willford Isbell King, National Bureau of Economic Research, New York, 1930, p. 73. The true nature of these estimates appears to be commonly misunderstood. It is an everyday occurrence to see comparisons of the burdens of taxation or of debt service with King's figures for national income. The comparisons should properly be made with the gross incomes which differ widely in their amounts and in their fluctuations from the net incomes of individuals.

SUMMARY OF
CONSUMERS' OUTGO IN THREE MAIN CATEGORIES

(Based on Table 3)

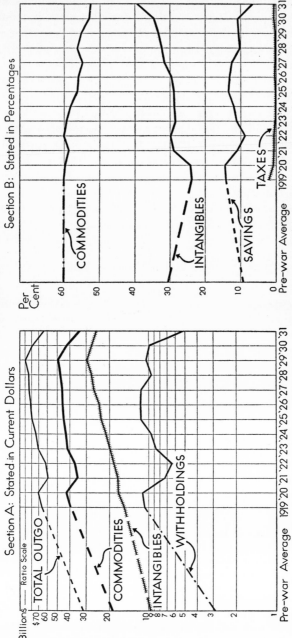

Section A: Stated in Current Dollars

Section B: Stated in Percentages

CHART B.—In Section A the upward sweep of intangibles is impressive, especially when compared with the lagging advance of commodities and the weakness of withholdings in recent years. The rising proportion of intangibles and the declining percentage of total outgo devoted to savings stand out even more clearly in Section B.

TABLE 3.—SUMMARY OF OUTGO IN THREE MAIN CATEGORIES, 1909–1931[1]

(In billions of current dollars)

Classes of Outgo	1909	1914	Pre-war Average	1919	1920	1921	1922	1923	1924	1925	1926	1927	1928	1929	1930	1931
Total Outgo	29.2	33.6	31.4	65.9	70.3	59.1	61.7	70.2	73.4	79.3	80.8	83.4	83.9	89.4	78.9	63.7
Commodities	17.4	20.5	18.9	39.6	42.0	34.7	37.0	41.7	42.8	44.8	45.3	45.7	47.3	49.3	41.9	33.6
Intangibles	9.0	10.1	9.6	15.6	17.0	17.1	18.3	19.9	21.1	23.1	23.9	26.2	27.1	29.7	27.2	25.0
Withholdings (Savings and Taxes)	2.8	3.0	2.9	10.7	11.3	7.3	6.4	8.6	9.5	11.6	11.6	11.4	9.5	10.4	9.8	5.1
Percentages																
Commodities	59.6	61.0	60.3	60.1	59.7	58.7	60.0	59.4	58.3	56.4	56.1	54.9	56.4	55.2	53.1	52.7
Intangibles	30.8	30.1	30.4	23.7	24.2	28.9	29.7	28.4	28.7	29.1	29.6	31.5	32.3	33.3	34.5	39.3
Withholdings	9.6	8.9	9.3	16.2	16.1	12.4	10.3	12.2	13.0	14.5	14.3	13.6	11.3	11.6	12.4	8.0

[1] Derived from Appendix A.

of Commerce. They were prepared with the cooperation of the National Bureau of Economic Research; and it is stated in connection with these estimates that a revision of King's figures, utilizing data not available to him, is in preparation.[3]

Table 4 presents a comparison of estimates of income, after required adjustments, with our estimates of outgo, and they are graphed in Chart C. The discrepancies in most years are slight. The year 1919 is a trouble-maker because of dis-

COMPARISON OF OUTGO AND INCOME ESTIMATES

Ratio Scale

(In billions of current dollars; Based on Table 4)

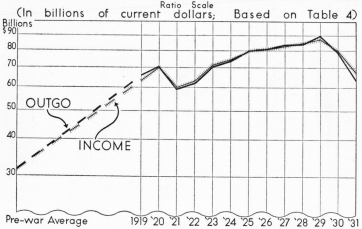

CHART C.—In general, outgo and income estimates are not far apart. The discrepancies between them may be increased by pending revisions of the income estimates.

turbances in prices. The unadjusted figures for 1930–1931 may not be truly comparable with the outgo figures. General agreement of the outgo and income estimates cannot safely be taken, however, as fully confirmatory evidence. In the first place, King's figures, as remarked above, are in process of revision. In the second place, comparison of the totals is unsatisfactory, particularly because both income and outgo estimates are to some extent compromises between the demands of logic and the limitations of the data. For this reason the totals may easily conceal inconsistencies of treatment or variations in comparable sub-totals which could be brought to light only by a thorough cross-checking. With closer definitions and further

[3] "National Income, 1929–1932," United States Government Printing Office, 1934, p. 10.

TABLE 4.—COMPARISON OF ESTIMATES OF NATIONAL INCOME AND NATIONAL OUTGO

(In billions of current dollars)

Procedure in Making Comparisons	Pre-war Average	1919	1920	1921	1922	1923	1924	1925	1926	1927	1928	1929	1930	1931
1. Estimates of Realized Income of Individuals..................	30.5	61.6	68.4	58.3	61.2	69.3	71.9	76.6	77.9	79.1	80.5	83.1	75.4	63.2
2. Addition of Imputed Rentals...........	1.0	1.4	1.6	1.7	1.8	2.0	2.3	2.5	3.0	3.4	3.5	4.1	4.0	3.9
3. Comparable Estimates of Income......	31.5	63.0	70.0	60.0	63.0	71.3	74.2	79.1	80.9	82.5	84.0	87.2	79.4	67.1
4. Our Estimates of Outgo...............	31.4	65.9	70.3	59.1	61.7	70.2	73.4	79.3	80.8	83.4	83.9	89.4	78.9	63.7
5. Excess or Deficiency of Income........	+0.1	-2.9	-0.3	+0.9	+1.3	+1.1	+0.8	-0.2	+0.1	-0.9	+0.1	-2.2	+0.5	+3.4

Line 1. King's estimates, *excluding* imputed income, as presented in "National Income and Its Purchasing Power," p. 74, are used through 1925. The figures for 1926–1929 are derived from "America's Capacity to Consume," Table 5, p. 152, by adding to Realized Incomes from Production the estimates for income from foreign investments and for residential rent; it is stated that the figures for the four years named are "from unpublished estimates of the National Bureau of Economic Research, continuing King's series." The Department of Commerce estimates for 1930–1931, appearing in "National Income, 1929–1932," are shown as they stand —i.e., without adjustments (for which we do not have the necessary data) to bring them into line with the income figures for earlier years. These three sets of income estimates are made up by somewhat different methods and are not properly continuous but are the best available at time of publication. From comments in the Department of Commerce study, it appears probable that King's estimates may be scaled down in a forthcoming revision.

Line 2. The adjustment consists of adding our estimates of imputed rentals of owned farm and non-farm homes occupied by owners. Our figures are considerably above those in the income estimates and are believed to be better-founded.

Line 3. Line 1 *plus* Line 2.

Line 4. Taken from Table 3.

Line 5. Line 3 *minus* Line 4.

refinements in procedure, a higher degree of accuracy in measurements of both national income and national outgo should soon be attained.

An apparent disparity between the outgo estimates and the income estimates requires cleaning up. Our estimates of outgo, as previously explained, are considerably below the figures which would be reached if all the spendings and withholdings of individual consumers were aggregated; for transfers from one consumer to another are ruled out. The national income, on the other hand, is the same as the aggregate of individual incomes.[4] This difference arises from the fact that the income of an individual is derived solely from his dealings with business, professional or institutional individuals or organizations, whereas the gross outgo of an individual by custom includes his payments or transfers to other individuals who are also acting in a consumer-capacity. It is only by eliminating such payments and transfers from one consumer to another that we can arrive at the net outgo of consumers as a body—in other words, at a figure comparable with accepted estimates of national income.

The foregoing remarks leave out of account one element which is frequently asserted to have played a large part in consumers' spending power, namely: the expansion of installment credit and of personal loans. We shall see a little later that consumers' borrowings have had in reality little net effect on total outgo.

CONSUMERS' COMMODITIES: RATIOS TO TOTAL OUTPUT

Of the three main categories of consumers' outgo—commodities, intangibles and withholdings—the first one offers by far the best data and fewest difficulties. The basic data of annual output of commodities are assembled from census records. It is then necessary (a) to allocate each class of output, as given in the census, between consumers' commodities and other commodities and (b) to add to each class of consumers' commodities its estimated "spread" between its value at point of production and its value at point of sale to ultimate consumers. The procedure and the percentages of allocation and of spread are set forth in detail in Appendix B.

[4] In making this flat statement, I follow King, *op. cit.*, p. 42. The statement is rejected by the authors of "America's Capacity to Consume" (pp. 145–146), but on grounds which seem questionable. See further comments in Appendix G.

The findings as to allocations of the annual output of movable commodities, which are summarized in Table 5 and in Chart D, throw new light on a question of prime importance in the national economy, namely: the proportion of productive activities *directly* governed by consumers' demands. The term *movable commodities* excludes all forms of construction and includes all forms of raw, semi-finished and finished articles of commerce. The raw and semi-finished articles are eliminated in the formula adopted for calculating the annual output of all *finished* commodities. Finished commodities other than those for consumers are not here itemized but consist mainly of equipment, construction materials, and commodities destined for public utility and other service enterprises. All the figures—and particularly those for all finished commodities—are only rough approximations.

As might have been expected, the output of consumers' commodities (Line 4) is much less subject to fluctuation than is other output which consists in a broad sense of producers' commodities. Yet consumers' goods, too, show some signs of increasing instability. Observe especially how much more sharply they dropped in 1931 than in 1921. Many factors, of course, enter into this showing. The comparison between 1921 and 1931 is highly significant, however, if it be taken to indicate, as I think plausible, that consumption during the intervening 10 years had become flabbier and less resistant to deterioration. To this question we will return in later chapters.

The percentages in Table 5, graphed in Section B of Chart D, measure for the first time the enlarged proportion of productive effort in years of depression devoted to consumers' goods. Of still greater interest is the persistence with which the ratios revert to what are apparently established relationships. In post-war prosperous years the output of finished consumers' commodities has run consistently close to 38% of the output of all movable commodities that pass into commercial channels (about 20% of all unmanufactured commodities; about 43% of all manufactured commodities); and it has approximated 56% of the output of all *finished* commodities.

The tendency toward uniformity of the ratios in most years of the period adds one more bit of evidence to the convincing demonstration in other studies that our productive system as a

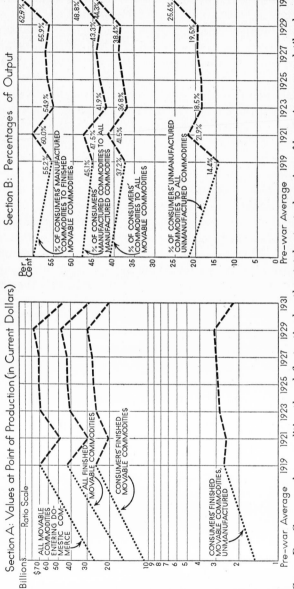

ALLOCATIONS OF
ANNUAL OUTPUT OF MOVABLE COMMODITIES
(Based on Table 5)

Section A: Values at Point of Production (in Current Dollars)

Section B: Percentages of Output

CHART D.—Consumers' commodities, though fluctuating less than total output, show signs of becoming more volatile; observe the sharpness of their fall from 1929 to 1931. They form in prosperous years about 38% of all commodities entering domestic commerce and about 56% of all finished movable commodities.

TABLE 5.—ALLOCATIONS OF ANNUAL OUTPUT OF MOVABLE COMMODITIES
(Values at point of production in billions of current dollars; deductions in italics)

Procedure in Deriving Output	1909	1914	Pre-war Average	1919	1921	1923	1925	1927	1929	1931
1. Output of Unmanufactured Commodities Entering Domestic Commerce.	6.4	7.3	6.9	18.0	11.4	15.1	15.6	15.3	15.9	8.6
1a. Farm Products (gross cash income)	4.8	5.5	5.1	14.4	7.7	9.5	10.2	10.0	10.3	5.8
1b. Products of Mines and Quarries...	0.8	0.9	0.9	2.2	1.7	2.5	2.3	2.3	2.4	1.3
1c. Petroleum (crude) Production....	0.1	0.2	0.2	0.8	0.8	1.0	1.3	1.2	1.3	0.6
1d. Products of Forests, Fishing and Hunting....................	0.8	0.8	0.8	1.3	1.1	1.6	1.6	1.4	1.2	0.6
1e. *Plus* or *Minus* Balance of Imports over Exports................	*0.1*	*0.1*	*0.1*	*0.7*	0.1	0.5	0.2	0.4	0.7	0.3
2. Output of Manufactured Commodities Entering Domestic Commerce.	18.1	21.0	19.5	51.7	37.3	53.4	54.9	55.0	61.5	36.5
2a. Census of Manufactures (unadjusted totals)................	20.5	24.0	22.3	62.0	43.7	60.6	62.7	62.7	70.4	41.4
2b. *Minus* Interplant Transfers and Receipts for Contract and Repair Work..................	*1.4*	*1.9*	*1.7*	*5.0*	*3.5*	*4.8*	*5.0*	*5.0*	*5.9*	*3.3*
2c. *Minus* Service and Public Utility Industries..................	*0.6*	*0.7*	*0.7*	*1.5*	*1.5*	*1.8*	*1.7*	*1.6*	*1.6*	*1.1*
2d. *Minus* Balance of Exports over Imports....................	*0.4*	*0.4*	*0.4*	*3.8*	*1.4*	*0.6*	*1.1*	*1.1*	*1.4*	*0.5*
3. Output of All Movable Commodities Entering Domestic Commerce.....	24.5	28.3	26.4	69.7	48.7	68.5	70.5	70.3	77.4	45.1
4. Output of Consumers' Commodities..	9.8	11.8	10.8	25.9	20.2	25.2	26.7	27.3	29.7	20.0
4a. Consumers' (ready-to-consume) Unmanufactured Commodities .	1.3	1.6	1.5	2.6	2.5	2.8	2.9	3.0	3.1	2.2
4b. Consumers' (ready-to-consume) Manufactured Commodities....	8.5	10.2	9.3	23.3	17.7	22.4	23.8	24.3	26.6	17.8
5. Output of All Finished, Movable Commodities..................	14.5	16.7	15.6	42.2	29.5	40.8	42.3	42.8	47.6	28.3
5a. Raw Materials and Fuels Utilized in Manufacturing.............	5.0	5.6	5.3	15.0	8.5	11.8	12.4	12.0	12.5	6.2
5b. *Plus* Transportation Charges on Raw Materials, Fuels and Semi-Manufactures..............	1.1	1.4	1.3	2.4	2.7	3.1	3.1	3.2	3.2	2.2
5c. *Plus* Value Added by Manufacture	8.4	9.7	9.0	24.8	18.3	25.9	26.8	27.6	31.9	19.9
6. Percentages of Consumers' Commodities to Output of All Movable Commodities..................	40.0	42.0	41.0	37.2	41.5	36.8	37.9	38.8	38.4	44.3
7. Percentages of Consumers' Unmanufactured Commodities to Output of Unmanufactured Commodities Entering Domestic Commerce........	20.3	21.9	21.1	14.4	21.9	18.5	18.6	19.6	19.5	25.6
8. Percentages of Consumers' Manufactured Commodities to Output of Manufactured Commodities Entering Domestic Commerce..........	47.0	48.6	47.8	45.1	47.5	41.9	43.4	44.2	43.3	48.8
9. Percentages of Consumers' Manufactured Commodities to Output of All Finished Movable Commodities	58.6	61.1	59.9	55.2	60.0	54.9	56.3	56.8	55.9	62.9

Line 1.   Aggregates of Lines 1a to 1e, inclusive; data taken from various government sources listed in the Census of 1930 report on "Wholesale Distribution—Summary for the United States," p. 32.
Line 2.   Census of Manufactures totals (Line 2a) with adjustments indicated in Lines 2b, 2c and 2d. The formula for calculating "total value of goods distributed" presented in the above-mentioned report has been slightly modified in order to obtain comparable figures for earlier years, as shown in Lines 1 and 2.
Line 3.   Line 1 *plus* Line 2.
Line 4.   Computed by applying the percentages of output allocated to finished consumers' commodities as detailed in Appendix B.
Line 5.   Aggregates of Lines 5a, 5b and 5c.   These figures run somewhat above the estimates for total net value of manufactured products given in *Statistical Abstract of the United States*, 1933, p. 398.
Line 5a.   Line 1 *minus* Line 4a with a further deduction for fuels destined to railroads, service enterprises, etc.
Line 5b.   Total railroad freight charges *plus* allowances for trucking and for water-borne traffic *minus* computed transportation charges on finished consumers' commodities.
Line 5c.   Derived from Census of Manufactures.
Line 7.   Line 1 divided into Line 4a.
Line 9.   Line 5 divided into Line 4b.
Line 6.   Line 3 divided into Line 4.
Line 8.   Line 2 divided into Line 4b.

whole maintained a reasonably sound, well-balanced development through the post-war boom.[5]

Noteworthy is the perceptible downward movement of all these ratios between the pre-war and the post-war periods, confirming the commonsense opinion that a gradually declining ratio of all productive effort goes into the final stages of turning out consumers' commodities. Production becomes year by year more roundabout; that is, allots a larger share of capital and labor to preliminary operations, because that is the way to pour out an increasing volume of consumers' goods.

CONSUMERS' COMMODITIES: DECLINING COSTS OF DISTRIBUTION

After the values of consumers' finished commodities at point of production have been computed, the final step in our computation consists of applying percentages of "spread" between values at point of production and values at point of sale to consumers. The spread for each commodity covers transportation charges and the customary margins of assemblers, of brokers and other wholesale dealers and of retailers. The margins in both pre-war and post-war periods are ascertainable with a fair degree of reliability; and they have been found much more stable than appears to be commonly assumed. The margins and other charges added to each class of goods constitute the costs of distribution borne by consumers.

The over-all percentages of spread for manufactured, for unmanufactured, and for all consumers' commodities are presented in Table 6 and are plotted in Section A of Chart E. These percentages, let me make clear, do not represent the ups and downs of the expenses plus profits (or minus losses) of the distribution system; for these ups and downs do not directly affect consumers' pocketbooks. Ignoring the elementary distinction between middlemen's expenses, which fluctuate considerably,

[5] Among the studies here referred to are Snyder's estimates of growth of production (see especially "Overproduction and Business Cycles" by Carl Snyder, *Proceedings of the American Academy of Political Science*, June, 1931); Mills' calculations of rates of growth in the pre-war and post-war periods ("Economic Tendencies" by F. C. Mills, National Bureau of Economic Research, New York, 1932); and Nourse's thorough examination of the prevalent notion that an extraordinary excess capacity was built up after the war ("America's Capacity to Produce" by Edwin G. Nourse and Associates, Brookings, Washington, D. C., 1934).

COSTS OF DISTRIBUTION PAID BY CONSUMERS

(Based on Tables 6 & 7)

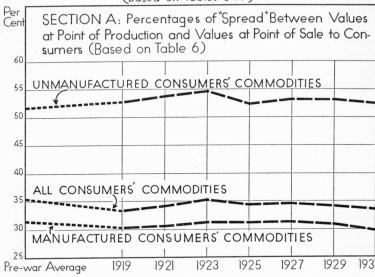

SECTION A: Percentages of "Spread" Between Values at Point of Production and Values at Point of Sale to Consumers (Based on Table 6)

UNMANUFACTURED CONSUMERS' COMMODITIES

ALL CONSUMERS' COMMODITIES

MANUFACTURED CONSUMERS' COMMODITIES

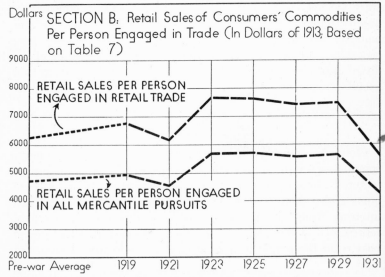

SECTION B: Retail Sales of Consumers' Commodities Per Person Engaged in Trade (In Dollars of 1913; Based on Table 7)

RETAIL SALES PER PERSON ENGAGED IN RETAIL TRADE

RETAIL SALES PER PERSON ENGAGED IN ALL MERCANTILE PURSUITS

CHART E.—Contrary to the popular impression, the ratio of consumers' costs of distribution to their purchases of commodities is slowly tending downward. The underlying explanation is found in the slight upward tendency of sales of consumers' commodities per person engaged in trade.

and the costs of distribution paid by consumers, which change slowly and moderately, breeds confusion and misstatements.[6]

Section A of Chart E makes unmistakable the definite, though slow, downward trend of distribution costs *paid by consumers.* The trend arises not so much from changes in margins as from gradual modification of the make-up of consumers' purchases— a perceptible swing toward classes of commodities, such as automobiles, for example, which carry relatively low spreads. The high rate on unmanufactured commodities, chiefly coal and raw foods, is occasioned by heavy transportation charges on coal in proportion to its retail value and by heavy assembling costs (not true distribution costs) on raw foods.

Table 7, graphed in Section B of Chart E, is an explanation and independent verification of the trend shown in Section A. Section B represents the average retail sales of consumers' commodities, deflated into 1913 dollars, (a) per person engaged in mercantile pursuits and (b) per person engaged in retail trade. The upward tendency indicates a slow gain in efficiency, as measured by the amount of sales per person. It reveals why costs of distribution have followed a slightly downward course.

The essential facts represented in Chart E run directly contrary not only to popular impressions but also to the peculiarly unscientific attitude on this question assumed by many economists. Yet the facts are, I believe, indisputable. If they were generally understood, perhaps part of the ignorant carping at the distribution system would be replaced by more intelligent and useful criticism.

Consumers' Commodities: Rising Proportion of Processed Goods

Chart F breaks down the total retail values of consumers' commodities into (a) manufactured commodities (b) unmanufactured commodities and (c) extra-commercial consumption of home-grown foods and fuels. The figures are so easily picked up from Appendix A that a separate tabulation of the data represented in the diagram is omitted. The chart brings out in bold relief the long-continued decline in total annual values of

---

[6] In all the mass of published material on costs of distribution that I have seen, only one paper ("Marketing Problems under a Planned Economy" by Wroe Alderson, *Bulletin of the Taylor Society*, Feb., 1934) clearly recognizes this distinction.

TABLE 6.—AGGREGATE SPREADS (COSTS OF DISTRIBUTION TO CONSUMERS) ON MANUFACTURED AND UNMANUFACTURED COMMODITIES, 1909–1931[1]

(In billions of dollars)

Procedure in Determining Spreads	1909	1914	Pre-war Average	1919	1921	1923	1925	1927	1929	1931
Manufactured Commodities at Retail Values	11.1	13.4	12.2	31.9	25.5	32.6	34.6	35.3	38.4	25.4
Less Manufactured Commodities at Producers' Values	7.6	9.2	8.4	22.3	17.7	22.4	23.8	24.3	26.6	17.8
Manufactured Commodities, Costs of Distribution	3.5	4.2	3.8	9.6	7.8	10.2	10.8	11.0	11.8	7.6
Costs of Distribution (in percentages of retail values)	31.5	31.3	31.4	30.1	30.6	31.3	31.2	31.2	30.7	29.9
Unmanufactured Commodities at Retail Values	2.7	3.3	3.1	5.5	5.4	6.2	6.1	6.4	6.6	4.6
Less Unmanufactured Commodities at Producers' Values	1.3	1.6	1.5	2.6	2.5	2.8	2.9	3.0	3.1	2.2
Unmanufactured Commodities, Costs of Distribution	1.4	1.7	1.6	2.9	2.9	3.4	3.2	3.4	3.5	2.4
Costs of Distribution in Percentages of Retail Values	51.9	51.5	51.7	52.7	53.7	54.8	52.3	53.1	53.0	52.2
All Consumers' Commodities at Retail Values	13.8	16.7	15.3	37.4	30.9	38.9	40.7	41.7	45.0	30.0
Less All Consumers' Commodities at Producers' Values	8.9	10.9	9.9	24.9	20.2	25.2	26.7	27.3	29.7	20.0
All Consumers' Commodities, Costs of Distribution	4.9	5.9	5.4	12.5	10.6	13.7	14.0	14.4	15.3	10.0
Costs of Distribution in Percentages of Retail Values	35.5	35.3	35.4	33.4	34.3	35.2	34.4	34.5	34.0	33.3

[1] This table excludes corrections for inventory changes, values of commodities manufactured on retail premises, payments for alcoholic beverages (in pre-prohibition years as well as during the prohibition regime) and extra-commercial consumption of home-grown foods and fuels, since none of these elements in consumers' total purchases of commodities carry calculable and/or fairly comparable costs of distribution. Because of these omissions, the totals are less than the inclusive totals of outgo for commodities in Tables 3 and 5.

TABLE 7.—RETAIL SALES OF CONSUMERS' COMMODITIES PER PERSON ENGAGED IN TRADE

Procedure in Computing Sales per Person	1909	1914	Pre-war Average	1919	1921	1923	1925	1927	1929	1931
1. Numbers Engaged in All Mercantile Pursuits (in thousands)	3,582	3,907	3,745	4,261	4,483	4,791	5,120	5,472	5,848	6,254
2. Numbers Engaged in Retail Trade (in thousands)	2,742	2,927	2,835	3,125	3,285	3,536	3,807	4,098	4,411	4,749
3. Total Retail Values of Consumers' Commodities (in billions of 1913 dollars)	16.8	18.7	17.8	21.1	20.3	27.1	29.1	30.4	33.0	26.6
4. Retail Sales per Person Engaged in All Mercantile Pursuits (in 1913 dollars)	4,690	4,786	4,738	4,952	4,528	5,656	5,684	5,556	5,643	4,253
5. Retail Sales per Person Engaged in Retail Trade (in 1913 dollars)	6,127	6,389	6,258	6,752	6,180	7,664	7,644	7,418	7,481	5,601

Line 1.   Estimates for censual years based on data in Census of Occupations as reclassified in "America's Capacity to Produce" by Edwin G. Nourse and Associates, Brookings Institution, Washington, 1934, p. 386; the numbers engaged for intervening years have been derived by interpolation (logarithmic); for 1909 and 1931, by extrapolation.   Since no allowances are made for the unknown amount of exceptional unemployment in 1921 and 1931, the figures for these two years, especially 1931, are doubtless somewhat distorted.

Line 2.   As above.

Line 3.   To the values (in current dollars) of commodities in Appendix A have been applied the specific indexes cited in Chap. V.   Extra-commercial expenditures and alcoholic beverages have been excluded for the prohibition years; but in 1909, 1914, and 1919 expenditures for alcoholic beverages passed through normal retail channels and for that reason have been included.

Line 4.   Line 3 divided by Line 1.

Line 5.   Line 3 divided by Line 2.

SUMMARY OF OUTGO FOR COMMODITIES
(Based on Appendix A)

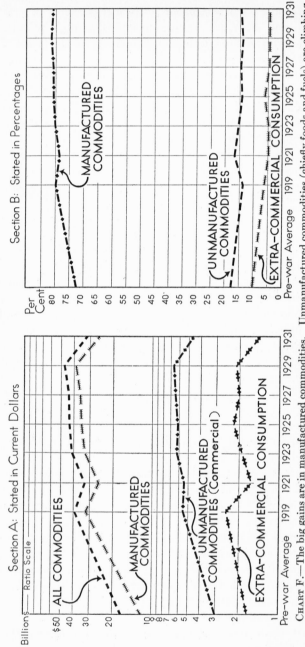

CHART F.—The big gains are in manufactured commodities. Unmanufactured commodities (chiefly foods and fuels) are climbing slowly in dollar volume; are definitely declining in terms of percentages of total outgo for commodities. Extra-commercial consumption has been rapidly going down both in dollars and in percentages. Inventory adjustments, alcoholic beverages and commodities manufactured on retail premises are omitted in this chart.

products raised and consumed by farmers, owners of vegetable gardens, and other grower-consumers. This does not of course imply a corresponding decline in quantities, for the prices of such products have been exceptionally depressed. The shrinkage in money values is in itself, however, an important factor affecting willingness to raise foods and fuels for home consumption.

The chart shows also the more rapid growth of manufactured than of unmanufactured commodities. Consumers' demands for raw products do not keep pace with advances in their total spending power. Processed goods form a steadily increasing proportion of consumption—a proportion which can now be measured.

Intangibles: A Field of Rapid Expansion

The growing proportion of intangibles, already remarked, stands out as one of the most prominent and illuminating trends of post-war consumption. In itself it goes far to explain why both producers of commodities and their employees have had great difficulty in adapting themselves to changing conditions. It has drawn billions of capital and millions of workers away from their former fields and into the so-called "service" enterprises.

The breakdown of total spendings for intangibles in Table 8 (graphed in Chart G) into eight groups indicates more clearly what has been going on. The largest group comprises the expenses of home occupancy—that is, rentals paid, rental values imputed to owned homes, and taxes, interest and upkeep on owned homes, all of which are detailed in Appendix A and explained in Appendix C. Before the war home occupancy took 38% of the outgo for intangibles. By 1919 its proportion had shrunk to 32%; and it required 10 years of steady climbing to get back to the 38% ratio in 1929. In 1931, because of the accustomed lag in times of depression in reducing rentals and other contractual expense, the proportion rose to nearly 43%. Throughout the post-war period, then, home occupancy outgo has gone up much faster than total outgo for intangibles. We shall find reason later on to view this development as one of especial importance and promise.

Chart G depicts a struggle for supremacy among the next four groups which epitomizes the inexorable passing of old

SUMMARY OF OUTGO FOR INTANGIBLES

(Based on Table 8)

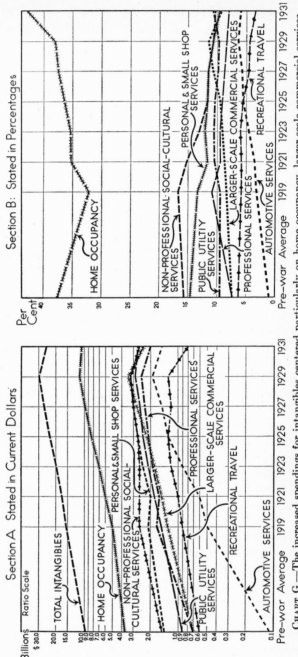

CHART G.—The increased spendings for intangibles centered particularly on home occupancy, larger-scale commercial services, public utility services and automotive services. The changing allocation of spendings for intangibles, as it appears in Section B, reveals important modifications of social habits.

ways of living and the triumph of the new. The four groups
are:

Personal and small shop services: comprising domestic services, personal appearance services (barbers, hairdressers, and so on), moving expenses and repairs,
tailoring and clothes-pressing, and two or three small items.

Larger-scale commercial services: laundries, dry-cleaning establishments,
theaters, hotels.

Non-professional social-cultural spendings: tuition, contributions, dues and
postage are the main items.

Public utility services rendered by street railway and other local transportation
agencies, electricity and gas companies and telephone companies.

Two of these groups—small shop services and non-professional
social-cultural spendings—have run quite closely parallel for
the most part. They have made fairly steady progress and have
stood up reasonably well—especially social-cultural spendings—
under the impact of depression. Their records are overshad-
owed, however, by the other two groups. The larger-scale
commercial enterprises shot up at high speed to their 1929 peak;
then dropped their gains with even greater celerity and no
effective resistance in the slump of 1929–1931. Public utility
services had a somewhat less spectacular ascent, but also avoided
the subsequent debacle; their retreat through 1931 was slow and
orderly.

A little lower down on the chart comes the group of professional
services—chiefly physicians and nurses, though taking in also
services to individuals by lawyers, artists, musicians and so on.
Spendings in this group have been relatively stable, but have
fallen to a constantly decreasing percentage of the total outgo
for intangibles.

Automobile services and expenses, on the other hand, as
would have been expected, have enjoyed a phenomenal rise.
But the showing should not be assigned an exaggerated importance. Seen in its true perspective, as delineated in Chart G,
it plays a brilliant, yet rather a minor, part in the sweeping forward movement of all intangibles.

Recreational travel—which includes spendings by individuals
for hotels and railway and steamship transportation, but *not*
automobile transportation—barely held its own in volume
through the prosperous years and fell off easily in 1931. Its
percentage of total outgo for intangibles has declined throughout
the period.

TABLE 8.—SUMMARY OF MAJOR GROUPS OF SPENDINGS FOR INTANGIBLES[1]

(In billions of current dollars)

Groups of Intangibles	Pre-war Average		1919		1921		1923		1925		1927		1929		1931	
	$	%	$	%	$	%	$	%	$	%	$	%	$	%	$	%
Total Intangibles	9.6	100	15.6	100	17.1	100	19.9	100	23.1	100	26.2	100	29.7	100	25.0	100
Home Occupancy	3.7	38.5	5.0	32.1	6.0	35.1	7.0	35.2	8.4	36.4	9.8	37.4	11.3	38.0	10.7	42.8
Personal and Small Shop Services	1.4	14.6	2.1	13.4	2.0	11.7	2.4	12.1	2.7	11.7	3.0	11.5	3.2	10.8	2.4	9.6
Larger-Scale Commercial Services	0.7	7.3	1.3	8.3	1.5	8.8	1.8	9.0	2.2	9.5	2.8	10.7	3.4	11.4	2.3	9.2
Non-Professional Social-Cultural Services	1.5	15.6	2.6	16.7	2.6	15.2	2.6	13.1	2.7	11.7	3.0	11.4	3.2	10.8	2.6	10.4
Public Utility Services	0.9	9.4	1.5	9.6	1.8	10.5	2.1	10.6	2.4	10.4	2.6	9.9	2.9	9.8	2.7	10.8
Professional Services	0.7	7.3	1.7	10.9	1.6	9.4	1.9	9.5	2.1	9.1	2.3	8.8	2.5	8.4	2.0	8.0
Automotive Services	0.1	1.0	0.5	3.2	0.6	3.5	0.9	4.5	1.3	5.6	1.5	5.7	1.9	6.4	1.5	6.0
Recreational Travel	0.6	6.3	0.9	5.8	1.0	5.8	1.2	6.0	1.3	5.6	1.2	4.6	1.3	4.4	0.8	3.2

[1] Based on Appendix A.

WITHHOLDINGS: TAXES AND SAVINGS

Taxes and savings are not intimately associated with each other; but both are quite distinct in character from all the other classes of outgo. Taxes and savings are withheld from current consumption and devoted to the purchase—whether forced or voluntary makes no difference—of protection against future mischances. They are reasonably placed in a distinct group.

Only taxes directly paid by individuals and not elsewhere counted are here taken into the reckoning; they include income taxes, both federal and state, personal property taxes, poll taxes, licenses, fees and fines. Taxes on owner-occupied homes fall under home maintenance, and motor vehicle and gasoline taxes fall under transportation. Customs duties, internal revenue taxes and other indirect payments made in the first instance by business enterprises enter into costs of production and distribution. We are not concerned for the present purpose with the final incidence of taxes but only with consumers' traceable disbursements. The totals of taxes directly paid have been presented in Table 1 and require no further comment.

Estimates of savings by individuals in their consumer-capacity are the most difficult and most uncertain of all the measurements of consumers' outgo. The procedure and formulae used in making the estimates are fully explained in Appendix D. The estimates are tentative and may be substantially modified whenever better data or better methods become available.

Savings of individuals go into four classes of acquisitions, namely: (a) payments of life insurance premiums; (b) increases or decreases in cash holdings; (c) payments for holdings of securities; and (d) payments for holdings of real property. The estimated amounts acquired by individuals are stated at the end of Appendix A and are graphed in Chart H, Section A. Throughout the period payments for life insurance climbed steadily, subject to moderate checks in years of depression. A glance at the chart is enough to show the great irregularity of the other classes of acquisitions. The irregularities do not offset each other but on the contrary tend to synchronize; in consequence, the totals of annual acquisitions fluctuate over a very wide range.

Since savings, by definition, come entirely out of current income, we deduct from total acquisitions (a) the annual totals of realized profits from sale of assets and capital gains and (b)

SUMMARY OF OUTGO FOR ACQUISITIONS AND NET SAVINGS

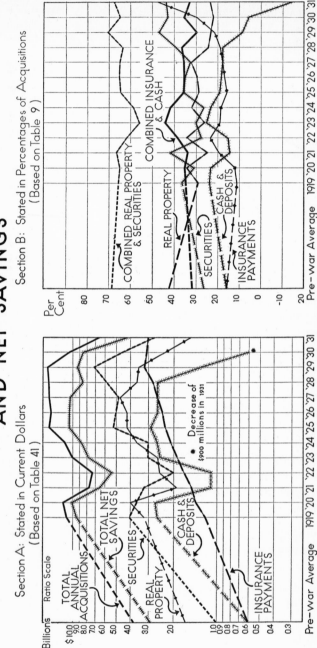

Section A: Stated in Current Dollars
(Based on Table 41)

Section B: Stated in Percentages of Acquisitions
(Based on Table 9)

CHART H.—The movements depicted at first sight appear highly irregular with the exception of payments for life insurance premiums. However, when percentages of acquisitions are combined in two groups—(a) life insurance and cash holdings and (b) securities and real property—we find a surprising approach to steadiness in the division of saved dollars between these broad groups.

withdrawals of capital from life insurance companies. These items do not properly belong to income.[7] Savings by consumers in prosperous years run, as shown in Chart B, from 10% to 14% of the national outgo.

Section B of Chart H (based on Table 9) presents the annual percentages of total acquisitions devoted to each of the four classes above named. The most interesting lines on the chart are those representing the combined percentages of (a) *funds*, consisting of life insurance premiums *plus* or *minus* changes in cash holdings, and (b) *properties*, consisting of real estate *plus* securities. The combination into the two groups smooths out the separate fluctuations of the four classes of acquisitions.

The implication is plain. Savings shift easily from one form of funds to another and from one kind of property to another, but not so easily from funds to properties or *vice versa*. Individuals normally place about one-third of their savings either in life insurance or in cash; about two-thirds either in securities or in real estate. The two last-named forms of property are in direct, constant competition for the favor of the public. Broadly speaking, what one of them gains the other loses.

CONSUMERS' BORROWINGS: HEAVIER DEBTS WITHOUT INCREASED SPENDING POWER

A question somewhat outside the main subject of this inquiry, yet closely

[7] For further discussion of this point see Appendix G.

TABLE 9.—PERCENTAGES OF CONSUMERS' ACQUISITIONS TO TOTAL ACQUISITIONS[1]

Classes of Acquisitions	Pre-war	1919	1920	1921	1922	1923	1924	1925	1926	1927	1928	1929	1930	1931
Payments of Life Insurance Premiums	15.8	10.9	12.0	19.5	23.3	19.0	18.6	15.7	16.9	17.7	18.9	21.2	29.5	46.9
Increases or Decreases in Cash Holdings	15.8	23.6	23.1	14.3	15.1	25.0	23.0	19.9	18.3	17.7	17.6	8.6	5.7	−14.1
Payments for Holdings of Securities	26.3	36.4	30.8	41.5	27.4	30.0	26.5	35.6	35.2	32.6	39.2	47.0	42.9	43.8
Payments for Holdings of Real Property	42.1	29.1	34.1	24.7	34.2	26.0	31.9	28.8	29.6	32.0	24.3	23.2	21.9	23.4

[1] Based on Appendix A.

related, is the extent to which consumers' purchases are financed by borrowings. The question has been generally discussed with considerable prejudice and a great deal of exaggeration. The data here assembled make it possible for the first time to supply well-founded estimates of the amounts of open accounts and of installment accounts outstanding during the post-war period. Other estimates are accepted as a base for computing totals of personal loans during the same period by banks, insurance companies (on life insurance policies), the United States Government (loans to veterans) and small-loan agencies of various types. The methods of estimating are set forth in Appendix E.

The load of debt per family rose alarmingly from 1919 to 1931. However, the increase was not in mercantile accounts or other debts arising from purchases but from loans granted by financing agencies. The findings are graphed in Chart I, Sections A, B and C.

The striking development of post-war personal borrowings is the rapid spread of the habit of turning easily to financial agencies, including Uncle Sam, whenever money for current expenses begins to run short. Borrowing at times is a necessity, and modern agencies for extending personal loans offer a useful service; but the volume of loans has grown with so much speed through both prosperity and depression as to suggest a question whether the service has not become *too* convenient and inviting for the good of the people who use it. The question is particularly pertinent to the extraordinary expansion of debts arising from loans in the two years 1929–1931.

The unhealthy condition created by free loaning while incomes were falling is clearly depicted in Section B of Chart I. Apparently a ratio of about 10% of personal debts to personal outgo may be accepted as normal. The sudden jump to 17% by the end of 1931, however, can scarcely be regarded as anything better than an exhibition of national recklessness. It doubtless helped to stave off painful readjustments; but it certainly did not make them in the end any simpler or more agreeable.

Debts arising from purchases of commodities (installment and open accounts debts combined) seem to bear a normal ratio to total commodity purchases which is also about 10%. The ratio came up to this level, as shown by Section C, in 1923, mainly in consequence of the rapid growth of installment sales, and then remained on that level with insignificant variations until 1931, when the ratio dropped to 8.7%. The evenness of the ratio offers convincing evidence that by 1923 mercantile practice in selling to consumers on credit had become well established; thereafter it was a stabilizing factor in the economic system.

The increase of family indebtedness did not build up consumers' spending power in the period as a whole. On the contrary, between 1918 and 1931 approximately 2.5 billion dollars was subtracted from their spending power. The explanation of this apparent anomaly lies in the fact that interest and other carrying charges grew even more rapidly than the outstanding debt. In other words, during the post-war years consumers as a body actually disbursed more cash in meeting service charges on their debts than they received through increased borrowings. Though the amount of their payments in excess of their receipts from fresh loans is large in itself, it is insignificant in comparison with their aggregate income and outgo during the thirteen years studied. The net effect, so far as total spending power goes, is almost negligible.[8]

CHANGES IN CONSUMERS BORROWINGS

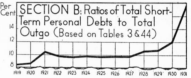

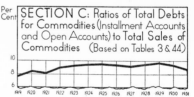

CHART I.—The growing burden of debt of the average American family is the result of loans, not of mercantile accounts. The ratio of debt to total outgo has risen alarmingly. The ratio of debt to purchases of commodities has remained fairly stable.

This chapter has sketched in broad outline our measurements of consumers' outgo, both spendings and withholdings, and has presented some of the chief findings. The detailed estimates

---

[8] For a discussion of two specific effects see Appendix E.

for major classes and sub-classes of objects of outgo are set forth in Appendix A, which is the source of the data used in all the subsequent analyses.

Before turning to the study, in Part Two, of underlying forces and long-term trends, it will be well worth while to get a better perspective of our national outgo by bringing it into comparison with outgo in other countries; this is the subject of Chapter III.

CHAPTER III

COMPARISONS

We are immediately concerned in the present study only with the behavior of consumption in the United States. However, a short digression is in order for the sake of getting a truer perspective—and incidentally correcting a warped impression, widely held, of alleged peculiarities of American consumption. The digression consists of introducing some comparisons with consumption in other countries.

DISTRIBUTION OF OUTGO IN GERMANY AND GREAT BRITAIN

So little attention has been paid to comprehensive studies of national outgo by consumers that only three estimates for foreign countries have been found. One is for Germany in 1913; another is for the United Kingdom in the period 1924–1927 (that is, an average year of the period); and the third is for the United Kingdom in 1932. In Table 10 the apportionment of German pre-war outlay is compared with the American apportionment in our average pre-war year. Similarly, the British apportionments for 1924–1927 and 1932 are contrasted with the American percentages for 1923–1927, averaged, and with 1931.

The comparisons in Table 10 obviously are far from accurate, because of divergences in classification of items and because strictly comparable estimates of average family spending power in the United States, Germany and the United Kingdom are not available. As a rough measure, estimates have been made of the average family income in the two European countries during the years covered by Table 10. These averages have been translated into dollars at the rates of exchange then prevailing. As indicated in the table, this procedure places the average pre-war spending power of German families at 53% of that of American families; and the average spending power of British families at 65% in 1924–1927 and 57% in 1932 of the corresponding figures for American families in the years shown in the table.

51

The last-mentioned showing is influenced by the more advanced stage of depression in Great Britain in 1932.

Table 10, in spite of its defects, brings to light some interesting and significant relationships. Broadly speaking, the similarities of distribution of consumers' outgo in the three countries are more striking than the contrasts.

AMERICAN AND EUROPEAN APPORTIONMENTS FOR FOOD

The percentages assigned to food in all three countries are probably the least questionable of all. Notable is the variation in the food percentage from the German pre-war 33% to the American post-war 21%.

Our estimates of spendings for food have been formed in the manner previously explained on the basis of census records of value of output while Feaveryear's British estimates are derived from physical quantities to which prevailing retail prices are applied; but no reason appears for rejecting the validity of comparison of results obtained by the two different methods. However, the fact that he applies retail prices to food consumed directly by farmers and by persons in institutions somewhat exaggerates the British figures.

Feaveryear's detailed study of physical volume of food consumption reveals a unique case of a nation bettering its food supply during a period of depression. His comment is worth quoting: "In the past two years the much lower level of food prices . . . has been one of the principal reasons for the comparatively happy position of this country. One wonders what might have happened in some of the depressed areas of Great Britain had this cheap food not been available." Along with this increase in food consumption "and perhaps not unconnected with it," there went a fall of nearly one-third in the consumption of alcohol.

The proportion of income required for food has long been recognized as the best single measure of average well-being. Ernst Engel formulated in 1857 his famous four laws of consumption, the outgrowth of his analysis of family expenditures in Belgium; and the first of these principles was, in substance, that as income increases, the proportion expended for food decreases. All subsequent studies, without noteworthy exception, have tended to confirm the principle. It must, of course, be qualified by giving consideration to the amount of food drawn from the

TABLE 10.—COMPARATIVE ALLOTMENTS OF NATIONAL CONSUMERS' OUTGO[1]

Major Classes	Pre-war			Post-war		
	Germany, 1913	United States, Pre-war Average	United Kingdom, 1924–27	United States, 1923–27	United Kingdom, 1932	United States, 1931
Approximate Average Family Spending Power (in current dollars)[2]	$850	$1,600	$1,900	$2,900	$1,200	$2,100
Percentages:						
Food	33.0	25.8	30.8	22.4	30.2	21.2
Clothing	10.0	11.9	11.2	12.5	8.6	11.1
Home Maintenance	19.0	25.6	13.4	24.1	16.8	29.8
All Others	38.0	36.7	44.6	41.0	44.5	37.9
Alcoholic Beverages	10.0	6.1	7.6	2.2	6.4	2.1
Tobacco	10.0	2.1	2.9	2.0	3.9	2.2
Transportation	2.0[3]	4.4	3.5	8.7	5.5	8.8
Sickness and Death	2.0[3]	2.8	1.7	3.4	2.0	4.0
Personal Appearance	[4]	1.5	[4]	1.8	[4]	1.8
Recreation	[4]	4.3	3.9	4.6	3.8	4.9
Social-Cultural Activities	[4]	6.5	2.8	5.3	2.9	6.2
Direct Taxes	[4]	......	9.5	1.2	11.1	1.5
Savings[5]	24.0	9.0	12.7[3]	11.8	8.9[3]	6.4
Totals	100.0	100.0	100.0	100.0	100.0	100.0

[1] The materials available for international comparisons of habits of expenditure are scanty. The major items shown in this table, however, are thought to be fairly comparable, subject to the qualifications stated in the text. All six of the estimates cited are the results of studies of national statistics of production of goods and services. They may be assumed, therefore, to be considerably more reliable than are estimates based on fragmentary records of family expenditures. The percentages for the United States are derived from Table 1 in the preceding chapter. The percentages for Germany, 1913, are based upon Prof. Ernst Wagemann's estimate given in "Economic Rhythm" (McGraw-Hill, New York, 1930, p. 40), somewhat modified by Prof. Jakob Marschak ("Encyclopedia of the Social Sciences," vol. IV, p. 296). The percentages for the United Kingdom are based upon Prof. A. E. Feaveryear's latest estimates reported in *Economic Journal*, Mar., 1934. Some liberties in reclassifying items have been taken to facilitate direct comparisons.

[2] These rough estimates of average family incomes stated in *current dollars* are not directly comparable without making allowances for important variations in living standards and costs. They are stated here merely for convenience in interpreting the percentages. For example, they make it evident that the smaller ratios allocated to food in the United States do not mean smaller expenditures on food.

[3] These percentages involve slight revisions or reassignments of those given by Marschak and Feaveryear respectively.

[4] Estimate not available or judged to be not fairly comparable.

[5] The differing definitions given to "Savings" and the difficulty of calculating this item make a comparison with the German estimate impracticable; and comparisons with the British estimates are by no means trustworthy.

soil without passing through commercial channels and to the extent of preparation of food products before they enter the home.

In the United States, both these factors have increasingly tended toward enlargement of expenditures for food. For instance, it is stated on acceptable authority that in 1901 two-thirds of our bread was baked at home, whereas in 1930 two-thirds was supplied by commercial bakers. Nevertheless, other factors have been powerful enough to make spendings for food, as shown in Table 10, a declining percentage of all outgo. Nor has the decrease in the food percentage been confined to well-to-do families. The living-cost-index budget for manual workers of the Bureau of Labor Statistics, to take one indication, allowed 43% for food in pre-war years against 38% in recent years; that of the National Industrial Conference Board cut down the food percentage from 43% to 33%.

The trend has been slowly making headway, with ups and downs, for generations. Waldron's estimate of national income and outlays in the United States as of 1890, when the country was predominantly agricultural, food was plentiful and its preparation was commonly carried on at home, nevertheless assigns 24.2% of all expenditures to food.[1] Going back farther, the account book of the family of a government employee in Washington, D. C., in the year 1816–1817, shows 46% expended for food.[2]

Cost-of-living budgets for workers in other countries make allotments to food, presumably expressing expert judgments, as shown on page 55.[3]

Budgets of workers in Leningrad in 1929, as published by the Soviet Government, allowed 46% for food.[4]

On the whole, it is safe to say that in no other country in our time and in no previous generation has any large body of people

---

[1] Estimate by G. B. Waldron cited in "Economic Principles of Consumption" by Paul H. Nystrom, Ronald, New York, 1929, p. 160.

[2] "The Standard of Living at a Professional Level, 1816–17 and 1926–27" by Charles Going Woodhouse, *Journal of Political Economy*, Oct., 1929.

[3] Abstracted from "Economics of Food Consumption" by Edith Hawley, McGraw-Hill, New York, 1932, pp. 123, 128. Note that these percentages apply to workers' budgets, not to national consumption.

[4] "Daily Life in Russia" by Alzada Comstock in *Current History*, Dec., 1930.

| | Percentage of
Income Spent |
Country	for Food
Canada	35
Australia	35
Chile	42
Sweden	43
Egypt	52
Germany	55
Switzerland	57
India	82

been able to exist with so small a proportion of its effort devoted to getting food as has been required of the American people during the past two decades.

APPORTIONMENTS FOR CLOTHING AND HOME MAINTENANCE

Turning back to Table 10, we find a significant approach to agreement among all the percentages of outgo apportioned to clothing. Apparently among modern industrialized peoples the allotment to this item in normal years falls between a tenth and an eighth of total outgo. The figures for both the United States and the United Kingdom indicate, however, that clothing gives way easily in years of depression. Price concessions do not bring out much additional buying. Feaveryear states that "the fall in expenditures upon clothing is mainly, though not entirely, accounted for by the fall of prices." Some supporting British evidence is a slight fall in the number of persons employed in the clothing industries, coupled with the increase of population, which "indicates that the nation as a whole was worse dressed in 1932 than at the earlier period."

Comparisons of spendings for home maintenance are unreliable because of the effects of government subvention, rate fixing, and disparities in the items included. However, some of the sub-classes under this head (not detailed in Table 10) yield points of interest. British percentages for rentals, fuel and light approximate those in this country and exhibit a similar rise in depression. American apportionments for furnishings and household services are much higher than British and drop more sharply in depression. In pre-war times the German percentages for furnishings and services were slightly above the American percentages, while those for rentals and fuel were considerably below.

APPORTIONMENTS FOR "ALL OTHERS"

When the residual items, grouped under *All Others*, are lumped, as in Table 10, the comparison suggests a well-marked tendency toward uniformity. However, the separate classes listed under this major heading reveal large variations in consumption habits.

The German pre-war percentage (10%) for alcoholic beverages and tobacco combined is about 2% above the American pre-war and almost precisely equal to the British post-war percentages. The American post-war apportionment for alcoholic beverages is not properly comparable. Attention has already been directed to the decreasing consumption of alcoholic beverages in the United Kingdom. Feaveryear attributes the increased apportionment for tobacco (based on Census of Production data) to "expenditure by women smokers, who, for some years, will probably increase in numbers, non-smokers being at present chiefly amongst the older women." Conceivably, data for alcoholic beverages and tobacco over a longer period would bring to view something like a universal ratio (in Western industrialized countries) of expenditures for these two forms of stimulants.

The apportionment to transportation in post-war America reflects the extraordinary popularity of automobiles in this country. Registration figures for Great Britain show that in 1932 there were only 1,100,000 cars and 600,000 motorcycles in use. Feaveryear allows 25% of the expenditure for operating cars as business expense against our 30% allowance. A more detailed comparison reveals a sharp rise in British ratios both for local fares and for vehicle purchase and upkeep, in contrast with little change in the American apportionments.

The British apportionment for sickness and death is about half of that prevailing here. Feaveryear allows average gross receipts for physicians of only £800, while our figure for the corresponding years is $8,000. Both nations show an increased percentage for this form of outgo in 1931–1932. The assignment by Feaveryear of only 0.2% for jewelry and cosmetics probably signifies that the estimates are not fairly comparable. Apportionments for recreation in the two countries are not widely different, and the differences are explainable by the rapid growth of motion-picture attendance on this side. The divergences in proportions going to social-cultural activities presumably arise from the large amounts expended in this country for reading matter and for contributions to churches and charities.

The heavy allotment to taxes in the United Kingdom, rising from 9.5% to 11.1%, no doubt distorts the comparisons of other items. Inasmuch as the British custom has been to raise an exceptionally large proportion of revenue through direct taxation, with a correspondingly lighter burden of indirect taxes, the effect is both to increase the percentages for taxes and to keep the costs of many commodities relatively low. But it should be observed in this connection that an exceptionally large part of the 10% expended for drink and tobacco in the United Kingdom in reality flows into the government treasury.

In his earlier estimates of savings Feaveryear used simply the average annual amount of new capital issues plus the amount spent for building or purchasing new homes. His later revision is more in line with the methods used in the present study (see Appendix D) and makes for a reasonably dependable comparison. The decline during depression in the amounts allocated to savings seems to have been even more precipitous here than in Great Britain. In both countries the decrease was more severe than in any other class of outgo.

INDICATIONS OF PARALLELISM OF CONSUMERS' DEMANDS

Especially illuminating is the parallelism between the American pre-war distribution of outgo and the British distribution in 1924–1927. In this comparison the difference in average family spending power, making allowances for prices, is not extreme. In fact, it is fair to say that the average British family of those years was on about the same plane of living as the average American family of 10 to 15 years earlier; and except for discrepancies in home maintenance and in taxes partly explained above, the two families had strikingly similar living habits.

Carrying the thought a step farther, a fair deduction from Table 10 is that the tastes and demands of average families in the United States, Germany, and Great Britain are not widely dissimilar. Additional evidence bearing on this point will be given in Chapter X. The notion, rather widely held abroad as well as by certain of our own best minds, that Americans are peculiarly obsessed by an itch for speed, swagger, and excitement gets little support from an examination of the facts. Nearer the truth in all probability is a judgment that all the modern industrialized peoples, *given equal spending power*, would use it for substantially similar objects.

PART TWO
ANALYSIS

CHAPTER IV

INDEXES

Part One has yielded the materials for a study of consumers' wants and buying habits, looking toward some tentative forecasting of demands. But before we can make much use of the materials, they must be put through a refining process. To make ready for the process is the function of this chapter.

One step in the process consists of eliminating the influence of population gains. The simplest method for this purpose is to restate over-all figures in terms of some common unit—for instance, per capita or per family. We have taken the family as the normal unit of consumption.

The second and main part of the process consists of removing so far as possible the effects of monetary change in price levels and price relationships. Plainly, before one can properly compare estimates for a series of years, which are stated in current dollars of widely variant purchasing power, it is necessary to reduce them to some common base.

By custom the reduction to a common base is accomplished by calculating the number of dollars endowed with the purchasing power which they possessed in a given base year that would be required in order to effectuate purchases made in each of the other years under review. The usual and most convenient base year is 1913. Our figures for consumers' outgo in the 1909–1931 period will rest on a common base when we get them all translated into terms of the so-called "dollar of 1913."

THE FAMILY AS A STATISTICAL UNIT

Chapter VII will present an estimate that well over four-fifths of consumers' outgo centers on family life, either in the home or outside. Only a minor fraction consists of spendings for strictly individual enjoyment. Though the percentages do not pretend to be exact, they serve to express the dominance of the family as the unit which governs the distribution of outgo among classes of objects.

61

Spending power, too, is better measured by families than by individuals. The number of gainful workers per family in 1930 was 1.63, a proportion considerably below that shown in previous censuses. In 32% of the families the number of gainful workers was two or more. One may safely assume that the larger portion of the earnings of the extra workers, additional to the main bread-winner, went into the family purse. Unless total spending power is calculated in terms of the family, the figures are likely to portray a distorted picture of actual living conditions.

In this study, therefore, per capita averages have been set aside in favor of per family averages. The number of families in census years has been taken from the census report and in intervening years has been derived by straight-line interpolation. The national outgo classified into major classes and main sub-classes, as in Appendix A, has been divided by the number of families to get national average family spendings and withholdings.

The average family, of course, does not exist in any other form than as a statistical unit. It is the same as the average family of the United States Census, which consisted in 1930 of 4.1 persons. It is neither a rural nor an urban family; neither rich nor poor. It has no locale. It is simply a convenient epitome of *the entire body* of American consumers.

An average by its very nature covers up variations—in this instance very wide variations among American families in respect to size, incomes, environment and tastes. Global estimates, such as are here presented, may easily create a delusion of uniformity and stability over a period of years which are far from characteristic of the component elements in the estimates. This possibility should be kept in view, especially through the earlier chapters of Part Two.

For some different purpose it may well be useful and interesting to classify families in smaller groups and examine the variations among them. The present study, however, is concerned solely with national totals and national averages. It would only breed confusion to try to fill in details before the picture as a whole has been sketched.

LIMITATIONS OF COST-OF-LIVING INDEXES

One easy method of reducing to a common base current dollar figures covering personal income or outgo of a series of years is to apply one of the general cost-of-living indexes. The method is unsuitable for our purpose, however, as will clearly appear in the following brief, non-technical recital of the methods of constructing these indexes.

Records of retail prices of a large number of consumers' commodities have been gathered by the United States Bureau of Labor Statistics since 1890 (enlarged and improved in 1907 and again in 1919) and by the National Industrial Conference Board since 1918. These records from scattered localities are combined into weighted index numbers representing the national movements of prices of each important class of commodities. The separate index numbers are then again weighted on the basis of a predetermined family budget which assigns to each class of commodities its proportionate share of family expenditure; and the separate indexes thus weighted are combined into general cost-of-living indexes.

Plainly a cost-of-living index is governed to a considerable extent by the weights assigned in the basic family budget. Both the B.L.S. and the N.I.C.B. indexes are founded on hypothetical budgets of workingmen's families.[1] For two reasons— (a) because the budgets are hypothetical and (b) because they pertain only to the families of industrial workmen—the general cost-of-living indexes are not well adapted to measuring the movements of prices of objects actually purchased by *the whole body* of consumers, which includes not only wage-earners but also farmers, business and professional men, salaried employees and all other elements in our population.

King undertakes to supply the deficiency by computing five distinct series of index numbers covering, respectively, urban workers, farm laborers, farmers, families spending about $5,000 for direct goods, and families spending about $25,000.[2] His index numbers "represent the estimated average fluctuations in

---

[1] The word "hypothetical" may be questioned on the ground that the base budgets used for weighting grow out of fairly extensive investigations of actual family expenditures. But the findings of such investigations, even if acceptable as truly typical of living habits at the moment, quickly become out of date. Cf. Douglas' criticism ("Real Wages in the United States, 1890–1926" by Paul H. Douglas, Houghton-Mifflin, Boston, 1930, Chaps. III and IV) and his remark (*op. cit.*, p. 61) regarding the error inherent in "the assumption that the relative amount spent on the various main groups of commodities remains constant throughout the period. This is not so." The N.I.C.B. base budget is quite frankly a product of judgment and "theoretical considerations."

[2] "The National Income and Its Purchasing Power," Chap. III.

the prices of commodities supposed to have been consumed respectively by each of the five classes of families mentioned."[3] In some way not explained he derives, presumably from the five indexes, "a common price index which is believed to represent approximately the *average for the year* relative prices of goods consumed by all consumers in the United States."[4]

In the light of this review, brief as it is, the need for a new over-all index of the prices of objects purchased by the people of the United States must be evident. A sound basis can never be supplied by field investigations of family expenditures unless (*a*) future investigations are far more comprehensive than any hitherto conducted and (*b*) they are kept up currently, indeed almost continuously. It is highly improbable that these two essential conditions will be fulfilled in the near future. A better basis than has been previously available is supplied by estimates of total national outgo of consumers, such as have been presented in Part One; provided, of course, that the estimates are reasonably dependable.

An Aggregate Price-Level Index of Consumers' Purchases

In order to reduce our estimates, so far stated only in current dollars, to a common base—and, as a by-product, to arrive at the desired new index—we have utilized, first, the retail price indexes of various classes of commodities and intangibles published by the Bureau of Labor Statistics and by the National Industrial Conference Board. They are supplemented by the B.L.S. wholesale price indexes of the following groups which consist largely of finished consumers' goods: furniture and house furnishings, petroleum products, automobiles, and automobile tires and tubes. The wholesale price indexes of these lines are reasonably applicable to retail prices because, as indicated in Appendix B, the ratios of wholesale to retail prices are

---

[3] *Op. cit.*, p. 70.

[4] *Op cit.*, p. 170. See also "Retail Price Level" by Willford I. King, a *News-Bulletin* of the National Bureau of Economic Research, Sept. 10, 1928, in which King explains the derivation and weighting of the series of index numbers therein presented "indicative of changes in the price of consumers' goods in general." But the series given in the *News-Bulletin* differs markedly from the series referred to in our text which we have derived from "The National Income and Its Purchasing Power," a later publication.

nearly uniform throughout the period. The indexes referred to in this paragraph are applied not only to the specific articles covered by them but also to various other articles which are closely analogous or related.

The sources above mentioned are so well known and their indexes so easily available that the notes subjoined to Table 13, in the next chapter, will be found sufficient, we believe, to indicate how they have been applied. In only one case does further explanation seem to be called for; that is, the application of the B.L.S. index of rents to our estimates of spendings for housing (commercial rents paid for leased homes, imputed rental values of owner-occupied homes and operating expenses of such homes). In Appendix C the B. L. S. index is rejected as a guide to the total rents paid for leased homes on the ground that it is based on identical properties and fails to allow for gains in size and quality of housing. For this very reason, however, the index is well adapted to the present purpose; that is, measuring variations in the command over housing of consumers' dollars.

Our estimates of consumers' spendings for professional services, domestic and personal services, hand trades and other services have been computed, as set forth in Appendix C, on the basis of average annual gross compensation received by the individuals rendering the services. Rates of compensation do not conform closely to changes in the cost-of-living. We have found it advisable, therefore, to derive from our detailed estimates of rates of compensation a separate index for each major occupation; and this index has then been applied to the payments by consumers for the services rendered by each occupation. The study reveals some interesting relationships but is too lengthy to be reported at this point.

The items covered by indexes of well-defined classes of consumers' commodities and intangibles aggregate nearly 70% of the total of consumers' outgo. Moreover, the items include substantially all the essentials of comfortable living in our generation—the entire outgo for food, tobacco and clothing, fully three-fourths of transportation, nearly nine-tenths of home maintenance and of sickness and death, and about four-tenths of personal appearance. The proportion is large enough and the nature of the items is such that these computations yield a *comprehensive index of the price-level of annual purchases of consumers' goods by the whole body of American consumers.*

The aggregate price-level index of consumers' purchases is obtained by totaling the national spendings for all items above mentioned (a) in terms of current dollars and (b) in terms of the number of dollars of 1913 that would have been required to purchase these items; then taking the relative of the two totals in each year as the over-all index number for that year. The index will be found in Tables 11 and 12. Before presenting it, however, a number of related questions should be treated.

The method of computing the index, it will be observed, avoids the necessity of relying upon some hypothetical budget in order to assign weights to the component items; for the weighting is automatically provided in our estimates (Appendix A) of national spendings each year for each item.

CONSUMERS' PURCHASES NOT COVERED BY SPECIFIC PRICE INDEXES

We still have to deal with the remaining 30% of consumers' outgo. This remainder comprises two widely different groups of items:

(a) Spendings for a variety of non-essentials, such as alcoholic beverages, a considerable number of specialties—for example, household electric appliances, radio sets, musical instruments, sporting goods and cosmetics—and an assortment of services rendered by commercial or sociable enterprises, including garages, theaters, amusement parks, hotels, travel agencies, clubs, private schools, churches and fraternal or benevolent societies.

(b) Withholdings—that is, payments for direct taxes and for the different forms of savings.

The first group amounts, on the average, to somewhere near 18% of total outgo; the second group, 12%. But both percentages are highly variable.

The first group is made up of spendings for new or wholly unstandardized goods; to collect comparative prices, therefore, is impracticable. The National Industrial Conference Board, to be sure, offers an index of spendings for recreation based on records of motion picture theater admission charges; but the movements of the index in the post-war period are slight and apparently meaningless, since they are not related to standards of performance. Failing usable specific indexes in this field, we are driven to the assumption that the forces which govern the broad swings of prices of other consumers' goods operate equally on prices of unstandardized commodities and services.

To the first group we apply, therefore, the aggregate price-level index of consumers' purchases already described.

AN AGGREGATE INDEX OF PRESENT WORTH OF CONSUMERS' ACQUISITIONS

To translate annual withholdings from their estimated amounts in current dollars into values stated on a comparable basis—that is, in terms of dollars of the purchasing power of 1913—presents a quite distinct problem. The problem has not, to my knowledge, previously been attacked. The ultimate aim may be defined as follows: to ascertain the comparative present worth in a series of years of assets which either were acquired or could have been acquired with money not spent for current consumption but withheld for the sake of assuring future consumption.[5]

Two factors must enter into the reckoning of anyone who is logically debating with himself whether to spend his money on current pleasures or to withhold it from the present and invest it in the future: (a) the amount of future money income which he expects to receive as the fruit of his self-denial; (b) the purchasing power of his anticipated money income—that is, its future command over consumers' goods. These are the two factors which govern the present real-income worth of money withheld from spendings.[6]

Both the essential factors can be approximately measured: (a) the amount of future money income on the basis of yields of securities; (b) *anticipated* purchasing power of future money income on the basis of the purchasing power of money at the moment of withholding. Neither of the two measurements is wholly satisfactory; but they will have to serve until something better is proposed.

---

[5] This definition of the problem presumes acceptance of the concept of direct taxes, presented in Chap. II, as being essentially amounts withheld from spendings in order to provide future social security and protection. The concept places taxes in the same general category with savings; and the same index is applied to taxes and to savings. Taxes might be viewed in some different light. But the sums involved are scarcely large enough to demand extended discussion of this particular question.

[6] Far be it from me to imply that decisions to spend or to save are customarily reached by reflective logic. All I mean to say is that a thoughtful observer, who is attempting to gauge the comparative values in different years of current dollars withheld from spending, would have to make the simple analysis above indicated, irrespective of how irrational the actual decision might be.

Savings, as treated in Chapter II, go into four main forms of acquisitions: life insurance premiums; cash holdings; securities, both stocks and bonds, both new and old; and real property. As implied above, we start with the postulate that the ups and downs of valuations of stocks and bonds, measured by their yields, are representative of the movements of valuations of other forms of assets. The postulate is obviously subject to qualification. Yields on stocks at times move under the influence of speculative excitement and take a different course from that set by the forces which synchronously play on the yields of other forms of acquisitions. However, it is plain to any observer that prices of equities in real property tend to rise or fall with corresponding movements in prices of stocks, though not necessarily at the same rate. Monies withheld for other uses—taxes, insurance premiums, cash deposits—are not directly responsive to changes in security prices; but they are reasonably valued on the basis of the yields they would obtain if devoted to the purchase of income-producing securities. Hence, a fair approximation to the potential yields of all acquisitions is supplied by taking into account both speculative yields on stocks and investment yields on good to prime bonds.

The next question is how to weight, respectively, speculative and investment yields. The answer is wholly a matter of judgment. The only time, as shown in Table 11, when a marked discrepancy occurs between the stock yield index and the bond yield index is during a period of universal inflation or deflation of property valuations. In any such period people of all occupations and income classes are powerfully affected. In inflationary periods they enlarge their speculative purchases of equities. In deflationary periods the weaker holders sacrifice equities because they cannot continue to save; but those who are financially stronger acquire the equities. In both periods the proportion of savings devoted to equities is doubtless larger than in normal times. In the light of these considerations it seems sensible to assign equal weights to the two yields; and this is done by using an arithmetic average of the two indexes of yields (reversed). This forms the best index we have been able to devise of the potential income-producing capacity of withholdings.

When it comes to measuring the command of anticipated income over future purchases of consumers' goods, the most suitable indicator is the current price-level index of consumers' purchases. It would be absurd to suppose that consumers as a body can foresee movements of prices. The present is their only guide.

In summary: to ascertain the present worth in current dollars of withholdings for future consumption, it is necessary to apply the index of income-producing capacity; and to express on a comparable basis the purchasing power of future income, it is necessary to apply the current index of the price level of consumers' purchases. The product of the two indexes forms the final index of comparable present worth of consumers' acquisitions. This index is applied to all withholdings. The calculation of the index is shown in Table 11 below.

TABLE 11.—CALCULATION OF INDEX OF COMPARABLE PRESENT WORTH OF
CONSUMERS' ACQUISITIONS

Procedure in Deriving Index	1913	1919	1920	1921	1922	1923	1924	1925	1926	1927	1928	1929	1930	1931
1. Index of Stock Yields (reversed)	100	88	80	73	94	80	91	106	107	119	141	149	108	84
2. Index of Bond Yields (reversed)	100	88	79	81	94	94	94	96	99	101	104	99	103	99
3. Arithmetic Average of Indexes of Stock and Bond Yields	100	88	80	77	94	87	94	103	104	112	123	124	106	92
4. Aggregate Price-Level Index of Consumers' Purchases	100	169	188	158	147	149	147	149	149	147	145	146	139	125
5. Resultant Index of Present Worth of Consumers' Acquisitions	100	149	150	122	148	130	138	154	155	165	178	181	147	115

Line 1. Record of average yields of dividend-paying common stocks dealt in on New York Stock Exchange, compiled by Cleveland Trust Company, and cited in "Prices" by George F. Warren and Frank A. Pearson, Wiley, New York, 1933, p. 286.
Line 2. Average yields of 60 domestic bonds, compiled by Standard Statistics, and cited in the *Survey of Current Business*, United States Department of Commerce.
Line 3. Arithmetic average of Line 1 and Line 2.
Line 4. Computed as explained in the text.
Line 5. Product of Line 3 and Line 4.

AN OVER-ALL REAL-VALUE INDEX OF CONSUMERS' PURCHASES AND ACQUISITIONS

Having now covered all the objects of consumers' outgo with indexes, it remains only to calculate the total outgo of each year in terms of dollars of 1913 and to take the relative of this sum to the total outgo in terms of current dollars as the over-all index number for that year of the combined price-level of purchases of consumers' goods and present worth-level of acquisitions of assets by consumers.

The resultant over-all "real-value" index appears in Table 12. It is *not* a price-level index of consumption; for that purpose the index based on consumers' purchases alone is better. The significance of the over-all index is reserved for discussion in Chapter V. It is enough to say here that it is submitted as a reasonable approximation which makes it possible to come closer than before to a true measurement of alterations in the average well-being of American consumers.

Interpolations and Comparisons

The price-level index of consumers' purchases (and consequently the over-all index of consumers' purchases and acquisitions) is calculable only for the years in which itemized estimates of spendings are available (that is, Census of Manufactures years). No basis exists in our estimates alone for ascertaining the index figures of intervening years.

However, a quite definite relationship emerges from a comparison of the index of consumers' purchases with the B.L.S. index. Our index number for 1919 is 90% of the B.L.S. number; for 1921, 89%; for 1923, 87%; for 1925, 1927, 1929 and 1931, each 85%. The striking regularity of the decline in this ratio from 1919 to 1925 and its steadiness thereafter can scarcely be fortuitous. Presumably the initial ratio (90% in 1919) is in large part a consequent of the differing rates of advance from 1913 to 1919 in (*a*) the price-level of items in workers' budgets covered by the B.L.S. index and (*b*) the price-level of articles consumed by the population as a whole covered by our index.

The decline in the ratio from 1919 to 1925 is ascribable, one may suppose, to an increasing disparity between the hypothetical budget used by the Bureau of Labor Statistics and the actual spendings of the whole population. The B.L.S. budget assigns heavy weights to a limited list of prime necessities. Prices of these necessities have apparently remained above the average price-level of actual purchases by consumers. By 1923, on this hypothesis, the budget of the average American family had reached a stable relationship with the B.L.S. budget, which has since persisted. Whether the explanation here suggested be

TABLE 12.—COMPARATIVE TABLE OF INDEXES

Indexes	1913	1919	1920	1921	1922	1923	1924	1925	1926	1927	1928	1929	1930	1931
1. Over-All Real-Value Index of Consumers' Purchases and Acquisitions..	100	166	181	152	147	146	146	150	150	149	148	149	139	124
2. Price-Level Index of Consumers' Purchases..........	100	169	188	158	147	149	147	149	149	147	145	146	139	125
3. B.L.S. Cost-of-Living Index........	100	188	209	177	167	171	171	176	175	173	171	171	164	148
4. Ratios (in per cent) of Index of Consumers' Purchases to the B.L.S. Index	100	90		89		87		85		85		85		85
5. N.I.C.B. Cost-of-Living Index......	100[1]	169	197	166	156	161	163	168	168	165	162	161	156	140
6. Ratios (in per cent) of Index of Consumers' Purchases to the N.I.C.B. Index..........	100	100		95		93		89		89		90		89
7. King's Over-All Consumers' Index (derived)........	100	174	197	173	162	165	165	169	171	167	165	165		
8. Ratios (in per cent) of Index of Consumers' Purchases to King's Over-All Index..........	100	97		91		90		88		88		88		
9. Ratios (in per cent) of our Over-All Index to King's Over-All Index....	100	95		88		88		89		90		90		

[1] 1914.
Line 1. Covers all objects of consumers' outgo weighted on the basis of national spendings and withholdings; see text.
Line 2. Covers all consumers' goods for which specific indexes are available (about 70 % of total outgo) weighted as above; see text.
Line 3. B.L.S. index weighted in accordance with an assumed workingman's budget.
Line 4. Line 2 divided by Line 3.
Line 5. N.I.C.B index weighted as above.
Line 6. Line 2 divided by Line 5.
Line 7. Relatives of King's estimates of national income for 1913 to 1927, inclusive, (a) in current dollars and (b) in dollars of 1913 ("The National Income and Its Purchasing Power," pp. 74 and 76). Index numbers for 1928 and 1929 supplied by National Bureau of Economic Research. King does not directly present the index figures here cited but does supply somewhat different figures in another connection (op. cit., p. 170). The reason for the discrepancy is not apparent.
Line 8. Line 2 divided by Line 7.
Line 9. Line 1 divided by Line 7.

accepted or not, the ratio between the two indexes appears to have sufficient consistency to justify us in interpolating numbers for the missing years in our index of consumers' purchases by applying the following percentages to the B.L.S. index figures: 90% in 1920; 88% in 1922; 86% in 1924; 85% in the remaining even years.

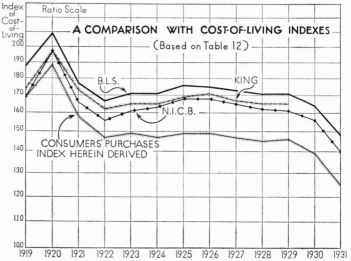

CHART J.—The divergence of our consumers' purchases index from the cost-of-living indexes is ascribable mainly to different methods of weighting.

Table 12 and Chart J present comparisons with other consumption price-level indexes which reveal similar relationships. The N.I.C.B. index (Line 5 of Table 12) is considerably lower than the B.L.S. index and much higher than our index of consumers' purchases, especially from 1925 on.   King's over-all consumers' index (derived by relating his estimates of national income in current dollars to his estimates in 1913 dollars) rather closely parallels the N.I.C.B. index.   The ratios of his index to both our index of consumers' purchases and our over-all index (Lines 8 and 9 of Table 12) show a rapid decline from 1919 to 1921 and a fair degree of steadiness thereafter.

VALIDITY OF THE NEW INDEX OF CONSUMERS' PURCHASES

Now that the price-level index of consumers' purchases and its relationships with established indexes have been presented, some further discussion of its make-up is required. It will be recognized as a variation of what Fisher calls an "aggregative" index.[7] It is complicated, however, by lack of data as to quantities of goods purchased; furthermore, new and substitute goods to an unknown amount are introduced each year. All that we really have is a record of total sums paid out each year for consumers' goods reckoned (a) at current prices and (b) as they would have been at 1913 prices.

At first sight the procedure in forming the index may seem to create hopeless confusion through continual changes of base. In point of fact, if the differences in goods purchased from one year to the next in the series were great, an index computed by the method here used would be worthless. It would measure neither price movements nor demand movements; it would be neither fish nor fowl.

But we have seen in Chapter II that alterations in the distribution of national outgo among the 12 major classes of objects take place gradually. This is so even when outgo is stated in current dollars. The truth of the observation will become clearer in subsequent analyses after fluctuations in the purchasing power of money have been eliminated. Over a term of several years, to be sure, the alterations in distribution of outgo may be large; for an example, turn to Chart K in the next chapter. But the essential point for the present purpose is that the changes come little by little through a steady process of substituting new articles for old and slowly forming new habits of living.

It is quite possible that more refined treatment of the data would improve the index. It is also possible that the series of index numbers if extended over a much longer period would become seriously distorted by excessive alterations in consumption. So far as the series is now carried, however, it displays a

---

[7] The method of constructing the index does not conform precisely to any of the accepted formulae, but is believed to be justifiable because of the relatively slight changes from year to year in the distribution of consumers' outgo among classes of objects. It is adopted as the most practical method for utilizing the data at hand. For helpful treatments of the problem of computing indexes when both price and quantity are variables see among others: "The Making of Index Numbers" by Irving Fisher, Houghton Mifflin, Boston, 1927; "Money, Credit and Commerce" by Alfred Marshall, Macmillan, London, Appendix B, pp. 275ff.; "The Construction of Index Numbers" by Warren M. Persons, Houghton Mifflin, Boston, 1928; and "A Treatise on Money" by J. M. Keynes, Harcourt Brace, New York, 1930, Chap. 8.

consistency of relationships with other indexes which may fairly be taken to indicate that distortions are not yet perceptible.

Chart J makes clear the parallelism in recent years of all the general indexes there represented. This is not in itself surprising since all are built up from approximately the same secondary indexes. At the same time, it goes to reinforce the view that broad price changes, arising out of movements of credit, affect at about the same time nearly all consumers' goods; for if this were not so, large modifications in weighting would in all probability introduce into the indexes not merely different levels but conflicting trends.

Need for an Improved Consumption Index

Index numbers are indispensable tools in efforts to master the intricacies of economic relationships and to discover underlying trends. When a general index is misleading or is wrongly applied, the consequent unsound judgments may have far-reaching influence. Three misinterpretations growing out of the misuse of cost-of-living indexes are worth citing.

1. The B.L.S. and N.I.C.B. indexes, though specifically designed to apply to workingmen's families, have been quite commonly taken—in the absence of an inclusive index—as gauges of the general purchasing power of consumers' dollars. Exaggerated estimates of the actual damage suffered by the entire body of consumers in the first years of the current depression have been one of the results. It is not yet possible to say whether a like comment applies to the later years.

2. Both the standard indexes above referred to, though compiled with due care, are probably misleading even when restricted to workingmen's incomes. The rapid upward sweep of intangibles and slower, but unmistakable, rise of processed commodities in total consumption, as set forth in Chapter II, could scarcely have left workingmen's outgo unmodified. These movements at the least constitute indications that the basic budgets of the two indexes allow excessive weights to prime necessities and insufficient weights to services and to non-essentials. If so, a true cost-of-living index of workingmen's families would run much closer to our aggregate index. Insofar as the indexes now in use overstate the price levels of goods purchased by workingmen's families, real wages are correspondingly underestimated.

3. King's over-all consumers' index seems clearly too high—by 10% or more from 1921 on. If so, the American people, instead of suffering a loss from 1919 to 1921 of 3%, as King figures it, actually had a gain of 3% in real income; and their gain in real income from 1919 to 1929, instead of being 43%, approached 58%.[8] These corrections make a large difference in judgments as to the true effects on consumption of periods of slump and of boom.

[8] Based on extension of King's estimates in "America's Capacity to Consume," p. 152.

In general, the price-level indexes of consumption previously available appear to have failed to keep in step with consumers' takings. Some slight revisions have been made, it is true, in the budgeted weights of the B.L.S. and N.I.C.B. indexes. But the revisions are plainly inadequate as allowances for the changes set forth in Chapter II.[9] The new aggregate price-level index presented in this chapter, though far from perfect, is offered as an improved device for gauging the movements of national consumption. The realities of consumption at best are seen obscurely through the monetary fog; and increased care is called for if harmful misconceptions are to be avoided.

[9] A like comment applies in some measure to the Snyder index of general price level (see "Business Cycles and Measurements" by Carl Snyder, Macmillan, New York, 1927, pp. 286–287) and to other indexes, not here discussed since they are only in part indexes of consumption.

CHAPTER V

TAKINGS

A plain distinction exists between the sums disbursed by consumers and what they get for their money. They pay out dollars which are uniform. They take in exchange an immense variety of objects designed to satisfy their wants.

Two Distinct Methods of Deflating Current Money Outgo

When it comes to reducing consumers' disbursements from their original expression in current dollars to a common base expressed in terms of dollars of 1913, one can look at the transactions from either of these viewpoints. If the purpose is to appraise consumption in its relation to other factors in the national economy, only the money side need be considered; for it is only through paying out money that consumers as such directly affect exchange and production of goods. The suitable procedure, then, is to apply a general index of the consumption price-level, preferably the aggregate price-level index of consumers' purchases given in the preceding chapter. Since the all-important consideration is the purchasing power of money passing through the hands of consumers, the aggregate index is properly applied to all disbursements for all classes of objects, including acquisitions as well as consumers' goods.

On the other hand, if the purpose is to survey the course followed by each of the main components of consumption, the foregoing procedure is inadequate, in that it does not take into account changes in price relationships among these components. For this purpose it is necessary to apply to each major class and main sub-class of objects of consumers' outgo the particular price-level index which best fits it; and in order to evaluate withholdings on an equivalent basis, it is necessary to apply an index which is a product of indexes of their income-producing capacity and of the purchasing power of their anticipated income, as set forth in the preceding chapter. When all these separate

76

indexes are applied, the outcome is a restatement of total outgo in conformity with the over-all real-value index of consumers' purchases and acquisitions described in the preceding chapter.

The principal aim of Part Two is to discover the characteristics and trends not of consumption as a unit but of the main classes of objects of consumers' spendings and withholdings. The principal aim of Part Three is to forecast under assumed conditions changes in the distribution of spending power among classes of objects. The inclusive purpose, in short, is to study the elements in consumption, their movements and their interactions. The purpose requires adopting the second of the two procedures above sketched; and this has been done in translating the current dollars of Table 1 (detailed in Appendix A) into the figures of takings per average family stated in dollars of 1913 which will be found in Table 13.

An Index of the Price-Level of Well-Being

Before examining the table, it will be advisable to give some further thought to its true meaning. The foregoing discussion has made clear that the dollar figures in the table do not measure changes in disbursements for the various classes of objects; the deflated values of disbursements would properly be obtained by applying the general price-level index. The figures do measure approximately changes in *real values received by consumers*.

The total of real values received might be called *real income*. But the term seems to me inapt in the present connection, because it connotes reactions by consumers, whereas the values here referred to are values-in-exchange, market place values, not values-in-use. The words *intake* and *takings* are chosen with the thought of centering attention on the objects purchased rather than either the money paid for them or the pleasure experienced in using them.

Of course, "real values" in an absolute sense cannot be calculated. All that can be done is to approximate changes in real values received in relation to some base year—in this case, the year 1913. By applying an index of prices of equivalent units of each class of consumers' takings, we ascertain the number of units purchased with the current money outgo of each year. The increase or decrease measures the gain or loss from the base year in real value received.

TABLE 13.—BASE TABULATION OF COMPARABLE VALUES OF TAKINGS PER FAMILY[1]

(In 1913 dollars)

Classes of Takings	1909	1914	Pre-war Average	1919	1921	1923	1925	1927	1929	1931
Totals of Average Family Outgo[2]	$1,000	$1,550	$1,575	$1,686	$1,575	$1,861	$1,958	$1,978	$2,036	$1,689
1. Foods and Soft Drinks (including home-grown foods consumed by farmers and others)	$409	$402	$406	$415	$365	$406	$409	$407	$416	$368
Commercial Only	333	330	331	368	311	354	358	357	369	314
Groceries and Delicatessen (Canned Goods, Coffee, Flour, etc.)[3]	73	72	72	78	65	77	77	77	81	68
Meat and Fish[3]	105	96	101	105	72	83	88	84	83	66
Dairy Products[3]	66	65	65	66	60	77	77	81	79	73
Bakery Products[3]	28	24	26	32	30	33	33	35	38	34
Fresh Fruits, Vegetables and Nuts[3]	45	51	48	51	50	49	48	47	53	42
Confectionery, Ice Cream and Soft Drinks[3]	15	21	18	34	32	33	33	33	33	30
2. Payments to Industry for Alcoholic Beverages and Other Illegal Commodities[4]	100	92	96	50	36	39	42	43	47	34
3. Tobacco[5]	33	34	33	34	35	42	41	42	45	37
4. Clothing	193	183	188	167	194	214	194	200	199	168
Women's Apparel (Clothing, Millinery, Furs, Dry Goods, Fabrics, Gloves, Umbrellas and Services)[6]	77	75	76	69	81	94	84	89	90	82
Men's and Boy's Apparel (Clothing, Furnishings, Hats, Gloves, Umbrellas and Services)[6]	58	50	54	45	51	54	49	50	48	37
Boots and Shoes (Includes Repairs)[6]	42	41	41	36	39	41	36	36	36	30
Knit Goods (Men's and Women's Hose, Underwear, Outerwear and Fabrics)[5]	15	16	16	18	23	26	24	25	25	20
5. Transportation	56	84	70	146	144	265	329	319	340	245
Vehicles (Includes Operating Cost)	36	60	48	126	123	241	303	292	315	226
Automobiles, new[7]	9	24	17	53	53	125	134	107	125	64
Gasoline and Oil[7]	5	9	6	22	25	30	42	41	51	41
Automobile Parts and Accessories (Parts and Tires)[7]	4	8	6	35	28	61	96	108	97	82
Repair and Storage[4]	3	5	4	6	6	12	16	18	21	16
All Other (Includes Motorcycles and Bicycles, Horse-drawn Vehicles, Insurance, Licenses, Gasoline Taxes, Chauffeurs, Blacksmiths[4]	16	14	15	10	9	13	15	18	21	23
Local Fares	20	23	22	21	22	24	26	27	26	18
Bus, Taxicab, Hack[5]	1	2	2	3	3	5	8	10	12	8
Street Railway Fares and Ferries[8]	19	21	20	18	19	19	18	17	14	10
6. Home Maintenance	424	383	403	349	330	387	407	446	494	442
Housing (Includes imputed rentals)[9]	195	178	188	176	152	165	187	217	250	253
Fuel and Light (extra-commercial and commercial)[5]	56	62	59	57	53	63	56	61	61	52
Furniture and House Furnishings (Includes Merchandise Manufactured on Retail Premises)[4]	89	68	79	56	67	90	94	94	104	68
House Furnishings[5,7]	71	52	62	35	46	62	63	61	62	42

Item										
Electrical Appliances and Supplies[4]										
Radio[4]	8	8	8	11	6	6	7	11	13	13
Musical Instruments[4]	5	5	6	6	2	2	7	9	15	6
All Other (Repair and Storage; Flowers, Plants, Seeds)[4]	7	10	11	8	12	12	9	8	8	1
Household Supplies[5]	13	11	8	8	8	10	10	8	11	9
Household Services[10]	$71	66	68	52	51	59	60	64	69	61
7. Servant Hire[10]	$35	30	33	25	22	26	27	28	29	24
Laundering and Dry Cleaning (Includes laundresses)[10,11]	20	19	19	14	14	16	16	18	20	16
All Other (Telephone, Ice, Moving Expenses)[4]	16	17	16	13	15	17	17	18	20	21
Sickness and Death	$43	44	44	46	41	45	43	43	47	41
Medicine and Supplies[5]	$10	11	11	14	12	14	11	13	15	13
Services of Doctors, Nurses, Hospitals, etc.[10,11]	30	29	30	28	25	27	27	26	27	23
Undertakers' Supplies and Services[10,11]	3	4	3	4	4	4	5	5	5	5
8. Personal Appearance	$24	23	23	25	26	31	31	32	34	26
Jewelry, Cosmetics, etc.[4]	$13	13	13	17	16	21	19	20	21	15
Barbers, Hairdressers, Manicurists, etc.[10]	11	10	10	10	9	11	12	12	13	11
9. Recreation	$68	67	68	59	66	82	87	109	109	83
Admission to Theaters, Games, etc.[4]	$19	18	19	18	20	26	30	39	47	33
Holidays and Travel for Pleasure (Hotels, Foreign Travel, Railroad Fares)[4]	40	41	40	33	38	46	48	48	51	41
Articles apparently designed for recreation[4]	9	8	9	8	10	10	9	10	11	9
10. Social-Cultural Activities	$106	98	102	90	95	95	99	103	108	100
Contributions (Including Immigrant Remittances)[4]	$50	42	46	41	39	37	36	38	40	36
Reading Matter[4]	18	18	18	12	16	15	16	17	19	19
Correspondence (Writing Materials, Postage, etc.)[4]	15	15	15	13	17	18	21	22	22	21
Tuition Privately Paid[4]	11	10	10	10	10	12	12	13	13	13
Dues of Fraternal Orders, etc.[5]	9	9	9	11	10	10	10	10	11	8
All Other (Services of Lawyers, Artists, Music Teachers, etc.)[10]	4	3	4	3	3	3	3	3	3	3
11. Taxes[12]	$1	1	1	38	27	22	23	23	23	28
12. Savings[12]	$143	139	141	268	217	233	255	224	175	117

[1] Some of the items above are not in fact allocable among all sections or population groups. The table presents averages for the entire country. Inventory changes are distributed among both the major classes and sub-classes.

[2] Only major classes and main sub-classes are shown in this table, although all items appearing in Appendix A have been included in the calculations. Hence the sub-classes do not exactly correspond with the figures (uncorrected for inventories) in Appendix A for the years affected by inventory changes, namely 1909, 1921, 1923, 1931. See Appendix B for explanation.

[3] Prices at retail, collected by the Bureau of Labor Statistics, of the sub-classes of items composing each group have been used to derive the basic inflating-deflating indexes applied to these expenditures.

[4] The price-level index of consumers' purchases herein derived (see Chap. IV) has been applied to all items for which no specific index could be found. This is not to be confused with the over-all price-level index of consumers' purchases and acquisitions.

[5] Indexes based on data gathered by National Industrial Conference Board applied to these items.

[6] Commodities are adjusted to retail price quotations of National Industrial Conference Board; services, to indexes of services; see text.

[7] Indexes of wholesale prices of Bureau of Labor Statistics are used; automobile index applied to automobile parts as well.

[8] Index of street car fares of National Industrial Conference Board.

[9] Indexes of housing costs of the Bureau of Labor Statistics.

[10] Indexes of personal services derived as explained in the text.

[11] Index of consumers' purchases herein derived applied to commercial services.

[12] Index of present worth of consumers' acquisitions is applied; see Chap. IV.

The accuracy of the measurements obviously depends in part on whether the records of prices over a series of years cover units which are in fact equivalent. In some lines of consumers' goods the units are physical quantities and are identical year after year. In most lines, however, alterations in quality and other intangible characteristics make it impracticable to keep the units strictly equivalent. Because of the difficulty of appraising alterations of this nature, they are usually ignored or minimized in constructing price indexes. Since most of the alterations are improvements, the effect is to magnify prices above what they would be if the units were strictly equivalent; and correspondingly to understate gains in real values received. Though the measurements are regrettably inaccurate, yet they create a clearer picture of actual movements and relationships of consumers' takings than can be formed in any other way. The picture differs markedly, we shall find, from the correlative picture of consumers' disbursements.

We are ready to return now to the question deferred from the preceding chapter. What is the meaning of the over-all real-value price-level index of consumers' purchases and acquisitions. The foregoing explanation makes evident that it is an index of takings, not of disbursements. It is an approach toward a measurement of the price-level at which consumers could purchase units identical with or equivalent to corresponding units purchasable in 1913. It is, in effect, an index, admittedly imperfect, of the price-level of consumers' well-being.

THE UPWARD COURSE OF AVERAGE FAMILY WELL-BEING

The first feature of Table 13 to strike one is a tendency toward uniformity both of total intake per family and of most classes of takings. The tendency is exemplified in a comparison of pre-war and post-war totals. The average American family absorbed goods and acquisitions to the value of $1,575 in the pre-war average year; and after all the shouting and the turmoil of the Great War, the family came back to a level only 7% higher (in 1913 dollars) in the year following the war. Many classes of takings were very slightly altered; for example, food (excepting the big gain in candy and soft drinks), tobacco, and personal appearance. The main increases were in transportation, taxes and savings. Offsetting decreases were in clothing (perhaps ascribable in part to the large number of persons still in uniform during the first half of 1919), in home maintenance and in recreation.   In these cold figures those who recall the period vividly will see a reflection of some noticeable changes in popular habits of living; yet the changes, viewed in their true proportions, are less impressive than the continuities.

Two features of the post-war years call for special comment.

It is apparent that the estimates for alcoholic beverages are distorted by lack of data during the prohibition nightmare; and to this extent the figures for total takings and their distribution among classes of takings are askew.   However, the distortion is approximately a constant throughout the post-war years and is not a large enough factor in any year to have a marked effect on the broad conclusions to be presented later.

When savings are deflated by the formula discussed in the preceding chapter, we find that the peak of genuine savings is placed in 1919 (no doubt associated with the Liberty Loan drive of that year); a secondary peak appears in 1925; and thereafter follows a rapid decline to a low point in 1929 and a record low for the entire period in 1931.   The showing may surprise those who have been in the habit of thinking of heavy purchases of real estate and securities in 1927 and 1929 as evidence of huge savings by the public.   In reality, the purchases were made at insanely high speculative prices, while at the same time the purchasing power of dollars over consumers' goods was relatively low.   Hence comes the necessity for double and drastic deflation of the current dollar figures if we are to get them down to a basis of genuineness—a basis that will make 1927 and 1929 figures truly comparable with those of earlier years.

The decade from 1919 to 1929 witnessed a $350 rise (21%) in total takings per family.   All the major classes of takings shared in the rise except foods, alcoholic beverages, sickness and death, taxes and savings; and only the last two showed sizable declines.   The gains were unequal.   Transportation heads the list.   The other outstanding increases, relative to the 1919 figures, were in recreation, personal appearance, home maintenance and tobacco.

The two instances of slump in consumers' total takings are of particular interest.   From 1919 to 1921 a moderate recession brought total family intake back to the pre-war level; but the chief post-war shifts of distribution were retained in 1921.   The 17% drop between 1929 and 1931 was much more precipitate— though it still left the total intake in 1931 7% ($114) above 1921. Most classes of objects fell off almost to the 1921 level.   The largest losses from 1921 to 1931 were in savings and in clothing. Three outstanding gains were in transportation, in home maintenance and in recreation.   In the other seven major classes, the parallelism between the two years of depression is noteworthy. It is depicted in Chart K.

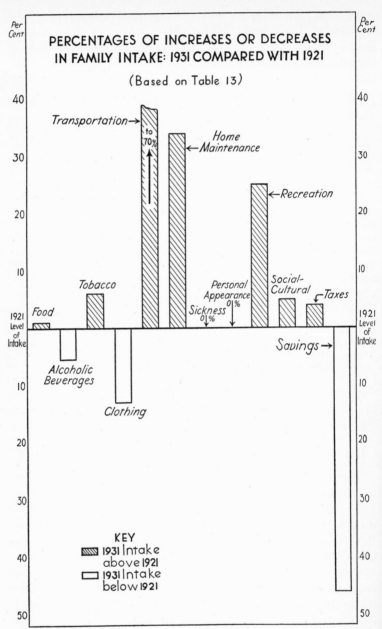

CHART K.—In five classes of takings notable gains or losses are revealed by a comparison of the two depression years. In the other seven classes, changes were slight.

Two broad conclusions emerge from this preliminary review of Table 13: First, the upward course of average well-being to its peak in 1929, though fairly steady, was slower and more hesitating after 1925 than was imagined in the midst of the hallucinations of the "new era." Second, in years of approximately

TABLE 14.—MAIN DIVERGENCES IN PERCENTAGE DISTRIBUTION OF OUTGO AND INTAKE[1]

Major Classes	Average of 1923–1927		1931	
	% of Outgo	% of Intake	% of Outgo	% of Intake
Food...........................	22.1	21.2	20.2	21.8
Clothing........................	12.3	10.8	10.6	10.0
Home Maintenance...............	23.7	21.7	28.4	26.2
Transportation..................	8.7	15.1	8.4	14.5
Sickness and Death..............	3.3	2.3	3.8	2.4
Savings........................	13.1	11.9	10.7	6.9
Other Classes[2].................	16.8	17.0	17.9	18.2
Totals.......................	100.0	100.0	100.0	100.0

[1] Based on Tables 10 and 15.
[2] Divergences slight.

equal total intake, even when the years are separated in time, a well-marked tendency appears toward equality of takings of the larger classes of consumers' goods.

DIFFERENCES IN DISTRIBUTION OF OUTGO AND OF INTAKE

The data for classes of takings set forth in Table 13 are presented in Table 15 in the form of percentages of total takings. It has already been remarked that the distribution of intake, or total takings, in the sense here given to the word, differs from the distribution of outgo, or total disbursements. The difference is a consequence of variations in the price relationships of classes of objects. Table 14 above lists the more important divergences between distribution of outgo in the post-war years, as shown in Table 10 of Chapter III, and the corresponding percentages of distribution of intake, as shown in Table 15.

Wherever the price index of a given class of objects rises above the over-all price-level index, the percentage of outgo is greater;

TABLE 15.—PERCENTAGE DISTRIBUTION OF TOTAL TAKINGS AMONG CLASSES OF OBJECTS[1]

Classes of Takings	Pre-war Average	1919	1921	1923	1925	1927	1929	1931
1. Food and Soft Drinks	25.8	24.6	23.2	21.8	20.9	20.6	20.4	21.8
Extra-commercial (home grown)	4.8	2.8	3.4	2.8	2.6	2.5	2.3	3.2
Commercial	21.0	21.8	19.8	19.0	18.3	18.1	18.1	18.6
Groceries and Delicatessen	4.6	4.7	4.2	4.2	4.0	3.9	4.0	4.1
Meat and Fish	6.4	6.3	4.6	4.5	4.4	4.2	4.1	3.9
Dairy Products	4.1	3.9	3.9	4.1	4.0	4.1	3.9	4.3
Bakery Products	1.7	1.9	1.9	1.8	1.7	1.8	1.9	2.0
Fresh Fruits and Vegetables	3.1	3.0	3.2	2.6	2.5	2.4	2.6	2.5
Confectionery, Ice Cream and Soft Drinks	1.1	2.0	2.0	1.8	1.7	1.7	1.6	1.8
2. Payments to Industry for Alcoholic Beverages and Other Illegal Commodities	6.1	3.0	2.3	2.1	2.1	2.2	2.3	2.0
3. Tobacco	2.1	2.0	2.2	2.3	2.1	2.1	2.2	2.2
4. Clothing	11.9	9.9	12.3	11.5	9.9	10.1	9.8	10.0
Women's Apparel	4.8	4.1	5.1	5.0	4.3	4.5	4.4	4.8
Men's and Boy's Apparel	3.5	2.6	3.2	2.9	2.5	2.5	2.4	2.2
Boots and Shoes	2.6	2.1	2.5	2.2	1.9	1.8	1.8	1.8
Knit Goods	1.0	1.1	1.5	1.4	1.2	1.3	1.2	1.2
5. Transportation	4.4	8.7	9.1	14.2	16.8	16.1	16.7	14.5
Local Fares	1.4	1.2	1.4	1.3	1.3	1.4	1.3	1.1
Vehicles (Including Upkeep)	3.0	7.5	7.7	12.9	15.5	14.7	15.4	13.4
6. Home Maintenance	25.6	20.7	21.0	20.8	20.8	22.6	24.3	26.2
Fuel and Light	3.7	3.4	3.4	3.4	2.9	3.1	3.0	3.1
Furniture and House Furnishings	5.0	3.3	4.2	4.8	4.8	4.8	5.1	4.0
Household Services	4.3	3.1	3.2	3.2	3.1	3.2	3.4	3.6
Household Supplies	0.7	0.5	0.5	0.5	0.5	0.5	0.5	0.5
Housing	11.9	10.4	9.7	8.7	9.5	11.0	12.3	15.0
7. Sickness and Death	2.8	2.7	2.6	2.4	2.2	2.2	2.3	2.4
8. Personal Appearance	1.5	1.5	1.6	1.7	1.6	1.6	1.7	1.5
9. Recreation	4.3	3.5	4.2	4.4	4.4	4.9	5.3	4.9
10. Social—Cultural Activities	6.5	5.3	6.0	5.1	5.1	5.2	5.3	5.9
11. Taxes	....	2.2	1.7	1.2	1.1	1.1	1.1	1.7
12. Savings	9.0	15.9	13.8	12.5	13.0	11.3	8.6	6.9

[1] Based on Table 13.

per contra, wherever the price index of a class is lower, the percentage of intake is greater. The largest variation, it will be seen, is in transportation; an outgrowth of the remarkable decline in automobile prices while the over-all price-level was either moving up or at least maintaining itself far above the level of 1913. The next largest variation is in savings; an outgrowth of post-war prices for securities and other assets at prices which were extravagant, especially in view of the reduced purchasing power of the income to be derived from investment of savings. The table reflects the relatively sharp fall in food prices in the years preceding 1931; the less drastic decline in clothing prices; and the characteristic inertia of prices of the lengthy list of commodities and intangibles grouped under home maintenance. The higher ratios of outgo than of intake for sickness and death are explainable chiefly by the exceptional rise of the price index for professional and hospital services.

DISTRIBUTION OF INTAKE AMONG CLASSES OF OBJECTS

An examination of Table 15 must deepen, I think, the impression created by Table 13 of the gradualness of change in most habits of living. The takings of the great majority of both major classes and sub-classes fluctuate only within very narrow limits of percentages of total intake. The average family, it is evident, tends strongly to persist in its established mode of life— in good years enlarging, in bad years retrenching, its purchases of most lines of goods in rough proportion to its gain or loss in spending power.

This predisposition toward stability of takings, though not surprising, is often overlooked. For instance, a popular idea is that spendings for personal appearance (a group comprising articles of adornment, cosmetics, perfumes, services of barbers and hairdressers and the like) jumped up alarmingly during the post-war boom; yet Table 15 shows it to possess a stability in relation to total takings that is rivaled only by tobacco, fuel and light, household services, bakery products and dairy products. Social-cultural activities, the table reveals, not only hold their own in good years, but resist retrenchment so vigorously that their percentage rises in bad years. It is readily understandable that home-grown foods, taxes and sickness and death should react similarly. A later chapter will discuss the elements of stability in present-day consumption.

However, the unsettling elements disclosed in Table 15 are not to be ignored. Chart L depicts the main shifts in relative position among the major classes of takings. The dominating features of the chart are (*a*) the phenomenal rise of transportation from 4.4% of total intake in the average pre-war year to a

MAIN SHIFTS IN RELATIVE POSITION OF CLASSES OF TAKINGS
(Based on Table 15; In Percentages of Total Takings)

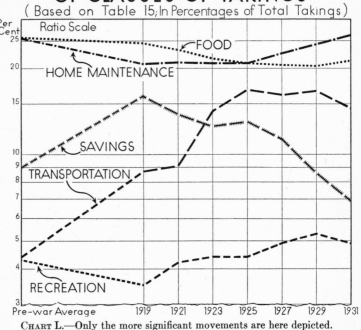

CHART L.—Only the more significant movements are here depicted.

height of 16.8% in 1925 and (*b*) the almost equally swift decline of savings from a high point of 15.9% in 1919 (Liberty Loan) to 6.9% in 1931. At first glance one is tempted to assume that the two movements are causally related—that money was taken out of savings to put into automobiles; and to some unknown degree this may be true. Much the greater part of both shifts, however, is ascribable to the contrary trends of prices in these two fields.

Food required a slowly declining percentage of total takings through the prosperous years, as would be expected, and a somewhat higher percentage in 1931. Home maintenance throughout the post-war period increased its ratio; and it is well worth noting that its rate of increase picked up when transportation stopped climbing. Recreation gained ground steadily after 1919 except for a moderate falling-off in 1931.

The comments in this chapter on consumers' takings, which have been set forth in dollars of 1913 and in percentages, are intended to be only preliminary to the main lines of analysis in the succeeding chapters of Part Two. The analysis will endeavor to bring out more plainly the forces at work beneath the surface which have modified consumption in recent years.

Chapter VI

WANTS

Human wants for economic goods are frequently referred to in the older texts as if they were insatiable and unlimited. And that proposition, stated in the abstract, is still defensible. But wants for many specific goods may become so nearly satisfied that demand for them at any practicable price shrinks far below productive capacity. When that occurs on a large scale affecting many lines of industry, the entire system of production and exchange is liable to suffer a disastrous breakdown.

In our present-day economy capital investments—in farm lands, in transportation facilities, in plants and equipment, in dwellings, in business organizations and in numerous other forms —commonly come to fruition only after a period of years; and their operating life, if the investments are to be profitable, must then go on without grave disturbance for succeeding years or decades. Investment, in short, is compelled to look far ahead. In the event that fixed capital ceases to cater to human wants, directly or indirectly, or oversupplies satiable wants, it can seldom be adapted economically to other ends; it remains nothing better than a monument to shortsightedness and loss. On the other hand, capital which is fortunate enough to serve expanding demands growing out of fundamental wants contributes heavily to national well-being and normally earns rich rewards.

Reference to these elementary truths is enough to emphasize the cardinal need of learning more about the actual and potential wants of consumers. Accurate measurements of the relative strengths of all the habits and motives which impel people to buy or refuse to buy would point the way toward accurate forecasts of their demands. True, the problem would still be complex; but it would no longer be insoluble. Better knowledge of potential wants would bring within reach an orderly development of all economic activities, a world in which gross miscalculations leading to devastating losses and suffering would be rare and inexcusable.

Unhappily that day is far distant. The most we can hope for now is to take a few groping steps; perhaps to form a somewhat clearer conception of the probable lines of growth of consumers' demands.

UNEXPLORED TERRITORY

Preceding chapters have presented estimates of takings of consumers' goods; some of the estimates are uncertain, but at least they are concerned with readily identifiable objects. The present chapter ventures, albeit somewhat timidly, into even less explored territory—into the dim and boggy region of hazy concepts in which social psychologists live out their days. Stated more prosaically, the chapter will attempt to infer from regroupings of our estimates the strength and influence of the chief motives which govern spendings.

The regroupings will be unavoidably somewhat arbitrary and under broad heads. The aim, be it remembered, is to discern the shadowy outlines of sweeping, powerful forces in the background—forces not to be seen through a microscope.

At the same time, the purpose of this chapter is to measure the forces *objectively;* to disregard wishful prejudgments in favor of unbiased analysis. An easy task for any writer is to list his own tastes and ascribe them to all his fellow-consumers. Stuart Chase, as one example, offers "an appraisal of genuine human wants, as distinct from the goods and services currently sold and delivered."[1] But his "genuine human wants" turn out to be simply the things which people, according to Mr. Chase's ideas, *ought* to desire. A similar assumption is made by many others; in fact, it underlies the entire body of doctrine known as "social planning." Though the data now available will not yield conclusive results, we should be able at the least to form better-grounded views as to the relative urgency of basic human wants at various levels of national income.

FIVE BASIC WANTS

A number of elaborate lists of consumers' buying motives, or wants, have been drawn up.[2] They are useful aids to salesmen

[1] "The Tragedy of Waste" by Stuart Chase, Macmillan, New York, 1929, p. 42.

[2] Examples will be found in: Chapter VI of "Principles of Merchandising" by Melvin T. Copeland, Shaw, Chicago, 1927; Chapter IV of "Economic Princi-

and advertising copywriters; but no one has yet succeeded, so far as I know, in utilizing them as bases of measurement of market demands.   The classification below is much simpler and for our purpose more workable.   It makes no pretense to being "scientific"; rather, it is the product of a long period of personal observation.

Subsistence.   The term is here broadly interpreted to cover all the prime requirements of the average American family.   It is possible to make up, by means of a comparative study of recorded expenditures of low-income families and of so-called "minimum comfort" budgets prepared by social workers, by the National Industrial Conference Board, and by others, a reasonable estimate of the expenditures required in order to maintain a passable standard of living. The "subsistence budget" to be presented below includes not only stark necessities but also allowances for habitual expenditures which are not given up except under severe pressure.

Enjoyment.   Under this head may be placed expenditures for personal and family pleasures and comforts, excluding those which seem to fall definitely within what Professor Young has well termed "the area of social pressure"; these latter expenditures are better allocated to the two groups following.

Approval.   The term refers to the reactions of friends and neighbors—in other words, to social approval in accordance with usages of the group to which each family belongs.   A considerable fraction of the family outgo in all income classes above the minimum comfort level is devoted to meeting conventional social standards—entertaining friends, driving a car of the "right" price class, dressing and living in correct style.   In many families these expenditures are maintained even at the cost of giving up expenditures in the group just above.

Prominence.   Many families aspire to outshine their neighbors—to attain social prominence in their own circle—through "conspicuous consumption," to adopt Veblen's term.   These families are the pace-setting Joneses.   The rest of us to a greater or less extent try to "keep up."   It is an error, however, to restrict this motive to high-income families; it is widespread.   Another considerable fraction of average family takings comes under this head.

Security.   The balance of family intake, not assignable to any of the foregoing motives, consists of withholdings—that is, direct taxes and savings.   They are placed here under the heading "Security"—meaning security against future mischances.

Taking the foregoing list of basic wants as a guide, let us see what can be ascertained as to the average American family's buying habits and motives.

---

ples of Consumption" by Paul H. Nystrom, Ronald, New York, 1929; and a paper on "Driving Forces in the Sales Plan" by Stuart DuBois Cowan in the *Taylor Society Bulletin*, June, 1931.

SUBSISTENCE: ESSENTIALS UNDER AMERICAN STANDARDS

The first question to consider is the amount of each major
class of takings required in order to maintain the minimum
standard of living of the *average American family*. The words
just preceding are italicized with a view to making clear that
we are dealing here with an abstract statistical unit—not with the
requirements of workers' families or of farm families or of high-
income families or of any other special class of families, but with
the requirements of a composite family representative of the
country as a whole. The subsistence budget for the average
family presented in Table 16 could properly be criticized as
inadequate for some groups and excessive for others if its broadly
representative character were to be overlooked. The allotments
to clothing and to housing, as two outstanding examples, are
much below requirements to maintain minimum standards of
decency for urban families; but when we take into account village
and rural families, including Negro and foreign-born families
in economically backward sections, the allotments appear
reasonable.

The main sources of information utilized in constructing Table
16 are: the numerous family expenditure studies of distinct
groups which will be found cited in Chapter X; Winslow's[3]
summary and critique of such studies; and the hypothetical
workers' budget of the National Industrial Conference Board[4]
which includes allotments for sundries not elsewhere detailed.
Data from these varied sources have been roughly weighted in
proportion to the size of population groups represented. The
results of these computations have been compared with our
figures for average family intake, as set forth in Table 13, and
some corrections made on the strength of the marked stabilities
in depression years of certain classes of takings. The composite
budget of requirements for subsistence, thus derived, is detailed
in Table 16.

On the face of it, the composite budget is an approximation;
more accurate measurement will remain impossible until a mass
of additional data has been collected. It is submitted, however,
as a usable recapitulation of the irreducible needs of the average

[3] "Purchasing Power of the Consumer," Book II, by Emma A. Winslow, Shaw,
Chicago, 1925.
[4] "The Cost of Living in the United States, 1914–1930," pp. 44–55.

American family—not "irreducible," of course, in an absolute
sense; but likely to be reduced only at the risk of such serious
dissatisfaction as to threaten social upheaval.   The amounts

TABLE 16.—A COMPOSITE ANNUAL BUDGET OF REQUIREMENTS FOR SUBSISTENCE
OF THE AVERAGE AMERICAN FAMILY[1]
(Sub-items in italics)

Classes of Takings	Expressed in 1913 Dollars		Post-war Budget Expressed in Current Dollars[2]			
	Pre-war Budget	Additions in Post-war Budget	1919	1921	1929	1931
Food and Soft Drinks.......	360		680	556	577	435
Alcoholic Beverages.........	20		34	32	29	25
Tobacco..................	20		35	34	26	25
Clothing..................	125		255	209	213	173
Women's Clothing.........	*75*		*153*	*125*	*127*	*104*
Men's Clothing...........	*50*		*102*	*84*	*86*	*69*
Transportation.............	30	20–60[3]	59	61	76	68
Vehicles and Upkeep.......	*10*	*20–60[3]*	*31*	*30*	*48*	*37*
Local Fares..............	*20*		*28*	*31*	*28*	*31*
Home Maintenance.........	240		352	407	378	346
Housing................	*120*		*144*	*203*	*191*	*169*
Furnishings.............	*30*		*68*	*58*	*50*	*47*
Supplies................	*10*		*21*	*19*	*18*	*16*
Fuel and Light...........	*50*		*67*	*80*	*73*	*72*
Household Services........	*30*		*52*	*47*	*46*	*42*
Sickness and Death........	30		59	59	68	62
Personal Appearance........	10		17	16	17	15
Recreation................	15		25	24	22	19
Social-Cultural Activities....	25		42	40	38	33
Withholdings (Taxes and Savings)..............	25	40[4]	97	79	118	75
Totals..................	900	60–100	1,655	1,517	1,562	1,276

[1] See text for explanation of terms.
[2] Approximations based on price indexes of major classes of spendings; see Chap. IV.   The
figures under this head are merely for convenience of comparison with post-war family expenditure
records stated in current dollars.
[3] In 1919 and 1921, $20 added to pre-war base; in 1923, $40; in all subsequent years, $60.
[4] In all post-war years, $40 added.

listed in Table 16 may be taken as practical minima so long as
the average family possesses resources of income and cash savings
sufficient to cover them.

The table shows two changes—and only two—between the pre-war and the post-war budgets of subsistence. Comparisons of low-income family expenditure records in the pre-war and the post-war periods, when outlays are reduced to a common price level, indicate that most classes of expenditure were but slightly modified. However, in the post-war studies automobile upkeep appears as an added item; and life insurance, one of the universal forms of saving in this country, shows a decided gain. Direct taxes, though not an item in low-income requirements, must be included in the subsistence budget of the average family; this form of taxation was insignificant before the war. We have enlarged the post-war budget, therefore, by adding for vehicles and upkeep (in 1913 dollars) the following allowances: $20 in 1919 and 1921; $40 in 1923; $60 in subsequent years. A combined allowance of $40 for direct taxes and savings has also been added in the post-war years. These two additions fully represent, in our judgment, the actual changes in the minimum living standards of the average American family.

That no greater revision of the pre-war budget should be called for may appear incredible to those readers who have been beguiled by oft-repeated assertions that during the war years the American people cut loose from their past and emerged with radically new standards of living and spending. Some notable alterations in apportionments of enlarged family income did occur, as the preceding chapter has indicated. But the takings of most classes of objects, when stated in 1913 dollars (see Table 13), were surprisingly uniform; and it is these stable classes for the most part that are prominent in the subsistence budget.

The Expanding Area of Free Spendables

Inasmuch as our composite subsistence budget is uniform throughout the period under survey, except for the variations just noted, the proportion of total takings unassigned to the budget goes up rapidly whenever general prosperity increases. The average family feels free to spend as they like money not required for the subsistence budget. They can save all of it if they choose; or they can devote all of it to personal enjoyment or to conformity with social standards which will assure the approval of their neighbors or to attaining a certain prominence within their own group if that is what they crave. Carrying out this

SUBSISTENCE REQUIREMENTS AND FREE SPENDABLES
IN SELECTED YEARS
(Based on Tables 13 & 16 ; In Dollars of 1913)

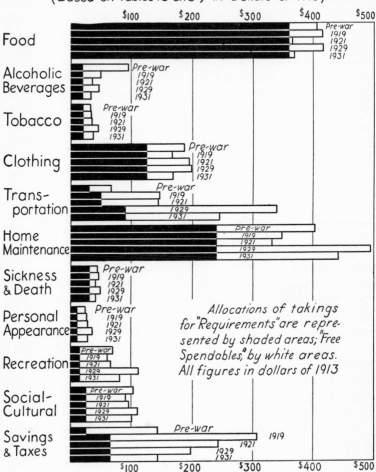

CHART M.—The white areas indicate graphically the non-essential elements in the major classes of takings per family.

conception, we will refer to the excess of average family intake above subsistence requirements as "free spendables."

Chart M represents the relative areas in selected years of subsistence requirements and of free spendables in each of the major classes of takings. Excepting alcoholic beverages (a distorted showing, as previously pointed out), the post-war years clearly allowed much greater scope for free spending than did the average pre-war year. Within the 13 post-war years, the large advances of free spendables were in transportation, home maintenance and recreation; a notable decline occurred after 1919 in savings and taxes. All these four classes are particularly sensitive to fluctuations of spending power. They are danger spots in present-day consumption. Succeeding chapters will return to these and other elements of instability in the economic system.

An Experimental Analysis of Free Spendables

The aim of this chapter is to discern, though it may be uncertainly, the influence of basic human wants on takings at various levels of spending power. The method employed is to allocate predetermined percentages of each year's free spendings (by major classes and main sub-classes) to the four basic wants apart from subsistence. To the want which has been designated "security" we assign all spendings above subsistence requirements under the two heads, taxes and savings. The percentage allocations of other free spendings to the three remaining wants, "enjoyment," "approval," and "prominence," are set forth in Table 17.

The percentages in Table 17 are obviously expressions of unproved personal judgments. At the same time, they are not so wholly arbitrary as they may appear at first glance. They have been derived from a painstaking review of the details of each class of takings; and the percentages have been assigned in the light of a certain degree of familiarity on the writer's part with the sales appeals which have proved successful in marketing representative commodities and services. One may fairly remark, too, that rough judgments of this kind, if not entirely unreasonable and if consistently applied, may yield valid indications of general trends in spite of their unreliability for finer measurements.

The allocation of family intake in 1929, as determined in accordance with Table 17, is represented in Chart N. An examination of the chart will reveal at once that the great bulk of food, clothing and home maintenance fall in the subsistence

TABLE 17.—PERCENTAGE ALLOCATIONS OF FREE SPENDABLES TO THREE TYPES OF WANTS[1]

Major Classes	Enjoyment	Approval	Prominence
Food...........................	50	25	25
Alcoholic Beverages...............	50	25	25
Tobacco........................	100	..	..
Clothing			
Women's Clothing..............	20	40	40
Men's Clothing................	40	40	20
Transportation			
Vehicles and Upkeep............	30	30	40
Local Fares....................	100	..	..
Home Maintenance			
Housing.......................	30	40	30
Furnishings....................	40	30	30
Supplies......................	75	25	..
Fuel and Light................	100	..	..
Household Services............	40	30	30
Sickness and Death[2]..............	50	30	20
Personal Appearance..............	30	35	35
Recreation......................	75	15	10
Social-Cultural Activities..........	30	50	20

[1] The percentages in this table apply only to expenditures in excess of the subsistence budget.

[2] To assign half the spendings for sickness and death (above the subsistence budget) to Enjoyment and the other half to Approval and Prominence may seem strange. But these terms should be interpreted in their defined sense. Enjoyment is meant to include physical and mental comfort; and certainly a large fraction of expenditures for doctors' fees, medicines and hospital services are not strictly essential but are designed to reduce discomfort. Other considerable fractions of payments to physicians and hospitals and of funeral expenses seem clearly assignable to desires for social approval and prominence.

budget, while the other classes are assigned largely to the other four basic wants. Corresponding allocations have been made for all the years for which we have classified estimates.

RELATIVE STRENGTH OF BASIC WANTS AT VARIOUS LEVELS OF SPENDING POWER

In Table 18 average family takings for all the years studied are classified, on the basis of Tables 16 and 17, under the five basic wants. Chart O rearranges the data of Table 18 by years ranked

AMILY INTAKE OF 1929 ALLOCATED TO MAIN TYPES OF BUYING MOTIVES
(Based on Tables 17 & 18; in, Dollars of 1913)

SUBSISTENCE — $1000	ENJOYMENT $316	APPROVAL $334	PROMINENCE $252	SECURITY $133
All Others $80	All Others $54	All Others $124	All Others $37	
Taxes & Savings $65	Liquor & Tobacco $39	Liq. & Tobc. $6	Liq. & Tobc. $6	
Liquor & Tobacco $40	Transportation $79	Transportation $73	Transportation $98	Taxes and Savings $133
Transportation $90	Home Maintenance $96	Home Maintenance $86	Home Maintenance $73	
Home Maintenance $240	Clothing $20	Clothing $30	Clothing $24	
Clothing $125	Food $28	Food $14	Food $14	
Food $360				

CHART N.—The amounts assigned to Enjoyment, Approval and Prominence, of course, represent only personal judgments, as explained in the text.

TABLE 18.—TAKINGS PER FAMILY ASSIGNED TO MAIN TYPES OF WANTS[1]

(In 1913 dollars)

Expenditures Primarily for	Pre-war		1919		1921		1923		1925		1927		1929		1931	
	$	Per Cent	$	Per Cent	$	Per Cent	$	Per Cent	$	Per Cent	$	Per Cent	$	Per Cent	$	Per Cent
Subsistence	900	57.2	960	56.9	960	60.9	980	52.7	1,000	51.0	1,000	50.5	1,000	49.2	1,000	59.2
Enjoyment	213	13.5	179	10.6	148	9.4	248	13.3	262	13.4	280	14.1	316	15.5	196	11.6
Approval	207	13.1	178	10.5	172	10.9	251	13.5	272	13.8	294	14.9	334	16.4	240	14.2
Prominence	138	8.8	129	7.7	117	7.4	192	10.3	213	10.9	223	11.3	252	12.4	173	10.3
Security	117	7.4	241	14.3	179	11.4	190	10.2	213	10.9	181	9.2	133	6.6	80	4.7
Totals	1,575	100.0	1,686	100.0	1,575	100.0	1,861	100.0	1,958	100.0	1,978	100.0	2,036	100.0	1,689	100.0

[1] Based on Table 17; see text.

not in chronological order but in the ascending order of the average family spending power in each year. This involves placing 1921 ahead of 1919. It also involves presenting arithmetic averages of the figures for the years 1921 and 1931; this is partly because it would be confusing to attempt to depict separately two years with almost identical spending power ($1,686 per family in 1919 and $1,689 in 1931), but is also for the more important reason explained below. The other four years (1923, 1925, 1927, 1929) appear in chronological order, since spending power moved up in each of those years above its preceding level; but the spacing is determined not by time intervals but by dollars of spending power.

The arrangement of years in Chart O, which will be followed in several of the charts in later chapters, has been adopted as the simplest and most practical method of measuring roughly the *joint effects* of two distinct factors: (*a*) the spending power factor, which powerfully influences the amounts of different classes of takings; (*b*) the time factor, which brings with it changes both in offerings and in tastes and thus also powerfully influences takings. If the chronological order throughout were the same as the ascending order of spending power, the problem of measuring their combined effects would be relatively simple; but in fact the two orders coincide only during the seven-year term, 1923–1929. By averaging the two widely separated years 1919 and 1931, however, we get a tabulation of takings in a hypothetical year with a spending power of $1,688 which may fairly be accepted as representative of post-war takings at that level. Thus the broad lines of expansion of classes of takings, under the combined influence of rising spending power and of temporal changes up to 1929, are set forth with less bias by either factor than would be attainable with any other arrangement of the data.[5]

Chart O makes evident that takings for enjoyment and for the sake of social approval and social prominence expanded in a steadily increasing ratio to total intake; but withholdings for security refused to conform to any consistent rule of progression.

[5] Other arrangements have been considered. Trend lines of the data in strict chronological order might conceivably be more reliable indicators. Unfortunately they are distorted by unusually large variations of takings in the two end years, 1919 and 1931. Another possibility would be to leave out 1931. Here again, however, the exceptional conditions in 1919 give an obvious bias to some of the important trend lines.

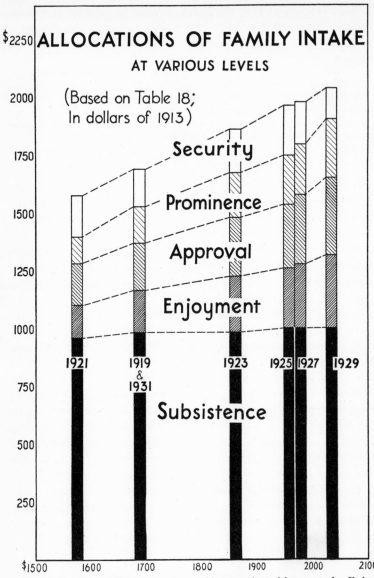

CHART O.—As spending power rises, takings motivated by wants for Enjoyment, Approval and Prominence gain at nearly twice the rate of gain in total spending power.

Chart O suggests that ultimately it may be possible to formulate new "laws of demand," which will perhaps state the relationships between basic wants and total intake somewhat as follows:

As total average family spending power rises:
Subsistence requirements remain nearly stationary, thus leaving a rapidly increasing proportion of free spendables.

Takings for enjoyment, for approval and for prominence gain at rates approximately double the rate of gain of family spending power.

Takings for security constitute the residue, the amount of which is not governed by any apparent autonomous principle.

The foregoing generalizations, it should be emphasized, are put forward only as very tentative hypotheses. Motives for buying are elusive; and it would be absurd to attempt at present to express their influence in mathematical formulae. Yet a real possibility exists, with additional data and an improved technique, of approaching much closer to accurate definitions of the relative strength of basic wants at various levels of spending power.

The possibility is alluring and deserves further study. Insofar as it is eventually realized, it opens the way to substantial progress in appraising and forecasting consumers' demands. These demands, let us remember, are not wholly formed out of thin air. They express persistent wants—wants that rise to the surface, whenever spending power expands, in some kind of predetermined order of precedence. When we learn more about the relationships of basic wants at different levels of spending power we shall gain a much clearer insight than anyone now has into the trends and prospective movements of demands for consumers' goods.

To develop this type of insight is necessary in order to make better-assured profits in a world of incessantly shifting demands. More than that, it is essential in order to operate the economic system at all. But that is a subject for later chapters.

Chapter VII

STABILITIES

"It is the beginning of wisdom," writes Whitehead, "to understand that social life is founded upon routine. Unless society is permeated, through and through, with routine, civilization vanishes. So many sociological doctrines, the products of acute intellects, are wrecked by obliviousness to this fundamental sociological truth. Society requires stability, foresight itself presupposes stability, and stability is the product of routine."[1] The philosopher has here defined with keen insight the nature of the problem which is to be dealt with in this chapter.

The problem is to ascertain what varieties and what proportion of consumers' takings possess a high degree of stability. Stability is a manifestation of inground habits of wanting, of living, of buying. Consumers' routine habits are the true subjects of our study.

The problem bears directly on the causes of economic breakdown and on the processes of recovery. The experience of generations had led economists to suppose that a decline of 20% to 25% in production and trade marks the low point of the business cycle, partly because at this point consumption, it was believed, must resist further decline with unbreakable strength.[2] Yet in 1932 and again in 1933 standard indexes of business activity went down more than 40% below a calculated normal. Many factors doubtless contributed to the unprecedented debacle. Among them all, however, none was plainer or more devastating than the unexpected vulnerability of consumption. Consumers' demands for many articles gave way with only a shadow of resistance.

Is this experience likely to be repeated in future, perhaps with even graver consequences? The first phase of the answer is

[1] "On Foresight" by Alfred N. Whitehead, an introduction to "Business Adrift" by Wallace Brett Donham, McGraw-Hill, New York, 1921, p. xiv.

[2] Cf. "Forecasting Business Cycles" by Warren M. Persons, Wiley, New York, 1931, p. 28.

to be given through an effort to classify and measure the dependably stable elements in consumers' takings. Three lines of classification, which unfortunately cannot be dovetailed into a combined scheme, are to be followed: (a) stabilizing wants; (b) stabilizing habits of living; (c) stabilizing habits of purchasing.

BASIC WANTS AS STABILIZERS

The two preceding chapters have sufficiently established, I think, the unchanging psychology of the average consumer. Chapter V makes clear that the consuming family of pre-war days and the consuming family of the hectic post-war boom were substantially one and the same. The popular assumption to the contrary has but a slight factual basis; for the parallelisms of major classes of takings are far more impressive than the divergences. When the dollar figures are restated (in Table 15) as percentages of total intake, the strong tendency toward continuity becomes still more evident. Chapter VI, though inconclusive, offers reason to believe that basic wants, except the want for security, control determinable proportions of different levels of spending power. Wants, therefore, are regularizing. Thus, the two chapters lead to the conclusion that consumers themselves are the constant factor in consumption. Their spending power fluctuates over a wide range and the goods offered to them assume innumerable forms; but people remain the same.

The dry meat of statistical data can be seasoned in this instance with some interesting comments by the executive vice-president of R. H. Macy and Company.[3]

I have had the privilege of observing the behavior of what is probably as large and representative a cross section of the public as comes into any store—150,000 or so a day. . . . The total of their behavior, I take it, is the national consumer attitude. . . . On the first day the state sales tax went into effect, they bought in precisely the proportion of requirements that they showed on the same day in 1932. . . . I challenge any store, any newspaper, to adduce convincing mass proof that the consumer wants change for its own sake.

Though consumers' basic wants do not appear to change perceptibly from year to year or even from generation to generation, they are obviously unequal in force and urgency. The requirements of subsistence in the present-day mode of life may

[3] Article by Paul Hollister in *Nation's Business*, Oct., 1933.

be thought of as forming the last line of resistance against innovation or deterioration; they are the most reliable stabilizers of consumption. Consumers' desires for enjoyment, for approval and for prominence respond more readily, as we have seen, to gains or losses in spending power; but when they are forced to fall back, they beat an orderly retreat and continue to exercise some measure of stabilizing restraint on fitful fluctuations in consumption. On the other hand, the desire for security, as expressed in annual withholdings, appears to be particularly irregular and undependable.

Wants are transformed into effective demands only insofar as they are associated with spending power. Whatever their inherent stability may be, they cannot in themselves guarantee a corresponding stability of actual consumption. Nevertheless, it is essential to recognize their fundamental importance in maintaining an orderly social-economic system.

HABITS OF LIVING AS STABILIZERS

Another line of analysis is tried in Table 19, which classifies average family intake on the basis of focal points, as follows: (a) intake centering mainly on family life in the home; (b) intake centering mainly on family life outside the home; (c) intake centering mainly on individual interests and activities likely to be disassociated from family life. The classification is based on the percentage allocations to these three groups shown in the table. Each reader will doubtless find reasons for disagreeing with some of the percentages, and he may easily make his own realignment. My opinion, however, after a number of tests, is that finer sub-divisions and other reasonable modifications will not materially alter the relationships discussed below.

In Chart P the estimates detailed in Table 19 are represented not in chronological order but in the order of an advancing scale of total spending power as was done in Chart O. This arrangement is adopted, as previously explained, in order to visualize more clearly the inseparably combined effects of changes in spending power and of changes in habits of living.

The most striking feature of Chart P is the rapid rise of intake centering on family life outside the home. The chief element in the rise was the increasing expenditure for automobile transportation. The growing habit of eating in restaurants was also a considerable factor. The amount centering on individuals

TABLE 19.—CLASSIFICATION OF AVERAGE FAMILY TAKINGS ON BASIS OF FOCAL POINTS
(In 1913 dollars)

Allocations to Three Focal Points	Pre-war	1919	1921	1923	1925	1927	1929	1931
Total Family Takings........................	$1,575	$1,686	$1,575	$1,861	$1,958	$1,978	$2,036	$1,689
Centering mainly on family life in the home......	*$1,094*	*$1,043*	*$970*	*$1,089*	*$1,109*	*$1,137*	*$1,174*	*$1,021*
	(69.5%)	*(61.8%)*	*(61.6%)*	*(58.5%)*	*(56.5%)*	*(57.5%)*	*(57.6%)*	*(60.4%)*
Food served at home (95% in pre-war years; 90% in post-war)......	386	373	328	365	368	366	374	331
Clothing classed as essential (80% pre-war; 65% post-war)......	150	108	126	139	126	130	129	109
Home Maintenance (75%)........................	403	349	330	387	407	446	494	442
Sickness and Death (75%)........................	33	34	31	34	32	32	35	31
Social-Cultural Activities (50%).............	51	45	47	47	49	51	54	50
Savings (50%)........................	71	134	108	117	127	112	88	58
Centering mainly on family life outside the home......	*209*	*292*	*295*	*436*	*507*	*508*	*545*	*415*
	(13.3%)	*(17.3%)*	*(18.7%)*	*(23.4%)*	*(25.9%)*	*(25.7%)*	*(26.8%)*	*(24.6%)*
Food served in restaurants (5%; 10%)......	20	42	37	41	41	41	42	37
Transportation (100%)........................	70	146	144	265	329	319	340	245
Recreation (100%)........................	68	59	66	82	87	96	109	83
Social-Cultural Activities (50%).............	51	45	48	48	50	52	54	50
Centering mainly on individual activities......	*271*	*314*	*284*	*314*	*321*	*310*	*295*	*225*
	(17.2%)	*(18.6%)*	*(18.0%)*	*(16.9%)*	*(16.4%)*	*(15.7%)*	*(14.5%)*	*(13.3%)*
Alcoholic Beverages (100%).............	96	50	36	39	42	43	47	34
Tobacco (100%)........................	33	34	35	42	41	42	45	37
Clothing classed as non-essential (20%; 35%)......	38	59	68	75	68	70	70	59
Sickness and Death (25%)........................	11	12	10	11	11	11	12	10
Personal Appearance (100%).............	23	25	26	31	31	32	34	26
Savings (50%)........................	70	134	109	116	128	112	87	59
Unassigned: Direct Taxes........................	*1*	*38*	*27*	*22*	*23*	*22*	*23*	*28*
		(2.3%)	*(1.7%)*	*(1.2%)*	*(1.2%)*	*(1.1%)*	*(1.1%)*	*(1.7%)*

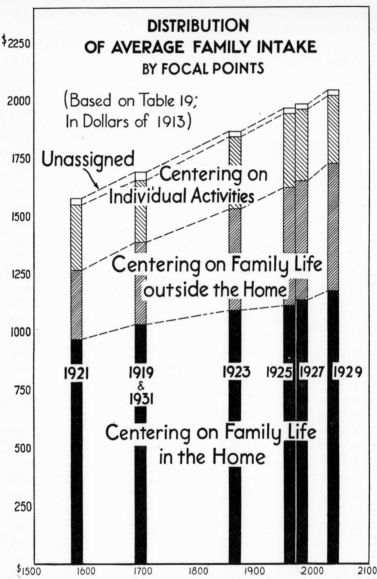

DISTRIBUTION OF AVERAGE FAMILY INTAKE BY FOCAL POINTS

(Based on Table 19; In Dollars of 1913)

Unassigned

Centering on Individual Activities

Centering on Family Life outside the Home

1921   1919 & 1931   1923   1925 1927 1929

Centering on Family Life in the Home

CHART P.—Increased spending power during the post-war years centered more and more on family life outside the home.

remained nearly uniform; but its proportion of total intake, surprisingly enough, slowly declined.

Though the absolute amount of takings centering on the home rose slightly, the ratio of takings in this group to total intake went down from 70% in the pre-war average year to less than 60% during most of the post-war years. Time was when a man's home was his castle and a large share of his savings were devoted to it. Social conventions called for a dwelling as pretentious as the family could afford. Those who loved display lavished their money on ornate trimmings and furnishings. These motives are no doubt fully as strong as they have ever been; but in our generation they have found expression in many other forms—in high-priced cars, in expensive wardrobes and beauty treatments, in night club parties, in round-the-world excursions. Perhaps the next turn of the wheel will make the home once more the focal point for entertainment and display. If that occurs, however, takings centering on the home will infallibly become far more subject to sudden fevers and chills.

From one-fourth to one-half of family takings centering outside the home are included under subsistence requirements. The remainder express desires for enjoyment, approval and prominence. The swift rise of this group does not necessarily denote strength or stability; for the basic wants motivating these takings, as we have seen, are not steadily persistent. The group could collapse—indeed, probably has collapsed since 1931—with yet higher speed than it expanded.

Only about one-fourth of the takings classed as centering on individuals fall under subsistence requirements. This proportion consists of habitual disbursements for liquor, tobacco, hair cuts, and similar minor items. The balance is made up mainly of numerous other small purchases. Such items, because they are habitual and in small units, stand up fairly well against moderate declines in spending power; but we may find them liable to quick retrenchment when spending power falls more sharply. That question will be answered when estimates for 1933 become available.

About three-quarters of takings centering on the home are included in our list of subsistence requirements, leaving only about one-fourth subject to the more volatile buying motives. Evidently the high proportion of subsistence budget expenditures is one underlying reason for the relative stability of the group.

A comprehensive study of the question whether consumers' takings, as influenced by living habits, are tending toward greater or toward less stability would take into account many other factors not here studied, including:

Size and composition of families
National-racial cultures
Population growth, and changes in the age distribution of the population
Distribution of spending power among income classes
Political and social ideology; particularly the rising or declining strength of traditions of conservatism
The relative prevalence and social authority of well-integrated vs. unstable personalities
Velocity of industrial changes affecting living conditions.

One may hazard a guess that a large majority of qualified observers would assign greater weight to the unsettling forces in American habits of living than to the stabilizing forces; but this is merely a guess.

So far as is shown by the study here reported, the most significant trend is that toward a decreasing proportion of takings centering on family life in the home. To the extent of the decrease, stability of consumption arising from the routine of home living has doubtless been undermined. No warrant is given for pushing this tentative conclusion to an extreme. The home still dominates and is still a powerful stabilizer. But we cannot safely shut our eyes to the tendency toward an increasing ferment of living habits which makes consumption less and less dependable.

Habits of Purchasing as Stabilizers

One more line of analysis will help to define and measure the stabilizing elements in demand. Consumers' purchases may be classified on the basis of their normal frequency of repetition into three groups:

Those frequently repetitive, such as food, small household supplies, rentals and home services, automotive services and the like; items commonly recurring once a month or oftener have been placed in this group.

Those less frequently repetitive, such as articles of clothing, some portions of automobile upkeep expenses, household supplies, travel and other recreational spendings, savings and the like; most of the items in this group commonly recur at intervals of more than a month and less than a year.

Those infrequently repetitive, consisting of automobiles, furnishings and fixtures of all kinds, foreign travel and the like; commonly recurring at intervals of more than one year.

All items of family takings have been assigned to the above groups, in accordance with the percentages detailed in Appendix F. As in all such compilations, the percentage allocations are subject to question; but it is unlikely that differences of opinion on these points would be wide enough to affect substantially the conclusions here drawn. The results are summarized in Table 20 below.

TABLE 20.—SUMMARY CLASSIFICATION OF AVERAGE FAMILY TAKINGS ON BASIS
OF GOVERNING CONDITIONS OF PURCHASE
(In 1913 dollars)

Group	Pre-war	1919	1921	1923	1925	1927	1929	1931
Frequently Repetitive............	$ 867	$ 821	$ 762	$ 868	$ 920	$ 944	$1,005	$ 910
Less Frequently Repetitive.......	569	710	650	758	798	806	785	607
Infrequently Repetitive..........	139	155	163	238	240	228	246	172
Totals......................	$1,575	$1,686	$1,575	$1,861	$1,958	$1,978	$2,036	$1,689

(In percentages of total family intake)

Group	Pre-war	1919	1921	1923	1925	1927	1929	1931
Frequently Repetitive............	55.1	48.7	48.3	46.6	46.9	47.7	49.4	53.9
Less Frequently Repetitive.......	36.1	42.1	41.3	40.7	40.8	40.8	38.5	35.9
Infrequently Repetitive..........	8.8	9.2	10.4	12.8	12.3	11.6	12.1	10.2

The three-fold classification in Table 20 naturally conforms closely, so far as commodities are concerned, with retail channels of sale. "In marketing consumers' goods," says Copeland, "a manufacturer can seek to have his product placed on sale in as many stores as possible, located at easily accessible points; he can place it in the stores in the central shopping districts; or he can arrange for the promotion of its sales by selected retail stores, in each city, that attract customers from large trading areas."[4] This grouping of outlets is the guide for a useful classification of commodities into (a) convenience goods (b) shopping goods and (c) specialty goods. The three categories in Table 20 —(a) frequently repetitive purchases (b) less frequently repetitive and (c) infrequently repetitive—are in general parallel.

[4] "Principles of Merchandising" by Melvin T. Copeland, Shaw, Chicago, 1927, p. 27.

Our classification also includes, however, intangible goods, direct taxes and savings—that is to say, the whole of consumers' intake. Moreover, we are immediately concerned not with retail channels but with consumers' habits of purchasing.

One manifest deduction from Table 20 is that alterations in allotment of takings among the three classes are associated not so much with the ups and downs of total spending power as with temporal modifications in offerings, tastes and marketing methods. Note, for example, the striking differences in percentage allotments between the average pre-war year and 1921, two years of equal spending power; and to a somewhat lesser degree between 1919 and 1931, also two years of equal spending power.

Frequently repetitive purchases sank to a low level during the post-war readjustment but climbed steeply thereafter up to a high plateau in 1923–1929 from which there was a considerable recession (in dollars) in 1931. The expansion of distribution of convenience goods through chain stores and other small-unit outlets was probably one important factor; another was the rise of contractual obligations for rentals, for upkeep of owner-occupied homes, and for home services. Less frequently repetitive purchases, consisting largely of clothing, recreational goods and savings, moved upward (in dollars) after 1921 but with considerable hesitancy; stated in percentages of total intake, they moved downward steadily through the post-war period and broke badly in 1931. Infrequently repetitive purchases advanced to a high plateau, mainly because of automobiles, in 1923–1929, but revealed their inherent weakness by a sharp drop from 1929 to 1931. The year-by-year movements of the three groups are represented in Chart Q.

A clearer view of the relative stabilities of the three groups in the early part and in the later part of the period studied is supplied by Table 21. Frequently repetitive purchases appear to have become more rather than less dependable. They fell off in close correspondence with the 7% decline in total takings from 1919 to 1921. But in the face of the 17% drop in total takings from 1929 to 1931, they lost only a scant 9%. Millions of unemployed, threatened with desperate poverty, continued to buy their daily newspapers, cigarettes and enough gasoline to run their cars. Less frequently repetitive purchases also went down at about the same rate as total takings in 1919–1921, whereas in 1929–1931 they fell much faster. In times of stress

RELATIVE MOVEMENTS
OF AVERAGE FAMILY INTAKE
ON BASIS OF GOVERNING CONDITIONS OF PURCHASE
(In chronological order; Dollars of 1913;
Based on Table 20)

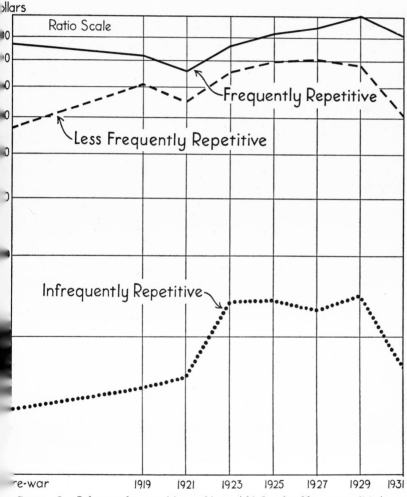

CHART Q.—Infrequently repetitive takings (chiefly durable commodities) moved up to a high plateau from 1923 to 1929; then fell off sharply.

consumers give up or space at longer intervals replenishment of clothing and household supplies, visits to the dentist, payment of insurance premiums, and the like. The evidence points toward increased vulnerability of takings in this group. Infrequently repetitive purchases, which moved up against the general trend in 1921, have obviously become highly sensitive and undependable.

TABLE 21.—PERCENTAGES OF CHANGE IN CLASSES OF AVERAGE FAMILY TAKINGS
(In 1913 dollars)

Group	Pre-war to 1921	1919–1921	1923–1931	1929–1931
Frequently Repetitive.........	−12	−7	+ 5	− 9
Less Frequently Repetitive.....	+11	−8	−20	−23
Infrequently Repetitive........	+17	+5	−28	−30
Total of Average Family Takings....................	0	−7	− 9	−17

A comparison of habits of purchasing in recent years with habits before the war, as indicated in Tables 20 and 21, suggests this tentative generalization:

Stabilizing habits—*i.e.*, purchases of frequently repetitive items—have grown in strength when measured in terms of dollar volume; but in prosperous years they form a smaller proportion of total intake.

An examination of the post-war figures suggests another probability:

The stabilizing influence of frequently repetitive purchases is gaining strength; but at the same time the unsettling elements—*i.e.*, less frequently and infrequently repetitive purchases—have become more easily liable to sudden deterioration.

Both these statements refer to the distributing-marketing system as it operates in present-day America. They may or may not be valid in other times or countries. And of course their validity remains to be established or disproved by further tests during the next few years.

An associated stabilizing factor—of secondary importance, yet far from negligible—is the rising proportion of purchases which are derivatives of other purchases, as for example:

Condiments for meats and vegetables
Accessories and garage services for automobiles
Small articles of dress to complete an ensemble
Upkeep expenses for dwellings
Fixtures and parts for all kinds of durable goods.

In Appendix F major initial purchases and all other spendings
which may be considered independently by the consumer are
classed as *primary* and listed in the left-hand column; spendings
necessitated or strongly stimulated by a concurrent or prior
purchase, such as the examples above, are classed as *derived* and
listed in the right-hand column.   The annual amounts of derived
purchases per average family and their percentages of total takings, as calculated from Appendix F, are shown below in Table 22.
The table reveals a steady gain (in percentages) of this type of
purchases.

TABLE 22.—AMOUNTS AND PERCENTAGES OF "DERIVED" PURCHASES

	Pre-war	1919	1921	1923	1925	1927	1929	1931
Amount per Average Family.........	$135	$165	$169	$204	$232	$230	$242	$217
Percentage of Total Outgo...........	8.6	9.8	10.7	11.0	11.9	11.6	11.9	12.8

Somewhat over half the derived purchases each year fall in the
"less frequently" group.   They introduce into this group particularly—to a smaller extent into the "infrequently" group as
well—a certain stiffness of resistance to reduction of spending
power.   Otherwise, the fluctuations in these two groups would be
even more erratic.   The influence of derived purchases is well
worth taking into account.

DECLINING INFLUENCE OF STABILIZERS

Family takings have been classified in this chapter from three
distinct angles.   Inasmuch as the classifications overlap to an
unknown extent, they do not yield unified estimates of the
proportions of comparable stable elements in consumption in
each year.   However, all the three analyses point toward a
common conclusion.

Consumers' basic wants appear to be, practically speaking, unchangeable.
Their urgent, irreducible wants, however, are the first to be satisfied; and these
wants control, therefore, a declining ratio of total takings when spending power

rises. Hence, as spending power goes up—which is, and presumably will continue to be, the secular trend—the stabilizing influence of wants goes down.

Spendings focused on family life in the home show a marked tendency to govern a smaller ratio of total takings. Even if the tendency should be reversed, additional takings for home life are likely to be motivated by volatile wants—especially wants for social approval and prominence. Habits of living, it seems probable, are losing a good deal of their power as stabilizers of consumption.

Frequently repetitive purchases are growing in dollar volume but not fast enough to maintain in normal years their pre-war ratio of total takings. Less frequently and infrequently repetitive purchases show unmistakable signs of increasing instability. The expanding area of derived purchases is a partial offsetting factor. On the whole, habits of purchasing are becoming less effective as stabilizers.

The common conclusion is that the once overwhelming dominance of routine in consumption is plainly weakening.

This observation in itself is certainly not novel. On the contrary, it is often put forward in loose and exaggerated terms. The effort in this chapter has been to offer a reasoned appraisal of the extent of the decline in stabilizing elements. As a personal judgment, and nothing more, one may venture to say that in the years just prior to the war perhaps 70% to 80% of consumers' takings would stand up in the face of a drastic reduction of spending power; that is, consumers would draw heavily on savings before lowering their intake beneath that level. Because of the altered ratios of control by urgent wants and by established habits of living and of purchasing, the percentage of stable elements in post-war consumption during the prosperous years probably sank to, say, 60% to 65%. The difference in percentages is adequate to explain one of the most baffling puzzles of the depression, namely: the persistent refusal of consumption to fight its way back with its one-time vigor.

CHAPTER VIII

INSTABILITIES

The resistless current of a mighty river is a fitting symbol of the physical needs and social habits which govern the greater part of consumption. But the stream may be lashed into fury by storms; its whirlpools, eddies and waves may be fickle and dangerous. This chapter and the one following will be concerned with the swirling surface, as distinguished from the deeper current, of consumers' takings. It will endeavor to discover the types of consumption that are peculiarly subject to turmoil.

It should be made clear at the outset that disturbances go on, to a greater or less degree, in all classes of takings. They are not so conspicuous in social-cultural activities or food, to be sure, as in transportation or household furnishings; but sizable fluctuations are found throughout the whole range. Every class is represented in our subsistence budget (Chapter VI); at the same time, every class contains non-essentials, weakly motivated purchases, which are easily given up.

DEFINITIONS: ELASTICITY, DISPENSABILITY, VARIABILITY

Up to this point in Part Two terms have been used in their everyday sense, and it has seemed unnecessary to introduce formal definitions. Three technical words are now to be employed, however; and their meanings should be stated as precisely as possible. All three words refer to consumers' demands.

Elasticity. Alfred Marshall originated the expression "elasticity of demand" and defined it simply and accurately as "responsiveness of demand to change in price."[1] The definition implies that the influence of price changes is conceived to be isolated from other influences, such as changes in taste, in market offerings or in income. To the best of my knowledge, Marshall observed the distinction consistently. Unhappily, later writers have bred confusion by grafting onto Marshall's conception something quite distinct, namely: the influence of gains or

[1] "Industry and Trade" by Alfred Marshall, Macmillan, London, 1920, p. 181.

losses in consumers' purchasing power.[2]   This is more than a minor question of dialectics. The confusion obstructs straight thinking on a fundamental issue of the day, the issue between the advocates of fiat increases in consumer purchasing power and those who favor the restoration of a self-balancing economy. In the present discussion "elasticity" is restricted to its Marshallian definition.

Dispensability is the liability of a given class of takings to be curtailed when spending power (or purchasing power, which is the same thing) declines. A "degree of dispensability" may be measured by comparing (other things being equal) expenditures for selected objects at various levels of spending power.[3] Thus, while elasticity is related to prices, dispensability is related to spending power.

Variability is here used as a generic term for the effects of temporal alterations, other than the alterations ascribable to price changes (elasticity) or to spending power changes (dispensability), which produce deviations of given classes of takings from a calculated or assumed normal. The chief alterations under this head are (*a*) in offerings of consumers' goods, (*b*) in consumers' tastes and (*c*) in the social-economic environment. Plainly, this is a catch-all grouping of factors affecting demand not covered under the other two heads. These factors have in common, however, the fact that they operate over a span of time, whereas elasticity and dispensability are, strictly speaking, non-temporal.

The three definitions may be abbreviated as follows:

Elasticity is the responsiveness of demand to price changes.
Dispensability is the responsiveness of demand to changes in spending power.
Variability is the responsiveness of demand to temporal changes distinct from changes in price and in spending power.

No logical difficulty appears in distinguishing the three sources of fluctuations in demand. In principle, each one should be

[2] The reference is not of course to all later writers. Yet the error is widespread. Even such competent authorities as Nystrom and Waite do not escape it. Cf. Nystrom's definition (italics mine): "The demand for economic goods is limited *by purchasing power and considerations of the best use of that purchasing power.* Thus, as prices go up buyers purchase less and less, or drop out of the market entirely. This tendency on the part of consumers to purchase less as the price goes up and more as the price goes down is termed the elasticity of demand." ("Economics of Consumption" by Paul H. Nystrom, Ronald, New York, 1929, p. 38.) Waite starts with a correct definition; but, sad to relate, five pages later he slips into a calculation of "elasticities of demand" in relation to income levels. ("Economics of Consumption" by Warren C. Waite, McGraw-Hill, New York, 1928, pp. 90ff.)

[3] The term "dispensability" and the idea of "degree of dispensability" are borrowed from Professor Jakob Marschak; but Marschak's formula for computing degree of dispensability has been replaced in the treatment which follows by a very simple method of ranking classes of takings in respect to dispensability. See the article on "Consumption: Problems of Measurement" by Jakob Marschak in "Encyclopedia of the Social Sciences," vol. IV, pp. 295ff.; also, "Die Elastizität der Nachfrage" by the same author, Tübingen, 1931.

measurable in itself. Insuperable difficulties come up in practice, however, because of lack of sufficient information to permit unraveling the tangled threads. A highly imperfect and tentative approach toward measurement is the most that can reasonably be hoped for.

Both the elasticity and the dispensability of *classes* of takings may be expected to remain fairly constant over a considerable period of time, at any rate when the temporal factors lumped under variability are minimized. Hence, the calculations of elasticity and dispensability in this chapter will be founded on non-chronological arrangements of our data. Variability, on the contrary, being a product of temporal changes, the data will be presented in their chronological order. The two lines of treatment will be found consistent with each other if their distinct purposes are clearly understood.

A slight realignment of the classification of takings is necessary in order to get significant results. The estimates of spendings for alcoholic beverages are so incomplete, as previously noted, that measurement of their fluctuations would be meaningless; this class has been dropped. The estimates for direct taxes and for savings have been merged, for reasons previously explained, under the general head of withholdings. Spendings for home maintenance, on the other hand, cover sub-classes of such widely divergent tendencies that the major class has been split up into (a) a combination of household services, including fuel and light, and current payments for dwellings—that is, paid rentals, imputed rentals and expenditures on owner-occupied dwellings— and (b) home equipment, which includes both furnishings and supplies. Thus, the 11 classes of takings to be treated in this chapter do not exactly correspond with the 12 classes in earlier chapters.

METHODS OF MEASURING ELASTICITY

Attempts to calculate the elasticity of demand for selected products have generally ignored—indeed, without exception to the best of my knowledge—the influence of both spending power changes and temporal changes. So long as the measurements are confined to short periods, the resultant distortions are likely to be negligible.

The problem now before us, however, is different in character. The aim is to ascertain relative elasticities of demand for broad classes of objects through a 13-year term.   We have seen unmistakable evidence that demand for some of these classes is largely affected by the ups and downs of average spending power; and everyday observation tells us that variations caused by new offerings, marketing stimuli and other temporal factors are by no means small.   The problem is soluble, therefore, only insofar as responsiveness to price changes can be isolated from responsiveness to other changes.

The first step is to try to eliminate changes in demand ascribable to other factors than price movements.   Because spending power is a dominating factor, we start by arranging our post-war estimates in the order of an ascending scale of spending power, as previously exemplified; then computing for each class of objects its percentages of total intake; then plotting these percentages, taking their average for the whole period as a base; and, finally, drawing a least-square trend line, which then becomes our base line.   For convenience, it appears as a horizontal base line in the series of R-charts, four of which—those for food, personal appearance, transportation, and sickness and death—are reproduced on the opposite page.

This trend line measures—crudely, to be sure—the effect of increases in spending power on takings of the given class.   By making the trend our base line, therefore, we eliminate as nearly as possible the influence of spending power on the given class. Unhappily, the trend line is not "pure."   If there were no environmental changes during the period, it could be taken as a fairly accurate expression of the normal ratios of spending power at different levels devoted to the given class of objects.   As it is, the trend line is in fact a hybrid representative of the intermingled forces of spending power and environment.   In spite of its defects, the oscillations of the plotted line over and below its own trend line may be justifiably attributed chiefly to price movements—complicated, in some cases, however, by other quick-acting agents, such as fashions, which cannot be eliminated.

The second step is to represent price movements in as direct a comparison as possible with oscillations of demand.   Obviously, our interest here is not in the separate movements of prices of each class of objects but in the relationships of these prices to the composite of prices for consumers' goods.   These relationships are expressed by relatives of the price index of each class of objects to the aggregate index of all consumers' purchases.

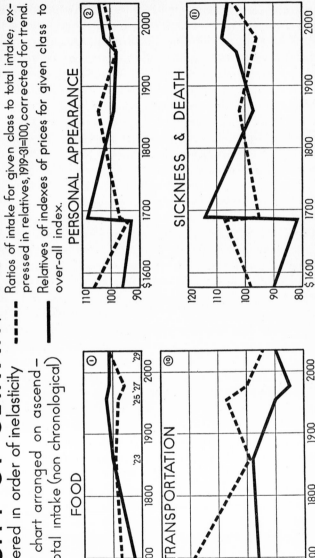

ELASTICITY OF CERTAIN CLASSES OF INTAKE

Charts numbered in order of inelasticity

----- Ratios of intake for given class to total intake; expressed in relatives, 1919-31=100, corrected for trend.

——— Relatives of indexes of prices for given class to over-all index.

Data on each chart arranged on ascending scale of total intake (non chronological)

PERSONAL APPEARANCE

SICKNESS & DEATH

FOOD

TRANSPORTATION

R-CHARTS.—Food and personal appearance are distinctly inelastic classes; transportation and sickness and death, highly elastic.

The relatives are plotted, in the series of R-charts, on a base of their 1919–1931 average.

When the two lines in one of the R-charts—one line representing oscillations of percentages of total intake about their own trend line and the other representing oscillations of relative prices—run closely parallel, the deduction is drawn that the class of objects in question is inelastic; for an advance or a decline in relative prices is accompanied by a corresponding movement of takings, signifying that consumption measured in equivalent units has not been perceptibly modified. When the two lines run counter to each other, the deduction is that the class in question is elastic: that is to say, the response to a rise in price is a falling-off in consumption or, in the contrary case, the response to a drop in price is a gain in consumption.

The number of points represented on the R-charts is too small to warrant calculating a correlation coefficient; instead, we have measured the point-to-point divergences. First, the *frequency* of conformance of direction of the two lines, clearly indicating inelasticity, is taken as one factor. On this count food ranks at the top; as shown on the chart, in only one of the six movements represented does percentage of intake vary inversely to relative price. At the other extreme, every one of the six movements of percentage of intake for sickness and death is inverse to the price movement. Second, *amplitude* of divergence of the two lines was taken as the other factor. Plainly, the greater the divergence the greater is the apparent elasticity of demand. By comparing the rankings, which are not widely different on the two bases, the 11 classes of intake have been placed in the following order of *inelasticity*:

1. Food
2. Personal Appearance
3. Social-Cultural Activities
4. Clothing
5. Tobacco
6. Recreation
7. Home Equipment
8. Dwellings and Home Services
9. Savings and Taxes
10. Transportation
11. Sickness and Death

No one will be disposed, I trust, to accept this ranking as a closed verdict. Certainly, it is not so intended. Apart from questions as to the method here employed, our data have two very serious deficiencies. They yield only six comparisons of movements of intake and of prices—far too small a number on which to predicate assured conclusions. In the second place, the

two-year interval between points of comparison leaves a wide
gap for extraneous factors, particularly changes in taste, to
creep in and distort the relationship between price movements
and percentages of intake.   Nevertheless, the ranking may have
some value if it is regarded as provisional and used with caution.

NOTES ON ELASTICITY

Elasticity of demand means much both to private business and
to the national economy.   High elasticity implies that a big
potential market can be tapped by lowering prices; and, con-
versely, that sales are liable to go off sharply if prices are raised.
Low elasticity implies a stubborn evenness of takings whether
prices move up or down.

Of course, it will not do to push these generalities beyond the
limits of a reasonable interpretation of the evidence.   A large
movement of prices may bring out an unexpected reaction, either
a sudden expansion of demand on one side or its disconcerting
collapse on the other.   For the purpose of the present study,
however, we may properly assume that the less elastic classes of
takings are relatively immune to fluctuations arising from any
price changes now foreseeable.

Inelasticity, we should remember, works both ways; that is,
while a reduction of prices for inelastic goods fails to enlarge
consumption and merely sets free increased spending power for
other objects, it is likewise true that a price rise instead of cutting
down consumption operates to withdraw spending power from
other objects.

Least elastic of all the 11 classes of takings is food.   A glance
at its R-chart will reveal a marked parallelism of prices and
takings.   The showing is in line with expectations and serves to
create a certain degree of restrained confidence in the remaining
R-charts; for the exceptional unresponsiveness of food sales to
price movements has been a commonplace for generations.[4]

The assignments of personal appearance to second place and of
clothing to fourth place in the inelasticity series are in spite of
rather striking instances of elastic response in certain years.

---

[4] As a recent example in point, the United States Summary of the Retail
Census for 1933 directs attention to the fact that while the decline in sales by the
food group of retailers between 1929 and 1933 was 37%, the B.L.S. food index
during the same period dropped 36.4%, "indicating that there occurred little,
if any, change in tonnage or the actual quantity of food consumed."

Undoubtedly, modifications of consumers' tastes affecting both classes occurred during the period. In the case of clothing, a shortage of supply coincident with an exceptional demand in one year (1919) distorts the picture. Nevertheless, the charts for both classes reveal inelastic response of takings to price changes in four movements out of six.

Social-cultural activities, which are placed third, are markedly inelastic in the lower levels of spending power, but seem to become more responsive to price changes in the upper levels. The tendency is plausible; for a certain volume of takings of education, reading matter, contributions, and the like is strongly motivated and therefore persistent whether prices are high or low, whereas accretions to this volume are more likely to be influenced by relative prices.

The relative prices of tobacco, the fifth group, follow an unbroken downward path. Tobacco consumption fluctuates considerably about its trend line but plainly tends upward while prices go down. Its chart indicates, therefore, a somewhat greater degree of responsiveness of demand to price changes than might have been anticipated.

Recreational takings, sixth in rank, have moved erratically, while relative prices have varied only slightly. Unfortunately, the price line for this class is largely fictitious, because specific price indexes in the recreation group are few and unreliable. If we take it, however, at its face value, we see that four out of the six movements of takings respond to opposite movements of prices. On this basis, recreation is placed among the more elastic classes; but it is the weakest finding of the entire series.

The next two classes in rank—(a) home equipment and (b) dwellings and home services—are so irregular that it is impracticable to trace any clear relationships between takings and prices. Their rankings in respect to inelasticity have been assigned by the method explained above but must be regarded as doubtful.

When we come to the last three classes in our ranking, we find ourselves on firmer ground. The data as to prices are sufficient to inspire considerable confidence and the fluctuations of both relative prices and relative takings are well marked. The savings and taxes class and the transportation class both exhibit unmistakable responses to price movements in four instances out of six. These two classes rank ninth and tenth, respectively.

In the sickness and death class, which ranks last, the response of demand to price movements is plain in five instances out of six and can be construed as a partial response in the sixth instance. Apparently expenditures for doctors, medicines and hospitals are exceedingly sensitive to the rise and fall of *relative* prices. "Relative" is emphasized, because the price fluctuations are larger in other goods than in medical fees and the like; but slight movements of price indexes in opposite directions may result, as they do here, in pronounced alterations of price relationships.

As the foregoing comments make manifest, our judgment is that the four classes near the top of the scale of inelasticity and the three classes near the bottom are properly ranked. The data are too scanty to permit fine gradations of the four intermediate classes. Mistakes in placing them, however, would affect only slightly the conclusions of the chapter summarized in Table 23.

METHOD OF MEASURING DISPENSABILITY

The most obvious and simplest method of measuring dispensability is to observe the ratio between takings of a given class in years of high spending power and the corresponding takings in years of low spending power. The figures appear in Table 13. Wherever the low point for a given class falls in 1931, that figure may properly be taken as a base; presumably it embodies in itself the influence of temporal changes during the period here under survey. Wherever the low point falls in an earlier year, as is true in four instances, an average of the low figure with the 1931 figure is taken as a more representative base. The classes of takings are ranked in respect to indispensability on the basis of the average ratios of takings each year to the base just described.

The method is crude. Short-swing fluctuations arising from variability and elasticity are not excluded. No attention is given to experiences outside the 1919–1931 period. The results may later be considerably modified. Nevertheless, for the limited purpose in view, which is merely to establish a ranking, the method appears to us adequate and has been adopted.

Following are the eleven classes of takings arranged in the order of their *indispensability:*

1. Social-Cultural Activities	7. Personal Appearance
2. Sickness and Death	8. Recreation
3. Dwellings and Home Services	9. Home Equipment
4. Food	10. Transportation
5. Tobacco	11. Savings and Taxes
6. Clothing	

Lest the list above be misinterpreted, it may be well to remind readers that the term *indispensability* is used in the technical meaning of unresponsiveness of demand to changing levels of spending power. It carries no connotation of either approval or reproach. Furthermore, we are dealing in this chapter only with entire classes of takings. A minimum quantity of food no doubt is the least dispensable of economic goods; in our generation, however, food consumption includes a sizable proportion of delicacies.

NOTES ON DISPENSABILITY

The comments following on various classes of intake are based not only on our estimates of deflated dollar takings (Table 13) but also to some extent on Lynd's tabulation of indexes of per capita output of consumers' commodities (in units of quantity for most items) and on his explanatory remarks.[5] Inasmuch as our figures for average family takings are stated in deflated dollars, they should be—and generally are—reconcilable with Lynd's.

Social-cultural activities stand at the head of the list—a showing which may excite surprise. The record, however, is clear. They neither climb very high in prosperity nor fall off severely in depression. As was remarked above, a certain minimum volume in this class appears to be so strongly motivated that it resists decline with exceptional force.

The high ranking assigned to sickness and death in the indispensability list, in contrast with its place at the bottom of the inelasticity list, offers a striking example of the distinction between the influence on consumption of spending power changes and of price changes. The method of measuring *elasticity* has the effect of *minimizing* the influence of changes in spending power. The R-chart for sickness and death makes it evident that the ratios of takings in this class rise whenever relative

---

[5] "Recent Social Trends," Chap. XVII on "The People as Consumers" by Robert S. Lynd, McGraw-Hill, New York, 1933, pp. 897ff.

prices fall and *vice versa*, signifying a high degree of response to changes in relative prices. The method of measuring *dispensability*, on the other hand, has the effect of *focusing* on the influence of changes in spending power. It then becomes equally evident that the response of sickness and death to changes in spending power is slight. Contrasts between ranks in the two lists appear in other classes—particularly in food, dwellings and home services, and personal appearance—all of which go to emphasize the usefulness of distinguishing between elasticity and dispensability.

Dwellings and home services, considered as one class, attains third place in the scale of indispensability because it is governed largely by continuing contracts and by fixed habits of living. Readjustments take time. Some of the constituent items, such as property taxes and payments for gas and electricity, are established by public authorities on a rate basis which does not readily conform to fluctuating price levels; takings of this kind must be kept up irrespective of changes in spending power. The prices of other items, such as rentals and servants' wages, are liable to give way abruptly at some stage of a long-drawn-out depression and sink to a point which will permit families to maintain their customary households. Both processes, in spite of their divergences, hold takings steady (when calculated in deflated dollars). However, the stability has a certain character of artificiality. It is questionable whether this class will retain its rank when it becomes possible to examine its record in 1933.

Food and tobacco, the next two classes in rank, show a moderately close approach to uniformity of takings both in good years and in bad. The fact that food, instead of heading the indispensability list, is in fourth place is explainable mainly by (*a*) the increasing proportion of food put up in labor-saving forms and (*b*) the growing habit of eating in hotels and restaurants. Lynd calls attention to the "sharp upward trends" in quantity takings of canned and prepared foods and of confectionery. In urban communities one out of every four persons eats at least one meal a day in restaurants, and millions eat all their meals away from their homes. Both these types of consumption are liable to suffer when spending power declines.

Next in order are clothing, personal appearance and recreation. Again, a natural question is why clothing, obviously a prime essential, should rank so low. The answer is two-fold: first, a tendency in good times, as noted by Lynd, to buy ready-made and high-fashion apparel which can be readily replaced by less expensive articles in periods of low spending power; second, the durability of clothing which makes it an easily postponable purchase.   More puzzling is the strong resistance of personal appearance and recreation, both composed of non-essentials, to declines in spending power.   The preponderance of small items in these two classes of intake may provide the clue.   Seligman estimates that in 1925 fully 55 % of sales of jewelry were of articles priced at less than $30.[6]   Other typical purchases, totaling large amounts, under the head of personal appearance are cosmetics, toilet soaps, razor blades, shaves and beauty treatments, all of which are relatively small items and frequently repetitive.   Similarly, the greater part of recreation consists of admissions to amusements and recreational commodities, for the most part a collection of small articles.

Two common characteristics of the last three classes on the list—home equipment, transportation and withholdings (savings and taxes)—are: first, they are made up mostly, though not entirely, of large purchases; second, by far the greater part of these purchases are postponable.   Consequently, their degrees of dispensability are large.   This is a sufficient explanation of the ranking of home equipment.

Of total takings of transportation, one-half in 1923 consisted of new automobiles against one-fourth in 1931; this is the chief factor in giving transportation its high degree of dispensability.   Unfortunately for the stability of the industry, purchases of new cars have proved to be more easily postponable than was formerly supposed.   An average useful life of 7 years was once thought an ample allowance; more recent estimates are from 8½ to 10 years.[7]   Consequently, the anticipated replacement demand has been slow in maturing.   A somewhat similar remark applies to tires.   On the other hand, expenditures for gasoline and maintenance have held up well; if separately grouped, they would take rank in the top half of the indispensability list.

    [6] "Economics of Instalment Selling" by Edwin R. A. Seligman, Harper, New York, 1927, vol. I, p. 116.

    [7] See *Standard Trade and Securities*, a publication of Standard Statistics Co., Inc., May 13, 1932.

Financial transactions, Snyder points out, form the most erratic group of all those which enter into his measure of volume of trade.[8] It is scarcely surprising to find them occupying the lowest place in respect to indispensability in family consumption.

It will be observed that the doubts expressed as to the ranking of some classes of takings on the score of elasticity have not been paralleled in the comments on dispensability. The method of ranking, though crude, is much simpler; the results are plausible.

Indispensability is a product of persistent motivations, fixed habits, continuing contractual obligations and frequency of repetition of small purchases. On the other hand, a combination of strong motivation, which carries expenditures up to a high level when spending power rises, with infrequent repetition of purchases, which makes them easily postponable, renders a high degree of dispensability unavoidable.

Method of Measuring Variability

Variability must be measured in time units. The shortest unit provided by our data is two years; the longest unit is the 13-year term 1919–1931. For convenience, we will refer to variability during these two time units as, respectively, short-swing and secular.

Short-swing variability is here measured by computing the coefficient of variation of the trend line of dollar takings in successive years. The relative variability of each of the major classes of intake is shown in the series of S-charts; the dotted line represents the takings of the given class reduced to relatives on a 1919–1931 base while the trend line fitted to these relatives is shown by the solid line. This trend line presumably gives expression to the influence of spending power and to the long-period influence of alterations in both price relationships and temporal factors. It does not of course cover short-period fluctuations in response to price changes; these fluctuations (elasticity) we have not been able to separate from fluctuations that properly belong to variability. Consequently, the ranking below may be distorted, especially in the case of classes of objects which possess high elasticity. The distortion can scarcely be great enough to shift the order of ranking by more than one place, with the possible exception of transportation.

[8] "Business Cycles and Business Measurements" by Carl Snyder, Macmillan, New York, 1927, p. 132.

Following is the ranking for *short-swing invariability:*

1. Social-Cultural Activities
2. Sickness and Death
3. Dwellings and Home Services
4. Food
5. Clothing
6. Tobacco
7. Savings and Taxes
8. Personal Appearance
9. Recreation
10. Home Equipment
11. Transportation

Secular variability can be only inferred from data limited to so brief a period as 13 years. The method adopted is to construct for each class of takings a postulated secular trend line, representing the product of three indexes: (*a*) total takings, or spending power (*b*) relative prices for the given class and (*c*) the ratio of the given class of takings to total takings. This trend line is plotted against its own 1919–1931 average as a base.

The index of total takings shows the movements of spending power; the index of relative prices of the given class shows the movements of prices affecting takings of that class; the index of ratio of takings of the given class shows the normal proportion of such takings to total takings, or spending power. The product of the three indexes, therefore (that is, the postulated trend line), in effect computes *what would have occurred* during the 13-year period if the takings of the given class had been determined solely by a composite of spending power and price movements—that is, if changes in popular taste, new offerings, market stimuli and other factors of variability had not intervened. The postulated trend is plausibly a reasonable indication of the normal course of demand for the given class of objects. The divergence between the actual trend and the postulated trend may be assumed, then, to represent the influence during the period as a whole of the factors of variability; and the degree of divergence, on that assumption, measures the degree of variation from the true secular trend.

Secular variability alone is ranked below; and the exact degree of divergence of the actual trend line from the postulated secular trend lines is shown. A plus sign in front of degree of divergence indicates that the actual trend at the end of the period runs above the postulated secular trend; a minus sign indicates that the actual trend runs beneath the postulated secular trend. If the postulated line is assumed to be a true trend line (which is of course merely a plausible assumption), then the plain implication is that those classes marked plus are moving toward a precarious position, whereas those marked minus will experience in time a decided upswing of demand. But the implication must not be treated as a probability unless it is confirmed by an examination of long-term trends of living and spending habits. This question is set aside for discussion in Part Three. At the moment we are concerned only with the *extent* of secular variability in the 1919–1931 period. Hence, the plus and minus signs are disregarded in the ranking, which is based solely on degree of divergence.

1. Social-Cultural Activities (+0.24)
2. Recreation (+0.72)
3. Food (+1.31)
4. Home Equipment (+1.51)
5. Personal Appearance (−2.23)
6. Clothing (+2.30)
7. Tobacco (+2.43)
8. Dwellings and Home Services (−3.29)
9. Transportation (+3.54)
10. Savings and Taxes (−4.05)
11. Sickness and Death (−4.96)

A comparison of the rankings for short-swing and for secular variability reveals wide differences—as instances, sickness and death, recreation, dwellings and home services and home equipment. This is not in itself surprising. It may easily happen that a strong upward or downward trend of actual takings, carrying it far above or below the postulated trend, is accompanied by exceptionally slight short-swing fluctuations from the actual trend. In order to measure variability as a whole, the two rankings, for short-swing and for secular variability, are combined. The final rankings (products of the two rankings above) appear in Table 23 and also appear in the upper right-hand corner of the S-charts.

Notes on Variability

The least variable class of objects of expenditure, as determined by this method, consists of social-cultural activities. At first thought so high a rank seems scarcely credible. It should be kept in mind, however, that desires for education, reading matter, stationery and the like, and voluntary obligations to pay dues and contributions, which are among the chief components of

SOCIAL-CULTURAL

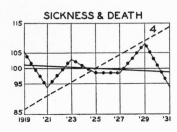

SICKNESS & DEATH

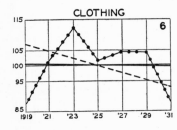

CLOTHING

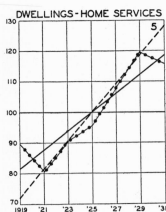

DWELLINGS-HOME SERVICES

VARIABILITY OF

Charts numbered in order of *invariability*

Data on each chart
arranged in
chronological order

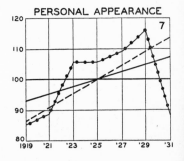

PERSONAL APPEARANCE

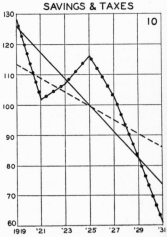

SAVINGS & TAXES

S-CHARTS.—Each chart indicates short-swing variability (responsiveness to
trend line; secular variability by the degree of divergence between the actual

CLASSES OF INTAKE

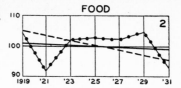

FOOD

KEY

 Average family intake for each class of objects ; expressed in relatives on a 1919-1931 base.

―――― Trend line fitted to above data.

― ― Postulated trend line; see text.

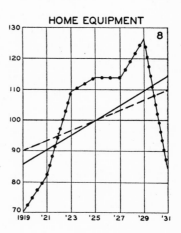

HOME EQUIPMENT

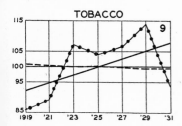

TOBACCO

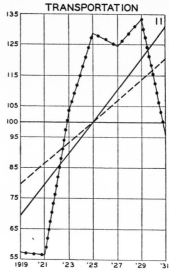

TRANSPORTATION

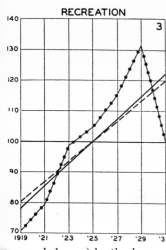

RECREATION

temporal changes) by the degree of oscillation of the intake line about its own trend line and the postulated trend line.

this class of takings, are strongly enough rooted to offer powerful resistance to changing conditions. Moreover, in this field inventions, new devices, and sales-building drives play only minor roles. Relative absence of disturbing factors is the best explanation of the slight variability of this class.

Food ranks second in respect to invariability. Food specialties, to be sure, are constantly appearing, but they agitate only the surface of demand; their effect is to shift purchases from one brand or style to another—the theme of the next chapter—rather than to set up large oscillations in total volume or to deflect total takings far from their normal course.

Recreation, the third in rank, is easily swayed by short-term factors; but its actual trend sticks so close to the postulated trend that it deserves a high rating for invariability. The same comment applies in principle to home equipment, though its amplitude of short-swing fluctuation brings it down to eighth place in the combined ranking. Both these classes may be described as vacillating, yet tenacious.

In contrast, three classes of takings—sickness and death, which ranks fourth, dwellings and home services, which ranks fifth, and savings and taxes, which ranks tenth—hold their own fairly well against temporary shocks but have lost a great deal of ground during the course of their post-war contest with the forces of change. Whether they are likely to regain their one-time status of dependable strength is a question for a later chapter. At this stage our rankings are governed by the records of the 1919–1931 period.

The remaining classes—clothing in sixth place, personal appearance in seventh, tobacco in ninth and transportation in eleventh—are highly variable in both short and long periods. Temporal changes are conspicuous in all of them. Clothing has lost much of its former value as a means of expressing desires for social approval and prominence. Personal appearance advanced steeply up to 1929; then fell off so sharply as to bring the actual trend well below the postulated trend, and this 1929–1931 decline is the primary cause of its low ranking for invariability. The use of tobacco has spread rapidly since the war; growth of the habit seems to have been jerky rather than steady. The case of transportation is too well known to require further comment.

Combined Ranking for Stability

In Table 23 the three rankings—for inelasticity, for indispensability and for invariability—are collated; and a combined ranking, showing the order of stability of the 11 classes of takings, is presented. The outcome contains no great surprises. Social-cultural activities, food, and sickness and death, in the order named, are rated as the most stable; transportation, savings and taxes, and home equipment, in the order named, as the most unstable. The preceding discussion of the separate rankings has sufficiently explained the factors taken into account.

TABLE 23.—ORDER OF STABILITY OF MAIN CLASSES OF TAKINGS DURING THE PERIOD 1919–1931

Classes of Takings	Ranking for Inelasticity	Ranking for Indispensability	Ranking for Invariability	Combined Ranking[1]
Social-Cultural Activities......	3	1	1	1
Food......................	1	4	2	2
Sickness and Death..........	11	2	4	3
Personal Appearance.........	2	7	7	4
Dwellings and Home Services..	8	3	5	5
Clothing...................	4	6	6	6.5
Recreation.................	6	8	3	6.5
Tobacco....................	5	5	9	8
Home Equipment............	7	9	8	9
Savings and Taxes...........	9	11	10	10
Transportation..............	10	10	11	11

[1] Combined rankings are products of rankings in the preceding three columns.

The stable classes of takings are very large, but so are the unstable classes. And it is particularly noteworthy that the more unstable classes, with the exception of savings and taxes, are growing rapidly. Dwellings and home services constitute the fastest-growing among the more stable classes; but the preceding chapter has suggested that further growth of this class will unsettle its stability. On the whole, then, our study of instabilities tends to confirm the judgment based on the study of stabilities, namely: that the stabilizing elements in consumption are losing their dominance.

Excepting the two classes of takings at the bottom of the "order of stability" (Table 23), the three lists of rankings are noticeably uncorrelated. Savings and taxes and transportation are readily responsive to price changes, to spending power changes and to temporal changes; hence, they are unstable on all counts. The other nine classes face the three types of changes with differing degrees of resistance. Their probable reactions can be more reasonably forecast if these differences are kept in view.

The validity of combining three dissimilar rankings into one ranking is open to serious question. The implied assumption is that all the three types of change exercise somewhere near equal influence on consumers' takings. The accuracy of the assumption remains to be tested. In the meanwhile, the "order of stability" set forth in Table 23 is distinctly an hypothesis, not a demonstrated result.

Indeed, the whole chapter is no more than a preliminary examination of the intricate problem of locating the sources of increasing instability of consumption. Whatever value it possesses consists in outlining a procedure for appraising with better judgment the elements of strength and of weakness in current consumption. If the chapter should succeed in opening up a fresh line of analysis of consumers' demands—if it should stimulate more expert statistical work in this field, particularly by well equipped younger men—its chief function will be fulfilled.

CHAPTER IX

OPTIONALS

The broad current of consumers' effective demands, to revert
to a metaphor previously employed, flows on with impressive
regularity. But closer examination has revealed seething
fluctuations in many classes of takings. And this is not the
whole story. Statistical classifications, while they expose to
view sweeping trends that might otherwise be overlooked, also
cover up subordinate movements. Day and Thomas call
attention to "the extraordinary complexity of changes in the
volume of manufacture. One line of manufacture expands
rapidly under the influence of the first widespread introduction of
its product; another disintegrates because of the collapse of
consumers' demand. . . . The general growth of manufacture
merges these diverse conditions into a single composite result.
In employing this composite the diversities which lie beneath
are not to be forgotten."[1] The comment was called forth by
the authors' review of the 15 years ended in 1923; it applies with
increased force to the 8 years which followed. Probably no
other short period has ever witnessed such turbulence in the
fortunes of industries catering to consumers' demands.

Preceding chapters have deliberately put aside mutations
within our classifications. These mutations are not statistically
measurable with the data supplied in this study. But this does
not mean that they should be ignored. They are in fact the chief
type of instability in present-day consumption.

The mutations to be considered in this chapter all arise from
consumers' choices among closely competitive goods. Plainly,
such options are numberless. Our purpose is not to discuss them
in detail but simply to review some of the evidence bearing on
the extent of free choice among competitive offerings, on the
tendency toward increasing variety of offerings and on the

[1] "The Growth of Manufactures, 1899 to 1923" by Edmund E. Day and Woodlief Thomas, Census Monograph VIII, U. S. Government Printing Office, Washington, 1928.

resultant aggravation of instability of consumption. The chapter is in the nature of a supplementary memorandum, somewhat outside the proper scope of this book; it is called for in order to avoid dropping the subject of instability at a half-way point.

TYPES OF OPTIONS

The main types of options which concern us here may be conveniently grouped under the following heads:

Directly competitive makes, brands or forms of commodities and services. The reference is to competition in the ordinary sense—that is, among producers of similar goods designed for substantially the same uses and markets. So-called inter-industry competition "for the consumer's dollar"—radio sets with pianos, automobiles with shoes, movies with candy, beauty shops with savings banks, and so on—is expressly excluded.

Rival designs and styles. The differences may be important or may be merely decorative features and gadgets which have little to do with worth or performance. They may be associated with competitive makes or may serve to distinguish essentially similar products of the same maker. High fashion goods belong in this group.

Innovations vs. established goods. The innovations may be marked improvements or may be superficial changes in appearance, packaging, and the like.

Slight differentiations in prices among closely similar goods. In some lines products and prices are ranged on a finely graduated, continuous scale.

It is plain to see that these groups are not mutually exclusive. A single purchase may involve choices under all four heads. However, one of the four types of options is likely to be uppermost in the buyer's mind.

The great variety of offerings of most kinds of commodities and intangibles, each offering differing from its fellows only in secondary characteristics, forces consumers to make innumerable choices.

CHOICES AT PRESENT UNPREDICTABLE

Selections among closely similar offerings are commonly determined by very slight shifts of emotional weights. One brand of coffee is preferred, perhaps, because its makers sponsored a snappy radio program the night before; a dress of one hue is taken because it "matches" something else, whereas an equally attractive dress "fights"; a higher-priced car is bought today than would have been chosen yesterday, because the purchaser for obscure reasons feels optimistic. Doubtless, the decisions to be made by individuals might be foretold if all the conditioning factors in each case were fully known.   But psychology has not yet reached so advanced a stage of scientific accuracy; it is not even making perceptible progress toward that stage.

A distinct, more readily soluble problem arises when one assembles the reactions of a sufficient number of individuals to make the law of averages applicable.   Three-quarters of a century ago Buckle put forward, as one convincing example, the "remarkable regularity" of statistical records of suicides and other crimes.[2]   Since his day studies of social statistics have invaded many other fields and have contributed immeasurably to a sound understanding of human behavior.   Regrettably, these conquests have not penetrated far into the subject of consumers' selective choices.   Some promising attacks on this special question have been started; but that is all.

One psychologist suggests, for example, an interesting method of appraising with fair precision *degrees of preference* of a group of consumers for competitive brands or grades "of coffee, tea, meats, motor cars, chewing gum, in fact anything for which comparative judgments are possible, as dependent upon the likes and dislikes of the buying public."[3]   So far as I know, however, the suggestion has not yet been put to use.   Nystrom's pioneer studies of fashion movements, their cycles and trends, yield much valuable information about one set of factors which influence popular reactions.[4]   A great deal of commercial research into the forces affecting sales of particular products is now carried on; indeed, it has come to be recognized as essential to modern business management.   Its results, however, are generally held confidential.   If a workable plan for correlating the non-confidential findings could be developed, important contributions to our knowledge of consumers' choices would probably be forthcoming. As it is, progress along this line is painfully slow.

Ignorance breeds uncertainty.   Statistical estimates, such as those given in this book, throw some light, flickering though it may be, on broad trends of consumption.   But the principles governing fluctuations of demand for particular products are for

---

[2] "History of Civilization in England" by Henry Thomas Buckle, Appleton, New York, 1906, vol. I, pp. 19ff.

[3] "Measuring Human Wants in Business" by J. P. Guilford, *American Economic Review*, Sept., 1929.

[4] See "Economics of Fashion" by Paul H. Nystrom, Ronald, New York, 1928, especially Chaps. II and IV.

the most part undiscovered; it is only here and there that private research opens up some fragmentary glimpses of them. In consequence, no basis exists for predicting the course of these secondary movements. "Executive planning" for business operations which will conform to consumers' demands remains at bottom, therefore, largely a matter of lucky or unlucky hunches.

Whether consumers' choices are actually capricious or not is for the present an academic question. Whatever laws may control them are so little understood that business management is compelled to accept them as unpredictably fickle and erratic. Under these circumstances, the greater the number of optionals in consumers' purchases the higher is the degree of instability in consumption—and the more unsettling is the influence of consumption on the economic system.

OPTIONAL MAKES AND BRANDS

An exact count of the number of options among closely similar products of competitive manufacturers open to consumers is obviously impracticable. The best available substitute is to review briefly the evidence bearing on the growth of competition within typical industries.

Almost universal is the impression of business men that competition has been growing more intense; and supporting data are not altogether lacking. For example:

Cherington states that while the output of woolen goods is now nearly three times as large as in 1900 the number of woolen mills in the meantime has been cut in two.[5]

Thorp's study of news items relating to changes in control of manufacturing and mining concerns shows that in the 10 years 1919–1928 nearly 6,000 sizable companies disappeared through merger or acquisition; and the annual number of such disappearances grew steadily from 311 in 1923 to 1,038 in 1928. No less than 300 makers of motor vehicles—a very high proportion—"disappeared" in spite of the notable growth and prosperity of this industry.[6]

Significant are the findings of two analyses of corporate income tax statistics revealing that from 1923 to 1929 the profits of manufacturing companies in relation to their sales (indicated approximately by ratios of net to gross incomes) remained on nearly the same level. Inasmuch as this was a period of high

[5] "The Commercial Problems of the Woolen and Worsted Industries" by Paul Cherington, Textile Foundation, Washington, 1932, p. 1.

[6] "Recent Economic Changes," Chap. II, Part 3, "The Changing Structure of Industry" by Willard L. Thorp, p. 186.

activity, declining costs and well-maintained prices, it seems plain that increasing competition, with its attendant expenses and disturbances, was in all probability the force that held profits down.[7]

Assuming then, that internal competition in numerous industries actually was intensified during the post-war boom, what was its influence on stability of consumption?

Most obvious was the large increase in varieties of goods offered to consumers. Productive processes and semi-finished materials were being standardized and simplified, partly under the impulse given to this movement by the well-known report on *Waste in Industry* published in 1921; but in consumers' goods the trend was the other way. Clark cites the case of one hosiery manufacturer who had lengthened his line from 480 items to 6,006. He quotes the advertisement of one automobile company enticing buyers with "50 body types and 500 color combinations."[8] Lyon has collected several examples from shoe making and retailing which indicate that the number of styles carried was about doubled between 1920–1921 and 1927–1928.[9] Every reader will recall the constant flow of slightly different models or patterns of all kinds of staple products. A natural consequence was to make customers more "choosy" and more fickle in their preferences.

Another outgrowth of intensified competition was the expanding custom of packaging numerous articles, particularly food staples, in handy cartons and cans. One indirect result was to preserve perishable goods in the unbroken package better than they could be kept after the package was opened in the home; and this fact powerfully favored a tendency, which was already growing, to buy goods for home use in small units. Small-unit purchasing, in turn, made it easy for consumers to experiment with unfamiliar products. Hence came the sometimes startling rapidity with which popular demand shifted from one make or brand to something slightly different.

Closely allied with packaging was the practice of playing up brand names and trademarks. The practice itself is almost as

[7] "Corporate Earning Power" by W. L. Crum, Stanford, 1929, p. 69 (covers years through 1927); and "A Decade of Corporate Incomes" by S. H. Nerlove, University of Chicago Press, 1932.

[8] "The Causes and Results of Hand-to-Mouth Buying" by Fred E. Clark in *Harvard Business Review*, July, 1928.

[9] "Hand-to-Mouth Buying" by Leverett S. Lyon, Brookings, Washington, 1929, p. 453.

old as commerce but never before has it been so nearly universal. Not only is it applied to nationally advertised goods but also to many which are local and unadvertised; indeed, the increase in the number and prominence of so-called "private brands" of wholesalers and large retailers has been especially notable in recent years. The brand may or may not be associated with a real distinction between the branded offering and competitive offerings. A report of the Federal Trade Commission remarks on this point: "The more brand-conscious the consumer can be made, especially for competitive articles, the better it is from the viewpoint of the manufacturer to whom advantage often accrues from placing a fanciful trademark or brand name on a well-known article, or substance, or simple mixture of substances, to obscure the fact that identically the same thing may be purchased under another name, and often for less money."[10] No matter what the motive behind the brand, its unquestionable effect is to reduce inspection of goods and discrimination in selecting them and thereby to facilitate shifts from one brand to another. Consider, for example, the rapid rise and fall of slightly differing makes of cigarettes, tooth pastes, breakfast foods, coffees, gloves, radio sets, gasolines, soaps and patent medicines, which have been conspicuous in the last few years.

The total influence of the three factors just named—greater variety of goods offered to consumers, small-unit packaging and selling and the general acceptance of brand names in lieu of specifications as guides to selecting purchases—works to intensify inter-company competition and thereby creates increasingly disturbed and shifting markets for many lines of merchandise.

OPTIONAL DESIGNS AND STYLES

Competition of growing intensity naturally leads not only to a larger variety of offerings, but also to ceaseless efforts to popularize distinctive designs and styles—ranging from peculiar treads of automobile tires to adaptations of period types of furniture. The average consumer finds himself bewildered by conflicting claims of superiority in respect to their beauty or utility. His choices tend to become more and more impulsive and undiscriminating.

[10] *Report on Resale Price Maintenance*, Part II, p. 8, U. S. Government Printing Office, 1931.

Still another wind to trouble the waters of consumers' demand blows fitfully from the uncharted regions in which fashions are born. It is a gusty wind; and the gusts have become perceptibly more frequent and more violent. Our primary concern here is not with the course of fashion movements but with their extent and timing. Obviously, the proportion of optionals among consumer expenditures grows as fashion changes spread over a wider area and speed up.

Up to about 1914, according to Nystrom, manufacturers "quite boldly and to some extent successfully fixed the fashions for the masses of the people and the people bought and used what was made for them." But during and after the World War "there began a series of baffling changes in consumer demand"; and in the post-war years of prosperity "consumers no longer apparently pay any attention to resolutions passed by trade associations concerning what they are to use and wear."[11] The transfer of the initiative in determining fashions from makers to consumers enormously increased the hazards of business. The dangerous situation thus created has been partially met, it is true, by intensive efforts to get an insight into the psychology of consumers and to appraise the force and direction of fashion trends. But the interacting influences at work are so complex that reasonable predictions necessarily remain exceedingly tentative and limited.

At the same time that fashion was freeing itself from the control of manufacturers and merchants, it was also asserting itself more vigorously in numerous lines of consumers' goods. "Prior to ten years ago," says one authority, writing in 1931, "fashion, although it always existed, was not the dominant factor in consumption and distribution problems that it has been since."[12] Fashion governs consumers' selections not only of dresses and trinkets but of automobiles, furniture, rugs, kitchenware, plumbing fixtures, watches, shoes, soaps, silverware, underwear, surgical services and even investments. The point is not merely that fashion is an important factor, which has been true for generations, but that it has become in our generation the *governing* factor in at least a very large proportion of consumers' selections.

[11] Address by Paul H. Nystrom published in the *Bulletin* of the National Retail Dry Goods Association, Mar., 1929.
[12] Chapter III, of Cherington, *op. cit.*, prepared by Amos Parrish & Company.

On top of the broadening scope of fashion, we must not over-look the accelerated tempo of fashion changes. "It used to take several years," remarks a du Pont sales executive, "for a new style to work from New York to San Francisco. Now it is a matter of days. The only style difference between women in New York and Keokuk is that the women of Keokuk dress in a little more extreme style."[13] Looking at markets for dry goods from the merchant's viewpoint, the United States Department of Commerce comments on a typical wholesaler's business as follows: "The great problem common to every department is the rapid rate at which hundreds of items lose their salability. Another large concern has estimated that 20% of all items carried become obsolete before they can be disposed of." The same report cites, as one example, a list of 60 colors "which had some vogue in 1927 in a single line of women's silk hosiery. . . . While some colors show purchases throughout the year others came in through the course of the year and completely disappeared from purchase lists before the year was over."[14]

Faster and faster, as the boom of 1923–1929 progressed, grew the dizzy dance of fashion demands. Automobile bodies must be redesigned each year if not oftener; otherwise, prospective pur-chasers would see no benefit in buying new cars. Oriental rug patterns, once the most popular of all, suddenly gave place to semi-modernistic designs. "Color in the kitchen" became a rallying cry for up-to-date housewives. And every novelty and shift of fashion brought with it loss, perhaps ruin, for some makers, increasing burdens of inventories and markdowns for merchants, and a growing sense of instability in the market for consumers' goods. Not without good cause did Knauth write in the spring of 1929: "Demand jumps from color to color, from fashion to fashion, from pattern to pattern in a most unex-pected way. Records of competitive sales of different types are baffling to study and they add a new terror to manufacturing and merchandising."[15]

[13] Paper on "Anticipating Changes in Consumer Needs and Habits" by C. F. Brown at Marketing Executives' Conference, Apr., 1929, of American Manage-ment Association, published in Marketing Executives' Series, No. 64.

[14] "Problems of Wholesale Dry Goods Distribution," Distribution Cost Studies, No. 7, issued by Bureau of Foreign and Domestic Commerce, 1930, pp. 5 and 41.

[15] "What Does the Consumer Want Today?" by Oswald W. Knauth, published in Marketing Executives' Series, No. 64, of American Management Association.

Something has to be said, too, about fads and frills, the bastard cousins of fashion movements. Tom Thumb golf, sun-tan lotions, King Tut jewelry, imitation reptile-skin shoes, storm-tossed bobs, purple lipsticks, out-of-season strawberries (generally sour), spiritualistic seances, sex-and-murder novels, quack cures, all have some of the characteristics of freak fashions; but they are scarcely worth dignifying with that label. "Fads may be defined," says Hoving, "as short-lived fashions that generally do not originate in the upper classes."[16] Most of our examples conform to that definition; the others and thousands more like them may be euphemistically described as frills.

Closely related was the popularity of shoddy imitations. The president of one of the largest woolen mills in the country is authority for the statement that the ascendancy of inferior goods gained momentum during the most prosperous years we have ever enjoyed, 1925 to 1929.[17] His opinion is supported by the observations of many other competent judges. This development is not to be excused, therefore, as the inescapable consequence of low incomes. It was the by-product of a restless longing for newness and display.

OPTIONAL INNOVATIONS

The rising tempo of fashion change has already been remarked. The observation is applicable over a much wider range. Never before have so many radically new products been introduced and quickly adopted.

The registration of automobiles in the United States in 1913 was 1,250,000; 10 years later it was 15,000,000; and in 1929 it was 26,500,000. Even more striking evidence of the rapid adoption of an improvement is the gain in the proportion of closed cars produced from one-third in 1923 to nine-tenths in 1929. The retail value of radio output in 1923 was less than $100,000,000; in 1929, more than $600,000,000. In 1923 the patent rights for cellophane (in the United States) were acquired; the demand for its use has expanded even since the beginning of the depression with such rapidity that it is now widely employed for packaging cigarettes, bakery goods and scores of other

[16] Address at Annual Convention of National Retail Dry Goods Association, Feb., 1929.

[17] Julius Forstmann, quoted in *New York Times*, Mar. 19, 1932.

products. Rayon, talking pictures, mechanical refrigerators and oil burners are other familiar examples.

The record of all these devices is in sharp contrast with the history of the majority of innovations in earlier generations. Thirteen years after a practicable typewriter was put on the market in 1873, for instance, it was still a commercial failure; its progress for more than two decades following was painfully slow; as late as 1896 the introduction of visible-writing machines aroused serious antagonism.[18] All observers agree, I think, that an accelerated speed of acceptance of new devices is one of the strongly marked characteristics of the post-war period. "Since 1922," says Copeland, writing in 1928, "changes in demand have been one of the chief marketing developments. As a consequence of the World War and of the boom preceding the crisis of 1920, various cakes-of-custom were broken. Old buying habits were changed and consumers subsequently manifested receptivity to new types of merchandise without all the customary delay and diffidence. New tastes and new buying habits developed more rapidly and more extensively than usually is the case under normal conditions."[19]

Especially noteworthy was the readiness of acceptance of all manner of innovations which reduce physical effort of even the mildest kind. Housewives bought bread and cake instead of flour. Men bought machine-made cigarettes instead of rolling their own. Purchases of ready-to-wear dresses moved up rapidly while piece goods and fabrics declined, until hard times reversed these trends for the time being. Household appliances and services made gains far above the average. The great increase in payments to barbers, hairdressers, and manicurists doubtless represents not only a widespread interest in personal adornment but also unwillingness to perform minor personal services for oneself. The tendency has been so commonly remarked that it needs no further comment here; but the persistent strength of distaste for physical labor must be kept in mind in attempts to forecast consumption during the years just ahead.

Quick acceptance of innovations involves scrapping many previously owned articles before their full term of usefulness has expired. While prosperity was in bloom, cars, typewriters, ice

[18] See an article in the *Wall Street Journal*, June 27, 1932.
[19] "Recent Economic Changes," vol. I, p. 321.

boxes, furniture were being traded in and junked with a light-heartedness which would have been incredible in any other generation. The practice has long been a favorite theme of moralizing essayists. Yet it is in truth simply the inevitable corollary of large spending power, especially when attractive new offerings are constantly being presented. Wastefulness is one important source of consumers' satisfaction in unnecessary purchases. So it has always been; and so it will continue to be whenever people attain a high level of free spending.

The significance of wastefulness, from the viewpoint of the present study, comes chiefly in the ease with which it can be checked. Great numbers of families, to take only one example, have recently made the discovery that their automobiles, form-erly replaced every second year, can be made to do for several years; and since the neighbors are reduced to a like extremity, the disgrace is no longer unendurable. Thus, the average length of service of American cars has gone up from the former standard of 7 years to somewhere between 8 and 10 years. The result was a drop in demand for cars so severe in its effects on industry as to amount to a national disaster. Similarly, defer-ments of purchases of improved models and new devices, because the old ones will serve without serious inconvenience, have created grave disturbances in hundreds of other industries.

Optional Prices

Less obtrusive, yet not less deadly in its consequences, is the effortless shift everywhere observable from higher priced goods to their near counter-parts on the next lower price level. The reference here is not to the general fall of prices but rather to the widespread exercise by consumers of innumerable options to take slightly inferior goods. In some lines, to be sure, habit dominates to such an extent that minor price differentials are commonly disregarded; and in other lines distinctions in quality are so conspicuous that the stepdown is strongly resisted. In the majority of staple lines, however, both quality gradations and price gradations are so fine that the shift can be made with a scarcely perceptible sacrifice of comfort or pride. Clothing and household supplies include many such lines.

It might be plausibly argued that a well-graded scale of prices is a condition favorable to stability, since it tends to substitute moderate movements for what would otherwise be extensive upswings or sharp breaks. But the argument overlooks the cumulative effects of shifts of demand up or down the scale of prices. The movement is like a snowslide; it may start with deceptive gentleness, but gathers mass and velocity until it sweeps everything before it. Once a well-defined tendency of consumers' demand toward lower priced goods becomes apparent, sellers all along the line begin to trim their prices in order to catch up with the slipping demand; but to the consumer this merely means more attractive opportunities to reduce his spendings still further. A system of closely graduated qualities and prices, for this reason, is peculiarly liable to foster instability of consumption.

Massed Decisions

The four types of options which have been treated—options among competing makes and brands, among designs and styles, between takings or deferments of innovations and between two closely graduated prices—are widely prevalent and overlapping. Moreover, they played a greater part in the post-war period than at any other time in economic history. Never before has a large body of consumers had so many chances to pick and choose.

If they had been prepared to exercise discriminating taste and judgment, their diversities of individual preferences would have matched the practically unlimited variety of offerings; and in that case multifarious personal idiosyncrasies would have been merged into a harmonious and inherently stable ensemble of demand. But they were not prepared. They were under the sway of forces which herded them into a consuming crowd and transformed their normally diversified consumption into massed demands.

The major forces which have stifled individuality in America and have regimented consumers' demands into formidable masses are too familiar to require lengthy discussion. It will be enough to make a few comments on those listed below.

Urbanization. In 1890 not much more than one-third of our population lived in places of more than 2,500; in 1930, nearly three-fifths. The preponderance of city masses is not measured by these bare figures. Their habits of living and of thinking dominate rural life as well.

Employeeism. The proportion of entrepreneurs to all income-gainers declined from 29% in 1909 to 22% in 1927.[20] An entrepreneur, whether he be farmer, professional man, or owner or executive of a business, is "on his own." Responsi-

[20] Derived from "The National Income and Its Purchasing Power," Chap. II

bility rests on him; and responsibility develops his self-reliance. The employee, on the contrary, habitually looks to others for guidance; as a type, he is the easy prey of propaganda and crowd thinking.

Mass Production. The aggregation of large numbers of workers in big establishments is in itself a powerful promoter of solidarity of feeling.

Common Experiences. The sudden emergence of some millions of low-income families into the "surplus economy" of 1923–1929 and their equally simultaneous descent into poverty have given them a common background which tends to weld them together.

Communication. New means of national communication and intercourse— the automobile, the popular magazine, the syndicated newspaper feature, the chain store, the motion picture and the radio—have broken down local barriers and have enforced uniform standards of ideas, manners and styles throughout the country.

Advertising. Because national advertising as well as other promotion addressed to popular audiences is designed to appeal to the largest possible number, it inevitably adapts itself to their mentalities; that is to say, it is essentially demagogic. Sophistry and ballyhoo are as necessary in successful advertising of many products as they are in successful vote-getting. Hence, the influence of much current advertising strengthens the tendency toward impulsive, follow-the-crowd decisions. And practically all advertising by its very nature favors uniformity of buying tastes and habits.

So brief a review of the main amalgamating forces in our national life does not warrant either approval or condemnation of them. Our sole concern here is with their effects on the American people as consumers.

Enhanced suggestibility is the prime effect. Psychologists have long recognized that crowd reactions differ in kind, not merely in degree, from normal individual reactions. Intelligent judgment is overborne by the weight of irrational feeling; excitability is stimulated; gullibility takes an exaggerated form; an extraordinary responsiveness to suggestion develops. The crowd spirit is engendered not only by physical assemblage but also by consciousness of active participation in the attitude and emotions of a large number of persons. It exists to a degree in all groups and communities. The forces named above cannot be said to create an American crowd spirit; but they do enormously increase the size of the crowd and its power. Thereby they make Americans as a body abnormally susceptible to suggestion.

Quickness of reaction is an associated effect. This is implicit, of course, in the nature of suggestibility. However, the speed with which a suggestion is acted upon by a crowd depends in part on the rapidity of its transmission. In this respect vital alterations have been generated during the past decade by the introduction of new means of communication, particularly the talking picture and the radio. Suggestions no longer spread slowly, as in pre-railroad days, nor at moderate rates and against the stubborn resistance of localized ideas, as in pre-radio days; they are simultaneously implanted from one end of the country to the other. The reaction is national and almost immediate.

These two factors—abnormal susceptibility to suggestion and speed of reactions on a national scale—go far toward explaining the violent, destructive swings of popular favor in consumers' choices among optional offerings. Decisions are less divergent and individualized than in earlier times; they are massed. And massed decisions are unrestrained by the inhibitions of self-reliant individuals. Like the loose gun-carriage in Victor Hugo's "93," they roll with terrifying mass and velocity from side to side of our economic craft.

Evidences of their growing power have already been given in this chapter: the sudden ups and downs of competitive makes and brands; the overnight acceptance or rejection of fashions; the swiftness with which innovations are adopted and established goods scrapped. So far as can be foreseen, the tendency toward massing decisions has not yet approached its climax. The majority of the forces supporting the tendency are plainly gaining ground. Everything points to an intensification of the extravagant fluctuations in consumers' choices, underlying the superficial steadiness of consumption, which threatens the stability of our whole economic system.

SUMMARY OF PART TWO

The aim of Part Two has been to uncover the broad trends of consumption from 1909 to 1931, more especially during the post-war years. These trends fall into two main groups: those which are ascribable to differences in spending power; and those which follow from temporal changes in tastes, offerings and environment.

As a necessary preliminary step, the estimates of national consumers' spendings and savings in Part One, there stated in current dollars, were reduced by means of price indexes (Chapter IV) to a common base. The common base selected for this purpose was the record of disbursements of the average family (a statistical unit) restated in terms of dollars with the purchasing

power of dollars of 1913. As by-products, a new aggregate
index of the price-level of consumers' purchases and a new
over-all real-value index of the price-level of consumers' purchases
and acquisitions were presented.

In Chapter V the reader's attention was directed to the general
upward course of average well-being and to the rather surprising
steadiness of takings of most classes of objects. As a basis for
subsequent analysis, the percentages of total takings each year
were calculated for the major classes and main sub-classes of
takings.

Chapter VI attacked the elusive problem of measuring the
influence of basic human wants on the apportionment of takings.
The method adopted was (a) to segregate the takings ascribable
to the requirements of subsistence and to the desire for security
(taxes and savings) and (b) to assign fixed proportions (unavoidably somewhat arbitrary) of the remaining takings to the other
three basic wants, enjoyment, approval, and prominence. A
tentative and qualified conclusion was drawn that takings for
the sake of enjoyment, of social approval and of social prominence
move up or down at a rate approximately double the rate of gain
or loss in spending power. It was deduced that these basic
wants may be accepted as constants which apparently govern
effective demands in definable ratios of total takings.

The next chapter endeavored to determine the extent of
stabilizing elements in present-day consumption, including (a)
the resistant influence of basic wants, (b) the volume of takings
which center on family life in the home and (c) the proportions
of frequently repetitive and of derived purchases. The conclusion was that the once overwhelming dominance of routine in
consumption is plainly weakening.

Chapter VIII analyzed major classes of takings in respect to
their (a) elasticity, (b) dispensability and (c) variability; and led
up to a combined ranking of classes of takings on the basis of
their relative stability. The chief sources of instability were
found to exist in certain large-volume classes, some of which
have experienced especially rapid growth since the war, thereby
reinforcing the judgment that the stable elements in consumption, though still strong, are definitely losing ground.

Finally, the present chapter has surveyed the widening range
of consumers' options, not statistically measurable with the
data now available, *inside* all classes of takings. It has empha-

sized the recent development and grave hazards of massed decisions which unsettle and undermine the economic system.

The net result of the analysis in Part Two is not encouraging.
Consumers as a body are motivated by a limited range of basic
wants which appear to remain nearly constant from country to
country and from generation to generation. Once these wants
are partially satisfied, they easily lose their driving power; hence,
consumption becomes volatile and non-resistant to decline.
Meanwhile, the enlarged output of goods places on the market
a bewildering variety of optional offerings. Consumers, lacking
the individuality and discrimination required in order to make
diversified choices, tend more and more to join in a massed
clamor for a small number of highly standardized commodities
and services and to swing violently from one favorite to another.
For the fundamental reasons here summarized, fluctuations in
consumption are rapidly growing both in steepness and in
amplitude.

The consequences, if the trend continues without effective
counteracting measures, are likely to prove unpleasant in the
extreme. Business enterprises will be called upon to endure
more frequent and more savage convulsions than at any time in
the past. Employment may attain renewed heights but will
also sink to lower depths. Returns from capital investment will
be less assured. These are among the possibilities to be explored
in the remainder of this inquiry.

PART THREE
PROJECTION

Chapter X

NORMS

If the estimates in Part One and the analyses in Part Two have any value, they should make it feasible to form reasonable estimates of consumers' demands in future years, which is the aim of Part Three. They should also contribute something to our understanding of the processes of collapse and recovery, which is the subject of Part Four.

The first question is: how would consumers use a much enlarged spending power if it were bestowed on them? To some readers, viewing the low state of employment and national income, the question may seem visionary. But it is well to recognize that when downswings are violent upswings may be equally abrupt and extreme. In any event, since our data are too gross to warrant fine measurements, the only course open is to foreshadow as best we can broad movements of large classes of takings; and this is the line of inquiry followed in Part Three.

The present chapter brings our national estimates per family into direct comparison with records of actual family expenditures. The comparison, as explained below, is in terms of money disbursed (outgo). Unfortunately it could not be worked out in terms of real values purchased (intake). Nevertheless, it supplies considerable guidance in forecasting demands at higher levels of average family spending power. The period 1909–1931, represented in our estimates, covers a band of average family spending power only about $400 to $500 in width, whereas for long-range forecasting we need to extend the trend lines to a width of not less than $1,000.

Spending power, however, is by no means the sole element affecting future consumption. Changes in consumers' attitudes, in offerings, in marketing methods and so on, cannot be ignored. These changes wrought by time—here called "variations"—are discussed in Chapter XI.

Chapter XII combines the judgments set forth in Part Two and in the preceding two chapters and endeavors to bring them to a focus in forecasts of probable takings of main classes of objects if and when spending power gets up to a $2,500 per family level.

UTILIZING FAMILY EXPENDITURE RECORDS

Records of actual expenditures of typical families form a source of information not yet utilized in this study. Perhaps they may supply clues to the apportionment of spendings at both lower and higher levels of family outgo than are covered in our national estimates.

The idea is not new. References have previously been made to the brilliant generalizations known as Engel's Laws, which Christian Lorenz Ernst Engel derived in 1857 from records of expenditures of workingmen's families in France and Belgium. Briefly put, the four generalizations are:[1]

> As the income of a family increases, a smaller percentage is spent for food.
>
> As the income of a family increases, the percentage of expenditure for clothing remains approximately the same.
>
> With all the incomes investigated, the percentage of expenditure for rent, fuel, and light remains approximately the same.
>
> As the income increases in amount, a constantly increasing percentage is expended for education, health, recreation, amusements, and so forth.

Naturally enough, these "laws" are not precisely applicable to the actual outgo of families living on a higher scale in other countries and in later generations. Yet they are fundamentally sound; and with relatively slight modifications they are true today of families in the lower income strata. They import the possibility of forecasting the expenditures of groups of consumers with some degree of certainty; just as many other social phenomena—births, deaths, marriages, suicides and accidents, for example—may be forecast.

The promising vein opened up by Engel has never been thoroughly explored. A considerable number of scattered records of family spendings have been accumulated. They are summarized in this chapter and certain tentative deductions drawn from them. Many more extensive and detailed investigations, however, will have to be carried on before such records can be made to yield the more accurate forecasts so urgently needed by private business, by governments and by social agencies.

---

[1] Cited from "Purchasing Power of the Consumer," Book II, by Emma A. Winslow, Shaw, Chicago, 1925, p. 168.

In the meantime, let us try some experiments with the records now available. A search has been made for all apparently dependable reports of annual family expenditures covering groups of sufficient size to constitute useful samplings. This requirement has perforce been liberally interpreted, since the number of records is too limited to allow much choice. Altogether, 72 reports of worthwhile investigations conducted at various times within the past 30 years have been collected. Any omissions are chargeable to oversight. The intention has been to bring together all records which measure the living and spending habits of families of Western culture since the turn of the century and to set them up as nearly as practicable in a comparable form.

One's first impression, on looking over the collection, is that it can never be more than a hopeless hodge-podge. The records come chiefly from America, because other nations have given even less attention to studies of family expenditures; mixed in with them are a few samples from Great Britain, Holland, Germany and Australasia, which are here stated in American currency. Some of the records cover rural families; some, urban. The average sizes of families vary considerably. The lack of uniformity in definitions of terms and in classifications of expenditures quickly becomes evident; this last-named defect has been to some degree repaired by reclassification of items according to a consistent scheme, but this is only a partial remedy.

Yet when all these scattered records are made roughly comparable, evidence appears of definable principles governing the consumption of industrialized peoples.

Comparisons Are in Terms of Outgo, Not Intake

Before examining the records, the method of reducing them to a common base needs explaining. In Chapter V and elsewhere a distinction is drawn between estimated outgo (disbursements) for classes of objects and estimated intake (takings) of the same classes. For the sake of clarity let me reiterate:

Outgo per family, first estimated in current dollars, is reduced to a common base by applying to all classes of objects an index representing the general price-level of consumers' purchases. This procedure yields a series of comparable figures for the period showing *how consumers spent* their money each year.

Intake per family, starting from the same estimates in current dollars, is reduced to a common base by applying to each class of objects the particular price-level index which best fits it. It thereby brings into account alterations in price relationships among the classes. This procedure yields a series of comparable figures for the period showing changes in *what consumers got* for their money each year.

Parts Two and Three deal by preference with comparisons of intake, not of outgo.

But the procedure must be adapted to such data as can be had. In the present instance the only workable method, in the absence of sufficiently detailed indexes for large classes of objects, is to apply general cost-of-living indexes indiscriminately to all classes of objects. The result is that we measure in this chapter only distribution of outgo, not of intake. As it happens, however, the main classes of objects here dealt with—food, clothing and home maintenance—form the great bulk of cost-of-living budgets; consequently, the differences between deflated estimates of outgo and deflated estimates of takings of these three classes are probably moderate, particularly in the lower levels of spending power. Considerable divergences from estimates of takings no doubt occur in the higher levels of spending power and in the unclassified group of objects called "All Other"; but they do not play a large part in our later forecasts.

The first move in reducing the figures to a common base was to translate the family expenditure records in foreign currencies into American currency at the rate of exchange then prevailing. The next move was to apply the cost-of-living index for each country given in the League of Nations *Yearbook*, using either 1913 or 1914 as the base year. The index applied to the American figures—both the family expenditure records and also our national estimates—was that of the National Industrial Conference Board, supplemented by the Douglas index for the years 1900–1914.[2] The chief reason, it will be apparent, for using here one of the well-known cost-of-living indexes, in place of our more comprehensive price-level index of consumers' purchases from Chapter IV, was to avoid the distortion of comparison that would follow from applying our index, which is widely different in type and scope from the other available indexes. Moreover, our index does not cover some of the years in which important family expenditure studies were carried on. Because a different index is adopted for the present purpose, our

[2] "Real Wages in the United States" by Paul H. Douglas, Houghton Mifflin, Boston, 1930, p. 60.

deflated estimates for total outgo per family in this chapter
differ from the deflated figures for total takings per family given
elsewhere. The discrepancy need cause no confusion if this
explanation is kept in mind.

FOUR SIGNIFICANT DEDUCTIONS

The 72 reports of family expenditure studies are graphed in
Chart T, which I will ask the reader now to examine. He will
see each bar, representing the average total outgo of one group
of families, divided into four broad classes of outgo: Food, Clothing, Home Maintenance, and All Other Expenditures. Note
that the bars are arranged not in chronological order but in the
order of an ascending scale of family spending power.

Even the most casual inspection can scarcely fail to suggest
the thought that each of the four classes tends to conform to a
pattern—a pattern with some rough spots in it, to be sure,
yet on the whole fairly clear. Each section grows as income
increases; but the rates of growth are quite distinct. In the
light of what has been said above regarding the heterogeneous
material collected from several countries and given only the
simple treatment just described, the emergence of the pattern,
imperfect though it may be, is a truly significant fact.

It implies, first, that however capricious individual tastes may
be, the major classes of consumption are predictable. At any
rate, a representative group of families at a given income level
may be counted upon to allocate outgo to food, to clothing and
to shelter in approximate conformity with well-established
norms. The residue of outgo, grouped under "all other," also
tends, though with less regularity, toward predictable ratios
of an ascending scale of spending power. Thus, the chart rein-
forces the suggestion previously made that the "laws of consumption" might be stated, if adequate data were available,
with a fair degree of precision.

Another inference has an important bearing on forecasts of
consumption. Loose assertions are frequent that a great change
in distribution of income is impending; and that the change will
involve radical alterations in modes of living and in objects
purchased. Chart T points toward almost the opposite conclusion. Moderate gains or losses in family spending power
obviously induce only small modifications of allocations of outgo.
This conclusion fortifies the findings of Part Two as to the

gradualness of changes of outgo accompanying the rise or fall of average family spending power. It seems highly improbable, then, that redistribution of the national income, taking away from high-income groups and giving to low-income groups, would produce anything more than a very slight effect on purchases by the national body of consumers.

A third inference is that the essential wants of families in all the countries dominated by modern mechanized civilization are not widely dissimilar. These wants find expression in the proportions of family outgo allotted to the four categories of expenditures. A comparison of the bars representing groups of families in European nations with the neighboring bars representing American families on about the same level of spending power, indicates, to be sure, a higher expenditure on food in this country; but this probably reflects relatively high prices for food rather than marked differences in consumption.[3] In other respects the broad divisions of spendings tally closely, with one or two minor exceptions. In view of the correspondence of low-income expenditures, one would reasonably expect the tendency to hold if like comparisons could be made in the higher ranges. To state the assumption in another form, the people of European countries, if raised to the same level of average income which prevailed here through the post-war boom, would presumably spend their new-found money much as Americans spent theirs. A like conclusion was drawn from the comparisons of national estimates in Chapter III.

The fourth inference from Chart T is worth especial emphasis. Since the bars do not follow any chronological order, records appear side by side showing expenditures of different groups in widely separated years—pre-war years, war years, post-war years. Nevertheless, one finds an almost steady rise at varying rates of each of the four divisions: Food, Clothing, Home Maintenance, All Other. Here, then, is further evidence of the relative freedom from temporal variations of the major elements in consumption. The demonstration should dispose—though doubtless it will not—of the baseless notion that in some mys-

[3] An excellent comparison of food consumption habits in this country and in a number of other countries is contained in "Economics of Food Consumption" by Edith Hawley, McGraw-Hill, New York, 1932. Her conclusion bearing on the point referred to in the text is: "Taken as a whole the diet of the workingman in the United States is not very different from those in other countries," p. 130.

terious fashion post-war America burst its cocoon and emerged
into the dazzling sunshine of a new way of life. The unsensa-
tional truth is that average income went up and that spending-
living habits were accordingly modified, much as they would
have been if the income rise had occurred a few years earlier.

The significance of the data assembled in Chart T may be
clarified by arranging on an ascending scale of total outgo all
the records of expenditures of American families with a spending
power in the range from $1,000 to $3,000, graphing the four
major divisions of expenditures and computing the trend lines
of these divisions; the trend lines appear in Chart U.[4] The
chart shows also the trends of our national estimates per family,
which will be discussed in a moment.

The "pattern" previously referred to now stands out somewhat more plainly in the trend lines derived from family records.
Numerous fluctuations appear, it is true, in the chart (not here
published) representing actual expenditures of each family group;

[4] In determining the trend lines for family records of expenditures the data
presented in Chart T for American families only were first ranked on the basis of
total outgo per average family in each group. Wherever two totals of family
expenditures were substantially identical—e.g., bars 34 and 35 in Chart T—only
the more recent record was taken. Spendings for each of the three main categories—food, clothing and home maintenance—were then separately graphed.
Outgo for all others was determined by deducting the first named categories
from total outgo; throughout the chart it is treated as a residual.

As the initial step in discovering the trend relationships, a straight line was
fitted to each of the three main categories of outgo by the method of least squares.
Deviations of the actual data from the trend points obtained by this method
revealed, however, that the single straight-line fit was not entirely satisfactory.
In the case of food, for example, the single straight-line fit understated the
amount of increment in the low income sector of the array and overstated it at
the high income level. Similarly the deviations of the actual data for clothing
and home maintenance from their respective single straight-line trends showed
clearly that the postulate, underlying the straight-line trend, of a constant
amount of increment as income rose, was unwarranted.

For food a more satisfactory trend line was obtained by fitting the data to a
second-degree equation, conforming to smaller increments in the high income
sector. For home maintenance and clothing no single equation, whether arith-
metically or logarithmically computed, was found that would truly reflect the
variations in increments in different sectors of the income array. However, these
variations formed in each case three or four clusters of increments. It appeared,
therefore, that the most satisfactory result was to be obtained by fitting a straight
line to each of these sectors. Thus the trend line for clothing consists of, first,
a straight line fitted from $1,000 to $1,300; second, a straight line fitted from
$1,300 to $1,800; third, a straight line fitted to the rest of the series.

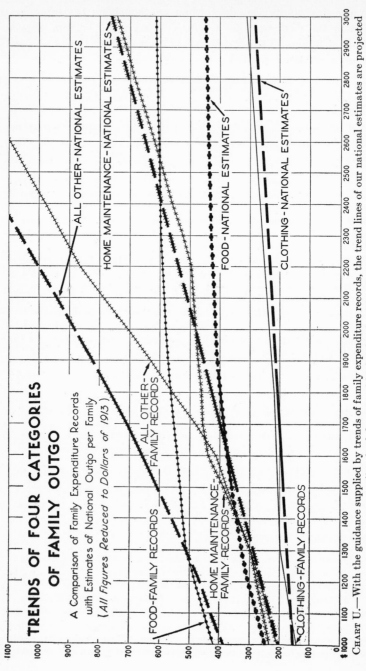

TRENDS OF FOUR CATEGORIES OF FAMILY OUTGO

A Comparison of Family Expenditure Records
with Estimates of National Outgo per Family
(*All Figures Reduced to Dollars of 1913*)

ALL OTHER - NATIONAL ESTIMATES

HOME MAINTENANCE - NATIONAL ESTIMATES

FOOD - NATIONAL ESTIMATES

CLOTHING - NATIONAL ESTIMATES

ALL OTHER - FAMILY RECORDS

FOOD - FAMILY RECORDS

HOME MAINTENANCE - FAMILY RECORDS

CLOTHING - FAMILY RECORDS

CHART U.—With the guidance supplied by trends of family expenditure records, the trend lines of our national estimates are projected into both lower and higher levels of family spending power.

yet the fluctations are slight when one considers the imperfec-
tions in the data that have been pointed out. Seldom does a
graph of figures drawn from such varied sources reveal so persistent a tendency toward well-defined trends.[5]

A Tentative Revision of Engel's Laws

On the strength of the trends of family expenditure records
graphed (above the $1,000 level) in Chart U, it appears permis-
sible to restate Engel's four laws in more exact terms somewhat as
follows:

*As the average spending power of groups of families living under the conditions
prevailing in the United States during the past 30-odd years increases from $600 to
$3,000, measured in dollars of 1913:*

1. The *proportion* spent for food decreases slowly up to a spending power of
about $1,300 and much more rapidly from that point on. The *amount* spent
for food per family rises from about $300 to slightly above $600.

2. The *proportion* spent on clothing decreases slightly. The *amount* grows
slowly from a minimum somewhat less than $100 to a height of around $300.

3. The *proportion* spent on home maintenance remains fairly constant up to a
spending power of about $1,300; and from that point on rises irregularly. The
amount increases at a rapid rate from a low of $150 to a high of about $750.

4. The *proportion* allotted to miscellaneous spendings rises slightly up to a
spending power of about $1,300 and with accelerating rapidity thereafter. The
amount climbs rapidly from about $75 to over $1,300.

The foregoing statements are, of course, tentative and likely
to be modified by future studies of family expenditures, which
will doubtless become more frequent and better standardized.

Comparison of Family Expenditure Records with National Outgo Estimates

Our estimates of national outgo per family may now be compared with the results derived from the foregoing review of
family expenditure records. In Chart U heavy lines representing the trends of national outgo are superimposed on the trend
lines of family records.[6]

---

[5] The number of cases in the income range between $600 and $1,800 is sufficient, in our opinion, to make the trend lines fairly dependable guides; in the
upper range they are unsafe, but nothing better is as yet available.

[6] The trend lines for our national estimates of average family outgo were in
general determined by methods similar to those employed for constructing the
trend lines of family records. As in the case of the family records, the trend line
for food was derived by a second-degree equation. Single straight lines were
fitted to the data for clothing and home maintenance; and a study of the devia-

The relationships shown in Chart U are so near to those which might have been anticipated as to constitute strong confirmatory evidence of the reasonableness of the trend lines derived both from family expenditure records and from national outgo estimates. The relationships may be summarized as follows:

Food. The national outgo per family for food is well below the normal amount for families on the same level of spending power as the national average. This is a necessary corollary of the fact that families with spending power above the national average spend little more for food than do families of near-average spending power. To put the thought in other terms, the median expenditure for food, if it could be ascertained, would presumably be considerably higher than the average expenditure. The extended trend line for national food expenditures per family, which runs roughly parallel to, but well below, the trend line derived from family records, appears plausible.

Clothing. For a like reason, the national average for clothing falls a little below the recorded expenditure of families on the corresponding level of spending power. The straight-extension trend line for average national expenditure maintains the relationship to the family-record line which one would reasonably expect.

Home Maintenance. The national average within the range of our estimates is below the trend line of recorded expenditure. However, the extended national trend line follows a sharper upward course under the influence of increasing proportionate spendings as average family spending power goes up.

All Other expenditures, a miscellany of unclassified items, on the contrary, takes a larger share of the national averages within the range of our estimates; but the extended trend line for the national average rises less rapidly.

The four national trend lines, it may be well to repeat, are offered with the reservation that additional data and analyses are needed to produce fully trustworthy guides. Meanwhile, however, American business is under the urgent necessity of utilizing whatever aids are available to grope toward sounder judgments of probable future demands for consumers' goods.

PROJECTED SPENDINGS AT VARIOUS LEVELS OF SPENDING POWER

The four categories of national outgo per family, calculated and projected on the basis of the national trend lines in Chart U, are presented in a cumulative form in Chart V. Thus we get a composite picture of the apportionment of average family outgo —calculated up to a total outgo of $1,877 (the average outgo for 1929 when deflated by applying the cost-of-living index used in

---

tions from these trend points revealed that the fit was satisfactory. For the income ranges not covered by our estimates the straight trend lines were extended.

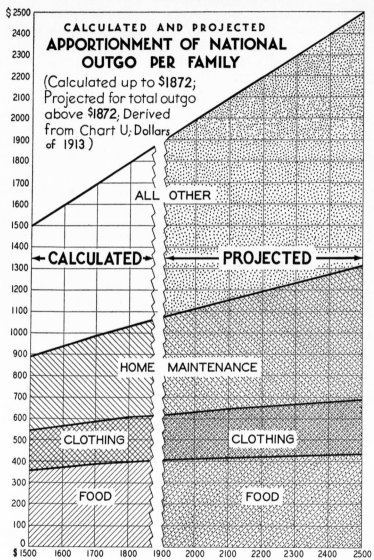

CHART V.—If average family outgo during the 1919–1931 period had risen to higher levels than were actually attained, it would probably have been distributed as represented on the "projected" side of the chart.

this chapter) and projected for the higher levels of total outgo.
The chart does not represent *future* spendings, this being a problem reserved for Chapter XII; it represents the *projected* spendings of consumers of the 1919–1931 period if these consumers
had possessed a higher spending power. Temporal factors
(variability) are not yet taken into account. The chart is
designed mainly as a provisional scaffolding while forecasts are
in the making.

At the same time, it serves also to emphasize some of the
fundamentals of consumption which are too often overlooked.
The slowness of expansion of spendings for food when spending
power rises is conspicuous. Clothing gains somewhat more
rapidly; yet it shows little promise of ever growing at a rate
greatly in excess of the increase of population. Home maintenance and "all other," in contrast, comprise classes of outgo
which are capable of providing immense and quickly expansible
markets.

But these are merely generalities long since gone stale. A
century and a half ago, wise Adam Smith wrote: "The desire of
food is limited in every man by the narrow capacity of the human
stomach; but the desire of the conveniences and ornaments of
building, dress, equipage, and household furniture, seems to have
no certain boundary."[7] Progress beyond Adam Smith's thinking on that subject can be made only by a laborious process of
mapping and measuring which will eventually convert the
generalities into precise statements of fact. The first faltering
steps in the process, now being taken in this study and in other
studies, are a century and a half overdue.

Table 24 below presents some of the figures which underlie
Chart V and adds corresponding figures for spending-power levels
outside the range of the chart.[8] The table brings out in dollars
and in percentages of total outgo the strength of the potential
demand for more and better food during the rise of average
family spending power from $1,000 to $1,500 and its declining

[7] "The Wealth of Nations," Book I, Chap. XI, Part II.

[8] The only attempt, with which I am acquainted, to set up a partly comparable
series of ratios for apportionment of outgo at different levels of spending power is
presented in Chap. XII of "Economic Principles of Consumption" by Paul H.
Nystrom, Ronald, New York, 1929. Nystrom's percentages, expressing his
authoritative judgments and no doubt taking into account many of the same
budget studies on which Table 24 is founded, are at some points nearly the same
as those here given; at others, rather widely divergent.

rate of advance thereafter; the relative weakness of demand
at the lower levels for clothing and its steadiness thereafter;
and the consistent expansion at an increasing rate of demand for
home maintenance and for "all other." By multiplying the
dollars by the number of families in the United States and
translating the result into current dollars it is possible to obtain

TABLE 24.—CALCULATED AND PROJECTED APPORTIONMENTS OF NATIONAL
OUTGO PER FAMILY[1]
(In 1913 dollars)

Four Main Categories	When Total Outgo Is $1,000		When Total Outgo Is $1,500		When Total Outgo Is $2,000		When Total Outgo Is $2,500		When Total Outgo Is $3,000	
	$	%	$	%	$	%	$	%	$	%
Food	250	25.0	360	24.0	415	20.8	437	17.5	450	15.0
Clothing	157	15.7	189	12.6	221	11.0	253	10.1	285	9.5
Home Maintenance	204	20.4	344	22.9	483	24.2	623	24.9	762	25.4
All Other	389	38.9	607	40.5	881	44.0	1,187	47.5	1,503	50.1

[1] Derived from Charts T and U.

an approximate measurement of the potential demands for these
four categories at any assumed level of average spending power.[9]

To ignore the relationships among the four categories of outgo,
as presented in the preceding table and charts, is to open the
door to serious misconceptions of the status and influence of
consumption. Tebbutt, as one example, offers a statistical
study, excellent in itself, of quantitative consumption during
the period 1928–1932 of a selected list of commodities—chiefly
foods, clothing, fuel and light, tobacco and gasoline—which he
introduces with the statement: "It is felt they are representative
of the relative movement of consumption in this prosperity-
depression period."[10] Yet his list cannot be construed as

[9] Of some interest in connection with Table 24, though not directly comparable,
is an analysis of German expenditures in 1929 for housing, including rent, fuel,
light and house furnishings, which shows the following percentages of the total
outgo of each group: agricultural workers, 15%; urban workers, 17.5%; salaried
employees, 20.5%; public officials, 22.1%. See article by Friedrich Luetge in
Jahrbuch für Nationalökonomie, Aug., 1930, abstracted in *Social Science Abstracts*,
Feb., 1931.

[10] "The Behavior of Consumption in Business Depression" by Arthur R.
Tebbutt, Harvard Bureau of Business Research, Boston, 1933.

truly representative, by any stretch of the term, of more than half of consumption, and that almost exclusively the more stable half. The selection creates a bias which accounts for his remarkable conclusion: "Actual consumption of goods remained practically the same in depression as in prosperity, excluding the abnormally depressed year of 1932, and then the declines were not great." Nor does Tebbutt stand alone. A similar opinion is expressed over and over again in economic literature; indeed, the assumption that consumers' demands are stable and dependable is commonly accepted as an axiom of economic thought. The root of the fallacy is failure to recognize the varying weights at different levels of spending power of the stable and the unstable elements in consumption.

An Increasing Area of Instability

If the apportionments, estimated and hypothetical, in Chart V and Table 24 are credible, they give ample support for the judgment that when average spending power rises, instability of consumption gains ground at a rapidly accelerating rate. The essential alterations in the character of consumers' demands are clearly seen in the following abridgement of Table 24.

A gain from $1,000 to $3,000 (200%) in spending power involves:

Four Main Categories	Gains (in dollars)	Gains (stated in percentages of spendings at $1,000 level)	Gains or Losses (in percentages of total outgo)
Food...........................	$ 200	80	−10.0
Clothing......................	128	82	− 6.2
Home Maintenance..............	558	278	+ 5.0
All Other.....................	1,114	286	+11.2

Our table of rankings of classes of intake in respect to stability (Table 23 in Chapter VIII) places both food and clothing in the upper half of the list. These two large classes include a large part of the dependable and resistant elements in consumption. They are the very classes which fall behind in relative importance when spending power moves up.

Home maintenance comprises (a) dwellings and home services, which ranks fifth in stability, and (b) home equipment, which is near the bottom of the list. Gains in this category intensify moderately the inherent instability of consumption.

The "all other" category, however, is made up overwhelmingly
of highly volatile classes of intake. Gains in this category, the
largest and most quickly expansible of all, increase enormously
the uncertainties and fluctuations of consumers' demands.

A truer and even more alarming view of the effect of growth in
spending power is to be had by considering the composition of
increments to total outgo. The tabulation above indicates that
an increase from $1,000 to $3,000 (in 1913 dollars) per family
would be allotted: less than one-sixth to food and clothing,
combined; a little over one-fourth to home maintenance; considerably more than one-half to "all other." Roughly, about
two-thirds of the increment would go to enhance the instability
of consumption. Increments to total outgo, once it gets above
the $1,500 level, are still more largely devoted to fickle demands.

The conclusion seems inescapable that gains in spending power
must inevitably enlarge the area of instability in consumption.
Assuming for the moment that prosperity, brighter and more
widespread prosperity than in the glamorous 1920's, lies ahead,
what will be its effects on the national economy?

As far as the eye can reach, we can only see consumption
becoming more and more feverish and unstable; not gradually
but with accelerating speed. Chapter VII ventured the guess
that before the war the proportion of dependable—that is,
moderately stable—consumption was perhaps 70 to 80%, and
in the post-war boom may have ranged between 60 and 65%.
In view of the large proportion of unstable elements in the
increments to outgo, it is plausible that a rise of average spending
power to $2,500 (1913 dollars) per family would carry with it a
reduction of the stable proportion to somewhere between 50 and
60%; and a rise to $3,000 would bring it down below 50%.

The effects of so sweeping a reduction could not fail to be
far-reaching. The potential amplitude of business fluctuations
spreading out from consumption would become so much greater
that in retrospect the heights and depths of 1929 and 1933 might
easily appear as merely moderate disturbances.

However, it would be premature to offer forecasts. So far we
have given thought only to the normal apportionments of
spending power at different levels—meaning by "normal" the
prevailing practice during the years up to 1931. But these

established norms cannot last indefinitely. Time will certainly introduce substantial variations. What are the principal prospective variations, and to what extent will they divert the golden stream of consumers' spendings from some groups of industries and turn it toward other groups? That question must be considered with care before intelligent forecasts can be attempted.

Chapter XI

VARIATIONS

The preceding chapter has yielded some broad apportionments of average family outgo over a wide range of spending power. These measurements have minimized temporal factors; they pertain to a static society of the post-war American type.

But American society is far from static. An effort to look ahead must take into account the influence of variability—that is, as previously defined, the effects of temporal alterations in consumers' tastes or in their environment. The effects are here called variations.

To undertake to foretell variations over a period of years would be nonsensical. The complications—particularly those arising from possible changes in technology and in government—are beyond grasping; the chances of error are numberless. Yet a few fundamental relationships and trends are observable. They are not safe guides, they will bear close watching; nevertheless, they have some usefulness, I believe, as indications of what the future *may* bring forth.

A Projected Rise of Spending Power

To begin with, it is necessary to delimit in some way the period to be surveyed and to set up some assumed level of spending power; otherwise, whatever forecasts may be developed will remain so vague as to be meaningless. The simplest procedure is to project the trend lines of our estimates of average family intake during the 1919–1931 period. The trend line shown in Chart W advances at an annual rate of 1.4%.[1] The $2,500 level, the chart indicates, should be reached between 1948 and 1949.

Let me add in haste that the chart is not a prediction; it is merely a projection. Obviously, it leaves out of the reckoning

---

[1] Not far from the average annual gain of *per capita* income from production which is estimated at 1.3% during the period 1900–1929. See "America's Capacity to Consume," pp. 17–18.

the severe slump subsequent to 1931. The omission involves an assumption that the decline was the consequence of non-recurrent monetary and political disturbances and formed only a temporary aberration. A further assumption is that political pressure through the coming years will be sufficiently restrained to allow the early restoration of a smooth-working, balanced

PROJECTION OF SPENDING POWER
TO $ 2,500 LEVEL

(In Dollars of 1913; Logarithmic Projection)

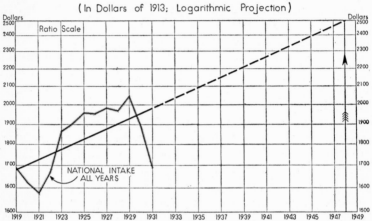

CHART W.—If the rate of gain through 1919–1931 is resumed, the $2,500 level will be reached in 1948–1949.

economy.   Both assumptions, though subject to serious question, are in harmony with and supported by the records of recovery from previous depressions.   The main source of doubt in this instance is widespread uncertainty as to the capacity of popular government to maintain self-discipline.   For the purposes of the present discussion, the question can best be put aside.   The continuance of a social order favorable to economic growth, then, is an underlying postulate; and on this basis the pro-jection represented in Chart W is submitted as a reasonable anticipation.

Furthermore, it is assumed that distribution of the national income among families will not change to such an extent as to create new ways of living.   The preceding chapter has given rea-sons for believing that moderate shifts in distribution of income would have little effect on *average* spendings.   And a violent shift involving a social upheaval is for the present purpose treated as an improbability.

This clears the way for stating the problem before us in somewhat definite terms. The endeavor in this chapter will be to form judgments as to large variations in prospect during the next 15 years, more or less; and the endeavor in the following chapter will be to forecast probable takings at the $2,500 level.

FACTORS CONDITIONING CONSUMERS' REACTIONS

"The unchanging psychology of the average consumer" has been stressed in earlier chapters. Both hopes and fears of any radical recasting of consumers' basic wants during the next few years may safely be dismissed as baseless. Variations will not spring from that source.

But the relative urgencies of wants and their expressions in purchases are conditioned by environment. Among the chief conditioning factors, some of which may induce marked alterations within the next decade or two, are the following:

Rate of growth of spending power, which is here assumed to expand as projected in Chart W. The effects of spending power depend in a great measure on how rapidly it is acquired. Waite's remarks on this point are well worth quoting: "Sudden and large increases of income are seldom of much immediate benefit to the recipients. Much of the increase will probably be squandered in ways which yield little lasting satisfaction, and often in ways which are a detriment to receivers. If, on the contrary, the rise has been gradual, or, better yet, if it comes in an unrecognized form, such as a gradual decrease in prices, the larger income will probably be well used, and result in a higher standard of living as well as level of consumption."[2] It should be kept in mind, accordingly, that our projected rise in spending power, on which this entire chapter is based, progresses at about the same rate as was experienced from 1919 to 1931. In the event that it should turn out to be much accelerated or retarded or abnormally jerky, the judgments which follow will need to be corrected.

Increased variety of offerings. Higher spending power implies greater output; and greater output, judging by the records presented in Part Two, will consist not so much of more abundant supplies of existing forms of consumers' goods as of innovations and improvements. The bewildering variety of offerings in the boom years will doubtless be enhanced in any future period of still greater spending power.

Rising proportion of mature people. This factor, though not previously considered in this study, is so well known that it needs little discussion. In 1930 persons over 20 years of age made up 61% of our population; in 1950 the corresponding proportion, according to competent estimates, will approach 70%.

---

[2] "Economics of Consumption" by Warren C. Waite, McGraw-Hill, New York, 1928, p. 118.

The designs and other optional features of all kinds of consumers' goods will be modified accordingly. However, I can see no traceable effects on the broad apportionments measured in this study.

Declining size of families. Associated with the lessening proportion of children is the marked decrease in number of persons per family. One might expect the tendency to cut down, for example, takings of clothing and of household space and furnishings. But our data do not confirm this expectation. The average family, a statistical unit, appears to be very little influenced by variations in average size.

Continued pressure of forces working toward the massing of popular decisions. These forces have been listed in the chapter on Optionals; and it would be impracticable to deal more adequately here with so large a subject. No one questions, so far as I know, their tremendous power, and I can see no probability of its weakening in the years just ahead. At the same time, one may expect without inconsistency a rising spirit of resistance on the part of individuals and small minorities.

The factors just named seem likely to modify considerably consumers' reactions to offerings of goods and marketing stimuli. We can perhaps get somewhat closer to useful forecasts by examining next the probable variations in offerings and in methods of selling them.

FUTURE OFFERINGS

A steady upward trend in number of patents issued annually has been evident for more than 40 years in both the United States and Great Britain. Its continuance is highly probable.[3] Patents include, of course, technological advances as well as innovations and improvements in consumers' goods. However, they all affect, either directly or indirectly, the forms, qualities or prices of goods for consumption. We may confidently anticipate an increasing outflow of inventions, most of them minor but some of far-reaching importance.

One or two major inventions might conceivably transform living and spending habits in the next two decades to an even greater extent than the automobile and the radio have done in the last two decades. Such inventions seldom spring to life full-blown; they develop by means of an accumulation of contributions from several fields. Hence, if any invention of the first magnitude likely to become widely salable in the next few years is in the making, some clear forerunners of its forthcoming should by this time be visible.

[3] See Chap. III, "The Influence of Invention and Discovery," by W. F. Ogburn in "Recent Social Trends," McGraw-Hill, New York, 1933.

The only consumers' goods that seem to me promising candidates for so important a role are (a) the fool-proof airplane and (b) the standardized-parts, low-priced dwelling. Both have advanced to a stage of near-practicability for general use. The airplane needs devices to make it safe and easy for amateurs to handle. The factory-built house needs designs to add attractiveness without sacrificing economy. To assume that these needs will shortly be met would be quite unjustified. Yet the prospect has enough plausibility to make it worth while to devote a moment's speculation to the potential effects.

As has often happened with concurrent inventions in the past, these two achievements would supplement each other; in fact, neither one could come to full fruition without the other. Family airplanes would find their best market among people who live in separate dwellings and travel considerable distances daily. Separate dwellings for the 6 million urban families (the chief potential market) now living in two-family or multi-family houses would become practicable only by placing the new dwellings on cheap land far removed from congested centers; obviously the family airplane or some other new mode of speedy, inexpensive transportation would be a prerequisite.

If the two inventions were to be perfected at about the same time, the consequences would be immense. Ogburn lists 150 noteworthy effects from the introduction of radio communication.[4] A comparable list for the two inventions in question would be longer and still more impressive. Cities would lose their residential character, would become mainly work-shops. Real estate values would be readjusted on a vast scale. Farms by the millions would be reborn as suburban homes. Industries and services catering to the home would multiply. Social customs and standards would be revised. Innumerable complementary inventions would appear. Most of our current economic troubles would vanish, and a feverish, uneven prosperity would quickly follow. The vista—at least part of it—is alluring. Unhappily it may be a mirage. In the absence of clear evidence of its reality, it is best to turn away and resume the duller task of cataloging probabilities.

The outstanding innovations in consumers' goods of recent years have been:

[4] *Op. cit.*, pp. 153ff.

Improvements in canned foods	Electric wiring in dwellings
Numerous refinements in automobiles and accessories	Mechanical refrigerators and other household appliances
Radio sets	Talking pictures
Airplanes	Rayon.

The list is short, partly because it is made up of groups but mainly because it is restricted to objects of large expenditure which also exercise a great influence on other spendings.   Electric wiring is not literally an innovation, but its approach toward universality is new.   Electrification of rural homes particularly has made rapid strides.

Among the most likely developments for wide adoption in the near future are:

Automatic heating and cooling appliances	Radio television sets
Air-conditioning appliances	Home talkies.

A significant characteristic of the second list is that it consists exclusively of devices for use in homes.   The first list, too, is made up largely of foods and appliances for the home.   We shall find other straws blowing in the same direction—all indicating that the home will be increasingly the center of consumers' interest and the focal point of their spendings.

Of at least equal weight, in the aggregate, with the important devices above listed, are the uncounted numbers of minor improvements constantly flooding the market.   In the same general class are fashions and other slight differentiations, such as are discussed in the chapter on Optionals.   It seems practically certain that changes in this class will come faster and faster in any future period of enlarged spending power.   Indeed, unless major inventions come to the rescue, the distinctive feature of the period, so far as I can see, will be an exaggerated emphasis on refinements and details of products offered to consumers. This is rather a sterile outlook, I grant; but an advance into more fruitful territory requires either (a) a radical remaking of consumers' wants, which we have ruled out as incredible, or (b) fresh, wonder-working inventions not yet in plain sight.

FUTURE MARKETING

The social-economic functions performed by selling-advertising-promotional-merchandising operations (all of which are comprehended in the generic term "marketing") are: (a) the static function of supplying pre-existing demands through a distributive system; (b) the dynamic function of creating or stimulating demands through skillfully directed appeals to basic wants. The first function can be, and commonly is, routinized and executed at a moderate expense; it makes widely available staples, semi-staples and small items of convenience goods. The second function calls for experienced judgment and resourcefulness in developing specialized methods and necessarily involves relatively high expense; it actively sells, not merely distributes, specialties, innovations, improved goods and strongly competitive goods. The distinction between the two functions, though usually ignored by critics, is vital to an understanding of present-day marketing methods and their probable future.

The two functions to a large extent apply to different products and operate through different channels. As a result, they may follow divergent courses. During the 23 years covered by our estimates the efficiency of the static function has doubtless been considerably increased by the growth of chains and of "one-stop" retail stores, and costs of distribution have thereby been somewhat reduced. The efficiency of the dynamic function also has quite obviously been raised; but meanwhile it has been called upon to care for an enlarging output of new and optional goods, and costs of distribution have thereby been somewhat increased. The net outcome, as shown in Table 6 of Chapter II, has been a truly remarkable uniformity of distributive costs, modified by a slight inclination downwards.[5] The trends just summarized appear likely to continue, keeping in step with the projected rise of spending power and with the anticipated gains in output of consumers' goods.

Channels of distribution may well be considerably modified within a decade or so. The larger variety of offerings may be expected to lead purchasers to demand a wider range of choice *at the moment of purchase* among competing brands and features. To satisfy consumers on this score retail stocks must be completely representative—inclusive, for example, of numerous color combinations and of a representative assortment of accepted makes of each line. This requirement is already generally

[5] The question is more fully discussed in the writer's paper "Are Marketing Costs Rising?" published in the report of the Boston Conference on Retail Distribution, 1932, p. 53.

met in groceries, drug stores and other retailers of convenience goods; but it is not yet met as fully as might be in apparel stores, furniture stores and other purveyors of higher-priced semi-specialties. Assuming that the practice expands, it will obviously favor the larger retailers strategically located where they can draw trade from a sufficient population to permit their carrying big stocks. Ease of travel by automobile is another factor working for larger stores in shopping centers. One may forecast with some confidence, then, that the United States of the late 1940's will contain fewer and better-stocked retail stores.

More fundamental is the prospective intensification of dynamic marketing. This will not be a matter of choice; not even if we find ourselves operating under the guiding hand of omniscient bureaucracy. It will be determined by the quantity of spending power and by the characteristics of offerings of consumers' goods.

The effects of enlarged spending power are not essentially different whether it arises in a capitalistic or in a communistic society. In either case those who have more money to spend than they care to devote to the satisfaction of their basic wants must be persuaded to try new goods and to form new desires; otherwise, the will-to-work, the mainspring of industrial progress, will infallibly lose its tension. If any communistic state ever grows prosperous enough to face the problem, it will be forced either to hold down standards of living or to adopt substantially the same dynamic methods of pushing sales as are required in the United States. In fact, their first faint stirrings are already perceptible in Moscow.

To expect a great body of consumers on the level of spending power attained in this country in the 1920's or a higher level to cultivate their own desires and to reach out for unfamiliar goods would be to repudiate all experience. Consumers, once their physical necessities are provided for, wait passively for further developments. "What the world has learned in the art of consumption," Mitchell well says, "has been due less to the initiative of consumers, than to the initiative of producers striving to win a market for their wares."[6]

The forms and media of intensified dynamic marketing during the coming years will necessarily be governed chiefly by the offerings of consumers' goods. Insofar as the offerings consist

[6] "Business Cycles" by Wesley C. Mitchell, National Bureau of Economic Research, New York, 1927, p. 166.

of widely distributed specialties and competitive items, advertising and other extensive promotion will grow. Insofar as they consist of innovations and minor improvements, retail merchandising and face-to-face selling will be the essential methods. The present outlook, for the reasons stated in the foregoing discussion of offerings, indicates more rapid expansion along the second line; but that highly tentative conclusion may be modified at any time by the appearance of unforeseeable new commodities or intangibles.

Conflicting Motivations: Goods vs. Leisure

The underlying factors which govern consumers' reactions; the characteristics of the goods offered to them; the scope and intensity of marketing dynamics; as well as social and political forces beyond reckoning: all these influences will be constantly playing upon American consumers in the future as in the past. They will reinforce some inclinations, prejudices, inhibitions, related to demands for goods; will weaken others. They will determine the dominant attitudes of consumers.

Accurate appraisal of the interworkings of these varied influences is of course impossible. However, if we are to look ahead at all, it is essential to give thought to some of the unending struggles in human society between conflicting motivations; for the effects on consumers' takings in the upper ranges of spending power will be decisive.

Most fundamental of these conflicts is the age-long duel between appetite and indolence. So long as elemental desires for food, warmth, sexual intercourse, play and some degree of family affection are ungratified, their urge is enough to drive men to labor. A supplemental set of compulsions is supplied by well-established social standards of living. All these strong motivations are provided for in our subsistence budget (Chapter VI). As average spending power rises to higher levels, however, it enters a more and more rarefied atmosphere. The law of diminishing returns of satisfaction—very rapidly diminishing—is at work.

Desires for sanitation, for culture, for esthetic enjoyments, for refinements, for future security and even for display are relatively feeble hot-house plants. True enough, they are powerful sources of energy for exceptional individuals; but among consumers as a body they are kept alive almost wholly by repeated doses of two pungent stimulants: attractive, novel offerings; the artifices of dynamic marketing.[7]   Naturally, the doses tend to become larger and less effective.

Distaste for work, on the other hand, needs no stimulants. It spreads fast, as the ancient social sanctions for habits of hard work give way.   It is fostered by the development of large-scale facilities for frittering away time at slight expense.   It expresses itself mainly in three forms: purchases of labor-saving devices and services; insistence on deliveries and other services by retail stores; shorter hours of work.

It is not my intention to treat the conflict between goods and leisure as a moral issue but merely to epitomize the contending forces.   The outcome is easily predictable: Leisure will increase as fast as enlarged productivity makes it possible.[8]

CONFLICTING MOTIVATIONS: HOMES VS. OUTSIDE INTERESTS

Chapter VII has given a rough measurement of the slowly increasing diversion of takings from the home to the automobile, the movie, the restaurant, the commercial laundry and other attractions or services outside the home.   If this tendency is to continue, it will exercise a strongly depressive effect on outgo for home maintenance.

Lynd offers the declining size of the average family and the weakening of marital ties as partial explanations of smaller living

[7] The weaknesses and limitations of human wants, the prime movers of all social progress, are completely ignored in many proposals for economic betterment.   One example is a thoughtful and illuminating article by Professor Adelbert Ames, Jr., on "Progress and Prosperity: a Suggested Program" (*Dartmouth Alumni Magazine*, Jan., 1932).   Ames develops the idea, which is sound in itself, that overproduction of tangibles could be corrected by diverting capital and labor to an enlarged output of beneficial intangibles; but how to build up corresponding desires to an equivalent volume is a problem left unsolved.

[8] If working hours are to be reduced, someone may reasonably ask, how is spending power to be increased to the extent projected in Chart W?   The answer is that a much larger gain would be attainable if it were genuinely desired. Chase, for instance, opines that in another decade we might produce, if his schemes were adopted, "$6,000 worth of consumers' goods [apparently per family] a year at 1929 prices," and this with a "thirty-hour average work week." ("The Economy of Abundance" by Stuart Chase, Macmillan, New York, 1934, p. 48.)   The figure may be within reason, considering solely productive capacity; but again, the weaknesses and limitations of wants effectively block such rapid progress.

quarters, which in turn hold down purchases of books, of furniture, of musical instruments and of many other articles.[9]   It should be observed, on the other hand, that the takings classified in Chapter VII as primarily for individual satisfaction show no tendency to absorb a higher proportion of total intake.   The family stubbornly holds its own as the paramount unit of consumption.   The primary cause of the trend toward outside activities, we may infer, was nothing more vital than an unusual concurrence of important innovations which drew money away from the home.   If so, the trend in all likelihood will be short-lived.   Recent and forthcoming innovations, it is pointed out above, belong for the most part to home maintenance.   On the whole, I believe it reasonable to surmise that the home will soon regain at least its former share of consumers' intake.

CONFLICTING MOTIVATIONS: ROUTINE VS. EXPERIMENTATION

The average mentality, one may safely take for granted, is inert, conservative, ruled by custom and habit.   Yet Chapters VIII and IX have established, I think, that the stabilities of consumption are losing ground.   Under the continual hammering of new offerings and dynamic marketing, consumers have become more and more receptive to novelties.   Any middle-aged observer can testify that shifts of demand have speeded up astonishingly in the past 30 years.   I see no reason to expect a reversal of this tendency.

On the contrary, with spending power larger and offerings more varied, consumers will doubtless accept new ideas and try new things with increasing alacrity.   As a corollary, they will discard the old lightheartedly.   In the next era of prosperity, for example, they will trade in or throw away usable automobiles, furniture, clothing, dwellings and food even more freely than at any time in the past.   One might suppose that the rising age level of the population would dampen their enthusiasm for untried ways, and perhaps it will eventually.   But it can scarcely become within a few years a factor of sufficient weight to retard perceptibly the accelerating tempo of change.

Wastefulness, obsolescence-in-use, fashion movements, all will step up to a faster pace.   Speculation, too—that is, experimentation with savable money—will take on fresh vigor; if not in

[9] "Recent Social Trends," vol. II, pp. 864–866.

securities, then in real estate, lotteries or horse races. A keen onlooker writes from Florida in the spring of 1934: "While the devil was sick, this past four years, many people predicted that we should never see again anything like the gaudy, wicked days of the boom. If Florida is any indication, they were wrong. The winter's tourist tide has already been enough to bring back the first faint symptoms of the old disease. . . . The big free buses to the scene of the crime are beginning to run again, filled with suckers all eager to buy something today and resell it tomorrow for more money."[10]

Conflicting Motivations: Thrift vs. Free-Spending

The analysis in Part Two has disclosed that real savings by consumers in the 1920's were irregular, in contrast with the orderly allocations of takings classified under the basic wants for subsistence, comfort, approval and prominence. The only plausible deduction is that a large portion of savings were merely a residue, a final resort for disposing of money after other wants had received their due allotments.

In the mind of the average consumer saving is no longer a primary obligation. It is not *his* duty to provide against old age and distress; it is the duty of employers or of the state.   On the other side, the pleasant doctrines of the cult of free-spending have been propagated with enormous success by a curious alliance of (a) manufacturers of popular specialties, grasping for sales in low-income markets, (b) labor union organizers, searching for arguments to justify high wages irrespective of labor productivity, and (c) a certain number of muddle-headed writers on economic subjects.   There can be no doubt, I think, that free-spending, as a rule of conduct for the everyday person, has gained the ascendancy; and it will probably go on for at least another decade or two, winning more and more converts.

Conflicting Motivations: Individuality vs. Herding

The principal conditions favoring regimentation of American consumers and concentration of their purchases on a few classes of objects have previously been reviewed (Chapter IX); and the opinion has been expressed that the combined influence of these conditions shows no convincing signs of lessening.   The outlook,

[10] Bruce Bliven in *The New Republic*, Mar. 7, 1934.

then, is for a continuation of the marked tendency toward herding; for an aggravated suggestibility and massing of decisions.

The resultant hazards can scarcely be overstated. Whitehead does not put the facts too boldly: "The canalization of the whole range of industry is in rapid progress. Apart from the dangers of economic prosperity, there is in this decay a loss to happiness. Varied feelings are fading out. We are left with generalized mass emotion."[11] Whitehead casts the blame on "great commercial corporations" with their mass production and standardized output, which is at the least an arguable point. In any case, wherever the responsibility may lie, the tendency toward canalization, among its other effects, undermines the stability of consumption which follows from wide diversification of demands. It bestows excessive authority on brand names, pat slogans and similar substitutes for sensible personal judgments of the suitability of offerings.

However, the tendency advances against stubborn resistance by a sizable minority of individuals possessing sufficient personality to maintain their own tastes and views. It is these scattered rebels who create demands for out-of-the-ordinary articles and services and offer a possibly expansible market for goods of superior craftsmanship and design.[12] Whether as a group they are holding their own or not is uncertain; but even if their number is decreasing, they seem likely to acquire in the not distant future a larger share of leadership in guiding consumption as well as other economic activities.

The same persons, or many of them, who refuse to run with the crowd when making purchases, also have the capacity to withstand popular trends along other lines. They will keep on working and saving long after their neighbors quit. They will place a high value on economic independence. In a free society these individualists are the natural accumulators of property and influence—the more easily and surely if the great majority are taking the opposite path. Thus, the forces that

[11] "The Study of the Past" by Alfred North Whitehead, in *Harvard Business Review*, July, 1933.

[12] For suggestive treatments of the possibilities of providing varied designs without giving up the main advantages of large-scale production see "Planning Standardized Components to Secure Variety in Products" by T. N. Whitehead in *Harvard Business Review*, Apr., 1932, and "Fine Arts in Mass Production" by John W. Higgins, in *Harvard Business Review*, July, 1932.

make for country-wide uniformity and standardization appear to
be rapidly forging at the same time a stronger and more compact
American bourgeoisie.

The grave social-political implications of a widening separation
into recognized classes do not at the moment concern us. The
probable effects on consumers' intake, however, are relevant to
this inquiry. Class distinctions will become more prominent
and more readily accepted; clothing, houses, furniture, amusements, reading matter, will be more plainly segregated into
well-defined groups, sold through different outlets, possibly with
less attention than at present to income ratings and more attention to social ratings. Popular fads and fashions will exercise
less influence on upper-class goods. Marketing stimuli for
popular goods will grow more blatant; for upper-class goods, more
subdued. Indeed, if the cleavage once becomes clear, almost all
successive moves will tend to broaden it.

In offering these observations, it may be well to add, I am not
advocating class distinctions but merely pointing toward a
drift. Unless the drift is checked in some way, the next 10
to 15 years will bring, in my judgment, an intensification of class
feeling which has to be reckoned with in a realistic survey of
probabilities.

A Summary of Indicated Variations

If the patient reader after going through this chapter feels
that it turns out to be rather a confused and inconclusive medley,
he will have the correct impression. The American scene is a
turmoil. The probable issues of numerous interacting conflicts
are more than usually obscure.

However, some of the variations that have been touched upon
stand out plainly enough to be carried over into the next chapter,
either as assumptions or as probabilities, particularly:

The projected rise of average family spending power to a $2,500 level toward
the end of the 1940's

A perceptible rise in the proportion of mature persons in our population

An anticipated flood of minor innovations, largely centering on the home;
possibly a new direction to be given to economic progress by the hoped-for
simultaneous presentation of a family airplane and an attractive low-cost dwelling

An intensification of dynamic marketing, which is an inevitable corollary of
high spending power

The demand for leisure fast outstripping the demand for goods

A probable comeback of the home to its full degree of dominance as a focal point of spendings

A speeding up of the processes of decay of long-established habits; freer experimentation with new things

Thrift giving ground to the cult of free-spending

Consumers rapidly splitting into two clearly marked classes: the suggestible majority; the resistant, individualistic minority.

Some of these elements in the present situation obviously are more assured of continuance than are other elements. However, none of them can be said to have the status of a well-defined and measurable trend. They are set forth only as hints and clues designed to give a little uncertain guidance to the next step—that is, attempting to arrive at reasonable estimates of future takings.

Chapter XII

FORECASTS

Provisos and qualifying statements in preceding chapters have given ample warning that this chapter is not going to attempt the visionary feat of predicting consumers' demands in detail. Unknown factors and incalculable cross-currents render that task impossible.

Yet a limited degree of foresight, I believe, is now attainable. It requires (a) setting up postulates and (b) projecting trends. Both processes involve uncertainties and debatable judgments. Some of the postulates no doubt will prove to be faulty; when this occurs the forecasts will have to be corrected accordingly. The trends are not so thoroughly established that they can be projected mechanically; on the contrary, I shall not hesitate to introduce modifications suggested by probable variations in population make-up, offerings, marketing methods and social-political-economic motivations, such as those reviewed in the preceding chapter.

Venturing on forecasts in the face of all these contingencies is a precarious business. Nevertheless, if the forecasts are understood to be tentative and subject to frequent revision, their potential value more than compensates for the risks of their being misread and misused.

Two questions are to be answered, so far as that is possible:

1. Assuming that average family spending power expands well above the 1929 level, how will the expansion be apportioned among the main classes of takings?
2. What will be the effect on stability of consumption?

In an effort to give some precision to the answers, the forecasts will be applied to an assumed spending power of $2,500 (1913 dollars) per family. Apportionments of intake at intermediate levels are not forecast but may be assumed to conform more or less to amounts indicated in Chart Aa by connecting lines between the $2,000 level and the $2,500 level.

184

FACTS OR FANTASIES?

The chapter aims to be factual and realistic. Our sole interest lies in finding out what people actually will buy whenever they have more money to spend, not what some amiable idealist would like them to buy. Moral values and personal tastes have no place in an effort of this nature; nor do flights of fancy. The economic scene of the 1940's and the people who act in it, so far as they are depicted in this chapter, will appear essentially similar to the scene and the people of the 1920's. The picture is more nearly analogous to an architect's sketch of an elevation, worked up from his blueprints, than to an imaginative artist's dream.

The foregoing precautionary statement is called for, I believe, because wishful thinking on this subject is easy, popular and liable to breed calamitous errors. Let me give one example from a writer who commands a wide audience.

The uniqueness of the individual consumer has only begun to make its impression on history. . . . The first movements of conscious tastes in a nation or class are largely imitative, taking shape in fashions sufficiently widespread and uniform to lend themselves to routine mechanical production. The self-assertion of the individual is a slower fruit of culture. But, as it grows, it will offer stronger opposition to the dominion of mechanical production. It will do this in two ways. In the first place, it will cause a larger proportion of demand to be directed to the classes of products, such as intellectual, aesthetic, and personal services, which are by their nature less susceptible of mechanical production. In the second place, weakening the traditional and the imitative factors in taste and demand, it will cause consumption, even of the higher forms of material commodities, to be a more accurate expression of the changing needs and tastes of the individual, stamping upon the processes of production the same impress of individuality.[1]

If these interesting predictions are to be read as pertaining to some far-distant Utopia, they have little bearing on present-day problems. But if they or other forecasts in a like vein are to be taken as a basis for planning, they are treacherous guides. Between the date of their publication (1921) and the date of our latest figures (1931) a large amount of evidence as to American consumption is now available. For the most part the evidence is quite definitely contradictory to the tendencies hypothesized by Hobson. If any perceptible progress has

[1] "Work and Wealth" by J. A. Hobson, Macmillan, New York, 1921, p. 76.

been made toward "the self-assertion of the individual," unless by small minorities, it requires sharper eyes than mine to discern it. Nor do the fragmentary data of British spendings, cited in Chapter III, indicate any different experience across the water.

Romantic fantasies about consumption make agreeable reading and normally do little harm. At this time, however, they have more influence than usual in that they supply a base for governmental activities in the supposed interest of consumers. It is especially important, for this reason, to insist that facts should be diligently sought, objectively analyzed, and given their due weight. These observations are respectfully referred to all the well-meaning bodies and persons, especially those now operating in Washington, that have undertaken to provide and prescribe for the American people.

MAIN POSTULATES

The necessary postulates have already been stated or implied in earlier chapters; but as a safeguard it may be wise to summarize them here. The underlying assumption is that during the next few years no fundamental changes in the social-economic structure will occur. Comprised within the general assumption are the following more specific postulates.

1. *Maintenance of political institutions and their powers substantially as they are.* The phrase is not intended to preclude normal alterations such as have been customary; but it does rule out of consideration here the effects of disastrous wars or of revolutionary shifts of control to one class or group. It excludes extreme forms of state ownership or domination of business enterprises. It presupposes that government will provide a reasonably stable money-and-credit system, without which foresight and planning become next to useless.

2. *Persistence of growth of volume of production at about the same rate as in the recent past.* Snyder[2] and Mills[3] agree in placing the rate in the United States between $3\frac{1}{2}$ and 4% per annum. The tendency toward uniformity and regularity of growth for several decades is strongly marked. Evidently growth cannot be determined mainly by technological improvements which are highly erratic. The real control rests, I am inclined to believe, in the human factor—

[2] See two articles by Carl Snyder, "The Problem of Prosperity" in *Journal of the American Statistical Association*, Mar., 1929, and "Overproduction and Business Cycles" in *Proceedings of the American Academy of Political Science*, June, 1931.

[3] "Economic Tendencies" by F. C. Mills, National Bureau of Economic Research, New York, 1932, p. 243. The exact rate, as figured by Mills, is 3.8% for the period 1922 through 1929. The pre-war rate he calculates to have been 3.1% (p. 2).

that is, in the limited capacity of organizations to effectuate improvements and of consumers to accept new products. The second postulate, then, appears to be well-grounded, regardless of the extent of impending technological changes.

3. *Adaptability of business enterprise to moderate vicissitudes.* Profit-seeking business is like one of nature's primitive organisms, awkward, seemingly defenseless, yet remarkably tenacious in the face of any adversity short of abolition of private ownership. It will presumably carry on through any conditions that can now be plausibly foreshadowed.

4. *Flexible and fairly stable price relationships.* This postulate does not refer to the general price level but to the coordination of groups of prices—for example, prices of farm products in relation to prices of industrial goods. In order to keep the problem of forecasting within practicable limits, it is necessary to assume, what seems probable, that alterations in price relationships will not be so violent as to invalidate the broad forecasts here attempted.

5. *Continuity of average consumer habits and reactions.* The reasonableness of this fifth postulate has been adequately shown, I think. Inherent in it is a judgment that the habits and reactions are irrational; for otherwise they would conform to the varied and changing circumstances of individuals and would be unpredictable in the present state of knowledge.

Granted these five postulates, it becomes feasible to project, with due caution, the main trends of consumers' takings.

MAIN TRENDS

Perhaps the outstanding feature of consumption emphasized by the analyses reported in this study is the normal continuity of relationships of the major classes of takings to total intake and to each other. This is quite consistent with another prominent characteristic, namely: the exceptional liability of certain classes of takings to sharp short-period fluctuations when submitted to stress.

The main trends in these relationships are associated with average family spending power, not with temporal changes. For that reason, the tables and charts in this chapter are based not on a chronological order but on an ascending order of average family spending power. For the sake of simplicity—also, in order to bring out plainly the hypothetical nature of the forecasts —the tables and charts, except Table 26, present *calculated* estimates for two assumed levels of average family spending power (all in 1913 dollars), $1,500 and $2,000 and *projected* estimates for the anticipated $2,500 level. The percentages and figures for the first two levels are calculated from data and estimates which have been fully treated in preceding chapters. The projections to the $2,500 level are computed, *except* in Tables

25 and 26 and Chart Aa, where the influence of changes in offerings, tastes, and so on, is taken into account. Hence, these concluding projections are partially expressions of judgment and are modified by anticipated variations in conditions during the next 10 to 20 years.

Trends cannot always be counted upon, of course, to persist indefinitely; especially when they have been established in the post-war years 1919–1931 and are now to be projected through a subsequent stage of deep depression, which in turn is to be followed presumably by a long and sweeping recovery up to an assumed new height of prosperity. On the other hand, a partial precedent has been supplied by our examination of apportionments of intake before and after the war; in spite of the hectic fluctuations of industry and of conditions of living during the war years, consumption emerged with only moderate changes in most classes of takings, and these modifications were generally in line with long-term trends, as revealed in the figures of later years. Variations now unforeseeable will doubtless bring innumerable minor shifts of demand. But our concern in this chapter is only with the broader, deeper-seated movements of consumption. Such movements may reasonably be expected to go on through one or two decades more.

Unfortunately, the trends that have been disclosed in this study do not mesh into a well-articulated system. They are usable only as indicators. A brief review will bring to mind those of chief value for forecasting.

Apportionments. Percentage distributions of total takings bring to light consistent and apparently dependable ratios (not necessarily uniform ratios) between total intake and the seven classes of takings which are charted and projected in Chart X. These projections are of particular value. Though they are not to be applied blindly, they seem unlikely to lead us far astray. The percentages for the other classes are more irregular and yield less acceptable projections.

Wants. From the classification of takings under five basic wants in Chapter VI we derive Chart Y. The chart, if taken at its face value, prognosticates almost uniformly large expansions of intake motivated by desires for enjoyment, for social approval and for prominence, and relatively slight expansions for subsistence and for security. However, it will not do to lean very heavily on mathematical projections of the spheres of influence

CALCULATED AND PROJECTED APPORTIONMENTS OF AVERAGE FAMILY TAKINGS

(Calculated for the $1,500 and $2,000 Levels of Total Intake; Projected to the $2,500 Level)

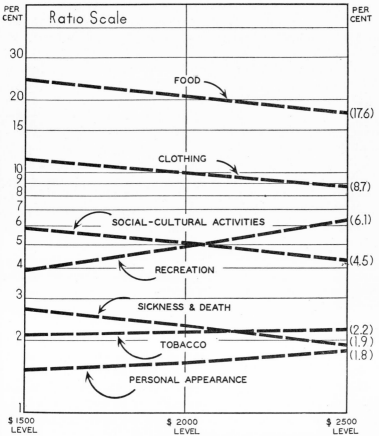

CHART X.—The ratios of these seven classes of takings to average family spending power follow a sufficiently consistent course to justify projecting their trend lines into higher ranges of spending power than have so far been experienced.

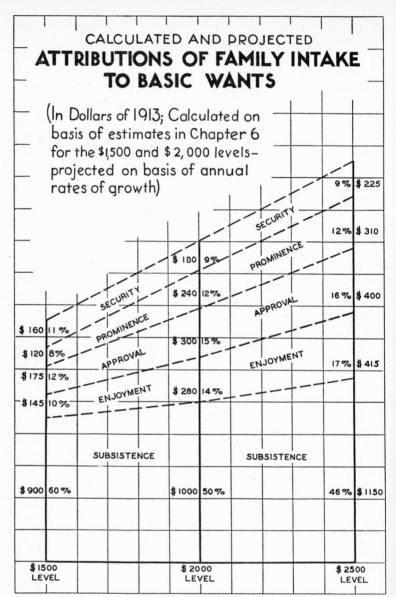

CALCULATED AND PROJECTED
ATTRIBUTIONS OF FAMILY INTAKE
TO BASIC WANTS

(In Dollars of 1913; Calculated on
basis of estimates in Chapter 6
for the $1,500 and $2,000 levels—
projected on basis of annual
rates of growth)

CHART Y.—The assignments of takings to basic wants (see Chart O) are here
projected into higher ranges of spending power.

of human motives.   It appears to me a more reasonable speculation that the wants for enjoyment and for approval will be so
far satisfied at an early stage of the assumed rise in spending
power that their control over intake will thereafter grow at a
decelerating rate, whereas the want for prominence will govern
a rapidly increasing proportion of total takings.   The whole
subject of motivation, as Chapter VI has stressed, is nebulous,
and needs a much longer record of experience before broad
generalizations can be safely attempted.   Meanwhile, projections
of the estimates in Chapter VI, though unreliable, at least serve
as partial checks on other means of forecasting demands.

   Stabilities.   Nothing is to be gained by projecting our estimates in Chapter VII of takings assignable, respectively, to the
home, outside the home, and centering on individual activities,
since the trends of 1919–1931 cannot reasonably be expected to
continue in the face of variations which are working powerfully
toward a renaissance of spendings on the home.   On the other
hand, the trends of purchases classed as frequently repetitive,
less frequently repetitive and infrequently repetitive, presented
in Chart Z, are apparently persistent and unlikely to be greatly
modified by any variations now in sight.   Chart Z presages a
relatively slow growth of the more stable elements in consumption; an alarmingly rapid growth of the volatile elements.   Note
that infrequently repetitive takings (chiefly durable goods) go
to 15.4% at the $2,500 level, which checks closely with an
analysis (based on Appendix F) of the takings listed in Table 25.

   Instabilities.   The data utilized in Chapter VIII and the conclusions of that chapter are too indefinite to make projection
possible.   They serve rather to emphasize the uncertainties that
beset attempts to forecast consumption.   If, for example, the
highly elastic classes of takings—sickness and death, transportation, and savings and taxes—should be subjected to large alterations in price relationships, their response might well be so
great as to invalidate the forecasts for these classes.   This
contingency has been taken into account in one of our postulates;
but a postulate, be it understood, carries no guaranty.   Our
measurements of degrees of dispensability are too crude to be
projected.   However, they supply useful clues to the more
expansible classes of takings *under the conditions which prevailed
in* 1919–1931; these conditions will be modified by such variations
as those treated in Chapter XI.   The study of short-swing

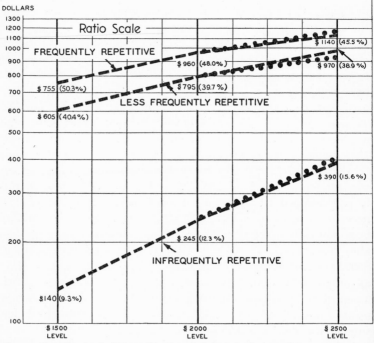

CALCULATED & PROJECTED DIVISIONS OF INTAKE ON BASIS OF NORMAL FREQUENCY OF REPETITION

Broken lines are the trend lines for data given in Table 20 rearranged in the order of an ascending scale of total intake   Dotted lines represent the calculated divisions at the $2,500 level obtained by applying the %'s in Appendix F to the forecasts in Table 25

CHART Z.—The projected rapid rise of infrequently repetitive purchases is plausible; if it occurs, consumption will become still more unstable.

variability in Chapter VIII contributes nothing of especial value to forecasting long-period movements. But the measurements of secular variability in the group of S-charts, though they are freely granted to be dubious, yield some indications worth observing of plausible long-term tendencies. They will be utilized cautiously as one factor in the forecasts.

Other factors to be considered will be taken from the chapters on Optionals, on Norms and on Variations. The variations to be allowed for will not include the simultaneous development, which has been referred to as a notable possibility, of a practicable family airplane and of a low-cost single-family dwelling.

SOME ANTICIPATED SHIFTS IN OBJECTS WANTED

The basic wants of people in America and Europe, as described in Chapter VI and graphed in Chart Y, may be presumed to be the fundamental springs of consumers' demands. Though the extent to which each want will become effective when spending power rises can be only vaguely foreseen, it is well worth while to consider what classes of objects are most likely to satisfy each basic want.

Subsistence. Our analysis (Chapter VI) of data for the 23 years ended in 1931 supports the judgment that the average minimum standard of living is unlikely to rise more than 10 to 15% while average family spending power moves up 25% from the $2,000 level. On this basis the subsistence budget, which was placed at $1,000 in 1925–1931, has been raised to $1,150 in our assumed $2,500 year. Allocation of the added $150 is necessarily a question of appraisal of tendencies which cannot be statistically weighed. The following is submitted as a reasonable expectation: Food, $5; clothing, $10; home maintenance, $50; transportation, $35; liquor and tobacco, $5; security, $25; all others, $20. The largest amounts, it will be observed, are assigned to the classes showing (see Table 13) decided trends upward, except security, which requires a larger allotment under subsistence because of the probable rise in direct taxes.

Enjoyment. Takings for enjoyment reflect personal tastes which are easily affected by variations in offerings and in marketing stimuli and may shift rapidly to new objects; but these shifts are likely to be minor and well diversified   The motive finds expression in all the main classes of takings, and I see no reason to expect it to distribute its future favors among classes in proportions much different from those prevailing in the past.

Approval. The classes of takings chiefly influenced by the want for social approval are clothing, housing and social-cultural activities, but most of the others are to some extent under its sway. Custom sets up norms which are regarded as essential for families in their various localities, occupations and income groups. As spending power goes up, the norms also rise but not necessarily in the same ratio. Shifts from one class of objects to another are mainly governed by widely accepted fashion movements. Of late years fashions, once confined almost exclusively to clothing, have more and more affected other objects, particularly automobiles and home furnishings; and the spreading tendency will probably continue. We may anticipate, then, that takings for the sake of approval will be perceptibly diverted from other classes toward the two objects just named.

ANTICIPATED SHIFT OF "PROMINENCE" TAKINGS TOWARD HOUSEHOLDS

About two-thirds of spendings for the sake of conspicuousness of consumption, according to estimates based on Table 17, are concentrated on automobiles and on home maintenance. A crucial question in any attempt to forecast consumption is whether a shift of public interest from one of these classes to another is in prospect. The number of objects suitable for a display of spending power by the average family, it should be recalled, is very limited.

"In former times," remarks Nystrom, "pretentiousness of home, size and appearance of yard and surrounding walls were eloquent symbols of social position and plane of living."[4] Employment of servants, also, has been for generations a common means of demonstrating prosperity. For reasons previously touched upon, however, the home has received since the war much less attention; the habit of living in apartment houses, the growing use of commercial services, such as laundering and baking, smaller families, scarcity of servants, less home entertaining, all have been contributing causes. Household expensiveness has become, therefore, a less effective medium of display.

[4] "Economics of Consumption" by Paul H. Nystrom, Ronald, New York, 1929, p. 385.

The automobile has been the chief beneficiary. It possesses three great advantages: (1) as a topic for conversation it ranks next to the weather; (2) it is often in plain sight; (3) when it is not at hand, a casual mention of its make is usually sufficient to "register" its approximate price. The prideful owner may still feel called upon to demonstrate that he has purchased his car recently; this is made convenient by yearly changes of body models.

However, the universal popularity of automobiles, combined with the growing acceptability of low-priced makes, reduces the interest and conspicuousness that formerly attached to ownership of an expensive car. As early as the spring of 1928 an acute observer reported that in roadhouses near New York nothing below a Rolls-Royce could command respect from the doormen. (If this notation appears frivolous, it is only because actual buying motives are not yet well understood.) Statistical evidence points plainly toward an indefinite continuance of a strong trend, begun in 1927, toward a larger proportion of cars retailed below $1,000.[5] The record is complicated, it is true, by the Ford shutdown in 1927; nevertheless, over a still longer term the downward movement of the average price per car has been unmistakable. Since it has gone on through prosperity as well as depression, it seems clearly to signify a changing attitude of buyers: greater interest in buying transportation for its own sake; less interest in buying prestige.

But the itch for prominence, which Chart Y indicates will be the impelling motive behind about one-eighth of consumers' intake at the $2,500 level, must find expression. If it turns away from one class of objects, it will infallibly seek other outlets. Its range of selection is closely restricted. Some of its influence no doubt will flow toward jewelry, clothes and entertainment. Much more attractive for this purpose, however, and more readily expansible, is the field of home maintenance; and within this field the suitable objects are housing, furnishings and servants.

In the light of these considerations, we have allowed in our forecast of takings at the $2,500 level for a more rapid rise of home maintenance and a slower rise of transportation than their 1919–1931 trends would signalize. The forecast does not imply an impending decay of the automobile industry but only a

[5] Based in part on an analysis in *Standard Trade and Securities*, May 13, 1932.

retarded growth of the market for extravagant styles and accessories—to the relief and profit of many manufacturers.   It does imply, on the other hand, greater attention to conspicuousness in housing; which in turn signifies a probable reversion of dwellings toward the useless roominess and over-ornamentation of the 1880's.

ANTICIPATED SHIFT OF "SECURITY" TAKINGS TOWARD REAL ESTATE

Chart Y shows a declining percentage of intake motivated by a desire for security from 11% at the $1,500 level to 9% at the $2,500 level.   The showing runs directly counter to the usual supposition that savings obtain a rising proportion of an enlarging national income.   On the strength of the analyses reported in Part Two, the supposition appears to be wrong.   If it is, some elaborate theories of the disastrous effects wrought by so-called over-saving and over-investment rest on an exceedingly questionable factual basis.   It should be observed, however, that we are dealing only with savings by individuals.   Conceivably a study of savings by business enterprises would tell a different story; that remains to be seen.

To forestall confusion, let me point out that the takings here attributed to the want for security do not include all savings and taxes.   The following amounts have been assigned to the subsistence budget: at the $1,500 level, $45; at the $2,000 level, $65; at the $2,500 level, $90.   Total savings (taxes omitted) approximate the following percentages of total intake: at the $1,500 level, 12%; at the $2,000 level, 11%; at the $2,500 level, 10.5%.

It is not my thought to intimate that any regularity of the ratio of savings to spending power can safely be predicated.   Withholdings seem to be residuals, the leavings after more pressing wants have been cared for.   As such, they fluctuate over a considerable range, as has been shown in Chapter VI.   One may hypothesize, however, that the number of families with a will-to-save is quite definitely limited, and these families by reason of their thrift possess exceptionally stable incomes; in an era of widening prosperity other families rapidly acquire fresh spending power but add relatively little to national savings.   On this hypothesis a generally downward trend in the ratios of savings, as average spending power goes up, is explicable and may be expected to continue. Moreover, powerful forces referred to in the preceding chapter have been set in motion to discourage thrift.

The chief forms of savings by individuals are life insurance, purchases of securities and purchases of real property. Starting with the postulate that some reasonable degree of stability in the money-and-credit system will be maintained, a steady expansion of insurance appears practically certain; for it is sustained not only by its universal acceptance and by well-grooved habits but also by unremitting, intelligently directed salesmanship. If the prior forecast of increased attention to housing is realized, it will involve a larger flow of savings toward owner-occupied homes. Once such a movement gets under way, real estate will again attract that considerable proportion of individual savings which gravitates toward speculation. Under such circumstances acquisitions of real property may quickly regain all the ground lost since 1927 and much more. This leaves only a reduced portion of the limited volume of savings available for purchases of securities. The outlook for a lasting revival within the next few years of heavy popular dealings in securities seems distinctly unpromising.

ANTICIPATED DISTRIBUTION OF FAMILY TAKINGS

All the clues to future takings which it seems possible to extract from the data at hand have now been assembled: customary apportionments at various levels of spending power; the extent of authority exercised by basic wants at various levels; prospective changes in the objects to be selected under the influence of basic wants; secular variabilities of classes of objects; norms of consumption at various levels, as derived from records of family expenditures; anticipated variations in offerings, marketing methods and social-economic forces during the next few years. The main postulates, too, have been stated; and I have tried to make plain that whenever the postulates require modification the consequent alterations in forecasts may be extensive.

Some of the clues are clear and plausible. For instance, the trend line of food in Chart U, where it is grounded in a parallelism between national estimates and family records, shows outgo of $430 at the $2,500 level; this is 17.4% of total outgo. The trend line for percentage apportionments to food (Chart X) strikes

17.6% at the $2,500 level.   Both the trend lines are unmistakable, and they are in part derived from separate data.   Their close approximation is scarcely to be dismissed as a coincidence. It justifies, in our judgment, placing anticipated food spendings quite confidently very close to $435 per family.

On the other hand, the two charts just named differ considerably in respect to clothing.   Chart U arrives at $250, or 10% of total outgo; Chart X at 8.7%.   The latter trend line, however, is given a downward bias by the excessive percentages for clothing in two years, 1921 and 1923, when the war-time shortage was being filled.   Some weight has to be allowed, also, for the probable diversion of some small part of "prominence" spendings from automobiles to clothing.   Considering these factors, we conclude that the apportionment to clothing at the $2,500 level will almost certainly fall somewhere between 9 and 10%, and probably nearer the upper than the lower limit.   The forecast, on this basis, is fixed at 9.6%, or $240 per family.

The other five classes of takings shown in Chart X maintain ratios which are consistent enough to be accepted as moderately good guides.   These ratios are applied, with slight modifications to allow for presumed variations, to tobacco, sickness and death, personal appearance, recreation and social-cultural activities. Alcoholic beverages, in spite of the apparent tendency toward moderation in their use, will certainly rise under the joint influence of enlarged free spendables and increased leisure. Accordingly, a somewhat higher percentage of total takings (3%) has been assigned to this class.

In all the eight classes so far treated the probable margin of error in the percentages of total takings is small.   These classes aggregate nearly half (46.6%) of total intake at the $2,500 level.

The remaining half presents more difficulties.   It comprises three large classes: home maintenance, transportation, and savings and taxes.   All are likely to be powerfully affected by the variations discussed in the preceding chapter and by shifts in the objects of basic wants.   Yet none of the three can fall far below the ratios of total intake established in previous years of prosperity unless living habits should change to a far greater extent than now seems conceivable; nor can any one of the three expand indefinitely in the face of stubborn resistance by the other two classes.   The ranges of feasible movements of their ratios within these limitations can scarcely be wider than the following:

home maintenance, 22 to 28%; transportation, 14 to 18%; savings
and taxes, 10 to 15%. The important factors favorable to home
maintenance, which have been sufficiently explained, justify
placing its ratio near the top of its range, at 26%. Inasmuch as

TABLE 25.—CALCULATED AND ANTICIPATED DISTRIBUTION OF FAMILY TAKINGS[1]
(In round figures; 1913 dollars; see explanation in text.)

Classes of Takings	$1,500 Level		$2,000 Level		$2,500 Level	
	%	$	%	$	%	$
Food.	23.2	350	20.6	410	17.4	435
Clothing	10.7	160	10.0	200	9.6	240
Women's	*6.3*	*95*	*6.0*	*120*	*6.0*	*150*
Men's	*4.4*	*65*	*4.0*	*80*	*3.6*	*90*
Home Maintenance	22.6	340	22.5	450	26.0	650
Housing	*11.6*	*175*	*10.9*	*220*	*13.6*	*340*
Fuel, Light, Supplies	*3.7*	*55*	*3.5*	*70*	*3.0*	*75*
Furnishings	*4.0*	*60*	*4.9*	*95*	*5.6*	*140*
Services	*3.3*	*50*	*3.2*	*65*	*3.8*	*95*
Transportation	10.9	160	16.5	330	15.0	375
Vehicles and Upkeep	*9.6*	*140*	*15.2*	*305*	*14.0*	*350*
Local Fares	*1.3*	*20*	*1.3*	*25*	*1.0*	*25*
Savings and Taxes	14.1	210	12.1	240	12.4	310
Savings	*12.2*	*180*	*11.0*	*220*	*10.6*	*265*
Taxes	*1.9*	*30*	*1.1*	*20*	*1.8*	*45*
All Others	18.5	280	18.3	370	19.6	490
Alcoholic Beverages	*2.4*	*35*	*2.2*	*45*	*3.0*	*75*
Tobacco	*2.1*	*30*	*2.1*	*45*	*2.0*	*50*
Sickness and Death	*2.6*	*40*	*2.2*	*45*	*2.2*	*55*
Personal Appearance	*1.5*	*25*	*1.6*	*30*	*1.8*	*45*
Recreation	*4.2*	*65*	*5.0*	*100*	*6.0*	*150*
Social-Cultural Activities	*5.7*	*85*	*5.2*	*105*	*4.6*	*115*

[1] Calculated for the $1,500 and $2,000 levels; anticipated for the $2,500 level.

part of its anticipated gain will be at the expense of transportation, the ratio for the latter is reduced to 15%. We have 12.4%
left for savings and taxes.

Within each of the three classes subdivisions of the ratios can
be assigned without overmuch risk of gross error. Certain items
are fixed by conditions that cannot be currently controlled by
consumers. Fuel and light and household supplies, for instance,
will require a few more dollars (of 1913) than in the past because
of the anticipated increase in size of dwellings; an allowance of
$75, 3% of total intake, is deemed adequate. Local fares, it is

safe to say, will remain approximately stationary at $25, or 1%. Taxes, an indeterminable item, are arbitrarily set at $45, or 1.8%. Deducting the last two percentages from their respective group percentages leaves the ratios for the only other sub-classes in each group, namely: Vehicles and upkeep, 14%; savings, 10.6%. The remaining three sub-classes under home maintenance— housing, furnishings, and services—stand in fairly regular relationships to each other; that is, furnishings run 35 to 45% of housing while services run 25 to 35% of housing. Using these relationships as guides, we are not likely to go far wrong in assigning to housing 13.6% of total takings; to furnishings, 5.6%; and to services, 3.8%.

Table 25 lists all the foregoing forecasts when spending power advances to the $2,500 level. For convenient comparison, the corresponding figures for the $2,000 and the $1,500 levels are also listed; the latter percentages are derived from Table 15 (Chapter V) by averaging those for the three years of largest intake to be applied to the $2,000 level and those for the three years of smallest intake to be applied to the $1,500 level. The Aa-charts present graphically the same estimates and forecasts. They show clearly not only the anticipated distribution of intake among classes of objects at the $2,500 level but also the gains in the various classes, both as estimated between $1,500 and $2,000 and as forecast between $2,000 and $2,500.

ARE FORECASTS RELIABLE

How far is it feasible to go in forecasting consumers' effective demands? Theoretically they are all predictable, under given postulated conditions. With the data now available, however, I see little more to be done. Here and there additional fragmentary records of consumers' takings of well-defined types of goods are to be had; now that a general framework has been supplied, from which the normal relationships of such types to larger classes of objects can be predicated, it is possible that some of the records will become usable as guides to reasonable forecasts. For the most part, however, the details of the classes of objects listed in Table 25 cannot as yet be filled in.

Many additional studies will be necessary before much further progress can be made. Those now in plain sight consist mainly of investigations on behalf of trade associations and large companies designed to throw light on the short-period trends of their

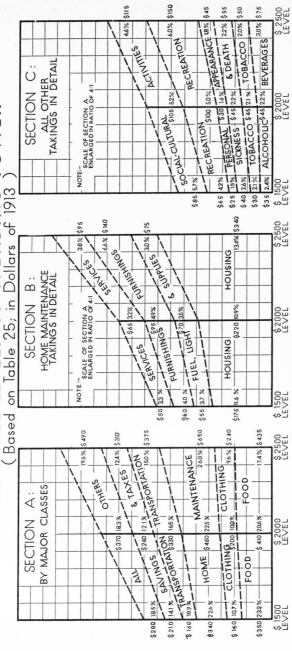

CALCULATED AND ANTICIPATED DISTRIBUTIONS OF FAMILY INTAKE
AT THREE LEVELS OF SPENDING POWER
(Based on Table 25; in Dollars of 1913)

CHART Aa.—All classes of takings, as here projected, share in enlarged spending power; but their rates of gain differ widely.

own markets.[6] Non-profit institutions may be expected to initiate from time to time a limited number of broader surveys of consumers' living standards and buying habits. The national government is of course the chief source of statistical data and should by all means extend its fact-gathering activities; among other things, it should provide regularly current data as to retail and wholesale sales of both commodities and services, current inventories in considerable detail, continuing records of family expenditures covering enough groups and localities to give reliable samplings, and current records of all important classes of payments into individual incomes. This is a large order, I grant, and not likely to be filled in the near future. Even after it is filled, several years will elapse before the new data will yield a great deal of fresh aid to the task of interpreting trends and forecasting consumers' demands some years ahead. On the whole, the prospect of rapid progress is not encouraging.

In the meantime (if our postulated conditions be fulfilled) the expectancies for classes of takings set forth in Table 25 are submitted as strong probabilities within moderate limits of tolerance. This assurance rests on the fact that the main inter-relations among classes of takings, as forecast in Table 25, are plausible and consistent with each other. Projections of apportionments; projections of amounts controlled by basic wants; projections of amounts frequently, less frequently and infrequently repetitive in comparison with the corresponding amounts derived direct from Table 25; projections governed by the "norms" of family expenditure records: all are in general agreement, after making adjustments for past and anticipated varia-

---

[6] Nystrom's well-known studies of fashion movements yield indications of probable shifts of demands from one line of clothing or furnishings to another. Forecasts of automobile sales have been common, but have proved particularly dangerous because of the absence of background information bearing on the place of automobiles in total takings. Elder reports some success in forecasting the sales of an anti-freeze mixture for automobile radiators. (See article by Robert F. Elder in *Factory and Industrial Management*, July, 1931.) Lewis W. Waters, vice-president of General Foods Corporation, is quoted to the effect that an important function of the company's 20-odd research laboratories is to predict food habits as much as five years in advance. (See *Weekly News Bulletin*, Sales Executives' Club of New York, Apr. 2, 1934.) Many unpublished investigations might be cited. All the serious attempts to forecast takings of specific products or a limited class of products, however, in the aggregate scarcely make a perceptible dent on the immense problem of mapping out in detail the anticipated developments of consumers' demands for some years ahead.

tions. The agreement, to be sure, is merely among different classifications of the same data; even so, it constitutes valid evidence of the existence of an orderly, even though constantly shifting, system of distribution of consumers' takings. Once we arrive at a correct understanding of the principles controlling the interactions of the elements in the system, it becomes possible to forecast their probable position at any assumed level of spending power.

I do not mean of course to claim any degree of probability in the present crude approximations which would be mathematically calculable; too many elusive factors of personal judgments are involved. Let us say simply that the forecasts in Table 25, being the results of analysis and cross-checking, are considerably better than hopeful guesses and emphatically better than fantasies.

PROSPECTIVE LINES OF EXPANSION

If we assume that the anticipations set forth in Table 25 have some degree of validity, their first use is to appraise probable lines of business expansion. For this purpose a further assumption is made that by the time the $2,500 year rolls around, in the latter half of the 1940's, the number of families in the United States will be 35 million. (If it should be 34 million or 36 million, the relative gains of the various classes of objects would not be much altered.) The anticipated distribution of national consumption, on this basis, is presented in Table 26. For convenience, their takings in the $2,500 year are placed in direct comparison with actual consumers' takings, according to our estimates, in 1929. The gains are stated in percentages and in money values (dollars of 1913).

The year 1929 is chosen for the comparison, in preference to some average or hypothetical year, with a view to making this particular forecast as specific and practical as possible. It should not be overlooked, however, that 1929 is by no means a typical year even of the new era boom. One of its peculiarities is an especially low volume of savings, when figured in deflated dollars; as a result, the expansion in this class (87%) appears much larger than it would if the comparison were made with normal post-war savings. If we take as a base the average deflated savings for the years 1923–1927, the expansion up to the $2,500 year is only

30%. Direct taxes have been more or less arbitrarily forecast at a figure more than double their amount in 1929.

All classes of takings in Table 26 show expansion well in advance of the assumed 17% gain in number of families. Food

TABLE 26.—ANTICIPATED EXPANSION OF CONSUMERS' ANNUAL TAKINGS BETWEEN 1929 AND THE ASSUMED $2,500 YEAR[1]

(In billions of 1913 dollars)

Classes of Takings	Esti-mated Takings in 1929	Antici-pated Takings in $2,500 Year	Anticipated Expansion of Takings	
			%	$
Total	59.9	87.5	46	27.6
Food	12.2	15.2	25	3.0
Clothing	5.9	8.4	42	2.5
Women's	*3.5*	*5.2*	*49*	*1.7*
Men's	*2.4*	*3.2*	*33*	*0.8*
Home Maintenance	14.5	22.7	57	8.2
Housing	*7.3*	*11.9*	*63*	*4.6*
Fuel, Light, Supplies	*1.8*	*2.6*	*44*	*0.8*
Furnishings	*3.4*	*4.9*	*39*	*1.5*
Services	*2.0*	*3.3*	*65*	*1.3*
Transportation	10.0	13.1	31	3.1
Vehicles and Upkeep	*9.3*	*12.2*	*31*	*2.9*
Local Fares	*0.7*	*0.9*	*30*	*0.2*
Savings and Taxes	5.8	10.9	88	5.1
Savings	*5.1*	*9.3*	*87*	*4.2*
Taxes	*0.7*	*1.6*	*129*	*0.9*
All Others	11.5	17.2	50	5.7
Alcoholic Beverages	*1.4*	*2.6*	*86*	*1.2*
Tobacco	*1.3*	*1.8*	*38*	*0.5*
Sickness and Death	*1.4*	*1.9*	*36*	*0.5*
Personal Appearance	*1.0*	*1.6*	*60*	*0.6*
Recreation	*3.2*	*5.3*	*66*	*2.1*
Social-Cultural Activities	*3.2*	*4.0*	*25*	*0.8*

[1] Derived from Table 25; assumes 35,000,000 families in the $2,500 year.

and social-cultural activities are relatively laggards, with only 25% increase in each case. Transportation comes next with 31%, a healthy growth yet greatly retarded in comparison with its headlong progress through the post-war years. Intermediate rates of expansion are those of men's clothing, sickness and death, tobacco, furnishings, fuel and light, and women's clothing, ranging from 33 to 52%. The fast-growers (expanding from 60 to 66%) form an interesting group: personal appearance, housing, household services and recreation, in the order named. Alcoholic beverages, because of uncertainty of data, cannot properly be assigned even an approximate rank in respect to expansibility.

The percentages of growth should of course be interpreted in connection with the amounts (in billions of 1913 dollars) shown in the right-hand column of Table 26. The largest dollar gains are there allotted to housing, savings, food, vehicles, clothing (combining men's and women's), recreation, and home furnishings; the smallest gains, to local fares, tobacco, sickness and death, personal appearance, social-cultural activities, and household fuel, light and supplies. Obviously, these amounts depend on what classification is adopted. At the same time, they yield indications of the most promising lines for enlargement of productive capacity during the next one or two decades.

Taking a long look ahead and ignoring technological changes, residential construction and materials clearly offer the largest fields for capital investment; the food, automobile, clothing and home furnishings industries, counting in all their varied branches, will keep on growing; commercial undertakings for providing recreation will expand at top speed; on the other hand, public utilities, hospitals, churches, publishing houses and tobacco factories are among the types of institutions and enterprises which will need relatively small accretions of capital.

If these indications were sufficiently definite and detailed, it would be possible to go on to estimate the anticipated requirements of consumer goods industries for materials, supplies, equipment and personnel and thus to work back step by step to a forecast of the entire complex of economic development. But reaching that stage of forecasting technique, quite obviously, will take some decades, if not generations.

PROSPECTIVE DEVELOPMENTS OF CONSUMERS' DEMANDS

The most that can now be attempted is to form a hazy picture of the main features of the market for consumers' commodities and services in the $2,500 year. Most conspicuous will be an insistent, apparently insatiable demand for larger and finer living quarters—not only by the wealthy but among all income groups. Since housing will once more be the chief medium for expressing desires for social approval and prominence, we may infer that the amount of tasteless extravagance and wastage in this field will be astounding. The number of domestic servants as well as the volume of impersonal services devoted to households will be far in excess of any previous experience. On the other hand, automobiles will be so completely taken for granted as an everyday necessity that they will be utilized less than at present as a medium for display; cheap cars in immense numbers will call for great public expenditures for highways and parking space. The heavy proportionate increase in outgo for personal appearance and for recreation will no doubt inspire strange fads sweeping in rapid succession from one end of the country to the other. Amusement resorts, entertainments, sports and beauty shoppes will flourish as never before. In most other respects the market scene of the 1940's will consist of further developments of the characteristics that became so familiar in the 1920's.

The picture may not appear highly attractive to all readers. I trust they will not hold me responsible. It is simply the logical outcome of the processes of measurement, analysis and projection which have been reported in this study. If the processes are seriously at fault, the picture is to that extent distorted. Otherwise, it represents a reasonable expectation, provided the postulated conditions are in fact realized.

Prospective Decline of Stability

It requires no extended argument to demonstrate that consumers' takings in the $2,500 year, unless the foregoing forecasts are wholly false, will be more volatile, more susceptible to sudden fluctuations, than has ever before been experienced.

The subsistence budget, after allowing liberally for a rise in standards of living, will take 46% of total spending power against 48% in 1929. The difference at this point is not great. But a large difference shows itself as soon as we start to examine the nature and motivations of the additions to "free spendables" between 1929 and the $2,500 year. Even the most stable classes —that is, food, social-cultural activities, housing and home services, and clothing—will acquire most of their increments above their 1929 records under the influence of wants that have already been largely satisfied. The increments, therefore, will have a high degree of dispensability. Moreover, a rapid rise in the proportion of infrequently repetitive, easily postponable purchases is strongly indicated by Chart Z.

Chapter VII has suggested, though only as an opinion, that perhaps 60 to 65% of outgo in the later post-war boom might be considered fairly dependable and stable; the remainder, unstable. Whatever the percentage may then have been, it will clearly be less in the $2,500 year by reason of (a) the smaller proportion required for subsistence, (b) the larger percentage of infrequently repetitive purchases and (c) the weak motivation of increments to takings. The sum of these reductions may reasonably be placed at 5 to 10%. This leaves in the $2,500 year a conjectured ratio of stability of 50 to 60%, which is in line with the ratio previously indicated by the discussion in Chapter X.

The exact percentage in itself is not significant; it merely tries to state the essential point in concrete terms. Consumption has been rapidly losing—and will in all probability go on losing—its former character of regularity and dependability: that is the all-important truth to be firmly grasped. Of all forecasts about consumption, this is the one that comes nearest to certainty.

The continuing trend toward instability of consumption is not to be viewed lightly. It is in cold fact one of the gravest of all menaces to the form of civilized society now existing. Unforeseeable shifts and fluctuations of consumers' takings create unending turmoil from one end to the other of the economic system. They aggravate convulsions, wherever the disturbances may start; and most observers recognize that an already shaky and nervous social-political-economic order is likely to go to pieces if convulsions are permitted to grow much more severe and more frequent.

The vital question still ahead of us is whether any counteracting forces are gathering strength; or if not, whether anything can be done to offset or damp down the combustible, not to say explosive, elements introduced into present-day economy by high-level spending power.

PART FOUR
DEDUCTION

Chapter XIII

PLANNING

If this book were written in normal times, it would stop at the end of Part Three. But the times are abnormal and perilous. The study here reported yields inferences which have a direct bearing on vital problems of national economy, and Part Four points them out.

Although the three preceding chapters offer only fitful and uncertain glimpses into the future, two general conclusions are scarcely open to serious doubt.

Spending power will presumably rise at some undetermined time well above its former peak; and as it rises, the inherent instability of consumption will progressively increase at an accelerating rate.

Instability of consumption already entails difficulties in forecasting consumers' demands far greater than were known to previous generations; and these difficulties will increase as consumption rises to higher levels. Statistical estimates and analyses of consumers' takings, it is true, make possible some limited and qualified forecasts. Further studies will probably produce marked improvements in forecasting technique. But there is little reason to look for even approximate reliability of detailed forecasts.

These two conclusions, in association with other observed tendencies referred to below, point toward notable changes in economic conditions and in business practice.

Economic Swings Tend to Grow Larger

A distinct tendency toward an increasing amplitude of business cycles appears in the American experience of the past 80-odd years. The evidence, to be sure, is open to question and certainly would not justify cocksure predictions.[1] Yet it strongly

[1] The showing depends of course partly on the statistical data and methods used in measuring fluctuations. Mitchell, writing before the 1929–1934 depression, calls attention to the relative stability of an index based on bank clearings and remarks: "It is rash to say that business cycles are growing milder because the cyclical fluctuations of outside clearings are less now than they were some forty years ago. The severity of the crisis of 1920 and the depression of 1921 is attested by abundant evidence." ("Business Cycles" by Wesley C. Mitchell,

suggests, at the least, that major cycles in future are likely to rise higher and sink deeper. That outcome, however, is not to be thought of as inevitable. More carefully considered, it rates as a threatening probability, which we must expect to be realized unless the persistent causes of the extraordinary violence of recent economic storms shall be weakened or offset.

A persistent cause, which has not heretofore been measured and has never, I think, been appraised at its true weight, is the growing instability of consumption. If it be granted that consumption exercises an absolute control in the long run over all forms of trade and industry—an axiomatic statement which no one questions—it follows that shifts and fluctuations in consumption set in motion disturbances that are bound to spread throughout the economic organism. This is enough in itself to excite some surprise that the influence of changes in consumption on the ups and downs of production has not been more thoroughly examined.[2]

But changes in consumption produce in fact *much larger disturbances* than their initial size would seem to warrant. As consumers turn either away from or toward a given class of goods, they start corresponding slumps or boomlets *which tend to increase in amplitude as they travel back through the distributing-producing system.* Kuznets has made a thorough study of correlations among retail sales of given commodities, wholesale sales and

---

National Bureau of Economic Research, New York, 1927, p. 349.) Obviously the once prevalent view that business cycles are growing milder cannot well be maintained against the record of the last five years.

[2] An explanation of the almost universal indifference of economists toward problems of consumption is offered in the introduction to this book. The particular question touched upon in the text—that is, the causal relationship of instabilities of consumption to cyclical movements—has had practically no attention, so far as I can find. There are of course innumerable discussions and theories of *total* consumption in relation to productive capacity and to output; but that is quite a different question. Even as to total consumption, two misconceptions are commonly accepted uncritically: (a) an implied assumption that the rise or fall of the total is spread more or less evenly over the whole range of consumers' takings, which is largely contrary to fact; (b) a widespread idea that no more than a minor fraction (usually thought to be in the neighborhood of 20%) of total consumption is subject to retrenchment, which is a long way from the present-day truth. In the light of recent experiences, it seems to me that a considerable recasting of unsupported judgments about the alleged "steadiness" of consumption would now be in order.

manufacturing output during the seven years 1919–1925. His general conclusion bearing on the point here stated is:[3]

There seemed to be an increasing rising variability in the flow of goods from one branch of economic activity to another, as we moved away from the ultimate consumers. Commodity sales by retailers fluctuated the least; those by wholesalers fluctuated more; manufacturing output to a still greater extent.

The explanation appears to center on the smaller stocks and more rapid turnover of retailers in comparison with wholesalers; and of wholesalers in comparison with manufacturers. Everyday observation indicates that the principle could probably be extended to the production of materials, supplies, equipment and buildings used by manufacturers of consumers' goods and on back to the capital goods required for the output of producers' goods; but statistical proof of these extensions, so far as I know, is lacking. If the soundness of the principle be accepted, which I see no reason to question, it signifies that a growing vulnerability of consumption carries with it a still greater liability to fluctuation of all business activity.[4]

Here, then, is an unsettling element of great power which deserves clearer recognition. In previous generations consumption was for the most part a stabilizer. Consumers' outgo was almost wholly devoted to predetermined objects, the fixed requirements of a low standard of living. As a source of cyclical movements it was negligible. But in our times consumption has grown capricious and subject to sudden deterioration. Perhaps the alteration in its character is a sufficient explanation of the apparent tendency toward an increasing amplitude of business cycles. In any case, our forecasts plainly indicate an enhanced

---

[3] "Cyclical Fluctuations" by Simon S. Kuznets, Adelphi, New York, 1926, p. 117.

[4] Cf. some recent remarks on nearly the same point by J. M. Clark: "If the demand for some consumable product begins to increase by 10 per cent instead of 5 per cent as formerly, demand for durable equipment to produce it may increase 30 per cent or more; and if the increase in demand for the product falls to $2\frac{1}{2}$ per cent, demand for durable equipment may suffer a positive drop of 15 per cent or more. When this happens, the purchasing power of the producers of durable equipment changes correspondingly, bringing about a further change in general consumer demand and still further intensified reactions on demand for means of production. Thus the cumulative process of expansion or contraction gets under way." *Journal of the American Statistical Association*, Mar., 1934, Suppl., p. 72.

instability in the period just ahead which will keep the entire economic system in a continual state of turmoil. We already know something about that condition from our experiences in the 1920's. We shall probably learn more before the 1940's are far advanced.

A MORE AGITATED, MORE EXPLOSIVE ECONOMY

Other unsettling forces, too, seem likely to gain in both mass and velocity. To discuss them here would lead far outside the scope of this book. Moreover, they are generally recognized and need only be mentioned.

The credit structure has been built up to such a size that it no longer rests securely on its gold foundation. It shivers and totters with every blow. So long as this condition persists—and no lasting repairs of the shaken structure have yet been seriously proposed—prices will remain unstable; long-term contracts will be unsafe; and fluctuations once started, whatever their source, will be intensified by the accompanying uncontrollable perturbations of prices and credit.

International trade and investment are peculiarly subject to social-political forces. At present the outlook for a re-establishment of well-ordered relations among governments is, to say the least, unpromising. If international commerce should revive under such circumstances, it might well serve merely to aggravate the danger of world-wide convulsions.

Technological improvements, whether directed toward bringing out new products or toward reducing costs, will presumably continue to create numerous disturbances.

All these causes of unsettlement have been to some degree operative in the past but not with equal force. One or two of them alone might be faced without grave apprehension. The real danger arises out of the possibility—more accurately, the probability sooner or later—of the concurrence of fluctuations separately generated in a "heterodyne" movement of incalculable power.

Whenever this occurs, the resultant swing of economic activities may easily be bigger and more violent than any previous y known. Prosperity in that event will soar to higher peaks of reckless spending; depression will plumb lower depths of despair.

These are unavoidable perils. We may suppose for the purpose of this discussion that price-and-credit movements are brought under intelligent control; that exports and imports again flow smooth'y; that technology advances at a steady, norma! rate. Nevertheless, the economic system will become more and more subject to chills and fevers, less and less resistant to booms and collapses, as average spending power goes up— especially spending power which is in the hands of highly suggestible masses of people and is largely concentrated on a few types of objects. This can be identified, I think, as a powerful, persistent cause, growing more forceful in each successive wave of prosperity, which makes inevitable the early development of a more agitated, more explosive economy.

CAN A WORKABLE BALANCE BE MAINTAINED?

Danger does not necessarily eventuate in disaster. Dynamite may be handled safely. Conceivably, the coming situation may be managed with boldness, skill and success.

The situation has many ramifications which cannot properly be treated here. One major sector, however, falls within the range of this study. That sector is comprised in the question: What can be done to maintain a workable balance between an enlarging productive capacity, on one side, and *a high level* of consumption, on the other side? The three italicized words are vital to an understanding of the question. It is a new question, not to be solved by the easy generalities that served well enough in times of scarcity and stability of consumption.

Moreover, the question daily grows more intricate on the production side. Improved processes and equipment call for larger investments in fixed forms of capital. Even more important, the time interval between investment and its fruition—that is, actual production on a scale commensurate with the investment— constantly tends to lengthen. This comment applies not only to expansion of industries but to training for the professions, development of real estate, establishment of trading enterprises and substantially all other undertakings requiring capital investments. Again, as the economic system becomes more complex, the gap widens between producers of raw and semi-finished materials and the ultimate consumers whose demands in the end determine their markets. These are not new factors; but it is well to remind ourselves of their continuing importance.

The crux of the question is not the balancing of current output and stocks with current demands. Forced adjustments at this point, whether by the government, by code authorities or by informal agreements, may be defensible at times as emergency measures but can have no lasting value. To attain a workable balance requires looking farther ahead. The equilibrium to be sought is between *future* productive capacity and *future* consumption. Moreover, it is not merely a balance between two grand totals, as one might infer from some current discussions; it is a delicate, shifting adjustment of capacity in each line to its corresponding demand.

No one expects a perfect adjustment. It is not essential. The economic organism can survive—can even keep on growing—in spite of an impressive array of gross miscalculations. At the same time, in the rarefied atmosphere of high spending power the organism is less hardy; an accumulation of bad guesses could be fatal. It is prudent to look ahead thoughtfully.

Two distinct procedures are open to us. One is to develop collective control and establish a "planned economy." The other is to put our faith in private enterprise and management, possibly to be further limited and regulated but to be left essentially free from direct control. Which procedure offers the better chance of escaping the dangers and reaping the benefits of the prospective large increase in productivity? The issue is clearly drawn. For reasons stated below no lasting compromise is feasible. The decision will be made soon.

PLANNED ECONOMY: TWO INDISPENSABLE FEATURES

"Economic planning" is proffered from various quarters as a a sovereign remedy for all our ills. Unfortunately its advocates hold such widely divergent views that it seems impossible to define the term. It covers schemes ranging all the way from a merely advisory board, possessing neither powers nor assigned functions, to an unlimited economic dictatorship on the Russian model. The only common characteristic I can find is faith— faith that edicts or agreements or political appointments will set up somewhere a body of men inspired by superior knowledge, insight, judgment and integrity. How far the faith is justified each reader can best decide on the strength of his own observations.

A related term, "planned economy," comes closer to a definable meaning, though its proponents appear to evade definitions. We may define it for them as an economic order in which some kind of governmental commission is empowered by law to draft a long-period (say, 5- to 10-year) national plan for development and control of at least the major industries, including farming, trading and financing; and thereafter to authorize or veto, in accordance with the plan, (*a*) investment of capital, (*b*) volume and prices of output and (*c*) payments and reserves of all kinds for the benefit of labor, ownership and management. This definition is rigorously restricted to the bare essentials of any regime that could be legitimately referred to as a planned economy. Anything less could be only an advisory or regulatory procedure, since it would leave large fields open to the unplanned activities of private interests. For that matter, "economic planning," if the term means anything more than compiling statistics and issuing fatherly advice, would have no stopping place short of the degree of supervision covered by the foregoing definition. In fact, it probably could not stop there; but that is beside the point of the present discussion.

Two features are indispensable to a planned economy:

1. *Specific, quantitative objectives.* The controlling authority must be prepared to state in figures, not in nicely rounded phrases, how many tons of coal shall be delivered, how many shoes of each size and style shall be made, how many apartment houses shall be constructed and where. Moreover, the figures must be approximated at least 5 to 10 years ahead; otherwise, no one can calculate capital requirements for buildings, equipment, raw materials, specialized labor and managing personnel, all of which must be provided well in advance of the assigned output. Without these figures, the "plan" will dissolve into a wordy fog.

2. *Predetermined administrative rules.* In view of the immense complexity of the task of exercising control over the proposals and operations of many thousands of business concerns (even though the control should be limited to a few industries) and of 6 million farmers, it is obvious that a large number of agents must be employed. They cannot be given wide discretion; if they were, the master plan would quickly be riddled by exceptions, not to speak of favoritism and wire pulling. Hence, the familiar, slow-moving processes of governmental administration will necessarily be adopted. Even supposing that action can be taken promptly on quotas of output and the like, questions of investment and business organization will inevitably either be settled by reference to inflexible administrative rules or wait long for decision by the central authority.

It is not my desire to exaggerate these two features, but simply to point out that they are inescapable elements in a planned economy.

Specific, Quantitative Objectives: How Will They Be Provided?

The practicability of the first feature—specific, quantitative objectives approximated at least 5 to 10 years ahead—has been

carefully explored in the present study. Any effort to set up
such objectives must start with forecasts of consumers' demands;
unless they are foreknown with reasonable assurance, it is impossible to calculate how much and what forms of textiles, leathers,
woods, metals, machines, structures and so on through the
infinite variety of materials, supplies and equipment will be called
for. The primary question that confronts economic planners,
then, is to determine how far they, or their proposed supervisory
board, will be able to go in forecasting consumption. The preceding chapter has presented the findings of a serious attempt to
answer the question.

The attempt has utilized, I think, substantially all available
data and whatever methods of analysis seemed at all promising.
With what results? A table of guarded forecasts of *main classes*
of takings based on postulated conditions and on broad assumptions as to numerous important variables. Even with these
limitations, the forecasts may have considerable value. But
they do not, and cannot, particularize the anticipated takings of
minor statistical classes; still less, of items comprised in these
classes or of the numberless types and styles which will be in
demand in 5, 10 or 15 years. Yet just such details, at the least
for the larger classes of objects, are prerequisites to setting up
the specific, quantitative objectives without which a planned
economy would be farcical.

Take one example: Let us suppose that the amount of housing
to be required could be accurately predicted. The information,
though valuable for some purposes, would be of little use to a
national planning board unless it were also possible to predict
the locations and types of dwellings, whether single-family or
multi-family, whether of frame, steel, brick or concrete construction, and the designs and appurtenances that would be
attractive to purchasers. Lacking these specifications, no human
intelligence could assign the correct productive capacity to each
kind of construction materials; not to speak of fixing the capacity
of the makers of equipment and supplies for producers of construction materials.

It is tiresome to belabor so obvious a point. I do so only
because it is fundamental and at the same time is universally
ignored or minimized in pleas for national planning.[5]

[5] The only reference worth mentioning to the necessity of working back from
forecasts of consumption to allocations of productive capacity, which I have yet

NATIONAL PLANNING REMAINS HAZY AND UNWORKABLE

Unless some primary flaw is found in the reasoning thus far, any responsible argument for a planned economy, or even for a recognizable dose of economic planning, should hereafter open with a proposed solution to the problem of overcoming the vital weakness emphasized by the present study, namely: the apparent impossibility of predicting (with reasonable allowances for error) consumers' demands *at a high level of spending power*. Permit me to repeat, too, that the problem here posed is just as critical in a socialistic as in any other form of planned economy. Four possible types of solution may be considered:

1. *Demonstrate* that sufficiently better data than those employed in this study are attainable and/or that sufficiently better methods are applicable to justify an expectation of adequate, detailed forecasts. (Not to be obscured by calling attention to desirable improvements in gathering statistics unless the improvements will yield the required forecasts.) This would be an entirely satisfying solution, one to be eagerly awaited.

2. *Equalize* incomes, or at least bring them nearer equality, with the hope of securing greater stability of takings.[6] Whatever the merits and demerits of this suggestion viewed as a device for reducing cyclical swings may be, its relationship

---

discovered among the rhapsodies on economic planning, occurs in the report on "Long-Range Planning" by a sub-committee (J. M. Clark, Chairman, J. Russell Smith, Edwin S. Smith, George Soule) of the National Progressive Conference. (Reprinted in *The New Republic*, Jan. 13, 1932.) It is perhaps the clearest, best-reasoned summation so far issued of the set of wholly unproved dogmas which make up the national planning credo. The authors are too well informed to ignore, as do their co-propagators of the faith, the need of *forecasts*, as distinguished from current statistics of consumption. "A more difficult but hardly less essential undertaking," they say in Part VI of their report, "is a study of potential demand, such as must be uncovered if industry is to operate more fully and the standard of living raised. This would be a very hazardous field of investigation." Indeed it would. However, the committee, after listing some of the hazards, waves them aside and centers its attention on "certain minimum comforts of life" which are presumably about the same as those in our subsistence budget. Apparently the committee has no conception of the large proportion of unstable, unpredictable elements in consumption. Now that the essential facts are laid before these gentlemen, just how do they propose to obtain those dependable measurements of *potential* demand which their own report declares to be essential?

[6] The suggestion is offered by the sub-committee mentioned in the foregoing footnote; but it must be said, to the committee's credit, that they advance it cautiously. It is something that "might help." Again: "If incomes were reasonably stabilized, the resulting sense of security would *probably* [italics mine] further stabilize the spending of them" (*op. cit.*, p. 11).

to the problem of forecasting consumers' demands some years ahead is almost negligible. This point has already been touched upon in Chapter X, wherein attention is directed to the fact that broad divisions of takings are only moderately and gradually affected by changes in the average spending power of groups of consumers. The present study, which has centered on statistical averages of family intake, makes evident that the average in any recent normal year includes a heavy proportion of unstable "free spendings"; and there is no reason to suppose that "free spendings" in the hands of middle-income families are more stable than are the same amounts in the hands of high-income families. In both cases they are "free"—that is, uncontrolled by fixed standards of living. Of course, if the average of all incomes were *reduced*, stability would be greater; that possibility is covered in the next paragraph.

3. *Reduce* spending power (and consumption) to so low a level that people will gladly take whatever goods are made available to them. Consumption will then be well stabilized and predictable. This seems to me the most likely eventual solution under any scheme of national planning. But it is not acceptable to the national planners themselves.

4. *Ration* consumption by eliminating the optionals treated in Chapter IX, restricting greatly the supply of postponable goods and of unstable classes generally, and prohibiting all forms of marketing stimuli—not only advertising but personal selling, promotions, displays, everything that might awaken desires or attract them unpredictably toward favored items. Assuming for the moment that this solution, which is implied in all planning projects so far broached, could be adopted and rigorously enforced, our national consumption would be obliged to conform to the tastes of the gentlemen of the planning board; and so long as their ideas remained unalterable, consumers' takings might be unerringly forecast. Our recently concluded experiment in liquor control, by comparison a very slight experiment, strongly suggests, however, that the American people are not yet spiritually prepared to accept this solution complaisantly.

All four solutions are open to overwhelming doubts or objections. At the least, it will surely be agreed that the advocates of a planned economy have not yet made a case for a reasonable judgment that adequate forecasts of consumption can be formulated either now or within the next few years. By "adequate" as here used, I mean forecasts from which specific, quantitative objectives of a national plan can be derived.

But without *specific, quantitative* objectives,[7] there can be no plan; there can be only a confused hodgepodge of guesswork notions. The conclusion, I submit, is inescapable: that a planned

[7] If I keep harping on the two words "*specific, quantitative*," it is to counteract the persistent tendency in discussions of the subject to substitute vague generalities for facts. To cite once more the forementioned report on "*Long-Range Planning*," a list of 11 "objectives" is duly presented; but on examination the list proves to be nothing more than a series of short paragraphs summarizing some of the committee's social and economic beliefs. These "objectives" are not the kind I am talking about.

economy (with which may be included any considerable degree of control through economic planning) remains as yet a hazy and unworkable project.

If we cannot look far enough ahead to plan, the only recourse left is to adapt production to potentially expansible demands, as fast as they show themselves, through a continual process of redesigning products, abandoning obsolete and building new productive capacity, and revamping marketing channels and stimuli. This is the solution resorted to by private enterprise. It is the antithesis of a planned economy.

CHAPTER XIV

FLEXIBILITY

If a planned economy cannot organize and maintain a workable balance between a rapidly growing and shifting productive capacity, on one side, and a rising and fickle consumption, on the other side, what chance has private business—private business with its ceaseless turmoil of conflict, scheming for advantage, self-seeking, odd mixtures of integrity and chicanery, lightheaded gambles and usual concentration on immediate profits? When viewed in contrast with the alluring picture of well-ordered development drawn by economic planners, private business is undeniably a good deal of a mess. Nor does its record, particularly in the post-war period, inspire confidence in its far sighted sagacity. That private business is under suspicion can scarcely excite surprise.

Yet its longer record, over the centuries, is not so bad. During its reign tremendous gains in human comfort have been realized. If these are to be ascribed, as some critics aver, wholly to science and the social increment, with private business merely playing the role of a leech, at any rate it has not put a stop to progress.

What is more to the point of the immediate discussion, private business has endured through the ages countless fiery trials— piracies, hostile or ignorant governments, wars, revolutions, financial crises, long-drawn-out depressions—and somehow has muddled through them all. Each time it has not only rebuilt its own fortunes but has opened the way for new advances in production and in prosperity.

PRIVATE BUSINESS FACES INCREASED HAZARDS

To meet dangers and take heavy risks is not a new trial. A compilation prepared by Dun and Bradstreet for the United States Department of Commerce shows that during the period 1900–1930 the failures and withdrawals from business *each year* averaged well over 20% of all the concerns listed.[1]

[1] *Domestic Commerce*, Sept. 20, 1933.

Some light on underlying causes may be derived from Hardy's classification of "the uncertainties of practical importance to the business manager" in the following five groups:[2]

Risks of destruction of property through the physical hazards of nature.

Closely related to the preceding are uncertainties in the productive process.

Social hazards . . . such as robbery, defalcation, and forgery . . . strikes, riots, wars, tariff changes, tax reforms, prohibitory laws.

Risks due to individual ignorance.

Market risks form the most important group of all.

Only the first of the five types of risk is decreasing, mainly through the spreading influence of insurance. Uncertainties in the productive process have doubtless been enlarged by rapidity of technological change. Social hazards, as above defined, may be increasing somewhat. Individual ignorance grows more costly as operations become more complex. Of chief importance, however, is the intensification of market risks. Leaving other factors out of the reckoning, the growing instability of consumers' demands, the incidence of which spreads throughout the entire economic system, cannot fail to generate more frequent and more threatening hazards.

Large risks imply correspondingly large profits for those who are skilled enough, or lucky enough, to escape disaster. It is a fair inference that bigger fortunes will be won, as well as greater losses incurred, by the entrepreneurs and investors of the 1940's.

Additional evidence of a distinct tendency toward increased hazards is supplied in studies by Kuznets and Burns. Kuznets presents the life histories of a number of typical industries, from which one may reasonably deduce that in general the newer, larger-scale industries grow much more rapidly than was true of the older industries at a corresponding stage of their development. He establishes a strong presumption that the faster the rate of growth of an industry, the greater as a rule is the amplitude of short-swing deviations from its primary trend line.[3] Obviously, the uncertainties and dangers of conducting rapidly expanding industries are extreme. Anyone who looks upon them

[2] Slightly adapted from "Risk and Risk-Bearing" by C. O. Hardy, University of Chicago Press, 1923, pp. 2 and 3.

[3] "Secular Movements in Production and Prices" by Simon S. Kuznets, Houghton Mifflin, Boston, 1930.

as relatively sure sources of easy profits would do well to review, for example, the records of the automobile and radio industries. Burns' investigation suggests, though it does not claim to prove, that the life histories of industries are becoming shorter; their death rate, higher.[4]

To be prudent, we can best take for granted that private business in the next few years will face greater hazards than any it has been called upon to meet for generations, perhaps even for centuries. The hazards are partly of its own making. Enterprise has created conditions which have fostered (a) wide diffusion of a fast-growing spending power, (b) popular education facilitating the rapid spread and massing of mercurial reactions and demands and (c) scientific research leading to large technological changes. Out of these developments have sprung the instabilities and the dangerous liability to intensified booms and depressions which make trade, production and investment more and more risky.

How well is private business equipped to navigate in these stormy waters? Can its equipment and its navigating methods be improved? To deal with these questions in all their aspects would lead far away from the subject of this book; but it seems appropriate to call attention to inferences drawn in part from our study of consumers' takings which bear on the two questions.

IMPROVED FORECASTING; INCREASED FLEXIBILITY

In times of incessant change the first requisite for survival is ready adjustability; guided, so far as practicable, by alert foresight. Few products can safely be left long unmodified. In all lines of consumers' goods frequent changes of engineering design, of pattern, of color, of accessory features—sometimes considerable improvements, sometimes merely catchy talking points—follow one another with bewildering speed; unless all signs fail, they will be still more frequent in the years to come.

The changes may easily call for large revisions of plant layout and equipment; witness the $9,000,000 devoted to revamping the Chrysler plant in the summer of 1932. Wholly new products may be required if a going organization is to be maintained. Makers of oil burners and makers of radio sets simultaneously take on electric refrigerators; a piano manufacturer attempts

[4] "Production Trends" by Arthur F. Burns, National Bureau of Economic Research, New York, 1933. Introduction by Wesley C. Mitchell, p. xviii.

to replace his vanishing sales by turning out power boats; a textile mill undertakes to dispose of its output by producing finished articles of clothing. Everywhere brains are being racked for fresh ideas; and this is only a foretaste of the unremitting pressure for improved and new products to which future management must be instantly sensitive and responsive—else it perish.

Marketing practice under these conditions will have to step up to a higher plane of quick adjustability and energizing power. Product changes in themselves usually involve fresh sales appeals and procedure. Channels of distribution will be increasingly subject to sudden mutations, each one requiring corresponding adjustments in marketing practice. Finer adjustments will inevitably call for enlarged use of selective and localized promotional-distributive-selling methods and media, complementing national campaigns.

More essential than in the past will be the marketing function of forecasting demands. The controlling factor in business operations, if spending power goes up, will be the heightened instability of consumption, as affected by fashions, prices, offerings and other variables. It will be more and more difficult to judge what is coming next. But business cannot be successfully carried on without some degree of foresight. Its former reliance on stability of consumption must be replaced, so far as possible, by more thorough research into the motivations and trends of consumers' demands. Marketing practice will become, then, much less a blind, stubborn effort to force the sale of such goods as the producer finds it convenient to make; much more an unceasing, intelligent effort to measure potential demands and to meet them speedily. The farther it goes in fulfilling this requirement, the greater will be its influence over business operations and its contributions to the maintenance of a workable balance between capacity, on one side, and consumers' expansible wants, on the other side.

Fortunately for private business, however, its continued success is not wholly dependent, as is the success of a planned economy, on an unattainable accuracy of forecasts of consumers' demands. Private business by its very nature possesses a high degree of flexibility; herein lies its overwhelming advantage over the rigidity of a planned system.

Improved forecasting is for private business an important aid, but not the vital principle of its existence. In the great areas where forecasting is uncertain or impossible, alert management can call into play its alternative master-policy—that is, heightened flexibility.

Private business is already flexible—but not flexible enough to measure up to the anticipated requirements of the next new era. In fact, powerful forces in the recent past have endeavored to substitute a contrary policy. Stabilization has been the watchword of industrial and financial management all over the world. The policy has taken such varied forms as trusts, holding companies, cartels, price agreements and understandings, territorial spheres of commercial influence, tariff walls, unionized wages, and restriction of output. It has proved itself a dismal failure. Its only success has been to procure a certain degree of temporary and deceptive quiescence which has prepared the ground for universal disaster. Stabilization is not a practicable policy in a world of incessant change and inherent instability of consumption.

Enhanced flexibility, even though it be an inescapable necessity, is not a policy to be adopted easily. It must break up innumerable petrifications of practice and of executive thinking. Some of its implications may be sketched in bare outline.

BROADER INFORMATION; MORE LIQUIDITY; TRUER ACCOUNTING

Flexibility in a skillfully managed business organization involves much more than willingness to try all sorts of doubtful experiments. It connotes well-thought-out decisions, made quickly but not impulsively. In a period such as is here envisaged, when changing currents of consumption set forces in motion that spread rapidly through the economic system, sound decisions cannot be based on narrow information. Even small business, not to speak of big business, will be forced to look far afield.

Information covering a wide area and a tangled maze of activities is for the most part incomprehensible unless it can be assembled and classified in statistical form. One characteristic of business management, then, in the coming period will be an increased use of statistical data and a habit of thinking in statistical terms. Such thinking has its own drawbacks but there is no practical alternative if the full potential flexibility of private business is to be intelligently utilized.

Financial and accounting practice must fall into line with the guiding principle of flexibility. Finance in all its phases will be far more consciously dominated by the vision—or the specter, as the case may be—of estimated potential sales and earnings. In the interests of flexibility, working capital will form a larger proportion of total assets. The experience of 1921 taught us to hold down inventories; of 1932, to keep up cash. The survivors of the debacle of 1929–1934 will value liquidity more highly than ever.

Fixed assets, on the other hand, will command less respect. Their inflexibility will be more generally recognized as a handicap. Their physical durability will count for less in estimating their commercial value. Independent clear-thinking accountants will insist on writing down fixed assets to a figure set by their actual and prospective earning power. They will not continue, I trust, to rest satisfied with outdated concepts of depreciation, taken over bodily from English practice, designed for little more than the measurement of physical deterioration. They will seek criteria of obsolescence, based in part on forecasts of consumption, by means of which they may give to managers and to investors more accurate and more helpful guidance.

Smaller Concerns; More Prudent Expansion

For some generations now, the standards of business success have been (a) size and (b) stability. Both these standards look toward moderate, sure profits in preference to quick and uncertain speculative profits. Respectable business thinking throughout the world has been dominated, though not always consciously, by the examples of famous British mercantile and financial houses—solidly established, fortified by world-wide connections, slow-moving, smug, yet admirable in their steadfast adherence to traditions of good faith. In this country, in spite of vicissitudes inseparable from pioneering and many other unsettling influences, intelligent management has constantly striven to approach the same standards.

Today these former standards are being rapidly altered or displaced; and the types of business enterprises which embody them will soon be as obsolete as the Spanish galleons which they resemble. New types will prove better fitted to ride successfully the stormy seas of shifting demands, unpredictable technological changes and uncertain prices.

Most imperative is the necessity for closer, sharper control of business operations. In practice, this usually means control by one man or by a tightly knit group. Quick-acting direction needs a free hand at the rudder. When the head of an operating enterprise must continually go to absentee owners or their bankers for approval of his moves, he carries too heavy a handicap; his strategy is usually relevant to the problems of day-before-yesterday.

Organizations, too, will have to be better disciplined, more thoroughly trained, more readily responsive to general orders, yet also more skillful and resourceful in their handling of tactical problems. Farflung distributive organizations, in particular, will need to be remodeled; they are too inflexible for quick maneuvers. Like the Macedonian phalanx, they can stand their ground and stolidly go down to defeat; but under the new conditions of accelerated changeableness they will be less able to cope with lighter and faster competitors.

These considerations point toward a judgment that the typical successful concern of the 1940's will be smaller than its counterpart of the 1920's. The so-called trust movement of the early years of the twentieth century grew out of the cost-cutting economies made possible by size and integration. It was sustained through the post-war boom by speculative financing. The first advantage has long since been matched in nearly all industries by the optimum-size plants of second-string competitors. The advantage of giant companies in respect to financing will be lessened if our forecasts of savings are well-founded; moreover, the next speculative frenzy when it does occur is more than likely to be fixated on some different delusion.[5]

The way seems to be cleared, therefore, for a renaissance of owner-managed, medium-size enterprises. Doubtless many large concerns, kept flexible by exceptionally intelligent direction, will continue to flourish. But sprawling agglomerations, created mainly for the sake of financing, managed through an interminable series of pointless conferences, infected from top to bottom with internal politics, can scarcely be expected to survive in a

---

[5] The improbability of a continuation of the post-war trend toward concentration of industry in large units is discussed from other angles in the writer's paper on "Adjusting Corporation Financing to Industrial Growth," *Journal of Business*, Oct., 1933.

kaleidoscopic environment. The age of industrial dinosaurs is probably over.

An allied inference is that well-managed enterprises in future will not be in such a hurry to expand as they were in the post-war years. "American business men," says a competent observer, "have been slow to grasp the fact that virtually no industry which starts out developing rapidly can maintain for long the same rate of growth. In consequence, many American industries tend to be overbuilt, and to have capital and a working force which have been assembled because the managers had assumed that business would continue to grow in the future as it has in the past."[6] As one example of the present tendency to watch trends of consumption more carefully and adjust investment to them, it is worth noting that *Iron Age*[7] thoughtfully reviews the evidence that steel consumption has been growing at a decreasing rate and forecasts an output sometime between 1935 and 1940 equivalent to 76% of today's capacity. If we had had between 1923 and 1929 a larger supply of this kind of dispassionate calculation and less ballyhoo, we might have possessed today a more diversified national industrial plant, organized in smaller units, far better fitted to prospective consumptive requirements; and the myth of general over-capacity would not have been heard.

A New Type of Business Ability

If all that has been said in this chapter, or any considerable part of it, is allowed to be sensible, it follows that business executives of a new type will be called for. A few of them are already at their posts. The special combination of experience and talents which will constitute outstanding business ability in the coming environment differs markedly from the combination that has previously been in the ascendant. The required combination includes as one major element an habitual thoroughness of reconnaissance, which has hitherto been lacking; that large risks are unavoidable must be more generally recognized as a good reason for surveying them in advance with the utmost care. The other major element is quick adjustability, which in turn demands (*a*) openmindedness plus (*b*) proficiency in forming

[6] "The Problem of Unemployment" by Paul H. Douglas and Aaron Director, Macmillan, New York, 1931, p. 54.

[7] Issue of Sept. 14, 1932.

and drilling organizations that can execute speedy changes of front to meet unforeseen contingencies.

Will a sufficient supply of the new type of business ability rise to the top in time to prevent disruption or decay of the economic system? If it does not, then mankind does not possess or cannot utilize at present the brain-power required to direct so complex and sensitive an organism. In that event, we may as well reconcile ourselves to a decadent future; whether under the sway of obsolete notions of business management or under the harsher stupidities of a bureaucracy makes little practical difference. However, the record of private business in earlier periods of trial gives ground for hopefulness. It is assumed in what follows that the new type of business ability will soon take command.

Business, operating under more unstable conditions, will necessarily be more of an adventure than it is in quieter days. Yet it need not be a gamble. American business men have never been slow to take chances; but they have done so often with a poker-playing faith in good luck. The time has probably arrived for less poker and more chess in business management. The executive of tomorrow will be spiritually akin to the great merchants of the Middle Ages who sent out their expeditions into distant lands, faced the hazards of the unknown with confident courage and guarded their solvency by diversifying their risks.

However, he will have to be even more alert; for his risks will be both more varied and more subtle. He will use all the facilities at his command for discovering not only the immediate demands of his markets but their trends and future probabilities. He will watch keenly the effects on his own undertakings of a broad range of social and economic movements. He will study unceasingly the reactions of his customers to new offerings and selling methods; and he will not hesitate to carry on research wherever the information in prospect seems likely to repay the expense.

Management confronting graver hazards will be forced to pay less attention to precedents. The remarkable advance achieved in manufacturing methods during the past 20 years has been brought about by discarding rules-of-thumb in favor of the rational procedure developed by able engineers. Comparable advances in managerial and marketing methods can be won only by means of a similar attack. This means incor-

porating into business thinking an outlook which may be called
for short "the scientific viewpoint."

The viewpoint of science is by its very nature impersonal
and professional. It implies a breadth of knowledge at least
sufficient to cover all the important factors bearing on a given
problem. Business has been gradually acquiring the scientific
viewpoint—gradually but at an accelerating rate—during the
past two to three decades. The process seems likely to go
forward with great rapidity in the period just ahead; not by
reason of anyone's conscious will, but mainly because the new
conditions will bring to the front new ideas and new men.

The results may be far-reaching. Writing some 30 years ago,
Thorstein Veblen argued with power and bitterness that business
enterprise rested upon archaic concepts, was devoted to exploit-
ing the fruits of the machine process, and was culturally repres-
sive. He drew a sharp contrast on all these points between
business men and technicians. "Business methods and the
apparatus of business traffic develop very promptly whenever
and wherever the situation calls for them; such is the teaching
of economic history. There is nothing recondite about them,
little that has to be acquired by a protracted, cumulative experience running over many generations, such as is involved in
technological development."[8] The machine process, on the
other hand, "inculcates thinking in terms of opaque, impersonal
cause and effect, to the neglect of those norms of validity that
rest on usage and on the conventional standards handed down
by usage. Usage counts for little in shaping the processes of
work of this kind or in shaping the modes of thought induced
by work of this kind."[9] Veblen's line of distinction has already
become far more shadowy than it seemed when he wrote; it
may altogether disappear under the growing pressure for better
informed and keener thinking business management. Insofar
as this occurs, not only will earnings be safeguarded but the
social order as a whole will be protected against such inexcusable
errors of imitativeness, rash plunging and short-sightedness as
those which plague us now. Moreover, a more intelligent
management of business cannot fail to bring with it a broader
interest in national welfare.

[8] "The Theory of Business Enterprise" by Thorstein Veblen, Scribner, New
York, 1927 (originally published in 1904), p. 303.
[9] *Ibid.*, p. 310.

LESS STABILIZATION; MORE STABILITY

Thus we arrive at a basically altered conception of business management. Under the shifting conditions inseparable from high-level spending power, stabilization of business operations on the basis of set formulas for products, production methods and costs, distributive channels, sales appeals, prices, financing, and accounting, is not to be long maintained in any industry; not even by the combined efforts of all the concerns engaged in that industry. The time will soon come—or perhaps has come—to discard the idea ruthlessly. Under the conditions now in prospect, the enterprises to prosper will be those that combine with foresight an ability to readjust their operations promptly to the new demands that each day brings forth.

Ready adjustability to changing circumstances as the guiding principle of business; medium-size enterprises, owner-managed and self-financed; thoroughly informed, flexible-minded executives: these are the essentials of success in handling dangerous instabilities.

Let us suppose these essentials to be fully realized. Drastic changes, even though unforeseen, would then have only temporary and limited effects; for business would be prepared and adaptable. Financial breakdowns on a large scale, paralysis of trade, and vast unemployment would be absent; for there would be no rigid resistances to dam up such movements until they acquire irresistible force.

Less stabilization will produce more stability. A flexible economic system does not collapse under a shock. It merely gives way in one spot. Its resilience permits it to go on functioning and shortly to regain its full strength. This is the universal experience of simple economic systems. It could just as well be true of complex systems if their operations were at all times kept elastic. It is the rigidity of inertia or forced stabilization that transforms minor defeats into disasters. Thus we arrive at the paradox that genuine stability may grow out of a timely recognition that instability is inescapable.

The paradox is something more, I trust, than the conventional bit of closing optimism. It is not, in point of fact, a true paradox; for the stability we are now talking about is a new kind—not the stability of a great edifice on a rock foundation but the stability of a seagoing vessel equipped with gyroscopes of

sufficient power to keep it balanced in any weather. Fixed
stability belongs to the dead past. Gyroscopic stability, given
able business management, can be achieved and maintained.

We cannot put an end to economic storm clouds; but we can
use ingenuity to ride out the storms. The metaphor is fortunately faulty; for when effective precautions are taken against
economic storms, the storms themselves become discouraged and
die down.

APPENDIXES

APPENDIX A

BASE TABULATION OF CONSUMERS' SPENDINGS AND WITHHOLDINGS, 1909 TO 1931

(In millions of current dollars)

Classes and Subclasses	1909	1914	1919	1921	1923	1925	1927	1929	1931
GRAND TOTALS	29,143	33,619	65,890	59,031	70,158	79,303	83,347	89,370	63,644
FOOD AND SOFT DRINKS¹	7,347	8,927	18,498	13,866	16,089	17,865	18,262	19,614	13,483
Commodities	7,347	8,927	18,498	13,866	16,089	17,865	18,262	19,614	13,483
Commercial Expenditures	5,896	7,358	16,149	12,337	14,297	15,876	16,402	17,705	12,161
Groceries and Delicatessen	1,395	1,650	3,565	2,506	3,108	3,379	3,346	3,516	2,406
Baking Powder and Yeast	15	15	28	32	28	25	27	21	17
Bee Products (farm made)	8	14	12	10	12	12	13	13	7
Canned Fish	38	47	75	46	72	85	95	106	67
Canned Fruits, Vegetables, Preserves, Jellies, etc.	162	254	575	488	625	718	662	930	603
Chocolate and Cocoa	21	33	110	76	89	100	115	113	79
Coffee, Spice, and Tea²	140	191	412	304	377	556	523	537	374
Corn Sirup, Starch	33	35	124	53	77	89	90	111	63
Flavoring Extracts (includes Malt Extracts)	20	29	82	82	79	101	114	138	119
Flour and Other Grain Mill Products	557	547	895	553	512	562	493	392	226
Food Preparations: Cereals, Macaroni, etc.	75	129	390	230	382	397	499	504	350
Gelatin³	3	3	8	7	6	7	8	8	7
Rice	27	28	108	50	56	64	65	59	41
Salt	7	10	25	22	25	23	23	24	20
Sugar	279	308	695	583	755	628	607	549	425
Vinegar and Cider (part under Canned Fruits and Vegetables)	9	8	26	20	13	13	12	11	8
Meat, Sausage, Poultry and Meat Products (includes Lard)	1,639	2,065	4,364	2,600	3,015	3,711	3,845	4,451	2,841
Milk, Butter, Cheese and Eggs	1,172	1,393	2,817	2,239	2,972	3,159	3,421	3,514	2,553
Butter	261	321	756	626	823	879	950	960	595
Cheese	66	80	190	117	191	175	185	173	107
Eggs	268	266	473	387	420	520	490	594	361

Milk (fresh)	525	625	1,041	895	1,296	1,355	1,539	1,498	1,297
Milk (condensed and evaporated)	42	83	261	167	199	182	210	233	166
Oleomargarine	10	18	96	47	43	48	47	56	27
Confectionery and Ice Cream	214	361	1,076	900	1,102	1,133	1,201	1,252	953
Chewing Gum	4	29	85	65	68	80	103	101	83
Confectionery and Ice Cream	214	332	991	835	1,034	1,053	1,098	1,151	870
Non-Alcoholic Beverages	73	97	380	381	369	380	387	425	337
Beverages	73	97	362	376	363	377	384	423	336
Liquors, Vinous	5	5	18	5	6	3	3	2	1
Bakery Products	471	584	1,357	1,294	1,334	1,506	1,656	1,813	1,413
Vegetables	437	{1,101[6]	917	{2,166[5]	1,001	1,231	1,132	1,302	786
Fruits and Nuts (includes Processed Nuts)	401	77	1,406	201	1,154	1,137	1,184	1,201	696
Fish and Other Sea Food (fresh)	69	77	197	201	182	169	160	156	125
Merchandise Manufactured on Premises of Retail Stores	25	30	70	50	60	70	70	75	50
Extra-Commercial Consumption[7] (Farm and village-grown foodstuffs consumed by grower)	1,451	1,569	2,349	1,529	1,792	1,989	1,860	1,909	1,322
Payments to Industry for ALCOHOLIC BEVERAGES and Other Illegal Commodities[8]	1,800	2,000	2,000	1,400	1,500	1,700	1,800	2,000	1,800
TOBACCO—Commodities	623	727	1,418	1,471	1,465	1,510	1,606	1,688	1,392
Cigarettes	49	96	884	465	466	561	680	814	733
Cigars	367	402	676	625	614	581	573	526	336
Tobacco Pipes	7	5	15	9	12	9	9	7	7
Tobacco, Chewing, Smoking	200	224	343	372	372	359	344	341	317
CLOTHING	3,641	3,957	8,057	7,959	9,412	9,241	9,740	9,927	7,060
Commodities	3,387	3,718	7,659	7,600	9,007	8,832	9,926	9,518	6,781
Women's Clothing	584	719	1,789	1,532	2,068	1,910	2,188	2,490	1,890
Corsets	51	63	116	116	120	119	119	122	102
Women's Clothing	533	656	1,673	1,416	1,948	1,791	2,069	2,368	1,788
Clothing, Men's and Boys	635	599	1,519	1,222	1,542	1,419	1,412	1,390	884
Boots, Shoes and Other Footwear	752	844	1,876	1,453	1,742	1,605	1,657	1,675	1,110
Leather (including leather used in repairs)	664	746	1,662	1,296	1,511	1,402	1,440	1,496	1,011
Rubber	77	83	172	140	203	169	181	143	74
Other Rubber Shoes, Heels, Soles, etc.	11	15	42	17	28	34	36	36	25

BASE TABULATION OF CONSUMERS' SPENDINGS AND WITHHOLDINGS, 1909 TO 1931.—*(Continued)*

Classes and Subclasses	1909	1914	1919	1921	1923	1925	1927	1929	1931
Men's Furnishings	248	279	612	513	595	582	620	610	406
Collars, Men's	27	29	73	46	66	43	21	14	10
Furnishings	65	81	166	119	159	186	224	234	141
Shirts	114	133	284	282	335	313	335	317	230
Suspenders and Garters	42	36	89	66	35	40	40	45	25
Millinery, Lace Goods, Handkerchiefs and Embroideries[9]	191	221	377	411	424	441	520	480	355
Fur Goods	73	53	193	154	216	288	336	287	178
Hats and Caps, Men's and Boys'[10]	133	129	244	182	254	239	248	243	151
Hats, Fur Felt	60	47	104	66	95	100	124	125	73
Hats, not Felt or Straw	21	28	67	56	65	66	62	54	25
Hats, Straw	46	51	65	54	83	62	51	53	45
Hats, Wool Felt	6	3	8	6	11	11	11	11	8
Dry Goods and Notions	69	58	151	137	199	208	227	269	177
Buttons	8	7	13	9	11	11	10	10	7
Combs and Hairpins	11	7	9	6	12	7	6	3	3
Cotton Small Wares	6	5	19	12	34	35	30	30	19
Fancy and Miscellaneous[11]	8	12	43	34	42	47	55	59	35
Hair Work	14	4	9	14	14	8	3	3	2
Leather Goods, Belts, etc.[12]	5	5	11	12	10	11	12	9	6
Linen Goods	8	9	9	10	14	14	13	43	29
Needles and Pins	3	4	15	10	11	9	10	12	10
Pocketbooks, Purses	6	5	23	30	51	66	88	100	65
Cotton Goods[13]	196	221	527	343	508	378	345	266	181
Silk Manufactures[14]	91	118	299	258	330	344	323	316	178
Woolen and Worsted Goods[15]	20	19	39	36	50	45	39	40	23
Knit Goods[16]	289	353	975	895	1,183	1,149	1,177	1,209	792
Gloves	44	42	114	74	104	98	108	119	84
Gloves, Cloth	17	17	39	21	39	41	42	42	30
Leather	44	42	75	53	65	57	66	77	54
Umbrellas	27	23	34	35	47	36	31	24	12

Merchandise Manufactured on Premises of Retail Stores	35	40	90	75	95	90	95	100	70
Corrections for Changes in Retailers' Stocks			−1,180	+280	−350				+290
Intangibles	254	239	598	359	405	409	414	409	329
Dressmakers and Seamstresses (not in factory)	130	110	150	131	143	140	136	124	92
Milliners (not in factory)	20	19	27	23	24	23	22	21	15
Shoemakers and Cobblers (not in factory)	45	50	105	103	119	124	131	137	116
Tailors and Tailoresses (not in factory)	34	35	66	62	69	72	75	77	66
Repairs and Storage	25	25	50	40	50	50	50	50	40
TRANSPORTATION[18]	1,062	1,667	4,071	4,316	6,179	7,661	7,308	8,470	5,592
Commodities	547	957	2,861	2,851	4,349	5,407	4,698	5,550	3,220
Automobiles	177	443	1,381	1,230	2,433	2,562	2,119	2,749	1,208
Gasoline and Oil[9]	89	167	880	902	995	1,306	1,145	1,501	907
Automobile Parts and Accessories	71	145	932	584	1,019	1,495	1,395	1,233	944
Parts	11	25	354	201	520	779	568	721	636
Tires and Tubes	60	120	578	383	499	716	827	512	308
Motorcycles and Bicycles	12	26	46	8	37	19	17	28	14
Horse-Drawn Vehicles and Equipment	198	176	72	27	35	25	22	19	7
Carriages and Wagons	131	115	34	12	14	10	8	7	2
Harness and Saddlery	58	52	32	12	17	12	11	9	4
Horse Blankets	5	6	5	3	4	3	3	3	1
Whips	4	3	1						
Corrections for Changes in Retailers' Stocks			−450	+100	−170				+140
Intangibles	515	710	1,210	1,465	1,830	2,254	2,610	2,940	2,372
Blacksmiths	40	40	10	5					
Bus Fares			10	50	100	167	245	310	240
Chauffeurs and Hack Drivers	10	10	45	60	90	100	130	160	125
Ferries, Inland Water Travel	25	30	50	45	55	60	65	70	50
Gasoline Taxes					22	88	155	259	322
Insurance on Automobiles			132	169	200	231	290	316	260
Motor Vehicle Taxes	25	50	76	106	150	183	196	200	200
Repairs and Storage (includes private garaging)	50	100	250	300	450	650	750	900	600
Street Railway Fares	340	430	562	655	663	645	614	525	425
Taxicab and Hack Fares	25	50	75	75	100	130	165	200	150

BASE TABULATION OF CONSUMERS' SPENDINGS AND WITHHOLDINGS, 1909 TO 1931.—(*Continued*)

Classes and Subclasses	1909	1914	1919	1921	1923	1925	1927	1929	1931
HOME MAINTENANCE	7,398	8,274	12,093	13,410	16,491	18,289	20,490	22,865	18,998
Commodities	2,558	2,869	4,776	4,922	6,435	6,368	6,694	7,209	4,556
Commercial Expenditures	2,358	2,669	4,596	4,822	6,305	6,231	6,564	7,074	4,446
House Furnishings[20]	1,050	1,131	2,421	2,066	3,084	3,157	3,115	3,264	1,916
Awnings	4	6	15	12	15	16	16	17	11
Blankets and Other Woolen Goods	13	12	26	24	33	30	26	27	15
Carpets, Rag and Wool	110	107	202	176	290	318	292	274	149
Carriages, Children's	14	18	38	33	52	47	44	43	30
China-firing	1	1	2	2	3	3	3	3	2
Clocks	12	11	20	16	31	29	38	45	65
Curtains and Other Lace Goods	21	25	42	46	47	49	58	53	39
Flags and Banners	2	4	6	5	4	5	5	4	3
Furniture	271	317	671	636	907	1,014	1,035	1,107	561
Glassware	42	55	114	100	156	145	139	148	108
House Furnishings	33	39	93	84	106	121	135	196	133
House Furnishings Manufactured on Retail Premises	15	15	30	30	40	45	45	50	30
Lamp Shades, Bric-a-Brac and Other Fancy Articles	8	12	43	34	42	47	55	59	36
Linoleum and Asphalted-Felt Floor Covering	22	24	79	73	117	116	112	133	61
Mats and Mattings	4	3	8	4	7	6	3	3	2
Mattresses	36	39	84	75	108	111	99	120	77
Mirror Frames	20	17	28	23	28	32	32	30	16
Mirrors	9	9	19	15	30	32	29	29	33[21]
Oilcloth	12	12	26	23	30	30	29	40	23
Plated Ware	27	27	53	45	79	79	83	81	44
Pottery and Porcelain	44	22	43	46	79	78	80	82	44
Refrigerators, Non-Mechanical	9	13	22	28	42	48	48	48	34
Sewing Machines	27	23	55	36	48	52	43	42	20
Sheetings, Towels, Blankets and Other Cotton Goods	130	148	352	228	338	252	230	177	121
Silversmithing	40	33	53	45	49	59	56	56	27

Statuary, Manufactured	1	1	1	1	1	2	2	2	1
Stoves and Ranges	92	104	232	165	313	303	296	313	194
Velvets, Plushes and Other Silk Manufactures	10	13	33	29	37	38	36	35	20
Window Screens	5	6	7	8	14	15	15	16	9
Window Shades	16	15	24	25	40	35	31	32	17
Electrical Appliances and Supplies	46	67	186	151	242	293	441	571	445
Electrical Machinery (domestic appliances not elsewhere listed and incandescent bulbs)	18	28	83	70	105	116	124	158	100
Gas and Electric Fixtures	17	25	29	26	46	50	49	56	27
Refrigerators, Mechanical					22	22	140	211	226
Washing Machines	11	14	74	55	91	127	128	146	92
Musical Instruments and Radio	140	163	564	386	567	643	663	910	266
Musical Instruments	5	6	21	21	27	41	38	27	19
Pianos	109	103	204	141	222	212	139	87	29
Phonographs, Records, Needles	26	54	339	209	238	125	191	153[23]	
Radio Sets and Supplies				15	80	265	295	643	2183[24]
Household Supplies[20]	184	215	498	393	514	514	519	583	397
Aluminum		7	27	17	39	46	45	55	28
Baskets and Willow Ware	1	1	2	2	2	2	3	3	2
Blacking	8	9	24	17	25	23	21	22	16
Bluing	1	1	3	2	2	2	2	1	1
Brooms	19	19	40	24	36	29	25	25	17
Brushes, Non-Rubber	4	5	11	10	15	13	14	14	9
Candles	1	1	1	2	2	2	3	3	2
Cleaning and Polishing Preparations	6	9	27	23	35	34	41	46	47
Cork Products	2	2	5	4	4	5	5	6	4
Cutlery, Kitchen	9	9	21	19	27	28	28	27	20
Fire Extinguishers		1	2	2	2	3	3	4	2
Glass Cuttings	18	18	34	26	29	33	26	40	25
Matches	16	18	26	43	34	34	36	28	26
Rubber Goods	7	9	26	11	18	21	23	23	16
Soap, Laundry and Kitchen	54	62	148	116	134	185	140	155	126
Stamped Ware	20	25	57	39	66	59	58	77	47
Tinware	4	7	20	14	18	22	21	25	18
Wooden Goods	14	12	24	22	26	23	25	29	16

Base Tabulation of Consumers' Spendings and Withholdings, 1909 to 1931.—(Continued)

Classes and Subclasses	1909	1914	1919	1921	1923	1925	1927	1929	1931
Coal, Wood and Ice	839	1,013	1,251	1,525	1,818	1,866	1,566	1,471	1,077
Coal, Anthracite	358	411	516	699	782	507	667	564	431
Coal, Bituminous	253	336	408	472	626	520	586	595	410
Coke	12	13	42	29	67	50	50	55	30
Fuel, Manufactured					1	1	1	1	1
Ice, Natural	161	183	156	172	172	131	115	100	75
Ice, Manufactured	22	30	69	80	83	94	92	106	95
Wood	33	40	60	73	87	63	55	50	35
Flowers, Plants and Seeds	99	80	191	181	250	258	260	275	200
Corrections for Changes in Retailers' Stocks			−515	+120	−170				+145
Extra-Commercial Consumption (farm-grown forest products consumed by farmers)	200	200	180	100	130	137	130	135	110
Intangibles	4,840	5,405	7,317	8,488	10,056	11,921	13,796	15,656	14,382
Commercial—Personal Services	868	850	1,179	1,137	1,390	1,571	1,761	1,859	1,569
Housekeepers	90	75	130	145	160	170	185	190	125
Laborers (domestic and personal service)	18	15	18	18	26	33	39	44	32
Launderers and Laundresses (not in laundries)	235	210	300	270	310	325	335	325	210
Servants (not in hotels)	525	550	731	704	894	1,043	1,202	1,300	1,002
Commercial—Impersonal Household Services	530	705	1,160	1,360	1,686	1,928	2,199	2,552	2,333
Electric Current	85	135	271	315	400	475	524	619	686
Gas, Manufactured	130	150	225	280	350	375	390	408	356
Gas, Natural	30	50	89	115	141	168	195	225	201
Laundering and Dry Cleaning	150	200	250	300	350	400	500	600	425
Moving Expenses	30	35	75	60	75	80	90	100	75
Repairs and Storage (furniture)	25	25	50	40	50	50	50	50	40
Telephone	80	110	200	250	320	380	450	550	550
Total Outgo (cash or equivalent) for Occupancy of Owned Homes	1,562	1,850	2,433	2,939	3,432	4,378	5,313	6,240	5,840
Total Outgo (cash or equivalent) for Occupancy of All Homes	3,442	3,850	4,978	5,991	6,980	8,422	9,836	11,245	10,680

Commercial—Rentals Paid for Leased Non-Farm Homes	1,750	1,850	2,300	2,800	3,300	3,800	4,250	4,700	4,550
Commercial—Expenses of Occupying Owned Homes	629	788	1,079	1,211	1,467	1,728	1,919	2,121	1,935
Craftsmen's Services for Repairs and Upkeep of Owned Non-Farm Homes Occupied by Owners (includes costs of materials)	90	100	210	175	270	300	310	320	190
Insurance on Owned Non-Farm Homes Occupied by Owners	120	130	190	215	255	295	290	300	255
Interest on Mortgages on Owned Farm Homes Occupied by Owners	43	54	66	78	80	80	79	78	71
Interest on Mortgages on Owned Non-Farm Homes Occupied by Owners	130	160	230	275	300	390	480	565	565
Other Communal Services (snow removing, etc.)	50	50	75	75	100	100	100	100	100
Taxes on Owned Farm Homes Occupied by Owners	26	29	38	63	72	73	75	78	74
Taxes on Owned Non-Farm Homes Occupied by Owners	170	215	270	330	390	490	585	680	680
Extra-Commercial—Net Rental Values (Imputed)	1,063	1,262	1,599	1,980	2,213	2,894	3,667	4,424	4,195
Net Rental Values of Owned Farm Homes	143	142	221	207	205	213	209	199	195
Net Rental Values of Owned Non-Farm Homes	790	970	1,133	1,521	1,760	2,487	3,185	3,920	3,710
Rental Values of Homes on Leased Farms	130	150	245	252	248	244	273	305	290
SICKNESS AND DEATH	847	944	2,115	2,003	2,365	2,599	2,833	3,153	2,552
Commodities	249	296	599	562	640	710	786	903	745
Caskets and Funeral Supplies	49	53	129	110	112	141	150	172	139
Druggists' Preparations	59	64	134	92	92	109	127	155	144
Optical Goods	15	23	67	55	68	42	41	55	33
Patent Medicines	110	135	301	249	337	351	394	438	343
Rubber Goods	7	9	26	11	18	21	23	23	16
Surgical Appliances and Supplies	9	12	32	25	38	46	51	60	40
Corrections for Changes in Retailers' Stocks			−90	+20	−25				+30
Intangibles	598	648	1,516	1,441	1,725	1,889	2,047	2,250	1,807
Dentists	80	92	271	266	320	352	379	418	351
Hospitals	100	125	200	150	200	225	250	300	200
Physicians and Surgeons	324	329	795	765	886	921	981	1,041	846
Secondary and Sectarian Practitioners	36	36	91	97	129	149	170	198	160
Trained and Practical Nurses	40	44	116	119	135	180	198	216	181
Undertakers (services only)	18	22	43	44	55	62	69	77	69

BASE TABULATION OF CONSUMERS' SPENDINGS AND WITHHOLDINGS, 1909 TO 1931.—*(Continued)*

Classes and Subclasses	1909	1914	1919	1921	1923	1925	1927	1929	1931
PERSONAL APPEARANCE	441	503	992	1,016	1,255	1,347	1,493	1,680	1,155
Commodities	244	277	605	629	759	768	823	914	593
Brushes	4	5	11	10	15	13	14	14	9
Jewelry	117	118	302	243	253	253	250	291	120
Perfumes, Cosmetics	24	37	96	123	250	213	266	318	252
Razors, Blades	26	28	64	56	81	83	83	81	61
Soap (toilet)	54	61	148	116	134	135	140	155	126
Watches	19	28	74	56	56	71	71	55	26
Corrections for Changes in Retailers' Stocks			-90	+25	-30				+25
Intangibles	197	226	387	387	496	579	670	766	562
Barbers, Hairdressers, Manicurists	160	183	301	303	395	472	556	645	468
Bootblacks	8	9	16	16	20	22	24	25	15
Jewelers	15	18	35	34	40	41	43	45	37
Photographers	14	16	35	34	41	44	47	51	42
RECREATION	1,222	1,461	2,335	2,581	3,127	3,488	4,003	4,663	3,144
Commodities	142	171	304	311	381	369	410	456	346
Aircraft			2	1	2	2	3	9	4
Ammunition	22	26	50	23	43	31	34	37	23
Billiard Tables	2	2	5	2	3	2	3	3	2
Cameras, Developing, Supplies	15	24	45	38	41	43	52	56	41
Firearms	7	5	14	11	15	13	16	18	8
Fireworks	3	3	6	6	6	8	7	8	5
Rubber Goods	3	4	10	4	7	8	9	9	6
Ships and Boats	11	14	30	30	32	27	33	35	29
Sporting Goods	17	20	31	48	63	64	67	88	72
Toys and Games	20	32	65	60	91	79	92	102	80
	42	41	96	78	93	92	94	91	61

Corrections for Changes in Retailers' Stocks	+15				−15	+10	−50		
Intangibles	2,798	4,207	3,593	3,118	2,746	2,270	2,081	1,290	1,080
Admissions to Theaters, Sports, Carnivals, etc.	1,250	2,000	1,600	1,200	1,000	800	700	400	350
Airways	11	3						60	
Clubs, Dues and Fees (golf, tennis, etc.)	100	150	125	110	100	100	100	140	50
Foreign Travel	426	615	510	495	375	150	40	200	130
Hotels (includes meals), Tourists' Houses, Camps, etc.	600	800	650	550	450	400	350	490	150
Railroad and Pullman Fares	411	639	708	763	821	820	841		400
SOCIAL-CULTURAL ACTIVITIES	3,959	4,764	4,375	4,064	3,717	3,700	3,556	2,194	1,937
Commodities	1,183	1,411	1,301	1,204	1,049	1,056	831	561	469
Artists' Materials	7	11	10	10	10	8	6	4	3
Books, Newspapers and Periodicals	683	804	722	655	600	605	530	382	321
Envelopes	16	22	20	18	14	16	14	7	5
Glue	2	3	3	2	2	2	3	1	1
Ink, Writing	5	7	8	9	9	8	10	4	4
Mucilage	1	3	3	3	4	3	4	2	2
Paper	220	317	328	305	251	191	204	86	68
Paper Goods	113	105	95	86	83	89	83	40	31
Pencils	22	47	41	42	42	36	40	14	12
Pens, Points	35	52	41	38	36	20	31	9	13
Stationery	20	32	24	28	32	27	24	9	7
Typewriters	4	8	6	8	6	5	7	3	2
Corrections for Changes in Retailers' Stocks	+55				−40	+45	−125		
Intangibles	2,776	3,353	3,074	2,860	2,668	2,644	2,725	1,573	1,468
Tuition Privately Paid	500	550	500	500	450	400	400	220	200
Postage	325	350	340	300	250	232	213	150	125
Fraternal, Civic, Union and Grange Dues	350	470	400	400	350	350	350	200	175
Artists, Sculptors, Teachers of Art	49	57	50	44	38	29	28	13	12
Musicians and Music Teachers	61	73	66	59	53	44	44	35	22
Lawyers	118	141	128	117	107	89	90	35	34
Church and Charity	1,200	1,500	1,300	1,150	1,000	1,000	1,000	500	500
Immigrant Remittances	173	212	290	290	420	500	600	420	400

BASE TABULATION OF CONSUMERS' SPENDINGS AND WITHHOLDINGS, 1909 TO 1931.—(Continued)

Classes and Subclasses	1909	1914	1919	1921	1923	1925	1927	1929	1931
DIRECT TAXES—Intangibles	25	25	1,355	809	757	940	1,037	1,246	·969
Income Tax, Federal	.....	.....	1,270	719	662	845	912	1,096	834
Income Tax, State	.....	.....	35	30	30	25	55	75	60
Licenses, Fees, Fines	25	25	50	60	65	70	70	75	75
SAVINGS	2,800	3,000	9,400	6,500	7,800	10,600	10,400	9,300	4,100
Increases in Cash Holdings	600	600	2,600	1,100	2,500	2,900	2,600	1,300	−900
Payments for Holdings of Securities	1,000	1,000	4,000	3,200	3,000	5,200	4,800	7,100	2,800
Payments for Holdings of Real Property	1,500	1,700	3,200	1,900	2,600	4,200	4,700	3,500	1,500
Payments of Life Insurance Premiums	500	700	1,200	1,500	1,900	2,300	2,600	3,200	3,000
Total Annual Acquisitions	3,600	4,000	11,000	7,700	10,000	14,600	14,700	15,100	6,400
Less Realized Profits and Capital Gains from Sales of Assets	500	500	1,000	500	1,200	2,900	2,900	4,000	(+600)[2][7]
Less Receipts of Funds Withdrawn from Life Insurance Companies	300	500	600	700	1,000	1,100	1,400	1,800	2,300

[1] Includes expenditures for food purchased through food stores and through restaurants, but not hotel meals.
[2] Changes in method of presenting data in Census of Manufactures tend to understate values for earlier years.
[3] Of "Glue and Gelatin." 75% placed under edible "Gelatin."
[4] Under "Confectionery and Ice Cream."
[5] Under "Alcoholic Beverages."
[6] Includes "Vegetables."
[7] These are values *at the farm* and therefore represent larger physical quantities than do equal values for other foods.
[8] This item is designed to cover only that portion of payments for illegal commodities (but including Census figures for alcoholic beverages during the pre-war years) which may be assumed to have been made for such commodities as alcohol and bottles. This portion enters into estimates of national income. Services of bootleggers are excluded. The figures above under this head are obviously guesses; they find some basis, however, in the estimates of expenditures for alcoholic beverages made by Warburton and Gebhart.
[9] Curtains and other lace goods for homes to the amount of 10% of retail sales placed under "House Furnishings."
[10] Chiefly for men although a small portion enters women's wear.

[11] Lamp shades, bric-a-brac, burnt-wood articles, etc., to the value of 50% placed under "House Furnishings."

[12] Remainder placed under "Trunks and Leather Goods."

[13] Piece goods only; sheetings, towels and blankets (40%) placed under "House Furnishings."

[14] Piece goods only; 10% allowed for uses of velvets and plushes in "House Furnishings."

[15] Piece goods only; 40% allowed for blankets in "House Furnishings."

[16] Includes hosiery, underwear and knit fabrics and outerwear.

[17] Under "Men's Furnishings."

[18] The term "Transportation" is here used to designate local and customary movements, whereas consumers' expenditures for longer, less usual trips, including "Foreign Travel," "Hotels" and "Railroad and Pullman Fares," are placed under "Recreation." Obviously the distinction, though it can be clearly stated, is not readily applicable to our statistical groupings. Buses and private automobiles, for example, are frequently used for lengthy pleasure trips while railroads provide daily transportation for great numbers of suburbanites. However, it seems reasonable to place each item in the class to which it mainly belongs, trusting that minor exceptions will offset each other.

[19] Includes "Lubricants Not Made in Petroleum Refining Plants" and "Fuel Oils Used for Domestic Heating" (a very small percentage).

[20] Under "House Furnishings" are included items which are for the most part durable; under "Household Supplies," are included kitchen supplies and those items which are commonly used up or discarded within a short time.

[21] Includes "Glass Cutting" in 1931.

[22] Under "Electrical Machinery."

[23] Includes "radio-phonograph" combinations.

[24] Phonographs included.

[25] Under "Mirrors" in "House Furnishings."

[26] Included under "Clocks."

[27] Does not enter into total; see Appendix D.

ESTIMATES OF SPENDINGS FOR COMMODITIES

AS LISTED IN APPENDIX A

In order to formulate estimates of consumers' spendings for commodities, three major steps are required.

1. *Assemble* data as to producers' values of all classes of commodities which are, in whole or in part, ready-for-purchase by consumers.

2. *Allocate* the proportion of each class taken by consumers.

3. *Add* to the base figure thus obtained an allowance for the "spread" between producers' values and the prices paid by ultimate consumers.

In principle, the three steps are simple; in practice, they involve many difficulties. As to some items—including, fortunately, a number of the larger ones—information is available which makes the results fairly dependable. As to other items, one must rely on trade opinions or on even more arbitrary judgments; and the resultant estimates are questionable.

Yet it is fair to say that the majority of the estimates appear to be in themselves reasonable and consistent. They are carried through a period of 23 years of unusually rapid change; if the procedure were grossly wrong, the estimates would presumably reveal unexplainable fluctuations. Furthermore, many of the items have been checked for different years against wholly independent estimates and have generally been found in substantial agreement.

SOURCES OF PRODUCERS' VALUES

The chief source of data is, of course, the Census of Manufactures. The first task here was to make sure that the census figures were arranged in comparable classifications throughout the period studied. The well-known monograph on "The Growth of Manufactures, 1899 to 1923" by Edmund E. Day and Woodlief Thomas was taken as a guide.[1] In addition, it was necessary to make a further study of the classification in each later census. Without attempting to enter into details, it is believed that the classes of manufactured commodities presented in Appendix A are comparable throughout, with the minor exceptions indicated in the notes subjoined to the table.

[1] Census Monograph VIII, United States Government Printing Office, 1928.

Since 1921 the biennial Census of Manufactures has been limited to establishments reporting a total production of $5,000 or more, whereas the minimum in previous years was $500. As pointed out by Day and Thomas, the effect of this change is in general insignificant; and we have not attempted to make allowances for output of establishments below the census minima. It is possible, however, that the change may have considerable effect, which we have been unable to trace, on estimates for bakery products and other items manufactured in small establishments.

Another difference in procedure, which has been here disregarded as probably immaterial, is the change in the Census of Manufactures of 1929 (in part) from reports of the selling value of products at the factory, whether sold or not, to reports of the selling value of products actually shipped or delivered. It is entirely possible, however, that in certain industries this change introduces a perceptible variation.

Data for producers' values of unmanufactured commodities come from several different sources. The Census of Mines and Quarries, supplemented by annual releases of the Bureau of Mines, supplies the values of coal at the mines. This is the only important mineral product which reaches the consumer in an unmanufactured form.

For farm products, the figures used for the years 1924–1931 are the Department of Agriculture estimates of cash income from specified commodities. Corresponding figures for prior years are taken from the *Agricultural Yearbooks*, supplemented by some of King's estimates[2] of farm income from crops not clearly covered in the *Yearbooks*. These figures from different sources are not as closely comparable as would be desirable; but they appear to be the best available. Whatever differences exist probably tend to increase producers' values before 1924 and may to some extent distort particularly our estimates of poultry and dairy products.

Producers' values for both manufactured and unmanufactured commodities are adjusted by adding the values of imports and deducting exports. These corrections obviously cannot be exact, because of differences in classifications and in the timing of reports. For the larger items, however, the inaccuracies on this account are probably not serious.

ALLOCATIONS TO CONSUMERS' GOODS

Having determined for each class of commodities the producers' values available for domestic takings, the next step is to allocate the output respectively to (*a*) producers' goods and (*b*) consumers' goods. The latter class of commodities, as defined in Chapter I, is limited to

[2] "The National Income and Its Purchasing Power," Chap. XI.

those which are ready-for-consumers'-purchase.[3] The former class includes: (a) all forms of raw and partly processed materials for further processing; (b) machinery, equipment, tools and supplies; (c) all construction materials except those used directly by home-owners for upkeep or repairs (e.g., paint, household tools, and the like); and (d) that portion of finished commodities which is taken for productive uses, not for consumption (e. g., automobiles for business uses, gasoline for trucks, fruits and vegetables for canning factories, coal for factories and apartment houses, clothing and food for institutions and hotels, and so on). Most of the uncertainties of allocation arise in connection with the group (d) just described.

By far the best guide for allocations of manufactured goods is "Distribution of Sales of Manufacturing Plants," a publication of the Bureau of the Census in 1933, which shows what proportion of manufacturers' sales were made to industrial and other large consumers "buying in quantities for productive or business purposes." This proportion may be taken as the minimum percentage of the output of each industry to be allocated to producers' goods. In many cases the Census of Manufactures supplies details which permit finer allocations, with reasonable certainty; for example, consumers' purchases of brushes can be delimited by subtracting from the total value of output street-sweeping brushes, industrial brushes and a large proportion of paint and varnish brushes. Again, in the allocation of sugar, the percentage going to consumers is determined by subtracting from the total value the value of all sugar used as raw materials by industries in the food, chemical, and other groups.

Further guidance in allocating the output of several large industries is provided by special governmental or private studies. Of particular value is the monograph on "Apparent Per Capita Consumption of Principal Foodstuffs in the United States" by E. P. Montgomery and C. H. Kardell.[4] By employing quantities given in the foregoing study, it is possible to estimate, for instance, the proportions of fresh fruit consumed without further processing.

Table 27 states the percentages of allocation of manufactured commodities adopted. It would clearly be impracticable to explain separately each of the 150-odd allocations. The following notes refer only to a few instances in which special comment is called for.

Food. A blanket allocation to producers' goods of 5 % of all ready-for-consumption foods was made as an allowance for hotel and institutional purchases.

[3] This definition, it may be well to emphasize, cuts across output at a very different level from that which has been commonly used in estimating values of so-called "consumers' goods"; as, for example, in Snyder's index of consumers' goods ("Business Cycles and Business Measurements" by Carl Snyder, Macmillan, New York, 1927, pp. 88–91).

[4] United States Government Printing Office, 1930.

This may be too low in the light of trade estimates of 10 to 12%;[5] but as an over-all percentage, covering both manufactured and raw foods, it is probably not far wrong. It was necessary to make considerable changes for earlier years in the allocations of flour, sugar, and other unfinished food products, in order to take care of well-recognized alterations in living habits.[6] Allocations for ice, both manufactured and natural, are based upon King's estimates.[7]

Men's Clothing. This commodity might appear at first sight to belong entirely to consumers' goods; but a study of the component products reveals that allowances should be made for takings by the government and by other purchasers of uniforms, for duplications arising from the inclusion of contract work and for the value of "other products (not normally belonging to the industry)." The outcome in this case was an allocation of 85% of men's clothing to consumers' goods.

Textiles. The most puzzling question was how to allocate the output of piece goods. In 1924 the Bureau of Business Research of Harvard University esti-mated that cotton piece goods were apportioned as follows: 30% sold for industrial purposes; 26% used by cutters-up; 6% exported; 36% sold as piece goods by retailers; and 2% unclassified institutional sales.[8] Breyer states that consumers' demand for cotton fabrics expands when price recession occurs, and *vice versa*.[9] Having in view observed variations of this character, our final allo-cations of cotton goods for the period from 1909 to 1923 range from 35 to 30%; from 1923 to 1929 the percentage is scaled down to 20%; for 1931, it is raised to 25%. Allocations of woolen and worsted fabrics are approximated by deducting values of such fabrics used as raw materials by reporting factories, with allow-ances for additional uses by custom tailors and non-reporting plants.

Automobiles. From 6 to 8% of the registrations of passenger cars, according to R. L. Polk and Company, are in the names of business concerns. Doubtless, fully as many more cars are bought primarily for business use, though registered by individuals. In the absence of more exact information, we have assigned 15% of purchases of passenger automobiles to business; 85% to consumers' outgo.

Automobile Parts and Accessories. It proved especially difficult to ascertain the proportion purchased direct by consumers as distinguished from the propor-tion sold to automobile manufacturers. An approximation was arrived at by estimating from the Census of Distribution the total purchases at retail of auto-mobile accessories in 1929.

Gasoline and Oil. After determining the values of fully refined petroleum products, allowances were made (*a*) for purchases by large establishments and institutions (*b*) for purchases by farmers and (*c*) for purchases by salesmen and others who would normally charge such purchases to business expenses. The

[5] See "A Fact-Picture of the Food Fields" 1932, issued by *Food Industries.*

[6] Useful data for the years before 1923 were found in "The American Baking Industry" by Hazel Kyrk and Stancliff E. Davis, Stanford University, 1925.

[7] "The National Income and Its Purchasing Power," p. 374.

[8] "Distribution of Textiles," Bureau of Business Research, Harvard University, Bulletin 56, 1926, p. 9.

[9] "Commodity Marketing," by Ralph F. Breyer, McGraw-Hill, New York, 1931, pp. 240–243ff.

Department of Agriculture assigns half the cost of purchase and upkeep of an automobile by a farmer to his expenses of production.

Electrical Appliances.   The census classifications were found to be inadequate for our purpose.   The allocations were made largely on the basis of data supplied by Brookmire Special Reports and by estimates given in *Radio Retailing*, a trade publication.

Patent Medicines and Druggists' Preparations.   Important help in allocating these items was obtained from material cited in "The Costs of Medicines," issued by the Committee on the Cost of Medical Care.

Books, Newspapers and Periodicals.   Subscriptions to and sales of publications were estimated by deducting from the total value of products of the printing and publishing industry all sales of advertising and of commercial printing.

By good fortune two independent checks of our original allocations, leading to a number of revisions, were made possible through the courtesy of other investigators.   Allocations for a different purpose were made in 1931 by Dr. Edward R. Dewey, of the United States Bureau of Foreign and Domestic Commerce.   A comparison of Dewey's allocations with those adopted for this study brought to light considerable variations in the minor industries but a high degree of correspondence in the larger classifications.   The totals of the two estimates, after correcting for certain specific items, differed by less than 5%. The other comparison was with a series of closely parallel allocations prepared by the staff of the National Bureau of Economic Research from which valuable suggestions were derived.

The percentages of allocation referred to above and those listed in Table 27 were designed primarily to measure the division of output between producers' commodities and consumers' commodities in 1929 and 1931.   They have been applied with only a few slight adaptations, the most important of which have been mentioned, to the census returns for earlier years.   Naturally the farther they are carried back, the more doubtful they become.   We recognize, too, that considerable differences in the percentages for certain industries may develop in years of marked depression.   In most of the census classifications, however, the probable extent of such variations is very moderate. Large errors are not likely, therefore, in applying the percentages within the period here studied.

By applying the percentages of allocation shown in Table 27 to the census totals of values of output at point of production, we get the percentages of consumers' goods in the output of the census classes of manufactured commodities in 1929 shown in Table 28 on page 258. These percentages are not strictly germane to our main line of inquiry, but are reported as a finding of possible value for other purposes.

TABLE 27.—PERCENTAGES OF ALLOCATION AND SPREAD ON MANUFACTURED COMMODITIES

Industry	Allocated to Consumers	Allowed for Spread[1]
Foods:		
Beverages	95	40
Bread	95	20
Butter	90	30
Canned fish	95	25
Canned fruits	95	25
Cheese	90	30
Chewing gum	100	40
Chocolate and cocoa	70	25
Coffee and spice	95	25
Condensed milk	90	25
Confectionery and ice cream	95	40
Corn sirup	50	25
Flavoring extracts	80	25
Flour	30 (1929–1931) 35 (1925–1927) 40 (1919–1923) 50 (1909–1914)	25
Food preparations	40 (1929–1931) 45 (1909–1927)	25
Ice	50	[2]
Meat packing, sausage, poultry killing	85	25
Oleomargarine	90	25
Peanuts	80	40
Rice	90	25
Sugar	65	25
Vinegar	80	25
Textiles:		
Asphalted floor coverings	90	40 (35)
Awnings	20	40 (35)
Carpets	90	40 (35)
Clothing, men's	85	35
Clothing, women's	90	35
Collars, men's	100	35
Corsets	100	35
Cotton goods	20–35[3]	35
Cotton small wares	30	35
Flags and banners	65	40
Furnishings, men's	100	35
Gloves	90	35
Hats, not felt or straw	90	40 (35)

TABLE 27.—PERCENTAGES OF ALLOCATION AND SPREAD ON MANUFACTURED
COMMODITIES.—(*Continued*)

Industry	Allocated to Consumers	Allowed for Spread[1]
Textiles (*Continued*)		
Hats, fur-felt............................	75	40 (35)
Hats, wool-felt..........................	75	40 (35)
Horse blankets..........................	50 (1919–1931)	40
	75 (1909–1914)	
House furnishings.......................	100	35
Knit goods..............................	90	35
Linen goods.............................	80	35
Linoleum...............................	90	40 (35)
Mats and mattings......................	100	40 (35)
Millinery and lace goods.................	87	45
Oilcloth................................	100	40 (35)
Shirts..................................	90	35
Silk manufactures.......................	30	35
Suspenders.............................	95	35
Woolen goods⎰ Worsted " ⎱	5	35
Forest Products:		
Baskets................................	10	30
Billiard tables..........................	20	50
Caskets................................	100	50
Cork products..........................	20	30
Furniture..............................	70	40 (35)
Matches...............................	100	30
Mirror frames..........................	90	40
Refrigerators, non-mechanical............	50	40
Window screens.........................	40	40
Wooden goods..........................	25	40
Paper and Paper Products:		
Envelopes..............................	25	30
Paper..................................	15	30
Paper goods............................	50	35
Printing:		
Books and pamphlets....................	100	35
Subscriptions and sales of periodicals.....	100	35
Chemicals:		
Ammunition............................	50	40
Baking powder.........................	30–50[4]	25
Blacking...............................	70	25
Bluing.................................	75	25

Table 27.—Percentages of Allocation and Spread on Manufactured
Commodities.—(*Continued*)

Industry	Allocated to Consumers	Allowed for Spread[1]
Chemicals (*Continued*)		
Candles............................	30	25
Cleaning preparations................	60	40
Druggists' preparations..............	80	40
Fireworks...........................	75	40
Glue and gelatin.....................	20	40
Ink, writing.........................	90	40
Liquors, vinous[5]....................	60	40
Mucilage...........................	20	40
Patent medicines.....................	85	40
Perfumes, cosmetics..................	100	40
Salt................................	50	25
Soap...............................	70	30
Petroleum and Coal:		
Coke...............................	10	25
Fuel, manufactured...................	10	25
Lubricants..........................	50	25
Petroleum refining...................	50	25
Rubber Products:		
Boots and shoes......................	100	35
Rubber goods........................	25	40
Rubber tires.........................	60	25
Leather:		
Gloves..............................	90	35
Shoes...............................	100	35
Leather goods.......................	50	35
Pocketbooks.........................	100	35
Saddlery and harness.................	25 (1919–1931) 70 (1909–1914)	35
Trunks and suitcases.................	75	35
Stone, Clay, Glass:		
China-firing.........................	100	45 (40)
Glass...............................	25	45 (40)
Glass cutting........................	65	45 (40)
Mirrors.............................	50	45 (40)
Pottery and porcelain.................	35	45 (40)
Statuary and art goods................	10	40
Iron and Steel:		
Cutlery.............................	90	40
Firearms............................	50	40
Stoves..............................	70	40
Tinware.............................	5	40

TABLE 27.—PERCENTAGES OF ALLOCATION AND SPREAD ON MANUFACTURED COMMODITIES.—(*Continued*)

Industry	Allocated to Consumers	Allowed for Spread[1]
Non-Ferrous:		
Aluminum	20	45
Clocks	60	45 (40)
Fire extinguishers	25	35
Gas and electric fixtures	25	35
Jewelry	80	45 (40)
Needles	30	40
Plated ware	80	45 (40)
Silversmithing	100	45 (40)
Stamped ware	25	35
Watches	90	45 (40)
Machinery:		
Electrical machinery, radios and parts removed	15	40
Refrigerators, mechanical	80	45
Sewing machines	75	40
Typewriters	10	45
Washing machines	100	45
Transportation:		
Aircraft	10	35
Carriages, children's	100	35
Carriages, wagons	25 (1919–1931) 70 (1909–1914)	35
Motor vehicle parts	30 (1919–1931) 10 (1909–1914)	45
Motorcycles	75	35
Passenger automobiles	85	25
Ship and boat	10	35
Miscellaneous:		
Artists' materials	75	35
Brooms	80	40
Brushes	70	40 (35)
Buttons	20	40
Cigars and cigarettes	100	15–40[6]
Combs and hairpins	80	40
Fancy and miscellaneous	80	40
Fur goods	60	45
Hair work	75	40
Hats, straw	100	40
Mattresses	60	40
Musical instruments	75	55 (45)

TABLE 27.—PERCENTAGES OF ALLOCATION AND SPREAD ON MANUFACTURED COMMODITIES.—(*Continued*)

Industry	Allocated to Consumers	Allowed for Spread[1]
Miscellaneous (*Continued*)		
Optical goods	75	40
Pencils, lead	100	40
Pens, points	95	40
Phonographs	80	55
Photo apparatus	30	40
Pianos	90	55 (45)
Pipes, tobacco	100	20
Sporting goods	90	40
Stationery	25	40
Surgical appliances	50	40
Tobacco	100	25
Toys	85	40
Umbrellas	80	40
Whips	25 (1919–1931) 70 (1909–1914)	35
Window shades	50	40

[1] Percentages of retail values; figures in parentheses indicate change in spread during pre-war years.
[2] Spread included in values reported in Census of Manufactures.
[3] See text.
[4] Same as Flour.
[5] Post-war years only.
[6] Spread on cigarettes, 15%; cigars, 40%.

ADDITION OF "SPREADS" TO OBTAIN RETAIL VALUES

So far, we have only the values at point of production of those commodities which are the direct objects of consumers' expenditures. It is now necessary to add to each class of commodities the estimated "spread" between producers' values and values at retail. The term "spread" includes (*a*) the mark-ups of retailers and of wholesalers, (*b*) assembling and transportation charges from producer to retailer and (*c*) customs duties on imported commodities.

A large amount of data bearing on retailers' mark-ups has appeared in recent years. Operating expenses and profits of various types of retail stores have been reported by the Harvard Bureau of Business Research and several other universities, by the National Cash Register Company, and by the United States Chamber of Commerce. A smaller number of studies of wholesalers' operating expenses and profits have appeared. The Census of Distribution covers operating expenses of both retailers and wholesalers. Of particular value for the immediate purpose is the annual compilation of mark-ups and expenses in all reporting department stores issued by the Controllers' Congress of the National Retail Dry Goods Association. From these varied sources it is now possible to determine the average combined wholesaling-retailing mark-up for most classes of commodities sold to consumers. It is true that the percentages pertain, as a rule, to stores or to departments, not to commodities; but it is reasonable to assume

TABLE 28.—ALLOCATIONS OF CENSUS CLASSES OF MANUFACTURES IN 1929
(In billions of dollars)

Products	Total Values	Producers' Commodities		Consumers' Commodities	
		$	%	$	%
Foods...................	12.0	2.7	22.5	9.3	77.5
Leather.................	1.9	0.7	36.8	1.2	63.2
Miscellaneous............	3.4	1.3	38.2	2.1	61.8
Textiles.................	9.2	4.1	44.6	5.1	55.4
Transportation Equipment.	6.0	3.2	53.3	2.8	46.7
Rubber.................	1.1	0.6	54.5	0.5	45.5
Petroleum and Coal.......	3.7	2.5	67.6	1.2	32.4
Forest..................	3.6	2.7	75.0	0.9	25.0
Chemicals...............	3.8	2.9	76.3	0.9	23.7
Printing and Publishing....	3.2	2.5	78.1	0.7	21.9
Paper..................	1.9	1.6	84.2	0.3	15.8
Stone, Clay, Glass.........	1.6	1.4	87.5	0.2	12.5
Non-Ferrous Metals.......	3.6	3.2	88.9	0.4	11.1
Machinery...............	7.0	6.3	90.0	0.7	10.0
Iron and Steel...........	7.1	6.8	95.8	0.3	4.2
Railroad Repair Shops.....	1.3	1.3	100.0	....	....
Total.................	70.4	43.8	62.2	26.6	37.8

that the prevailing mark-up in the channel of distribution through which the bulk of a given commodity passes is applicable to that commodity. Minor exceptions and adjustments, based on personal knowledge or inquiries, have been made here and there.

Transportation charges on the main classes of consumers' commodities have been derived from Statement No. 3242, issued in March, 1932 by the Interstate Commerce Commission, which presents estimates for the year 1930 of percentages of freight revenue to values at destination. Customs duties have been taken into account only for the few commodities of which a large proportion is imported.

The census classifications and the classifications of commodities in the various other sources of data to which reference has been made unfortunately do not correspond closely. In the end, it is necessary to utilize percentages of operating expenses, mark-ups and transportation costs as guides rather than to rely on rule-of-thumb methods. For that reason, the percentages of spread on manufactured commodities finally adopted, as listed in Table 27, are stated in round figures.[10]

PAYMENTS BY CONSUMERS FOR DISTRIBUTION

The spreads between producers' values and retail values are added to producers' values and constitute in effect the payments made by consumers at the time of purchase for the distributive services of transportation agencies and of middlemen. They are, in other words, *consumers'* costs of distribution. The findings on this subject are summarized in Chapter II (Table 6). It seems advisable to add here, however, some further explanatory comments.

A clear distinction should be drawn between consumers' costs of distribution and middlemen's costs. Consumers' costs consist mainly of wholesalers' and retailers' mark-ups. Middlemen's costs consist of wages, rent, delivery expense and the like, the total of which middlemen naturally try to keep within their mark-ups in an effort to gain some profits for themselves. The percentages of expenses to sales among middlemen, even among those in the same line of trade operating under closely similar conditions, vary over a wide range. Some of

---

[10] It is of some interest to compare the spreads in the United States listed in Table 27 with *retail* margins in Great Britain, as given in an article on "Retail Profits" by W. R. Dunlop in the *Economic Journal*, Sept., 1929, pp. 357–370. "Generally speaking," says Dunlop, "fairly constant averages exist which enable us to group commodities under their respective margins." Following is Dunlop's list of standard English retail margins (based on selling prices):

Over 33⅓%	33⅓%	25%
Fashion goods (ladies' shoes, expensive millinery, etc.)	Jewellery	Fish
	Furniture	Fruit and vegetables
	Shoes	Margarine
Expensive flowers and fruits	Underwear	Jam
	Drugs	Metal polish
Ironmongers' scales	Toilet soaps	Underwear
	Chocolates	Shoes
	Newspapers	Wines and spirits

20%	14–18%	Under 14%
Meat	Cheese	Eggs
Marmalade	Flour	Butter
Laundry soap	Tea	Bacon (English)
Biscuits	Lard	Cheese (imported)
Cigarettes	Laundry soap	Meat essense
	Bacon (imported)	Condensed milk
		Sugar

them make money; some lose. Moreover, the percentages fluctuate considerably from year to year. But these variations have no direct effect on consumers. *Their* costs are determined primarily by remarkably stable, standard mark-ups or margins, established by trade custom for all important classes of commodities.

To be sure, constant minor disturbances, such as bargain sales and the use of advertised articles as "loss-leaders," influence average mark-ups. But most of these disturbances recur year after year with a close approach to regularity. They are taken into account, for example, in the compilation of the Controllers' Congress above mentioned; and an examination of the resultant actual mark-ups over a period of years shows only slight or quite exceptional variations. Even in the period of stress from 1929 to 1932 over-all gross margins of the distributive trades declined very little—in retail trade from 28.5% in 1929 to 27.8% in 1932 and in wholesale trade from 13.8% in 1929 to 12.7% in 1932.[11] (In passing, it should be explained that the percentages last given apply to *wholesale values* of the 50 to 55%[12] of consumers' commodities which pass through wholesalers' hands and are equivalent to an over-all burden of less than 6% on total retail values.)

It is doubtless true, also, that in the long run the spreads paid by consumers tend to conform to middlemen's costs of doing business plus a small average profit. But the adjustments are normally slow and moderate. During the entire 23-year period here studied the few adjustments we have been able to locate (indicated by figures in parentheses in the right-hand column of Table 27) are for the most part minor.

This explanation is called for because an incredible amount of misstatement and confused thinking about costs of distribution has been placed in circulation. It has been frequently asserted that consumers' costs of distribution were much higher in the post-war than in the pre-war period. The assertion appears to have no substantial foundation.

The best sources of information for the pre-war years are studies made by the Joint Commission of Agricultural Inquiry, the Factory Investigating Board, the Bureau of Labor and the Federal Trade Commission. Some further information has been obtained from "Keeping Up with Rising Costs" by Wheeler Sammons[13] and from a pamphlet

---

[11] Estimates of the Cost Analysis Division of the United States Bureau of Foreign and Domestic Commerce cited in "National Income, 1929-32," Government Printing Office, 1934, p. 110.

[12] These percentages are derived from rough estimates in the writer's paper, "Are Marketing Costs Rising?" in the Report of the Boston Conference on Retail Distribution, 1932, Retail Trade Board, Boston Chamber of Commerce.

[13] A. W. Shaw Co., New York, 1915.

on "Distribution" by William H. Ingersoll published by the American Fair Trade League.   From the printed data, supplemented by information given orally by Mr. Ingersoll, it has become evident that some slight increases actually occurred in post-war mark-ups in the apparel, piece-goods, furniture, chinaware and jewelry groups; all such changes are indicated by figures in parentheses in Table 27.   These increases are insufficient, however, to offset fully the downward tendency of distributive costs paid by consumers.[14]

High spreads, as a rule, are applicable to unmanufactured foods and fuels; for example, 50% on fresh vegetables and fresh fish, 45 to 55% on milk in bulk, 55% on fruits and nuts, 55 to 65% on milk in bottles, 65 to 75% on coal.   The spreads on these commodities must cover heavy costs of assembling, in the case of foods, and of transportation, in the case of fuels.   Indeed, they might logically be regarded as belonging to the costs of production rather than to the costs of distribution.   Corresponding costs are covered, to a large extent at least, in the producers' values of manufactured commodities.   Such factors as perishability, bulk and high instability of prices also enter into the spreads applied to unmanufactured foods.

ITEMS FROM OTHER SOURCES

Three important items are now to be added in order to make our estimates complete—or practically so: (a) illegal commodities (b) home-grown commodities and (c) commodities manufactured on retail premises.

As was stated in Chapter I, payments for illegal *services* rendered by one individual to another do not appear in national income estimates as now computed; and they have been omitted also in our estimates of spendings.   But payments for illegal *commodities* do find their way promptly into business accounts and governmental statistics.   During the prohibition era such payments were large.   We cannot properly ignore them.

Prior to the adoption of the Eighteenth Amendment, alcoholic beverages were of course distributed through legal channels, and their retail values for pre-war years were computed in the same manner as other retail values.   The commonly cited estimates of *American Grocer* for pre-war expenditures for alcoholic beverages, which were formed by adding the proper spreads to value at factory and checked by applying the prevalent prices of alcoholic beverages to total physical quantities, have been used for 1909 and 1914.   Warburton's estimates

[14] For a further examination of this question, see the writer's paper above referred to.

of the annual liquor bill prior to prohibition correspond closely to the *American Grocer* figures.[15]

Warburton presents also a thorough analysis of products used in production of liquor since prohibition. The data form the basis for the post-war liquor expenditures in Appendix A. Since the estimates are designed to cover only payments for commodities, they naturally fall below even the minima of estimated total expenditures for alcoholic beverages given by Warburton, Wheeler, Fisher, Feldman, Gebhart and others. Allowance has been made for the fact that prohibition prevailed only during the latter half of 1919.

Our estimates for value of home-grown, home-consumed foods and fuels are determined by deducting cash income of all crops as estimated by the Department of Agriculture from gross income, which includes cash income plus the value of products consumed in the farm household. For the pre-war period, for which the Department of Agriculture presents no estimates, data given in "Income in the United States" are used. It should be observed that values of farm-grown commodities consumed by farmers are stated as values *at the farm* whereas other estimates in the master table (Appendix A) are values at retail.

The Census of Distribution has revealed a considerable amount of merchandise which is manufactured by retailers on their own premises and is not covered by the Census of Manufactures. The total amount in 1929 was about $300,000,000. After making what appear to be suitable deductions for construction materials and other producers' goods, some $225,000,000 has been allowed for the retail values of retailers' manufactures; and the figures for other years than 1929 have been proportionately adjusted.

ADJUSTMENTS FOR INVENTORY CHANGES

By applying the spreads listed in Table 27 to producers' values (corrected for exports and imports) and adding values of commodities manufactured on retail premises, we get the retail values of the commodities produced in a given year. But output figures at retail values are not necessarily equivalent to retail sales in the same year. The difference arises from the accumulation or depletion of inventories in the hands of manufacturers, wholesalers, and retailers. In normal years the difference is probably slight, since stocks of ready-to-consume commodities are ordinarily kept in well-defined ratios to current sales. In years of rapid price changes, however, inventories do not follow sales so closely.

The only usable guide we have found for making the required adjustment between retail values at point of production and retail sales during

[15] "The Economic Results of Prohibition" by Clark Warburton, Columbia University Press, 1932.

the same period is the index of department store stocks reported in the *Survey of Current Business*. A rough check has been made of our results against the inventories of trading corporations published for recent years in *Statistics of Income*, and no noteworthy inconsistency has been discovered. The inventory figures in themselves, however, do not give a great deal of help, because (*a*) they include many corporations engaged in handling producers' goods and (*b*) they do not include unincorporated trading enterprises. That the department store index is representative of all retailers is of course a pure assumption, but it is unavoidable in the absence of better data. Inventory changes in stocks of *finished* consumers' goods held by manufacturers and wholesalers are not provided for but are quite unlikely to be large items.

Marked changes in the department store index, comparing only the end-of-year figures, occurred in 1919, 1921, 1923, and 1931. In the remaining years adjustments on this account do not appear to be called for. Corrections for the four years named were made by applying percentages of increase or decrease in the index figures to total stocks of consumers' commodities on hand at the beginning and at the end of each year; the stocks were estimated by assuming an average turnover of five times per annum. To illustrate: In 1923, department store stocks increased about 11%; total values at retail of consumers' commodities produced in that year came to about $38,600,000,000; if the average turnover was five times during the year, trade stocks were about $6,900,000,000 at the beginning and $7,700,000,000 at the end; hence, retail sales in that year were approximately $800,000,000 less than retail values produced. This amount was then pro-rated among the classes of commodities likely to be affected. A like procedure was followed in the other three years. The calculations are set forth in Table 29.

It is freely granted that this is rough figuring. If anyone can offer a more accurate method, we shall be happy to adopt it. Fortunately, inventory adjustments are not required in the majority of the years studied.

Comparisons with Independent Estimates

As remarked in the text, the Census of Distribution covering the year 1929 has made it possible for the first time to check computations of retail sales against census records. In order to reduce the totals to a comparable basis, however, it is necessary to make a considerable number of adjustments. The census total of retail sales includes, to take some outstanding examples, sales financed in part by trade-ins of cars and other commodities, an item omitted from our estimates for reasons already stated; also, items which are better classified as intangible services, such as automobile repair services, charges for

TABLE 29.—ANALYSIS OF CORRECTIONS FOR CHANGES IN INVENTORIES[1]

(In millions of current dollars)

Derivation and Distribution	1919	1921	1923	1931
Total Retail Values of Commodities (Less Extra-Commercial and Alcoholic Beverages).....	37,556	31,057	38,568	30,134
Less[2] Food.....	16,183	12,355	14,312	12,178
Tobacco.....	1,418	1,471	1,465	1,392
Coal, Wood, Ice.....	1,251	1,525	1,818	1,077
	18,852	15,351	17,595	14,647
Total Values to Be Corrected.....	18,704	15,706	20,973	15,487
Amount of Correction for Increases (−) or Decreases (+) of Retailers' Inventories[3].....	−2,500	+600	−800	+700
Amount of Correction Stated as Percentage of Total Values to Be Corrected.....	13.4	3.8	3.8	4.5
Distribution of Corrections for Inventories among Classes of Commodities:[4]				
Clothing.....	−1,180	+280	−350	+290
Transportation (Cars, Tires, etc.).....	−450	+100	−170	+140
Home Maintenance (Furnishings, Supplies, etc.).....	−515	+120	−170	+145
Sickness and Death (Medicines, etc.).....	−90	+20	−25	+30
Personal Appearance (Cosmetic, etc.).....	−90	+25	−30	+25
Recreation (Sporting Goods, etc.).....	−50	+10	−15	+15
Social-Cultural Activities (Reading Matter, etc.).....	−125	+45	−40	+55

[1] Corrections have been applied only to those years shown below in which the index of Department Store Stocks shows considerable changes.

[2] These commodities move rapidly into consumption. Annual changes in stocks of finished goods can scarcely be large. The corrections are concentrated, therefore, on other classes of commodities.

[3] See text for method of derivation.

[4] The total correction was applied to commodity sales by groups as given in Appendix A. Thus, retail values of clothing produced in 1919 would be $8,889,000,000 without correction for stock changes. Applying the percentage of correction (13.4%), the amount deducted for additions of clothing to stocks is $1,180,000,000.

TABLE 30.—DERIVATION OF RETAIL PURCHASES BY CONSUMERS FROM CENSUS
OF DISTRIBUTION

(In millions of dollars)

Total Transactions through Retail Channels Reported in Census		$49,115
Additions:		
Retail sales by wholesalers..............................	$ 690	
Additional milk sales....................................	130	
Direct sales by manufacturing bakeries...................	414	
Direct sales by manufacturing dairies....................	105	
Direct sales by planing mills............................	352	
Direct sales by power laundries..........................	421	
Direct sales by cleaning and dyeing establishments..........	157	
Direct sales of newspapers and periodicals................	460	
All other direct sales by manufacturers...................	517	
Sales of meals in hotel dining rooms......................	358	
Other *estimated* additions..............................	3,500	
Sales of farm products direct from farms to consumers and sales by hucksters and peddlers having no established place of business (1,500); direct retail sales by other manufacturers than those named above (500); sales of retailers who went out of business at any time between Jan. 1, 1929 and the date of census-taking or who operated seasonally and therefore were not reported in the Census (1,500).		
Total Known and Estimated Additions...................		7,104
Total of All Retail Sales................................		56,219
Deductions:		
Sales by retailers to other retailers.......................	707	
Receipts from auto repair and storage (service).............	909	
Receipts from other repair and storage (service)...........	365	
Second-hand store sales.................................	148	
Country buying and assembling..........................	450	
Hotel meals (service)...................................	358	
Sales of laundries and cleaners (service)...................	578	
Trade-ins..	1,500	
Direct sales of manufacturers of *producers'* goods (e.g. sales by planing mills).......................................	352	
Retail sales of commodities plainly classifiable as producers' goods (construction material, farm equipment, office supplies, etc.)..	4,869	
Retail sales to producers of commodities usually classified as consumers' goods (automobiles, household hardware and paints, gasoline, etc.).................................	1,361	
Total Known and Estimated Deductions.................		11,597
Retail Purchases of New Commodities by Consumers.........		44,622

storage of goods, laundry services, sales in hotel dining rooms and so on. On the other hand, the census total omits certain large items, notably (a) sales of food products through other channels than reporting retailers, (b) direct retail sales of some classes of manufactured goods and (c) sales in 1929 by retailers who were out of business by the time the Census was taken. The necessary adjustments are listed in Table 30; for the sake of clarity, some of the items are shown both as additions and as deductions.[16]

The adjusted total supplied by the Census of Distribution is approximately $44,600,000,000; our corresponding estimate is $45,200,000,000 (total commodity sales, $49,200,000,000 *less* alcoholic beverages, $2,000,-000,000, and extra-commercial items, $2,000,000,000). The discrepancy is less than 1.5%. Granting that some of the adjustments of the census figures are very loose estimates, nevertheless it seems probable that the actual discrepancy if it could be accurately determined would not exceed 5%. The total of our estimates of retail sales of commodities to consumers in 1929 appears to be in sufficiently close agreement with the census total to establish the general reasonableness of the percentages of allocation and of spread used in making our estimates. On the strength of this conclusion, we have felt justified in applying the same percentages, with such modifications as have been described, to producers' values in other years.

This is not to say that every percentage is indubitably correct. Conceivably, two or more gross errors may have cancelled each other. However, a number of independent estimates of the retail sales of specific classes of commodities have been compared with our estimates, and no large, irreconcilable disagreements have as yet come to light. The Census of Distribution provides through its so-called "commodity breakdowns" a certain amount of information as to national sales of classes of commodities. Other well-founded estimates for selected commodities are supplied by trade journals, by the publications of the Committee on Costs of Medical Care and by Lynd's contribution to "Recent Social Trends."[17]

[16] For a further explanation of the adjustments see the writer's paper on "Consumers' Retail Purchases, Pre-War and Post-War," *Bulletin of the Taylor Society*, Dec., 1931.

[17] Chapter XVII, "The People as Consumers," by Robert S. Lynd, with the assistance of Alice C. Hanson, in "Recent Social Trends," vol. II, McGraw-Hill, New York, 1933.

APPENDIX C

ESTIMATES OF SPENDINGS FOR INTANGIBLES

AS LISTED IN APPENDIX A

When we come to estimating individuals' spendings for intangibles, we find the figures more elusive than those for commodities. The greatest difficulty lies in determining what proportions of the various items are properly chargeable to consumers. Many of the answers, as will be indicated below, are merely more or less informed guesses. However, the best that can be done at present is to use guesswork tentatively and trust that item by item better data will in time become available.

Inasmuch as the explanatory comments below relate primarily to the sources of information used in our estimates for separate items, the comments will follow in a general way the order in which spendings for intangibles are listed in Appendix A. These items are regrouped in Table 8 of Chapter II under another classification which does not require further discussion here.

TOTAL PAYMENTS FOR PERSONAL SERVICES

Of the 71 items of intangible spendings in Appendix A, 30 items consist of personal services rendered by professional people, by commercial employees and by domestic servants. Although these 30 items are scattered under several main headings, it will be convenient to discuss them here together; for they are all derived from a common source, the Census of Occupations.

Since the census classifications have varied somewhat during the period studied, a few regroupings have been necessary in order to obtain comparable figures. A more serious difficulty was to gauge the number in each occupation in the inter-censal years. For the post-war years, the estimates of occupational shifts by Wolman in "Recent Economic Changes"[1] and by Hurlin and Givens in "Recent Social Trends"[2] were found helpful. For the pre-war years rates of increase from 1900 to 1910 were carried forward to 1914, thereby avoiding the war-time distortions which creep into interpolations of the 1910 and 1920 census returns. Corrections were made for exceptional

[1] Vol. II, pp. 472–473.
[2] Vol. I, p. 268ff.

267

TABLE 31.—DERIVATION OF PAYMENTS BY INDIVIDUALS FOR PERSONAL SERVICES
IN 1929

Occupations	Number Engaged (in thousands)	Average Annual Gross Earnings	Total Payments for Services (in millions of dollars)	Percentage Paid Directly by Individuals	Total Paid by Individuals (in millions of dollars)
GRAND TOTALS.............	5,594.9	$1,675	$9,366	57	$5,365
PROFESSIONAL SERVICES.....	1,179.1	$3,240	$3,817	58	$2,195
Artists, sculptors, teachers of art..	57.0	$2,000	$ 114	50	$ 57
Dentists......................	69.7	7,500	523	80	418
Lawyers, judges and justices......	156.7	4,500[1]	705	20	141
Musicians and music teachers.....	161.8	1,800	291	25	73
Photographers.................	38.8	2,000	78	65	51
Physicians and surgeons.........	153.1	8,500	1,302	80	1,041
Nurses.......................	432.0	1,250	540	40	216
Secondary practitioners; optometrists, osteopaths, chiropractors, midwives, healers, etc.........	110.0	2,400	264	75	198
DOMESTIC AND PERSONAL SERVICES................	2,992.3	$1,035	$3,090	82	$2,529
Barbers, hairdressers and manicurists......................	358.4	$1,800	$ 645	100	$ 645
Bootblacks....................	22.4	1,100	25	100	25
Housekeepers.................	253.5	1,000	254	75	190
Laborers, domestic and personal service......................	68.0	1,000	68	65	44
Launderers, laundresses (not in laundries)...................	364.0	1,000	364	90	325
Servants and cooks (not in hotels).	1,926.0	900	1,734	75	1,300
HAND TRADES................	500.0	$1,565	$ 782	52	$ 404
Dressmakers and seamstresses (not in factory)..............	166.0	$1,000	$ 166	75	$ 124
Jewelers......................	38.7	2,300	89	50	45
Milliners and millinery dealers....	48.1	1,700	82	25	21
Shoemakers and cobblers (not in factory)...................	76.3	1,800	137	100	137
Tailors and tailoresses...........	170.9	1,800	308	25	77
ALL OTHER SERVICES........	923.5	$1,815	$1,677	14	$ 237
Chauffeurs....................	890.0	$1,800	$1,600	10	$ 160
Undertakers (service only).......	33.5	2,300	77	100	77

[1] Net rather than gross earnings of lawyers were used in the belief that most of their office and other expenses are incurred for and paid by business clients.

unemployment in 1921 and 1931, using standard indexes of employment and other data.[3]

[3] See especially the National Industrial Conference Board *Bulletin*, Sept. 20, 1931, on "Economic Activities of the Population."

Having determined the number in each occupation for each of the years studied, the next step was to arrive at average gross earnings of the persons engaged in each occupation; their *gross* earnings, not *net*, are the same as the total payments to them for their services.[4] In estimating payments to professional people in 1921 and 1931 a 10% deduction was assumed to represent the decreased demand for their services. It would be impracticable to present in detail the evidence supporting each rate of average gross earnings (as shown for 1929 in Table 31) and the year-by-year adjustments. Suffice it to say that the data may be considered fairly adequate.

ALLOCATIONS OF PAYMENTS FOR SERVICES RENDERED TO CONSUMERS

The problem of allocating to consumers correct percentages of total payments for services can be handled only by drawing rough deductions from a variety of facts and observations and checking the results so far as possible with other estimates. The new industrial classifications in the Census of Occupations of 1930 have proved illuminating in certain cases. Following are instances requiring special comment.

The number of physicians and surgeons in 1929 was placed at 153,000 and their average gross earnings in that year at $8,500. The total payments to them, therefore, were $1,300,000,000. If we assume that 80% of the payments were made directly by individuals, which seems reasonable, we reach an estimate of $1,040,000,000; and this is the corresponding estimate of the Committee on Costs of Medical Care. The same percentage has been applied in other years. A similar allocation was made for payments to dentists.

Payments to lawyers in 1929 aggregated about $700,000,000. By far the greater part undoubtedly came from business. Yet the number of divorces in that year was 200,000. Taking them into account, as well as various other occasions when individuals seek legal advice, it would seem that an allocation of 20% to consumers' outgo cannot be far wrong.

Through the industrial classifications introduced in the Census of Occupations in 1930, the number of chauffeurs engaged in domestic service is shown to be about 90,000, or somewhat over 10% of the total number of chauffeurs listed under the occupational heading. Because of differences in the classification in preceding censuses, it was impracticable to carry back this percentage. With the 1929 figure as a base, the number for earlier years was adjusted to changes in the registration of high-priced cars.

[4] The chief sources of information were: publications of the Committee on Costs of Medical Care; extracts from an unpublished manuscript on "Life Earnings of Vocations" by Dr. H. F. Clark, Columbia University; Douglas' "Real Wages in the United States"; the 1917 and 1918 reports of *Statistics of Income;* Chap. XVI of the Federal Trade Commission report in 1926 on "National Wealth and Income"; indexes of earnings issued from time to time by the National Industrial Conference Board; and, particularly for the pre-war period, King's "Income in the United States."

Again, the industrial classification of the 1930 Census gives for the first time the division between servants employed in households and those employed as elevator tenders, janitors and sextons, guards, watchmen and charwomen in hotels, institutions, factories, etc. The latter receive their compensation directly from business enterprises and are therefore not included in our service bill. The breakdown in the 1930 Census was utilized as a guide in the allocations for earlier years.

Comparable estimates covering incomes of domestic servants of specified types (equivalent to our estimates of payments by individuals to these servants) have recently been issued by the United States Department of Commerce.[5] These estimates total: for 1929, $2,219,000,000 against our $2,019,000,000; for 1931, $1,396,000,000 against our $1,464,000,000. The discrepancies are surprisingly small, considering the considerable element of judgment in both sets of figures. Other estimates from the same source are not directly comparable with ours but appear to be consistent.

The numbers of dressmakers, jewelers, milliners, shoemakers and tailors, taken directly from the census industrial classification headed Independent Hand Trades, are used in determining percentages of total compensation paid directly by consumers. Thus, of total jewelers under the occupational listing, about 40,000, only 27,000 are shown to be included properly under the hand trades. The percentages paid by individuals given in Table 31 exclude services of those receiving payment from producers and those services which are incidental to retailing; both excluded factors have already been accounted for under commodities.

In some instances the allocations for services could be combined with associated commodities and checked against independent estimates of inclusive outlays for services and supplies. Thus, the services of undertakers plus funeral supplies are not far from Gebhart's figure for total funeral expenditures.[6] Shoemakers' services combined with shoe supplies at retail are in line with estimates for shoe repairing cited in Crain's *Market Data Book*. Payments to barbers, manicurists and hairdressers combined with spendings for perfumes and cosmetics agree fairly well with Crain's corresponding over-all figures.

In many occupations an overwhelming proportion of the service is rendered to consumers; or, if not, the problem of allocation is analogous to one of those discussed above. Table 31, showing how these payments were computed for 1929, will be found clear, we think, without further explanation. Similar tables have been constructed for other years.

Related items are payments to retail establishments for repair and storage services. For the year 1929 the amounts shown in Appendix A are taken from the Census of Distribution. Corresponding expenditures in other years within the clothing and home maintenance groups are calculated by applying the 1929 ratios of repair and storage to the total sales of commodities in those groups. Repair, storage and

[5] "National Income, 1929–32," U. S. Government Printing Office, Washington, 1934, Table 194, p. 151.

[6] "Funeral Costs" by John C. Gebhart, Putnam, New York, 1928.

servicing charges for automobiles, however, have been adjusted to year-by-year changes in passenger car registrations.

INTANGIBLE ITEMS IN TRANSPORTATION

Under the main head Transportation in Appendix A will be found a number of intangibles which require brief explanations.

Street Railway Fares. Total passenger revenue of all electric railways is taken as a basis; revenue from motor buses operated by electric railways is deducted and appears under Bus Fares; the best judgment we can form is that 20% of the remainder may properly be allocated to business expenses, leaving 80% charged to expenditures of individual consumers.

Bus Fares. Estimates of gross passenger revenue are from "Bus Facts," a publication of the National Association of Motor Bus Operators. Ninety per cent of the revenue from city service and 75% of inter-city revenue are allocated to consumer spendings.

Taxicab and Hack Fares. In the year 1929, according to records of city registrations collected by the National Automobile Chamber of Commerce, some 70,000 taxis were in operation. If we allow an average gross revenue of $5,000 to $6,000, a trade estimate, their aggregate receipts would approximate $400,000,000. Other estimates run as high as $700,000,000 to $800,000,000. Assuming that one-half the minimum is allocable to consumers' expenditures, we arrive at the $200,000,000 shown in Appendix A. The amounts of this item in other years have no better basis than a judgment that they bear a reasonable relation to the 1929 figure.

Ferries, Inland Water Travel. Estimates based on data presented in *Census of Water Transportation* by the Bureau of the Census, 1926.

Insurance on Automobiles. Over-all figures have been taken from the *Insurance Yearbook*. The percentages assigned to payments by consumers, based in part on our allocations of purchases of passenger cars explained in Appendix B, range from 70% in 1919 to 60% in 1929 and 1931. The allocations allow for greater coverage of buses, taxis and trucks in recent years.

Motor Vehicle Taxes. Under this head are included registration fees, permits, fines, etc. The totals are taken from annual editions of the *Statistical Abstract*. The percentages of allocation are determined as in the case of insurance. The *Statistical Abstract* for 1923, p. 381, indicates that about 80% of the total was paid for private passenger cars, but this doubtless includes some cars used primarily for business purposes.

Gasoline Taxes. Unlike most other taxes on commodities, which may be presumed to be included in producers' values, the gasoline tax must be calculated separately. Basic data have been taken from annual editions of *Statistical Abstract* and from the article on gasoline tax in the "Encyclopedia of the Social Sciences." Following the allocation of spendings for gasoline, as shown in Appendix B, 60% of the total is treated as having been directly paid by consumers.

HOUSEHOLD SERVICES RENDERED BY BUSINESS ENTERPRISES

The next important group of intangible items will be found near the end of the section headed Home Maintenance in Appendix A. The estimates for the various personal services have been reviewed above. A somewhat miscellaneous assortment of other items may be classed as household services.

Electric Current. Our estimates of household consumption are derived in large part from a useful article entitled "Basic Facts Regarding the Utilities" in *The Annalist,* Apr. 22, 1932. Supplemental data are given in *Commerce Yearbook.*

Gas, Manufactured and Natural. Estimates of household consumption for 1909, 1914, 1919, 1924, 1929 and 1931 were obtained through the courtesy of the American Gas Association. The figures for the intervening years are straight-line interpolations.

Telephones. Total operating revenues of telephone companies, as reported to the Interstate Commerce Commission, have been allocated one-half to business expenses and one-half to consumer expenditures. This division has been approved as plausible by men in the industry and is to some extent confirmed by the fact that at the end of 1929 about 57.5% of the telephones in the Bell System were in residences. The smaller telephone systems presumably have a higher proportion of residence installations. On the other hand, the average annual revenue from business telephones is larger than from residence telephones.

Moving Expenses. The number of families moving each year has been derived in part from telephone reinstallations. To this number has been applied an average figure for moving charges as given in trade journals.

Laundering and Dry Cleaning. Estimates for recent years, obtained through the courtesy of the Laundryowners' National Association, are based on census reports. Estimates for earlier years are formed from data in the Census of Manufactures. Of total sales, from 25 to 30% are allocated to business enterprises; the balance, to consumers' expenditures.

HOME OCCUPANCY

The remaining intangible items under Home Maintenance relate to the expenses incurred for dwellings, both rented and owner-occupied. For reasons stated in Chapter I, we include here the rental values of homes occupied by the owners.

Rentals paid for leased homes and rentals imputed to homes occupied by owners are derived directly or indirectly from census data throughout. The chief sources of basic information are the Census of Families and the estimates of the value of real property for 1922 and 1912 in the census report on "Wealth, Debt, and Taxation." For our purposes the 1922 data were adopted for use in constructing 1923 estimates; similarly, figures for 1912 were used as of 1914. In presenting the explanations below of expenditures for house occupancy, the order of the items under this head in Appendix A has been shifted somewhat.

Values of Owner-Occupied Homes. Line 1 in Table 32 represents the average values of owned non-farm homes occupied by owners for the three years used as bases. Values for 1914 and 1923 were obtained by deducting from total values of residential property, derived from data in "Wealth, Debt, and Taxation," values of leased residential property.[7] Having obtained the total values of owned residential property in these years, the average values were determined on the basis of the number of owner-occupied homes—derived from census figures by

TABLE 32.—RENTAL VALUES OF LEASED AND OF OWNED NON-FARM HOMES

Derivation of Rental Values	1914	1923	1929
1. Average values of owner-occupied non-farm homes	$2,000	$3,300	$4,500
2. Average values of leased non-farm homes.........	1,600	2,000	3,000
3. Average rentals of leased non-farm homes........	200	300	375
4. Ratios of average rentals to average values of leased homes (in percentages).................	12.5	15.0	12.5
5. Average rental values of owner-occupied non-farm homes......................................	250	375	550
6. Totals of rentals paid for leased non-farm homes (in millions of dollars)......................	1,840	3,300	4,725
7. Totals of rentals imputed to owner-occupied non-farm homes (in millions of dollars)............	1,625	3,075	5,885

Line 1. Values for 1914 and 1923 derived from data for 1912 and 1922 in "Wealth, Debt, and Taxation"; values for 1929 derived from the Census of Families, 1930; see text.
Line 2. Residuals of total values of residential property less values of owner-occupied homes; these balances then divided by numbers of leased non-farm homes, interpolated from census data.
Line 3. The ratios in Line 4 supplied the rental figures for 1914 and 1923, checked by comparisons with average rentals used for this period in "Income in the United States," and Ingalls' "Wealth and Income of the American People"; for 1929, the average of median and mean of census figures.
Line 4. See text.
Line 5. Ratios of 12.5% applied to Line 1, except in 1923; see text.
Line 6. Rentals in Line 3 multiplied by numbers of leasing families; 1914, 9,200,000; 1923, 11,100,000; 1929, 12,600,000.
Line 7. Rentals in Line 5 multiplied by numbers of owning families; 1914, 6,500,000; 1923, 8,200,000; 1929, 10,700,000.

straight-line interpolation. The average value of owner-occupied homes in 1929 is placed somewhat below the census median, $4,778. If, from the ranges of values given in the Census, a rough average be constructed by using the mid-points of each range and minimum values for the two extreme ranges, the average value of owner-occupied homes would be nearly $6,000. However, it seems quite probable that owners' replies to the census questions may have exaggerated actual values. An average value of $4,500 is consistent with estimates to be presented in Appendix D and may well be regarded as fair.[8]

[7] Consult Appendix D for detailed explanation of this procedure. Data in "Wealth and Income of the American People" by Walter R. Ingalls, Merlin, York, Pennsylvania, 1922, were used as guides to the 1914 estimate.

[8] The total valuation of residential property occupied by owners in 1929 ($48,000,000,000) contrasts with the commonly accepted estimate by King of $29,300,000,000 for 1927. King's estimate, it is fair to add, was presented as only rough and preliminary. "The National Income and Its Purchasing Power," p. 378.

Rental Values of Owner-Occupied Homes. The value of owner-occupied homes governs the allowance for imputed rentals. The customary ratio of *gross* rental value to market value of homes is about 12½ %;[9] and this ratio has been applied except in 1923 when it is slightly lowered in order to maintain a consistent progression of imputed rentals. For 1931, the average gross rental of owner-occupied homes, adjusted to changes in total assessed valuations in *Financial Statistics of Cities*, was lowered to $500; for 1909, the average rental of $250 in 1914 was retained; for all other years, *total* rentals were derived by interpolation.

Imputed rentals of owner-occupied farm homes are based on data collected by the Department of Agriculture.[10] The value of farm dwellings not used in production in 1929 was estimated by the department at $6,600,000,000. The ratio of gross rentals to values may be reasonably placed at 10%, making the total farm rent bill for this year $660,000,000. Of this total 54% is assigned to rentals on owned farm residences, this being the ratio of owned farm homes to all farm homes. The remaining $305,000,000 is placed under extra-commercial rentals; such rentals are paid mostly through crop-sharing or exchange of services. Similar calculations were made for all other years on the basis of Department of Agriculture data; for 1923 the final figures are $357,000,000 and $248,000,000, respectively; for 1914, $228,000,000 and $150,000,000.

King, in presenting his imputed rentals, reduces them to a *net* figure by assuming that net rentals (after expenses for upkeep, taxes, etc.) are two-thirds of gross rentals.[11] Our corresponding estimates may be derived from Appendix A by deducting from our figures for gross rentals derived above the totals of the items listed as commercial expenses of occupancy of owned homes.

Rentals Paid for Leased Homes. In Line 3 of Table 32 the average rental of leased non-farm homes for 1929, $375, is derived from the 1930 Census of Families. The census median rental for both urban and rural non-farm homes is $326. That the median is lower than the average is borne out by the construction of a rough average, using the same procedure as explained above for values of owned homes. Roughly, the average rental may be placed at over $400; the median, at $330. The mid-way figure of $375 was selected as the average rental for non-farm families in 1929.[12] The sum appearing under this head in Appendix A is

[9] Cf. Nystrom's remark that "a rental value fixed at 12½ per cent of a conservative real estate valuation is believed to be a fair estimate." "Economic Principles of Consumption," Ronald, New York, 1929, pp. 378–379.

[10] *Crops and Markets*, Apr., 1933, pp. 144–147; for pre-war years, Census of Agriculture.

[11] "Income in the United States," vol. II, p. 229.

[12] Other investigators working independently have derived various other rent averages. In "The Income of the American Family" by Daniel Starch, New York, 1930, pp. 8–9, the average non-farm rental is placed at $42 a month, or $500 a year. Dr. E. E. Wood in "Recent Trends in American Housing," Macmillan, New York, 1931, arrives at rentals of $10–20 per month for families at the *top* of the lowest economic third, i.e., with a $1,200 income. Our estimate of total expenditures in 1927 for occupancy of all homes, rented or owned, is $9,800,000,000 against Nystrom's estimate of $8,100,000,000. Several existing national rent bills (particularly Bader's $16,000,000,000 in the *Journal of the American Statistical Association*, Sept., 1931) place the total at a much higher

the product of this average and the number of non-farm homes rented, 12,600,000, correction being made for those homes reported under "tenure unknown."

Given the average rental for 1929, one possible procedure for obtaining the averages in other years would be to conform to changes in standard indexes of rentals. This method does not appear adapted to our purposes. Both the Bureau of Labor Statistics and the National Industrial Conference Board attempt to measure changes only in workingmen's rentals; the latter index covers but 30% of the population.[13] The Bureau of Labor Statistics obtains the rent on each index date of specified pieces of property. While this procedure gives comparable figures for identified properties, it makes no allowance for unquestionable gains in the size and quality of housing occupied by workingmen. The N.I.C.B. rent index is designed to take into account all types of houses, old and new; but it is definitely limited to rents of four or five rooms, with bath, such as are usually occupied by local wage earners.[14] These limitations explain why both rental indexes show a distinct decrease during the period from 1923 to 1929.

A preferable method, in our judgment, is to relate rentals to market values. The ratio of 1929 (Line 4 of Table 32), a known factor, was carried backward to 1914. Applying this ratio to the average values of leased homes for 1914, derived from "Wealth, Debt, and Taxation," we arrive at the average rental for leased non-farm homes, $200. The National Bureau of Economic Research, using a different approach, found that the average family income in 1910 was about $1,200 "and 17.65% [percentage of expenditure for rent derived from family budget studies] of this gives $212 average rental."[15] Although Nystrom states that "pre-war studies usually fixed rental values at about 10% of the actual total values of residence properties,"[16] the results obtained by the $12\frac{1}{2}$% ratio for the pre-war period check more satisfactorily with the N.B.E.R. estimate.

In 1923, however, to allow for the housing shortage during the years directly after the war, the ratio of rentals to values of leased homes is raised to 15%. An examination of cost-of-living data shows that the sharpest bulge in all standard rental indexes occurred about 1923. Although market values of residential property undoubtedly rose during this period of rising prices, it is believed that assessed valuations upon which estimates made in "Wealth, Debt, and Taxation" are based, did not reflect this rise proportionately. The switch to a 15% ratio for this period, then, seems to be required.

In interpolating total rentals for leased homes, allowance was made for the effect of rent laws during the war. The 1919 weight in interpolation, therefore, was fixed at half the weight of 1921. As in the case of imputed rentals of owner-occupied homes, the average rental of leased homes in 1931 was decreased about 10%.

---

figure, seemingly overlooking the decidedly lower scale of rents prevailing in rural and farm areas.

[13] "Cost of Living In the United States" by the National Industrial Conference Board, New York, 1926, pp. 34–42; pp. 83–84.

[14] *Ibid.*, p. 42.

[15] "Income in the United States," vol. II, pp. 291–294.

[16] *Op. cit.*, p. 378. Note that the $12\frac{1}{2}$% ratio previously cited refers to post-war, not pre-war, rentals.

EXPENSES OF OCCUPANCY OF OWNED HOMES

Practically all the items listed under this heading in Appendix A are based on the average values of owned homes occupied by owners, derived in the fashion outlined above. The methods used in estimating each of the items under this heading, as given in Appendix A, are:

Taxes on Owner-Occupied Non-Farm Homes. Tax rates were taken from data gathered by the President's Conference on Home Building and Home Ownership. City rates averaged $1.89 per $100 in 1910; $2.02, in 1918; and $2.07, in 1928. In addition, states were collecting $0.20 per $100 in a large number of cases and there were special taxes (averaging $0.12 per $100) in a small number of cities. "While no weighted general average covering county, city and special levies can be accurately computed, it is highly probable that the general average exceeds $3 per $100 for the year 1931."[17]   For the three base periods the general average used was $2.90 for 1929 and 1931; $2.50, for 1923; and $1.80 to $1.90 for the years 1909 and 1914.

The difficulty, as pointed out in the source mentioned above, comes in estimating the relation of assessed valuation to market valuation, since tax rates are based on assessed valuations. A comparison in 1922 of assessed real property and improvements subject to general property taxes (p. 15, "Wealth, Debt, and Taxation") with value of real property and improvements taxed (*ibid.*, p. 18) shows $92,400,000,000 for the former and $155,900,000,000 for the latter, or roughly a ratio of 60%. Using the same sources, 70% is the ratio for 1912 and 1902. By 1929 students of taxation believed "property may be valued for the purposes of taxation at anything from 20% to 100%."[18]   We have continued the trend evident from 1912 to 1922 and lowered the ratio for 1929 to 50%. To illustrate the method of deriving the figures in Appendix A, the procedure for 1929 was: Total value of owner-occupied homes equals the product of average value and number of owned homes; of this amount, at the 50% ratio, $23,500,-000,000 represents assessed valuation; a tax rate of $2.90 applied to this valuation results in $680,000,000. For 1931, after examining *Financial Statistics of Cities*, the tax base and rate were left unchanged. Unpaid taxes are not considered here, but appear in Appendix E as "Borrowings."

Taxes on Owner-Occupied Farm Homes. King has taken 30% of the total taxes paid by farmers as a reasonable charge against agriculture as an industry, the other 70% being charged against the farmer as an individual.[19]   The Department of Agriculture, however, assigns only 10% of total taxes on farm property as a cost of housing.[20]   The latter allowance seems more reasonable, and is used throughout; the estimates of total farm taxes are also taken from department data.[21]

---

[17] "Home Finance and Taxation," Washington, 1932, p. 104.

[18] "Housing America" by Editors of *Fortune*, Harcourt, Brace, New York, 1932, p. 103.

[19] "Income in the Various States," p. 181.

[20] *Crops and Markets*, Apr. 1933, p. 145.

[21] *Supra* and *Agricultural Yearbook*, 1932, p. 893.

Other Communal Services. Under this heading are included costs of snow-shoveling, street-watering, and other items not included directly under the property tax in data given in *Financial Statistics of Cities.* Of the total sum given in this source for these services, the amount paid directly by owner-occupiers is based on the ratio of owner-occupied property to total property.

Interest on Mortgages on Owner-Occupied Non-Farm Homes. Ryan estimates the total of home-mortgage debts in 1929 by families living in their own homes to be at least $10,000,000,000.[22] A fair check is obtained by taking the total value of owned non-farm homes of which 40% ($18,800,000,000) are encumbered with mortgages.[23] Assuming these homes to be mortgaged to 50% of their value, total mortgage debts on such property would be $9,400,000,000. Similar figures for 1923 and 1914 were calculated, using the census percentages of owned homes encumbered. Interest on such mortgages is figured at 6%.

Interest on Mortgages on Owner-Occupied Farm Homes. As in the case of taxes, we have followed the Department of Agriculture in assigning to farm dwellings 10% of total interest payable.[24]

Insurance on Owner-Occupied Non-Farm Homes. In the absence of better source material, a blanket coverage of 80% of the total value of owned homes was assumed, to which was applied the average rate of insurance during the year.[25] It was thought that homes without coverage would be approximately offset by insurance on personal property and furnishings, the value of which has been estimated at from $40,000,000,000 to $50,000,000,000. Insurance on farm homes, following Department of Agriculture procedure which does not attempt to separate this item but places all of it under costs of production, has not been included.

Craftsmen's Services for Repairs and Upkeep. No accurate measurement of this item was attempted. Retail sales of hardware, tools, paint, and similar commodities used for household repairs and upkeep were calculated from the sources given in Appendix B. To this was added a small allowance for craftsmen's services. The total allowance for 1929 is $30 a home, which is somewhat less than 1% of the total value of owner-occupied homes.

INTANGIBLE ITEMS OF RECREATION

Admissions to Theaters, etc. Steiner's estimate for 1929 made for "Recent Social Trends"[26] was approved by the leading trade journal in this field as the most plausible guess that had been offered. Starting with this estimate, we have made adjustments for other years in the light of taxes on admissions, values of motion picture films produced and trade opinions.

Clubs, Dues, and Fees. Here also Steiner's estimate for 1929 has been accepted as a base and rough adjustments have been made for other years.

Hotels, etc. The 1930 Census of Hotels supplies basic data. It has been assumed that the revenues of hotels catering mainly to permanent or to both

[22] "Internal Debts in the United States," p. 319.

[23] Data on mortgages were not collected by the Census for 1930; the 40% used here is suggested by Ryan.

[24] *Op. cit.,* p. 145.

[25] *Statistical Abstract,* 1932, p. 281.

[26] "Americans at Play," by Jesse F. Steiner, McGraw-Hill, New York, 1933.

permanent and transient guests represent expenditures by individuals; this is true also of resort hotels. A small proportion of the business of hotels for transients has been added. A further addition has been made for expenditures at tourists' camps, as estimated by Steiner. The sum thus reached for 1929 has been adjusted to the index of hotel occupancy in 1927 and in 1931 supplied in *Survey of Current Business.* The figures for earlier years are simply expressions of trade judgments as to the relative amounts of non-commercial travel plus hotel residence in those years.

Foreign Travel. Net expenditures by American travelers abroad in recent years appear in "Balance of International Payments," an annual publication of the United States Department of Commerce. Of these expenditures, 25 % are allocated to business travel; 75 %, to pleasure travel.

Railway and Pullman Fares and Airway Fares. Of the total passenger revenues two-thirds are allocated to consumers' spendings.

REMAINING ITEMS

The remaining items do not fall into any well defined group. The following notes are arranged in the order in which the items appear in Appendix A.

Hospitals. The amount directly paid by individuals for hospital care in 1929 is taken from "Medical Care for the American People."[27] For 1923, data presented in "Hospitals and Dispensaries," a report of the United States Department of Commerce, were used. Corresponding estimates for other years were computed as ratios of all other expenditures in the sickness and death group.

Tuition Privately Paid. This estimate attempts to exclude all outgo for education from public and endowment funds; also, such items as purchases of books, direct payments for services of instructors and travel expenses, all of which are covered elsewhere. The chief sources are: "Biennial Survey of Education" issued by the United States Bureau of Education; "Tax Burdens and Public Expenditures," a publication of the National Industrial Conference Board; and some private estimates of expenditures for adult education. The figures are of course largely expressions of personal judgments.

Postage. No sound basis for allocation between business and individual mailings was discovered. Fifty per cent of postal revenues was arbitrarily assigned to individuals.

Dues of Fraternal Societies, Unions, etc. Steiner's monograph, previously referred to, was accepted as a guide. His estimates were modified somewhat on the strength of various budget studies showing expenditures of this type by farmers and workingmen.

Contributions. The basic data comes from King's analysis of contributions by individuals in New Haven.[28] By applying the percentages of such contributions from living persons to the whole population of the country it was possible to arrive at approximations of national figures for the period 1909–1925. Since

[27] Committee on the Costs of Medical Care, University of Chicago Press, Chicago, 1932.
[28] "Trends in Philanthropy" by W. I. King, National Bureau of Economic Research, New York, 1928.

the trend of these estimates checked fairly well with the trend of contributions reported in *Statistics of Income*, the amounts for later years were based on the income reports.   Our totals are in line with estimates of the John Price Jones Corporation if allowance be made for contributions from estates and other sources.

Immigrant Remittances.   Net figures are taken from "Balance of International Payments" previously referred to.

As was remarked at the outset of this discussion, estimates of expenditures for intangibles are peculiarly uncertain. Yet, unless some unconscious bias has distorted all the estimates, it seems probable that the relationships and long-term movements of the major items are not seriously misrepresented.

APPENDIX D

ESTIMATES OF WITHHOLDINGS

AS LISTED IN APPENDIX A

The term "withholdings" by definition covers (a) taxes directly paid by individuals in their consumer-capacity and not elsewhere counted as elements of outgo and (b) savings out of current incomes of individuals.

The first-named form consists, as stated in the text, mainly of income taxes paid by individuals but includes also personal property taxes, poll taxes, and licenses and fees for personal activities (marriage licenses, hunting licenses, fines, etc.). Income taxes are easily derived from *Statistics of Income* and the financial reports of those states which impose such taxes. Estimates of other taxes directly paid by individuals, kindly supplied by the Finance Department of the United States Chamber of Commerce, have been adapted to the requirements of this study. Their amount is largely conjectural but in any case is relatively small. There appears to be little chance for gross error in the total figures for direct taxes, as given in Appendix A.

DIFFICULTIES IN ESTIMATING SAVINGS

When we come to calculating annual savings by individuals, however, we confront a truly formidable problem. If accuracy is insisted upon, the problem becomes insoluble. Essential data are lacking; admittedly dubious assumptions have to be used as substitutes. But even crude approximations to the figures for consumers' savings are well worth having, not only to carry through the present inquiry, but also because they contribute to a clearer understanding of the processes of economic growth.

The cardinal requirement in attacking the problem is to lay out a soundly reasoned procedure for utilizing such data as can be had. If the problem is to be mastered at all, it is not by frontal attack but by an enveloping operation in three stages. That is to say, estimates must first be built up of total acquisitions of assets by all types of owners; then suitable deductions must be made for acquisitions by institutions and business enterprises; third, allowances must be made for payments by consumers which are derived from other sources than their current incomes. Unless the operation is thoroughly and correctly planned, it will inevitably miscarry. On the other hand, if the main line of reasoning is sound, the defects in data, serious as they are, do not necessarily import complete failure. The findings may still fall within normal limits of tolerance for estimates of this nature.

The Concept of Consumers' Savings

Our objective, to repeat, is to measure *consumers'* savings out of their *current incomes.* The definition of *consumers* given in Chapter I holds good; we are concerned only with natural persons acting in their consumer-capacity. So far as practicable, savings arising out of an individual's main business or profession are to be separated from savings with which we are here concerned—those financed out of personal income.[1] Furthermore, the aim is to treat *consumers as a body;* this involves attempting to eliminate inter-individual transactions *except* in the cases described in the next paragraph. These are the same distinctions that have been drawn in formulating estimates of spendings for commodities and for intangibles.

Certain exceptions to the rulings previously applied must now be introduced. Since the objective is to measure savings out of current incomes, it is necessary to include in our estimates transfers of funds *from income accounts to capital accounts,* although the transfers may take place wholly within the circle of consumers as a body (that is, they may not involve dealings with institutional, business or professional individuals or organizations); indeed, the transfer may be from a person's income account to the same person's capital account. Thus when an individual deposits part of his income in a savings account, the transaction is obviously to be reckoned as an item of consumers' savings. Again, when real property is sold by one individual to another, neither one of whom is acting in his customary business-capacity, it may happen that a portion of the payment for the property comes from the purchaser's income account, while the entire amount is regarded by the vendor as capital; in that case the portion taken from income is properly treated as an item of consumers' savings. The principle applies equally of course to transfers of securities from one individual to another; but such transfers are relatively infrequent.

By far the greater portion of payments for property are made out of pre-existing capital; and especial care is needed to see to it that mere transfers of capital from one asset to another are rigorously excluded from estimates of current savings.

---

[1] Most previous estimates of savings (those of King, of Ingalls and of Friday are best known) lump business savings with personal savings. By so doing they avoid many of the pitfalls referred to in the text. But such estimates, though valuable in themselves, become misleading when they are placed in apposition with those estimates of national income which are in effect aggregates of individual incomes. The proper comparison is with incomes of both individuals and business enterprises.

To summarize: Consumers' savings as here conceived consist of payments or withholdings out of current income by the national body of individuals acting in their consumer-capacity for acquisitions of potential income-yielding assets. The payments may pass from the body of consumers to institutions, business enterprises or individuals acting in their normal business-capacity; or the payments may pass from the income accounts of some consumers to the capital accounts of other consumers; or withholdings from income may pass to the capital accounts of the withholders.

EFFECTS OF INFLATION AND DEFLATION

Another new element enters into the problem of computing savings. So long as we are dealing only with day-to-day spendings for consumption, it is permissible to ignore the effects of long-term swings of prices. But savings are devoted to assets; and important types of assets—that is, securities and real estate—are peculiarly subject to sweeping movements of price inflation and deflation. How do these movements affect computations of savings?

Inflationary. When prices follow a broad upward trend, borrowings for the purchase of assets grow apace and sales of assets yield profits. Such profits are not true income but nevertheless constitute funds available for reinvestment. Fortunately for our purpose, profits from sales of assets are reported by income taxpayers, and so the approximate amount for all individuals may be estimated with a fair degree of accuracy. By subtracting (a) profits and (b) accumulations of borrowed funds from current payments by individuals for property holdings, we get the net amounts of such payments which must have come out of their current incomes.

Deflationary. When prices follow a broad downward trend, the case is more puzzling. Individuals realize losses, not profits, from their sales of assets; on top of that, they usually have to cut down their indebtedness. At first blush one is tempted to assume that the losses and reductions of debt are paid out of incomes and constitute in effect forced savings. In fact some such statement could be applied to exceptional persons here and there. But to suppose that it is generally true of consumers as a body is to misjudge the nature of a deflationary movement. The movement consists essentially of throwing assets on the market, accepting the losses on them and using the proceeds to scale down debts. If it were otherwise—if holders as a rule were able to pay their debts and replace their losses out of current income—deflation would be stopped in its tracks. It follows that losses and reductions of debts *whenever they overbalance profits and debt increases* are properly treated as payments out of assets—or, if one prefers a more precise statement, as decreases in monetary values of assets. As such, they should be ignored in computations of current savings *out of income.*

Thus we arrive at what looks like a paradox: Inflationary profits on sales of assets and increases in debts to finance purchases of holdings are to be deducted in computing current savings. The effects of inflation are dealt with elsewhere by applying deflating indexes in Part Two. But deflationary losses on sales of assets and decreases in debts are not to be added.   Since our immediate aim is to find out how current dollar incomes are disbursed, we must not be misled into taking into account concurrent devaluations of assets and debts which take place outside the circle of current income and outgo.

The difficulty here discussed arises because our whole system of credit and valuation, no longer firmly anchored to its gold base, expands and contracts under the influence of irrational fevers and chills.   The consuming public hopefully acquires high-priced assets and piles up debts in good times; then helplessly shrugs its shoulders and watches both assets and debts shrink when times turn bad.

A Four-Fold Grouping of Acquisitions

The two chief forms of assets to which consumers' savings may be devoted, as tabulated below, are (a) *funds*, principally deposits and interests in life insurance policies, and (b) *properties*, both real and personal.   The amounts, in dollars, of these assets obtained each year are referred to as annual *acquisitions;* the amounts in some instances are minus quantities.

I. Funds

1. Interests in life insurance policies, which are here treated as accumulations of premium payments.[2]
2. Cash holdings, including savings deposits, time deposits, demand deposits. interests in building and loan associations and currency.

II. Properties

3. Holdings of securities and of other capital interests in business enterprises
4. Holdings of real estate, (a) urban and (b) farm.

Our estimates of consumers' savings will be substantially complete if they cover annual payments or withholdings devoted to these four groups of assets.

A Working Formula for Computing Consumers' Savings

Having now in mind the basic concept of consumers' savings, the method of handling broad inflationary-deflationary movements and the four-fold grouping of acquisitions, we are ready to consider a practicable formula.   The formula must of course be adapted to the data available, and this requirement has been kept in view.

As an illustration, the full formula, applied to the calculation of consumers' savings in 1929, is set forth in Table 33.   Similar calcula-

[2] An allocation of premium payments (a) to current protection and (b) to increase of cash surrender values might be made.   But from the viewpoint of the individual, his entire premium is in substance a low-interest form of saving.

TABLE 33.—CALCULATION OF CONSUMERS' SAVINGS IN 1929[1]
(In billions of current dollars)

A. Payments for Life Insurance Premiums (90%)..................... 3.2
B1. Increase in savings bank deposits (80%).................... 0.4
B2. Increase in time deposits (70%)........................... 0.3
B3. Increase in demand deposits (25%)......................... 0.1
B4. Decrease in outstanding currency (50%)....................−0.2
B5 Increase in assets of building and loan associations............ 0.7

　　B. Total Accretions of Cash Holdings, or Equivalents.............. 1.3

A + B. Total Payments or Withholdings for Acquisition of Funds...... 4.5

C1. New public issues (non-refunding) of domestic non-financial
　　corporations....................................... 6.4
C2. Net purchases of securities from foreigners............. 0.1
C3. Net reduction in federal issues........................ −0.7
C4. Net additions in state and municipal issues (non-refunding). 1.4

　　C5. Total of Addition to Publicly Distributed Securities... 7.2

　　　　C6a. Takings of securities by Federal Reserve
　　　　　　Banks................................. 0.3
　　　　C6b. Takings of securities by all reporting banks
　　　　　　(reduction)............................−1.0
　　　　C6c. Takings of securities by insurance companies 0.5
　　　　C6d. Takings of securities by non-profit institu-
　　　　　　tions................................. 0.3
　　　　C6e. Takings of securities by non-financial busi-
　　　　　　ness corporations........................ 0.9
　　　C6. Less takings by institutions and business enterprises.. 1.0

C7. Purchases by individuals of publicly distributed securi-
　　ties... 6.2
C8. Purchases by individuals of privately sold mortgages
　　(20% of farm mortgages; estimated takings by others
　　of urban mortgages deducted)............................. 0.3
C9. Capital supplied by individuals to business enterprises
　　not publicly financed..................................... 4.1

　　C10. Total Acquisitions of Securities and Capital Supplied in
　　　　Other Forms by Individuals.......................... 10.6
　　C11. Less accumulations of short-term bank loans to
　　　　individuals...−3.5

　　C. Total Payments for Securities and Capital Supplied
　　　　in Other Forms... 7.1

TABLE 33.—CALCULATION OF CONSUMERS' SAVINGS IN 1929.—*(Continued)*

D1. Acquisitions of non-farm real estate (acquisitions by business enterprises deducted)............................ 4.0
   D2. *Less* accumulations of long and medium term debts.. −2.0

   D3. Total Payments for Non-farm Real Estate............. 2.0
D4. Acquisitions of farms................................ 1.5
   D5. *Less* increase of farm debt........................ −0.1[2]

   D6. Total Payments for Farms............................ 1.5

   D. Total Payments for Equities in Real Estate.................. 3.5

   C + D. Total Acquisitions of Personal and Real Properties......... 10.6
   E1. *Less* realized profits and capital gains from sale of assets... −4.0
   E2. *Less* receipts from life insurance policy maturities and dividends (90%)...................................... −1.8

   E. *Less* Total Amounts Derived from Other Sources than Income.. −5.8

   (C + D) − E. Net Payments for Properties Derived from Income... 4.8
Total Savings in 1929 [A + B] + [(C + D) − E]...................... 9.3

   [1] The percentages indicate proportions allocated to consumers after deducting allowances for the estimated payments or acquisitions of institutions, business enterprises and individuals acting in a non-consumer capacity.
   [2] Does not enter into total; see text.

tions were made for other years. Some introductory comments, with indicated references to the table, follow.

Annual payments by individuals for premiums on life insurance policies (A) may be fairly estimated by deducting from total premiums an allowance of 10% for premiums paid by business enterprises.

Year-to-year increases or decreases in total cash holdings (B1 through B4, covering bank deposits and outstanding currency) are reported by the Comptroller of the Currency and the Treasury Department. The troublesome question is how much to apportion to individuals in their consumer-capacity. The answer can be only a series of rough approximations which are explained later. The annual increase or decrease in assets of building and loan associations (B5) is also placed in this group. The total of the group (B) forms our estimate of accretions (or decretions in some years) of cash holdings or their equivalents.

Adding payments of life insurance premiums and accretions of cash holdings (A + B), we get the total acquisition of funds during the year.

To compute the annual acquisitions of securities and of other capital interests in business enterprises, requires a somewhat elaborate process of assembling the annual additions to publicly distributed securities (C1 through C5) then subtracting the takings by institutions and business concerns (C6a through C6) in order to arrive at purchases by individuals (C7). To this sum are added purchases of privately sold mortgages (C8) and acquisitions by individuals of interests in enterprises not publicly financed (C9). From the total acquisitions by individuals thus computed (C10) we must deduct increases in bank loans to individuals (C11). The remainder (C) is an estimate of their annual payments for securities and other capital interests.

An analogous process (D1 through D) gives annual acquisitions of urban and farm real estate by individuals. Increases in long and medium-term debt are deducted in order to obtain annual payments for equities in real estate.

We now have (C + D) total acquisitions of securities and real estate. But some of the payments for these properties come from other sources than savings out of current income. One source consists of profits from sale of assets (E1) which may be derived from *Statistics of Income*. Another source consists of funds supplied by withdrawals from insurance companies (E2), an item which calls for some explanation.

These withdrawals consist of payments to individuals of death losses, matured endowments and surrendered policies, annuities and policyholders' dividends. The last two items might properly be treated as income; but we find no evidence that they have been included in the standard estimates of national income of individuals referred to in Chapter II. Hence, for the sake of comparability of the outgo estimates herein presented with income estimates, we class them among withdrawals of capital funds. Withdrawals by individuals from life insurance companies are in cash or its equivalent (in the case of dividends) and may be utilized for whatever purposes the individuals elect. Considering consumers *as a body*, however, their spendings are more than covered by their current incomes in all the years studied, without the necessity of using capital funds. Consequently, in estimating national outgo these withdrawals are best regarded as funds not derived from current income which are available for investment.

In passing, it may be well to remark that similar problems of handling withdrawals do not arise elsewhere. Whereas the full payments to life insurance companies are here regarded as acquisitions, the other items of acquisitions start with estimates of *net* changes in holdings of assets. It is of course true that capital is constantly being shifted from one form of holding to another; but the net changes reflect withdrawals as well as fresh investments.

We now deduct the total amounts derived from other sources than income (E) and thus arrive at net annual payments for properties out of current income [(C + D) − E)], or true savings.

The aggregate of payments for life insurance premiums (A), increase or decrease in cash holdings (B) and payments out of income for securities and other capital interests and for real estate [(C + D) − E], constitutes our estimate of consumers' savings. The working formula sketched above, as briefed for 1929 in Table 33, will be further commented upon in the following section-by-section explanation of estimates of savings devoted to each of the four groups of assets.

Setting up the formula is of course only a preliminary step. We still have to face the difficulties and uncertainties inseparable from an attempt to extract needed information from inadequate data. However, the formula should first be critically examined and judged as to its validity. If it is seriously wrong, no amount of data will cure it. If it is basically sound, the errors ascribable to defective data may perhaps be kept within moderate limits.

LIFE INSURANCE PREMIUMS

As a measurement of life insurance savings in this form, it is customary to use premium payments *less* operating expenses. But we are concerned only with savings by individuals and must therefore exclude corporate operations. A simple record of premium payments, as cited in the *Statistical Abstract*, meets the requirement.

However, an unknown proportion of the premiums comes from business enterprises as their contributions toward group insurance of employees and for policies which they hold on lives of officers and owners. A blanket allowance of 10% for premium payments by business is thought to be sufficient, leaving 90% paid out of individual incomes. Following is a record of the net amounts taken into our estimates.

TABLE 34.—ANNUAL PAYMENTS BY INDIVIDUALS OF LIFE INSURANCE PREMIUMS
(In billions of current dollars)

1909	0.5	1922	1.7	1927	2.6
1914	0.7	1923	1.9	1928	2.8
1919	1.2	1924	2.1	1929	3.2
1920	1.4	1925	2.3	1930	3.1
1921	1.5	1926	2.4	1931	3.0

The outstanding characteristic of these payments is the regularity of their growth, excepting only the slight falling-off in 1930 and 1931. Life insurance has taken rank in the American scheme as an element in decent standards of living, comparable in that respect with food, clothing, tobacco and home maintenance; in fact, because of its immunity from price fluctuations, it may be said to enjoy a superior status so long as consumers' outgo holds well above a subsistence level.

CASH HOLDINGS OR EQUIVALENTS

Savings which accumulate as cash holdings become easily visible to even the most casual observer. The amounts of deposits and of currency outstanding are reported in statistical tables issued from time to time by the Comptroller of the Currency, the Treasury Department, and the Federal Reserve Board; and the figures are widely publicized. As a natural result, popular writers often assume that the word "savings" is almost identical with "cash holdings," or at least that variations in cash holdings represent corresponding variations in other forms of savings. Neither assumption has a sound basis. Increases in cash holdings accounted for less than 25% of consumers' *savings* during the period 1919–1930 (omitting the decrease in 1931). *Acquisitions* of cash holdings in relation to total acquisitions during the same period, as shown in Table 9 of Chapter II, fluctuated widely and irregularly between 6 and 25%.

As implied above, statistical information regarding total deposits and currency circulation is sufficient for our purpose. The real problem is to decide what proportion of the annual increase or decrease of each form of holding should be allocated to individuals in their capacity as consumers. The only recourse is to rely on well-informed judgments wherever they can be found.

Savings Deposits. This item is restricted to deposit accounts in mutual savings banks. They are usually treated as if they were composed exclusively of savings out of the current incomes of individuals. Yet it is common knowledge that a sizable fraction belong to small business enterprises. We have made an allocation (partly based on Dailey's study referred to below) of 20% to business accounts, leaving 80% of the annual increment assigned to consumers.

Time Deposits. Here we have a slightly better basis for judgment. French's analysis of elements in the post-war expansion of time deposits leads him to the conclusion: "Bank statistics show clearly that there could have been no appreciable amount of shifting of deposits from the demand to the time category on the part of large depositors in national banks. If there was any such shifting it was on the part of small depositors. We may safely say that the same conclusion would be valid for other commercial banks."[3] It appears, then, that whatever difference in character exists between mutual savings bank deposits and time deposits in other banks is not radical. On the other hand, the exceptional gains in time deposits from 1921 to 1929 must certainly be attributed in part to a shifting of small commercial deposits.

Dailey reports a study of time deposits in national banks which "shows that those deposits evidenced by savings pass books have averaged almost 72% of the total time deposits since the autumn of 1928. . . . One is probably not far wrong in estimating that at the present time in excess of four-fifths of the time deposits reported by the national banks represent the accumulation of savings."[4] The general opinion, however, is that a larger proportion of time deposits than of savings deposits belong to business enterprises. We accept 30% as a fair allowance and reckon 70% of the annual increment from 1923 to 1929 inclusive as withholdings from current individual incomes. However, on the strength of observations as to the changing character of time deposits in less prosperous years, we have scaled the percentage assigned to consumers from 70% up to 80% both before 1923 and subsequent to 1929.

Demand Deposits. Little attention has been given, as a rule, to savings which take the form of checking accounts of individual consumers. Yet most families in the higher income groups maintain such accounts, and their aggregate is undoubtedly large. Moreover, they are important because of their immediate responsiveness to alterations in individual income.

The best guide we have found for allocating the total of demand deposits between business enterprises and individual consumers is Keynes' analysis of what he calls "income-deposits."[5] On the strength of admittedly loose calculations of transactions financed by checks and of probable velocities of income-deposits and of business-deposits, Keynes arrives at an estimate that about 25% of demand deposits in 1923 belonged to individual consumers.[6]

Some evidence bearing on the reasonableness of this percentage is supplied by the findings of the inquiry into size of bank deposit accounts as of February 15, 1934, conducted by the Federal Deposit Insurance Corporation. In the

---

[3] "The Significance of Time Deposits in the Expansion of Bank Credit, 1922–28" by D. R. French, *Journal of Political Economy*, Dec., 1931.

[4] "National Banks in the Savings Deposits Field" by Don M. Dailey, *Journal of Business*, Jan., 1931.

[5] Keynes' definition of "income-deposits" corresponds precisely to our conception of deposits of individual consumers. "Deposits of this kind, replenished by individuals out of their personal incomes and employed by them to meet their personal expenditure and their personal savings, we shall call *income-deposits.*" "A Treatise on Money" by John Maynard Keynes, Harcourt, Brace, New York, 1930, vol. I, p. 35.

[6] *Ibid*, vol. II, pp. 37–38.

TABLE 35.—ROUGH ESTIMATES OF ANNUAL ACCRETIONS OF CONSUMERS' CASH HOLDINGS, 1909–1931

(In billions of dollars; decreases in italics)

Classes of Cash Holdings	1909	1914	Pre-war Average	1919	1920	1921	1922	1923	1924	1925	1926	1927	1928	1929	1930	1931
1. Increases in Savings Deposits.....	0.1	0.2	0.15	0.6	0.6	0.9	0.5	0.8	0.8	0.8	0.8	0.9	1.1	0.4	0.5	1.5
2. Increases in Time Deposits.........	0.1	0.1	0.1	1.1	1.0	0.6	0.6	0.7	0.8	0.9	0.7	0.9	0.6	0.3	0.5	*-1.1*
3. Increases in Demand Deposits......	0.3	0.2	0.25	0.7	0.6	*-0.6*	*-0.3*	0.2	0.2	0.5	0.3	0.1	*-0.1*	0.1	*-0.5*	*-1.4*
4. Increases in Currency Holdings.....	0.0	0.0	0.0	0.0	0.1	*-0.2*	*-0.2*	0.2	0.0	0.0	0.0	*-0.1*	0.1	*-0.2*	0.0	0.5
5. Increases in Assets of Building and Loan Associations.............	0.1	0.1	0.1	0.2	0.4	0.4	0.5	0.6	0.8	0.7	0.8	0.8	0.9	0.7	0.1	*-0.4*
6. Totals of Annual Accretions of Cash Holdings or Equivalents.........	0.6	0.6	0.6	2.6	2.7	1.1	1.1	2.5	2.6	2.9	2.6	2.6	2.6	1.3	0.6	*-0.9*

Line 1. End-of-year deposits in mutual savings banks estimated by averaging successive June 30 figures as given in reports of the Comptroller of the Currency; 80% allocated to consumers' deposits.

Line 2. Includes postal savings; end-of-year deposits derived as above; allocations to consumers' deposits ranging from 70 to 80% as explained in text.

Line 3. Derived as above except for recent years in which end-of-year figures are available; 25% allocated to consumers' deposits.

Line 4. Approximately 50% of annual increases or decreases in circulation outside banks.

Line 5. Data issued by the United States League of Building and Loan Associations.

Line 6. Totals of Lines 1 through 5.

13,529 insured banks the deposit accounts of $2,500 or less came to 40.8% of total deposits, both demand deposits and time deposits. In this group were nearly 55,000,000 deposit accounts. In view of the low state of business at the time of the inquiry, many of these small accounts doubtless belonged to business concerns; but the bulk of them must have been personal accounts. Inasmuch as the published data do not separate demand deposits and time deposits, it is not possible to draw any exact conclusions; but at least an allowance of 25% of demand deposits to strictly personal accounts is not inconsistent with these findings.

Another crude check—this time for a relatively prosperous period—may be derived from the corporate reports in *Statistics of Income*. Cash holdings of all corporations at the end of 1929 were $22,500,000,000 of which $8,000,000,000 belonged to non-financial corporations. If we accept Means' estimate that at least 78% of American non-financial business wealth is corporate wealth,[7] we should add $2,000,000,000 for unincorporated business, giving a total of $24,-500,000,000 of cash holdings by business enterprises. Included in this figure are $7,500,000,000 of savings and time deposits which we have previously assigned to business enterprises, leaving $17,000,000,000 for demand deposits and till cash (an unknown quantity, possibly approximating $2,000,000,000). The total demand deposits in all banks at the same date came to about $22,500,-000,000. On the strength of these figures, we could fairly assign about 65 to 70% of all demand deposits to business and 30 to 35% to non-business accounts. However, among the non-business accounts a large proportion belong to governmental bodies, estates, and non-profit institutions. What percentage is left for individual consumers cannot be determined; but it would probably fall somewhere near 25%.

A thorough investigation of the whole question of ownership of demand deposits is greatly needed and would be likely to reveal considerable variations from year to year. Unfortunately the investigation remains to be made. In the meanwhile, we have applied the 25% allocation to individuals throughout the period studied.

Currency. Money in circulation, after deducting the sums held by Federal Reserve Banks, has fluctuated considerably. The fluctuations have been especially marked in years of large price changes and in 1931, when loss of confidence in banks induced hoarding. Whatever the causes of fluctuations, plainly the year-to-year variations in currency holdings of consumers should be taken into account. In order to estimate the amounts, we have been forced to make an arbitrary allocation: of the total circulation at any one time about one-half is assumed to be in the tills of retail stores and other business enterprises; and one-half, in the pockets (or the mattresses) of consumers. Possibly the division should be adjusted to fit the abnormal hoarding in 1931; but we have found no basis for supposing that the distribution of hoarded currency in that year was notably different from the distribution of ordinary till-and-pocket currency.

Building and Loan Assets. Gains in these assets, as shown by reports of the United States League of Building and Loan Associations, are assigned in their entirety to consumers and are taken to represent actual current savings out of

---

[7] "The Modern Corporation and Private Property" by Adolf A. Berle, Jr., and Gardiner C. Means, Macmillan, New York, 1933, p. 31.

income. The assumption is implied—as is true of all our estimates of increases or decreases in deposits—that accrued interest each year is properly included in consumers' income accounts.

Estimates based on the foregoing percentage allocations are presented in Table 35. The large year-to-year fluctuations in the five cash items—savings deposits, time deposits, demand deposits, currency and building and loan assets—are noteworthy, especially in contrast with the stability of payments for life insurance premiums. Cash holdings, in fact, are by far the most irregular of the four groups of consumers' acquisitions.

PURCHASES OF PUBLICLY DISTRIBUTED SECURITIES

It might be supposed that the volume of securities purchased by the public in recent years could readily be derived from the corporate balance sheets published in *Statistics of Income;* but it is a hopeless task to disentangle from these figures the large proportion which arise from intercorporate dealings. The more practical method is to utilize the excellent records of publicly announced security issues maintained by the *Commercial and Financial Chronicle* supplemented by corrections for other public issues. Having thus determined the net additions to the security market each year, the second step is to deduct known or estimated takings by institutions and business concerns. We thereby arrive at remainders which must represent purchases by individuals.[8]

It is first necessary to separate additions to the security market from issues designed for refunding or for acquisition of pre-existing securities; the latter purpose underlies, as is well known, most of the offerings of holding companies, investment trusts and other financial corporations. Both refunding and financial issues, as given in the *Chronicle* record, have been deducted to get the figures in Line 1 of Table 38. Lines 2 through 5 are self-explanatory.

Lines 6 to 10 inclusive show the takings each year by institutions and business enterprises. The takings of Federal Reserve Banks, of all reporting banks and of insurance companies are deduced from their total investment holdings at or near the end of each calendar year. At certain times, notably 1920 and 1929, the showing may have been distorted by revaluations at lower market prices; but no satisfactory method has been found for making corrections. Purchases for non-profit institutions have been loosely estimated as about two-thirds of the takings of insurance companies.[9] Takings by all non-financial corporations in recent years have been based upon the combined

---

[8] The method was suggested by an article on "Savings for which Banks Can Compete" by J. S. Lawrence, *American Bankers' Association Journal*, June, 1930; but Lawrence's computations have been revised and elaborated.

[9] The proportion indicated is suggested by the estimates of institutional assets in "Trusteeship of American Endowments" by Woods, Struther & Co., Macmillan, New York, 1932.

balance sheets of leading corporations prepared from time to time by Standard Statistics Company.[10]   As a guide to estimates for earlier years we have used Nerlove's compilation of net incomes reinvested[11] checked against corporate income from dividends of other domestic corporations as shown in *Statistics of Income*.   The totals of Lines 3 through 10, shown in Line 11, are believed to constitute reasonable approximations of combined takings from the security markets by other than individual purchasers.

Whether these takings are of new securities or of old securities makes no difference.   In either case whatever they remove from the market reduces by that much the volume of added securities to be absorbed. Unless we have left out of account some important class of purchasers—and this seems unlikely—the remainder must have gone to individuals. Their takings each year appear in Line 12.

PURCHASES OF PRIVATELY SOLD MORTGAGES

Another class of security consists of real estate mortgages privately sold to individuals.   The only practicable way to measure from existing data annual payments for mortgages is: (*a*) to ascertain as nearly as possible the amount of new mortgages issued each year; (*b*) to allocate the amount on the basis of the best information available between institutions and business enterprises on the one side and individuals on the other; and (*c*) to make allowances for the rising proportion of real estate mortgage issues included among publicly distributed securities.   The procedure rests on the assumption that dealings in mortgages outstanding before the beginning of the year did not involve heavy transfers from institutions and business enterprises to individuals or vice versa.   The assumption is plausible; for everyday observation indicates that new securities are sold as a rule to classes of buyers in rough proportion to their previous holdings.

Farm Mortgages.   The best source of information is a valuable study by Wickens.[12]   He offers new estimates of total farm mortgage debts for 1910, 1920, 1925 and 1928, from which we derive approximate annual increments as shown in Table 36.

Wickens also presents data as to the proportions of farm mortgages held by principal classes of lending agencies in 1920, 1925, and 1928, from which we derive allocations to individuals, except retired farmers, as shown at the top of p. 294.[13]

[10] See *Standard Earnings Bulletin*, Aug. 17, 1932, pp. 2–5.

[11] "A Decade of Corporate Incomes" by S. H. Nerlove, University of Chicago Press, 1932, p. 62.

[12] "Farm-Mortgage Credit" by David L. Wickens, Technical Bulletin No. 288, Feb., 1932, United States Department of Agriculture.

[13] Retired farmers are omitted on the assumption that their holdings were generally acquired through sales of farms, not through purchases out of income. Other individuals, it is presumed, bought their holdings for cash.

Years	Percentage
1909	45
1914	40
1919	30
1920	25
1921 to 1929	20

The resultant estimates indicate a remarkable falling off in purchases of farm mortgages by individuals as a body; in fact, they dwindle away to practically nothing after 1925. Obviously the figures are not to be read with overmuch literalness; but they probably conform in a general way to the actual trend of investment by individuals in this type of security.

TABLE 36.—ANNUAL INCREMENTS OF FARM MORTGAGE DEBTS
(In millions of dollars)

Years	Increment
1909 and 1914	$400
1919 and 1920	500
1921 to 1925	300
1925 to 1929	35
1930 and 1931	None[14]

Urban Mortgages. The data assembled in "Internal Debts of the United States" for the years 1913, 1921, 1929, 1930 and 1931 have been used as the main basis of our estimates.[15] For our purpose it is necessary, first, to segregate holdings of individuals from holdings by other lending agencies and, second, to allow for duplications between direct purchases of mortgages and purchases of publicly distributed securities based on urban mortgages which have already been counted.

The chief forms of urban mortgages held by individuals are: issues put out by real estate bond houses or other selling agencies, of which perhaps two-thirds in recent years are included under "publicly distributed securities"; guaranteed mortgages, of which perhaps four-fifths were publicly distributed; and individual mortgages acquired directly by individual investors, probably a declining amount.

The proportion of real estate bonds taken direct by individuals was no doubt larger in the earlier years; and a like remark applies to guaranteed mortgages. Mortgages given and taken by individuals were a common form of investment in the early part of the period but have been largely supplanted by the other two forms. Our figures start from the judgment that somewhere near $5,000,000,000 of such mortgages were outstanding in 1929[16] and possibly from $7,000,000,000 to $10,000,000,000 in the earlier years when the known holdings of real estate securities by financial agencies bore a relatively small ratio to real estate values.

[14] See "Internal Debts of the United States," Chap. 2, "Farm Mortgage Debts," Macmillan, New York, 1932, pp. 27ff. These debts decreased after 1929. The net decline may be presumed to represent losses by holders rather than repayments out of income.

[15] *Op. cit.,* Chap. 3, "Urban Mortgage Debts."

[16] See an article by Ditlew M. Fredericksen in *Harvard Business Review,* Jan., 1932, p. 144; also, "Internal Debts of the United States," p. 78.

Since net accretions after 1920 must certainly have been slight or non-existent, the item has been left out of account in the later years.

The following figures for the three forms of holdings take into account the data and the factors just referred to; but they are essentially no more than guesses.

TABLE 37.—ANNUAL TAKINGS BY INDIVIDUALS OF URBAN MORTGAGES NOT PUBLICLY DISTRIBUTED

(In millions of dollars)

Years	Real Estate Bonds	Guaranteed Mortgages	Individual Mortgages
1909 and 1914	20– 30	Negligible	150–200
1919 and 1920	80–100	10–20	60– 80
1921 and 1922	40–100	10–20	Negligible
1923–1927	100–200	20–30	Negligible
1928 and 1929	200–300	40–50	Negligible
1930 and 1931	0– 40	10–20	Negligible

From these figures we derive the rough estimates which are incorporated in Line 13 of Table 38. The estimates include takings direct by individuals of both farm and urban mortgages.

CAPITAL SUPPLIED TO ENTERPRISES NOT PUBLICLY FINANCED

Even more obscure, and at the same time more weighty, is the problem of estimating the volume of capital supplied by individuals to enterprises not publicly financed.

The question before us here is how much cash business men and others put into the securities of small or closely held corporations and into the purchase or development of unincorporated enterprises. We have located only one previous attempt, that of Nerlove, to formulate even a partial estimate: and Nerlove's figure—that is, $500,000,000 a year of new capital secured by small corporate units—appears to us plainly inadequate.[17] Means' study of his 200 "giant" corporations and their financing[18] throws some additional light on the question.

Means estimates roughly that the giants have controlled in recent years 35% to 45% of all business wealth other than banking; let us say 40%. He has also examined all public offerings of securities in the *Chronicle* record during the six years 1922–1927, and he finds that "66.5% of new capital obtained by this method was received by the large corporations." Presumably these offerings took care of the total

[17] *Op. cit.*, p. 72.
[18] "The Large Corporation in American Economic Life" by Gardiner C. Means, *American Economic Review*, Mar., 1931, and Chap. III of "The Modern Corporation and Private Property, *op. cit.*"

financing of the corporations owning 40% of business wealth. The remaining one-third (33.5%) of the public offerings presumably raised the capital needed by companies owning another 20% of business wealth. It follows that about 60% of American business has financed its new capital requirements through public offerings. Other estimates by Means indicate (a) that the proportion of capital raised by public offerings has probably fluctuated from year to year over a wide range and (b) that the proportion was lower in the early part of the post-war period than in the later part. In view of the impossibility of ascertaining the exact proportions, we have assumed the following percentages of all business to have been financed through public offerings: 1919–1922, inclusive, 50%; 1923–1926, 55%; 1927–1931, 60%.

Three other assumptions which we believe justified are:

(a) The new capital requirements of small business and of big business bear approximately equal ratios to their wealth. It is true that some allowance may properly be made, and has been made in our estimates, for the abnormal speculative attractiveness in boom years of the "blue chip" shares of well-known companies; but this is relatively a minor factor so far as *new* issues are concerned.

(b) The broad influences making for contraction and expansion from year to year of the new capital issues of large concerns affect simultaneously and almost equally the operations and financing of small concerns. The contrary assumption that small business capital requirements are quite stable from year to year appears to us untenable. However, a slight allowance for the greater need and willingness of their owners to keep small enterprises going, tending to smooth out the year-to-year fluctuations, has been made in our estimates.

(c) Substantially the entire capital of small enterprises is supplied by individuals. The individuals may borrow some of it (provision for which is made in Table 38); but none of it, practically speaking, is contributed by large business organizations and by institutions. (Financing of subsidiaries of large companies is included in Means' previously cited estimates of the new capital received from public offerings.)

Accepting the above assumptions and minor allowances, we have formulated the estimates, shown in Line 14 of Table 38, of new capital supplied by individuals to enterprises not publicly financed. These estimates are proportioned on the basis of the foregoing percentages of publicly financed business, to the total new public issues each year of domestic non-financial corporations shown in Line 1.

Payments by Individuals for Securities

Combining the estimates for publicly distributed securities, for privately sold mortgages and for capital supplied to privately financed enterprises, we get the total takings by individuals of securities and of other forms of ownership interests, which are presented in Line 15 of Table 38.

TABLE 38.—ROUGH ESTIMATES OF PAYMENTS BY INDIVIDUALS FOR SECURITIES, 1919–1931

(In billions of dollars; decreases in italics)

Derivation of Payments by Individuals	1919	1920	1921	1922	1923	1924	1925	1926	1927	1928	1929	1930	1931
1. Public Issues (Non-refunding) of Domestic Non-Financial Corporations	2.2	2.7	1.8	2.3	2.7	3.3	4.1	4.3	5.2	5.3	6.4	4.7	1.8
2. *Plus* Net Purchases of Securities from Foreigners	*0.7*	*1.2*	*0.8*	*0.7*	*0.0*	*0.6*	*0.6*	*0.7*	*0.8*	*0.7*	*0.1*	*0.3*	*0.2*
3. *Plus* Net Additions to Federal Government Issues	*4.8*	*1.9*	*0.6*	*0.7*	*0.8*	*0.9*	*0.7*	*1.2*	*1.0*	*0.8*	*0.7*	*0.1*	*1.7*
4. *Plus* State and Municipal Issues (Non-refunding)	*0.7*	*0.7*	*1.2*	*1.1*	*1.0*	*1.4*	*1.4*	*1.3*	*1.5*	*1.4*	*1.4*	*1.4*	*1.2*
5. Total Additions to Security Markets	8.5	2.7	3.2	3.4	2.9	4.4	5.4	5.1	6.5	6.6	7.2	6.3	4.5
6. Takings by Federal Reserve Banks	*0.0*	*0.5*	*0.0*	*0.2*	*0.3*	*0.4*	*0.2*	*0.1*	*0.3*	*0.5*	*0.8*	*0.2*	*0.1*
7. Takings by All Reporting Banks	*0.7*	*0.5*	*0.3*	*1.9*	*0.2*	*1.5*	*0.2*	*0.3*	*1.8*	*0.6*	*1.0*	*1.6*	*0.3*
8. Takings by Insurance Companies	*0.3*	*0.5*	*0.2*	*0.3*	*0.1*	*0.3*	*0.3*	*0.3*	*0.5*	*0.6*	*0.5*	*0.5*	*0.6*
9. Takings by Non-Profit Institutions	*0.3*	*0.4*	*0.1*	*0.2*	*0.1*	*0.3*	*0.3*	*0.2*	*0.3*	*0.4*	*0.3*	*0.4*	*0.4*
10. Takings by Non-Financial Business Corporations	*1.4*	*0.4*	*0.2*	*0.3*	*0.6*	*0.3*	*0.6*	*0.7*	*0.3*	*0.7*	*0.9*	*0.0*	*0.1*
11. Total Takings by Others than Individuals	2.6	0.4	0.2	2.9	0.7	2.7	1.1	1.4	3.2	1.8	1.0	2.7	1.5
12. Purchases by Individuals of Publicly Distributed Securities	5.9	2.3	3.0	2.9	2.2	1.7	4.3	3.7	3.3	4.8	6.2	3.6	3.0
13. Purchases by Individuals of Privately Sold Mortgages	0.3	0.4	0.1	0.5	0.2	0.2	0.2	0.2	0.2	0.3	0.3	0.1	0.0
14. Capital Supplied to Enterprises Not Publicly Financed (largely through purchases of securities of small companies)	2.3	2.7	1.8	2.3	2.2	2.6	3.3	3.5	3.6	3.6	4.1	3.1	1.2
15. Total Takings by Individuals	8.5	5.4	4.9	2.9	4.6	4.5	7.8	7.4	7.1	8.7	10.6	6.8	4.2
16. Payments by Individuals (accumulations of short-term loans deducted)	4.0	3.6	3.2	2.0	3.0	3.0	5.2	5.0	4.8	5.8	7.1	4.5	2.8

Line 1. Taken from the record of public offerings maintained by *Commercial and Financial Chronicle.*
Line 2. Derived from the "Balance of International Payments", issued annually by the United States Department of Commerce.
Line 3. From reports of the Secretary of the Treasury.
Line 4. From the *Chronicle* record of capital issues.
Line 5. Totals of Lines 1 through 4.
Line 6. From reports of the Federal Reserve Board.
Line 7. From reports of the Federal Reserve Board.
Line 8. From *Insurance Yearbook*, a publication of the Spectator Company.
Line 9. About two-thirds of insurance company takings; see text.
Line 10. Rough estimates based for recent years on combined corporate balance sheets prepared by the Standard Statistics Company.
Line 11. Totals of Lines 6 through 10.
Line 12. Line 5 *minus* Line 11.
Line 13. Rough estimates; see text.
Line 14. Proportioned on sliding scale (50 to 40% of total domestic new capital requirements) to public issues as shown in Line 1; see text.
Line 15. Totals of Lines 12 through 14.
Line 16. Approximately two-thirds of total takings except in 1919, when a large arbitrary allowance is made for bank loans on Liberty bond issues; see text.

But we have not yet reached our goal.   Obviously a good part of the money so invested was borrowed from bankers and brokers.   Some of the loans were short-time, and all of them called for repayment on demand or at a specified date; so it might seem proper to dismiss them as merely temporary accommodations.   On the other hand, new loans were made faster than the old loans were paid off; throughout the boom years loans incurred by individuals to finance purchases of securities and other ventures were accumulating.   In order to estimate how much was actually saved out of current income for such investments, it is necessary to deduct the accumulations of loans.

How much were they?   Only a rough guess is possible.   From the end of 1921 to the end of 1929 total bank loans and discounts increased about $15,000,000,000.   Other short-term loans (brokers' loans from own capital, life insurance policy loans for business purposes, and loans by small-loan agencies presumed to be for non-consumption purposes, and unrecorded obligations) had a probable growth of about $3,000,-000,000.[19]   The total expansion, then, in short-term debt (excluding loans for consumption purposes treated in Appendix E) was $18,000,000,000.

During the same period notes and accounts payable of industrial corporations, as compiled in *Statistics of Income*, went up some $3,000,-000,000; from the end of 1925 to the end of 1929, the same item for *all* corporations grew about $5,000,000,000.   These corporate increases are surprisingly moderate, particularly when brought into comparison with gains in gross income as follows (in billions of dollars):

Gross Income	1921	1926	1929
All Corporations.............................	91.2	142.1	160.6
Manufacturing and Trading Corporations........	65.8	103.4	115.6

Transactions of this size make huge demands on short-term credits. On the basis of an average two-month term of payment for goods sold by manufacturing and trading corporations, their operations must have involved total accounts payable outstanding at the end of each year as follows: 1921, $11,000,000,000; 1926, $17,000,000,000; 1929, $19,000,-000,000.   The expansion in mercantile short-term payables during the nine-year period was greater, it seems, than the expansion in all payables, including bank loans; this must mean that in the period as a whole (though not in the last three years of the period) bank loans to corporations were substantially reduced.   The data are not adequate for year-to-year reckoning; but this much may be said with some

[19] Based on "Internal Debts of the United States," Chaps. 6 and 10.

confidence: In the nine-year period little, if any, of the $15,000,000,000 increase in loans by banks and $3,000,000,000 by other financial agencies was absorbed by business corporations; most of it may reasonably be assigned to individuals for financing their operations of a business character. The operations best fitted for financing by short-term loans consist of purchases of securities or other ownership interests; and the whole accumulation of such loans has been charged against purchases in this category.[20]

The accumulation comes to approximately one-third of the purchases. The remaining two-thirds must have been paid by individuals from their own funds. This explains the entries for the years 1922–1929, inclusive, in Line 16 of Table 38. The same ratio has been applied in 1920, also a year of expanding loans.

The table covers, also, three years when bank loans were sharply curtailed, 1921, 1930, and 1931. For the reasons stated earlier in this chapter, it does not seem possible to accept the naive notion that deflationary decreases in loans represent repayments out of income. When the credit structure breaks in a storm of deflation, loans are repaid for the most part by selling assets at reduced valuations. At the same time, we find no reason to assume that any change occurs in financing fresh purchases. They are paid for in part by fresh loans in substantially the same way as in inflationary years. The two-thirds ratio used in the years of inflation has been applied, therefore, in the three years of deflation.

[20] The view taken above is in part confirmed by a study of the National Industrial Conference Board issued under the title "The Availability of Bank Credit" (New York, 1932, pp. 10–11) which says: "Following 1922 there was a marked shift in the nature of the financing functions of banks with respect to industry and trade. Less and less bank credit from that year on to 1929 was furnished to industry and trade directly through commercial loans, and more and more, indirectly through loans to consumers, loans on securities, and loans on real estate. In 1922 about 47% of all bank loans and investments in the United States were classed as commercial loans with responsibility for repayment residing primarily with industry and trade, 12% was security loans, and 9% was real estate loans; in 1929, by contrast, the corresponding percentages were 33%, 20%, and 18%, respectively. . . . Undoubtedly a factor in the declining proportion of commercial loans to industry and trade was the growing importance of personal and consumer loans, dependent for repayment not on a turnover of production and trade but on the stability of personal incomes." A rough calculation based on the foregoing percentages indicates that the increase in bank loans and discounts for account of individuals from the end of 1922 to the end of 1929 approximated $13,000,000,000, which is quite consistent with our assumed increase of $15,000,000,000 from the end of 1921 to the end of 1929. It should be noted in this connection that bank loans on real estate collateral may properly be presumed to have been used for current business transactions. More exact computations would be desirable but we find no way to make them.

An adaptation of the ratio is required for 1919 because of the extraordinary purchases by individuals of Liberty bonds. Bank loans to
finance the purchases were extended with the greatest freedom—indeed,
urged upon people of all classes. Moreover, previous issues of government bonds were readily taken as collateral up to a high percentage
of their face value. In the absence of any better-founded guess, we
have arbitrarily assigned to "payments by individuals" (Line 16)
two-thirds of their takings of non-governmental securities and only
one-fifth of their takings of Liberties.

HOLDINGS OF NON-FARM REAL ESTATE BY INDIVIDUALS

The fourth important form of savings by individuals consists of
payments for real estate—in preceding generations the preferred, indeed
almost the sole, object of permanent investment. Even in this generation, as Table 9 of Chapter II makes clear, real property held first
place before the war and in three of the earlier post-war years. Since
1924, however, it has lost ground before the rapid advance of investment in securities and the slow but steady progress of payments to life
insurance companies.

The first step toward an estimate of savings devoted to real estate
is to ascertain the volume of acquisitions by individuals. No single
source will supply the information for both farms and non-farm real
estate; but in each case some scanty data and some plausible relationships can be combined to form estimates which seem to be within reason.

Investments by individuals in non-farm real estate comprise both
owner-occupied homes and holdings of rented dwellings and business
buildings. However, a rising proportion of rented dwellings erected
since the war have been multi-family houses belonging to corporations:
and the interests of individuals in such property have been taken into
account in our estimates of their purchases of securities. A similar
comment applies even more plainly to business buildings. The immediate problem is limited to estimating the volume of acquisitions of
personally-owned properties.

As the best available base, we take the 1922 estimate of national
wealth in the form of business and residential real estate, apart from
the holdings of public utilities and manufacturing and mining companies. The estimate, as interpreted by Berle and Means, is:[21]

Residential real estate	$48,000,000,000
Real estate for business uses	24,000,000,000
Total	$72,000,000,000
Of which corporations engaged in trade and finance owned	$12,000,000,000

[21] *Op. cit.*, Appendix M.

Two refinements of the above figures may be made:

(*a*) The total for residential real estate may be split into two parts. Owner-occupied homes in 1922 were valued at about $26,000,000,000 (7,800,000 families in homes with an average value of $3,300), leaving $22,000,000,000 of the residential real estate for rented dwellings.

(*b*) The holdings assigned to specified classes of corporations may be taken as the foundation of an estimate of holdings of all kinds of business enterprises. Unincorporated retailers in 1929, according to the Census of Distribution, did over 50% of all retail business, and doubtless the percentage was considerably higher—say 60%—in 1922; on the plausible assumption that they owned proportionately as much real estate as incorporated trading concerns, we must assign at least $5,000,000,000 to them; to which $1,000,000,000 may be added for unincorporated service enterprises (small hotels, theaters, laundries, etc.). Furthermore, we must allow at least $2,000,000,000 for holdings of construction companies and of incorporated service concerns. The total of urban real estate owned by business enterprises, exclusive of public utilities and factories, comes, then, to $20,000,000,000.

Deducting the last-named sum from the total of rented residential property and business property, we get the amount of these two forms of property owned by individuals, namely: $52,000,000,000. Included in this amount is the value of owner-occupied homes, as given in paragraph (*a*) above, $26,000,000,000. It is in this way that we arrive at the estimates listed under the year 1922 in Table 39.

If these figures be accepted, it becomes possible to construct the remainder of Table 39. Line 1, Market Values of Non-Farm Real Estate, is based on the assessed valuations of real property in cities of 30,000 and over, as given in annual issues of the census report, *Financial Statistics of Cities*. The valuation in 1922 was 58% of the market value, $72,000,000,000, as given in the above cited estimate of national wealth. This percentage is *not* a ratio between assessed valuations in cities of over 30,000 and market valuations of real estate in the same cities; it simply states the relationship in the one year 1922 between the total of assessed valuations in these cities and the total of market values of all urban real estate, except that belonging to public utilities and to manufacturing and mining companies. In the absence of any more satisfactory method, we have applied this percentage to the assessed valuations of succeeding years and have thus obtained the over-all market values in Line 1.

The average values in 1922 of dwellings occupied by owning and by renting families are easily deduced, since the number of non-farm families in each group is supplied for census years. These average values are: dwellings occupied by owning families, $3,300; dwellings occupied by renting families, $2,000. For 1929, corresponding values based upon *median* figures from the 1930 Census of Families are, respectively, $4,500 and $2,500. The average values of intervening years are scaled. The scale for rented dwellings is roughly adjusted to the index of rents of the National Industrial Conference Board. In this way we obtain the aggregate valuations of owner-occupied homes and of rented dwellings each year from 1922 to 1929, inclusive, shown in Lines 2 and 3 of Table 39.

TABLE 39.—ROUGH ESTIMATES OF NON-FARM REAL ESTATE PURCHASES BY INDIVIDUALS, 1923–1929

(In billions of dollars)

Derivation of Payments by Individuals	1922	1923	1924	1925	1926	1927	1928	1929
1. Market Values of Non-Farm Real Estate..	72	76	82	89	96	105	110	115
2. Valuations of Owner-Occupied Homes.....	26	28	32	35	38	42	44	47
3. Valuations of Rented Dwellings...........	22	23	24	26	27	29	31	32
4. Valuations of Property for Business Uses..	24	25	26	28	31	34	35	36
5. Rented Dwellings and Business Property Owned by Business Enterprises.........	20	22	23	25	27	29	32	33
6. Rented Dwellings and Business Property Owned by Individuals..................	26	26	27	29	31	34	34	35
7. Total Non-Farm Real Estate Owned by Individuals............................	52	54	59	64	69	76	78	82
8. Annual Increments of Holdings by Individuals..............................	..	2	5	5	5	7	2	4
9. Payments by Individuals (accumulations of long and medium-term loans deducted)	..	1.0	2.0	2.5	2.5	3.0	2.0	2.0

Line 1.   Omitting real property owned by public utilities and by manufacturing and mining companies; derived from assessed valuations of real property in cities of over 30,000; see text.

Line 2.   Based on census reports of owner-occupied homes in 1920 and 1930 (numbers for intervening years interpolated) and assumed average values on a scale from $3,300 in 1922 to $4,500 in 1929.

Line 3.   Numbers of non-farm renting families obtained as above; assumed average values of dwellings per family on a scale from $2,000 in 1922 and 1923 to $2,500 in 1928 and 1929.

Line 4.   Line 1 minus Lines 2 and 3.

Line 5.   Derived from reported assets of certain classes of corporations given in Statistics of Income plus allowances for unincorporated business enterprises; see text.

Line 6.   Line 3 plus Line 4 minus Line 5.

Line 7.   Line 2 plus Line 6.

Line 8.   Derived from Line 7.

Line 9.   Derived from Line 8 on assumption that one-half each year's increment represents payments for equities; however, the more extreme fluctuations have been smoothed out on the strength of Dodge reports of valuations of new residential construction.

The balance of each year's total valuation, it must be presumed, consists of property for business uses, as presented in Line 4.

The non-farm real estate holdings of business enterprises (Line 5) are derived in the manner explained above from Statistics of Income, with allowances for unincorporated concerns. Subtracting these holdings from the combined valuations of rented dwellings and of business properties, we get the holdings by individuals of income-producing properties (Line 6). By adding the valuations of owner-occupied homes we arrive at the total holdings of individuals (Line 7).

The annual increments of holdings by individuals shown in Line 8 conform in a general way with the observed movements of real estate speculation. They are also consistent with the Dodge reports of new residential construction except for the sharpness of the rise in 1924 and of the drop in 1928. In such rough figuring year-to-year agreement is not to be expected. It seems proper to smooth out the two extreme fluctuations without altering the totals for the period; and this is done in Line 9.

PAYMENTS FOR NON-FARM REAL ESTATE

We have next to consider what proportion of the annual increments may fairly be reckoned as actual payments by individuals from their own funds. Obviously, accumulations of mortgage debts incurred in order to finance purchases of real estate should be deducted. At the end of 1929 the total mortgage debt resting on urban properties was probably about $35,000,000,000,[22] or a little over 30% of total market valuations. The ascertainable holdings or issues of financial organizations moved up from $9,000,000,000 at the end of 1921 to $27,600,000,-000 at the end of 1929, an increase of $18,600,000,000.[23] Inasmuch as properties owned and occupied by business concerns are often unincumbered or lightly incumbered, not less than two-thirds of the debt increase, it is safe to say, was on property owned by individuals; this would come to about 40% of the gain in market vaues of their holdings. An additional 10% of the gain may be ascribed to revaluations of assessments of unsold properties. On the whole, it would seem that somewhere near 50% of the annual increments may be taken to represent actual payments by individuals. Line 9 presents smoothed-out estimates based on the assumed percentage.

The reader may wonder why Table 39 is limited to an eight-year term. One obvious reason is that estimates through this period can be anchored at each end to census reports. A more cogent reason is that in these eight years prices were relatively stable, whereas both immediately before the period and immediately after real estate markets ran wild. Such large fluctuations make measurement of annual changes not merely difficult but impossible.

Nevertheless, in Table 40, Line 4, we have ventured to enter figures for the years preceding and subsequent to the eight-year term. These figures are put forward only as guesses which look plausible in their relationship to the figures taken from Table 39 for the eight years 1922–1929.

---

[22] Chapter 3 of "Internal Debts of the United States," p. 78. The estimate is for the end of 1931, but appears to be equally valid for the end of 1929.

[23] *Ibid*, p. 76.

TABLE 40.—ROUGH ESTIMATES OF TOTAL PAYMENTS BY INDIVIDUALS FOR REAL ESTATE, 1909–1931

(In billions of dollars; decreases in italics)

Derivation of Payments by Individuals	1909	1914	Pre-war Average	1919	1920	1921	1922	1923	1924	1925	1926	1927	1928	1929	1930	1931
1. Purchases of Farms by Individuals	1.2	1.4	1.3	2.7	2.5	1.4	1.6	1.8	1.7	1.7	1.7	1.7	1.6	1.5	1.3	1.0
2. *Less* Increases of Farm Debt	0.2	0.2	0.2	0.5	0.5	0.0	0.1	0.2	0.1	0.0	0.0	*0.1*	*0.1*	*0.1*	*0.1*	*0.3*
3. Net Payments for Farms	1.0	1.2	1.1	2.2	2.0	1.4	1.5	1.6	1.6	1.7	1.7	1.7	1.6	1.5	1.3	1.0
4. Assumed Payments for Non-Farm Real Estate	0.5	0.5	0.5	1.0	2.0	0.5	1.0	1.0	2.0	2.5	2.5	3.0	2.0	2.0	1.0	0.5
5. Total Payments for Real Estate	1.5	1.7	1.6	3.2	4.0	1.9	2.5	2.6	3.6	4.2	4.2	4.7	3.6	3.5	2.3	1.5

Line 1. Based on percentages of farms transferred to individuals; see text.

Line 2. For years since 1924 derived from estimate of farmers' indebtedness by the United States Department of Agriculture (see especially *Crops and Markets*, April, 1933); for earlier years based on rough year-to-year allocations of total increases in farmers' indebtedness.

Line 3. Line 1 *minus* Line 2 *except* that decreases in Line 2 are not deducted; see text.

Line 4. Figures for 1923–1929, inclusive, are taken from Line 9 of Table 39; figures for both preceding and subsequent years are merely crude relatives to the 1923–1929 figures which have been adjusted to observed market conditions.

Line 5. Totals of Lines 3 and 4.

FARM REAL ESTATE; HOLDINGS AND PAYMENTS

The question of how much farm property was purchased by individuals each year can be answered with some approach to definiteness on the strength of data collected by the Bureau of Agricultural Economics.[24] In the years 1927–1931 the combined percentages of farms which changed ownership by voluntary sales and trades and by administrators' and executors' sales were: 1927, 3.5%; 1928, 3.3%; 1929, 2.9%; 1930, 3.0%; 1931, 2.7%. (It is assumed that forced sales and transfers by inheritance and gift do not involve fresh money payments and may therefore be disregarded.) Corresponding percentages for earlier years are not given and can only be inferred. It seems best to take for granted that the 3.5% ratio is normal and may be adopted for the years 1923–1926 and for the two pre-war years. Suitable adjustments for years of greater or less activity would seem to be: 1919 and 1920, 4.0%; 1921, 2.5%; 1922, 3.0%. These percentages applied to total values of farm land and buildings give the estimates entered in Line 1 of Table 40.

The accumulations of farm indebtedness up to 1924 (roughly estimated) are entered in Line 2. Since 1924 the amount of farm debt has slowly diminished. For the reason previously given, the decline is ignored in our estimate of annual payments for farms (Line 3).

Payments for both major kinds of real estate are summed to give the grand totals in Line 5.

NET ANNUAL SAVINGS FROM INCOME

We are now prepared at last to bring together the estimates of annual payments for funds and for properties and of increases or decreases in cash holdings and thus reach the figures for total annual acquisitions in Line 5 of Table 41. These figures might perhaps be construed as actual savings; at any rate, they represent each year's gains in the holdings, measured in current dollars, of individuals.

But they are not savings from realized income. It remains to take out (a) profits and capital gains from sale of assets and (b) withdrawals from life insurance funds. Fortunately, *Statistics of Income* supplies satisfactory data as to profits and capital gains of income taxpayers. The figures in Line 6 of Table 41 are slightly adjusted to allow for small additions from incomes not subject to taxation. The annual disbursements by life insurance companies for death losses, matured and surrendered policies, annuities and policyholders' dividends are also recorded. After deducting 10% for payments to business concerns, the receipts by individuals from this source are shown in Line 7.

[24] See especially "The Farm Real Estate Situation, 1931–32," by B. R. Stauber, Circular No. 261, United States Department of Agriculture, Jan., 1933.

TABLE 41.—SUMMARIZING ESTIMATES OF CONSUMERS' SAVINGS, 1909–1931

(In billions of dollars; decreases in italics)

Derivation of Net Annual Savings	1909	1914	Pre-war Average	1919	1920	1921	1922	1923	1924	1925	1926	1927	1928	1929	1930	1931
1. Payments of Life Insurance Premiums	0.5	0.7	0.6	1.2	1.4	1.5	1.7	1.9	2.1	2.3	2.4	2.6	2.8	3.2	3.1	3.0
2. Increases in Cash Holdings	0.6	0.6	0.6	2.6	2.7	1.1	1.1	2.5	2.6	2.9	2.6	2.6	2.6	1.3	0.6	0.9
3. Payments for Holdings of Securities	1.0	1.0	1.0	4.0	3.6	3.2	2.0	3.0	3.0	5.2	5.0	4.8	5.8	7.1	4.5	2.8
4. Payments for Holdings of Real Property	1.5	1.7	1.6	3.2	4.0	1.9	2.5	2.6	3.6	4.2	4.2	4.7	3.6	3.5	2.3	1.5
5. Totals of Annual Acquisitions	3.6	4.0	3.8	11.0	11.7	7.7	7.3	10.0	11.3	14.6	14.2	14.7	14.8	15.1	10.5	6.4
6. Less Realized Profits and Capital Gains from Sales of Assets	0.5	0.5	0.5	1.0	1.0	0.5	1.0	1.2	1.5	2.9	2.4	2.9	4.8	4.0	0.0	0.6
7. Less Receipts of Funds Withdrawn from Life Insurance Companies	0.3	0.5	0.4	0.6	0.6	0.7	0.9	1.0	1.1	1.1	1.2	1.4	1.5	1.8	2.0	2.3
8. Net Annual Savings from Realized Income	2.8	3.0	2.9	9.4	10.1	6.5	5.4	7.8	8.7	10.6	10.6	10.4	8.5	9.3	8.5	4.1

Line 1. From Table 34.

Line 2. From Line 6 of Table 35.

Line 3. From Line 16 of Table 38, except pre-war years which are inferred from the relative amounts of new capital issues in the *Journal of Commerce* record.

Line 4. From Line 5 of Table 40.

Line 5. Totals of Lines 1 through 4.

Line 6. Derived from *Statistics of Income*; see text.

Line 7. Ninety per cent of total payments to policyholders for death losses, matured endowments, annuities, surrendered policies and dividends; the remaining 10% is ascribed to business enterprises.

Line 8. Line 5 *minus* Lines 6 and 7.

Subtracting these two items, we get the final estimates of annual savings from income. These figures, it may be well to reiterate, are tentative and subject to change. It has been our aim to show frankly their weaknesses and to invite criticisms which will eventually improve them. For the time being, however, they are treated in this study as acceptable approximations.

Appendix E

ESTIMATES OF CONSUMERS' BORROWINGS

The question here taken up lies a little outside the main subject of this book. Yet it is too closely related to be easily thrust aside; and mis-statements are too frequent to be ignored. Moreover, the estimates of commodity purchases at retail set forth in Appendix A supply a new factual basis for computing changes in mercantile credits through the post-war period.

Scope of Problem

At this point we are dealing only with *borrowings for current expenditures*. Borrowings by individuals for acquisitions of potential income-producing assets have been taken into account in the preceding estimates of savings devoted specifically to real estate and securities. Short-term borrowings to finance current expenditures are now to be separately computed and treated as additions to or deductions from consumers' spendable monies.

The word "borrowings," as here used, needs a word of explanation. It covers both debts incurred by deferring payments for purchases and debts incurred by obtaining loans of money. Our primary concern is with the total debts outstanding, however they may have been incurred; and, more particularly, with the year-to-year movements of total debts.

The entire problem should be treated as a unit. Some useful studies, to be cited later, of distinct forms of consumers' borrowings have been made. But the various forms interlock. Most direct loans to families by insurance companies and financing companies, for example, are used in large part to settle outstanding debts; and installment accounts to a considerable extent take the place of open accounts. Ryan's first-hand investigation among personal finance companies indicates that the percentage of personal loans used to pay off old debts falls somewhere between 65% and 80%.[1] A study of clothing sales on credit under Seligman's direction reveals that "the ten-payment plan [installment selling] has led not to any increase of consumption credit in general, but rather to a substitution of fractional credit for lump-sum

[1] "Family Finance in the United States" by Franklin W. Ryan, *Journal of Business*, Oct., 1930, p. 413.

credit."[2] These examples illustrate the ease with which consumers' borrowings may shift from one form to another and the consequent danger of drawing misleading conclusions from an examination of one form alone—a remark which is particularly applicable to numerous discussions of installment selling as if it were an isolated phenomenon. Certainly the growth of any one form of borrowings cannot safely be accepted as an index of the movements of borrowings as a whole.

In the present study we are concerned only with *consumers*, in the sense in which the word has been defined in Chapter I. Credits and small loans extended to individuals for business purposes have been excluded so far as practicable. The exclusion is responsible for some discrepancies between the estimates here to be presented and preceding estimates which generally cover some transactions of a distinctly commercial character.

Moreover, consumers are here regarded as a body—for the reasons stated in Chapter I. Inter-consumer dealings, such as loans from one person to another when both are acting in non-business roles, are left out of the reckoning.

METHODS OF COMPUTING INSTALLMENT CREDIT OUTSTANDINGS

In order to compute consumers' installment debts outstanding at the end of each year, we have employed Ayres' method[3] modified by Seligman's corrections. Briefly put, the method is:

1. Ascertain and apply the estimated percentage of installment sales to total sales of each commodity. The figures for total sales are taken from Appendix A, except sales of second-hand passenger automobiles, which are calculated from the commodity breakdown supplied by the Census of Distribution (for 1929) and from data issued by the National Association of Finance Companies. The percentages of sales on installment have been derived for the most part from Seligman with some corrections indicated by the *National Retail Credit Survey* of the United States Department of Commerce. The percentages applied to automobiles, however, are adjusted from year to year to accord with estimates of the above-mentioned Association.

2. Apply to sales on installment the average percentages (derived from the above sources) of down payments; then add to the remaining balances increments to represent carrying charges calculated on the basis of normal percentages of carrying charges to original debt. The result is the amount of installment paper issued on each class of commodities each year.

3. Calculate the percentages of installment paper issued each year which will be outstanding at the end of the year. These percentages are functions of the

[2] "Economics of Instalment Selling" by Edwin R. A. Seligman, Harper, New York, 1927, vol. 1, p. 296.

[3] Explained in "Installment Selling and Financing" by Milan V. Ayres, a paper read at the Third National Automotive Financing Conference, Chicago, Nov., 1926.

average time each class of paper remains outstanding; this information also comes from Ayres as modified by Seligman.[4] Inasmuch as the average time for piano paper is two years, the percentage in this instance exceeds 100%.

Table 42 below lists the main commodities sold on installment and the percentages, corresponding to the three paragraphs above, which we have applied. They are sufficient, in conjunction with the information

TABLE 42.—PERCENTAGES USED IN COMPUTING CONSUMERS' INSTALLMENT DEBTS OUTSTANDING AT END OF EACH YEAR

Main Commodities Sold on Installment	Percentages of Total Sales Made on Installment	Percentages of Down Payments on Installment Sales	Percentages of Total Obligations, Including Carrying Charges, Incurred Each Year Which Will Be Outstanding at the End of the Year
New Passenger Automobiles	58 to 63	33	55
Used Passenger Automobiles	45 to 65	33	55
Furniture.................	50	15	75
Pianos...................	85	15	130
Phonographs.............	80	10	45
Radio Sets...............	75	25	30
Washing Machines........	80	10	55
Vacuum Cleaners..........	85	15	40
Sewing Machines..........	90	10	80
Gas Ranges..............	70	15	50
Mechanical Refrigerators...	90	10	80
Jewelry..................	10	20	45
Clothing.................	4 to 5	25	15

given above, to reconstruct our estimates of installment paper outstanding at the end of each year, which will be found summarized in Line 1 of Table 44.

METHODS OF COMPUTING OPEN ACCOUNT OUTSTANDINGS

The procedure for computing open accounts of consumers with merchants at the end of each year is much simpler. The percentages of chief classes of commodity sales made on open account, as listed in Table 43 are derived mainly from the *National Retail Credit Survey*. The percentages supplied by the *Survey*, however, are for types of retail outlets; hence it has been necessary for some commodities sold through varied outlets to utilize other sources, particularly the

[4] *Op. cit.*, vol. 1, pp. 92–119.

Census of Distribution.[5]   Thus, in the case of foods, to take the largest item, sales on open account were estimated at 25% by combining the percentages of credit sales of each type of outlet in the food group.

In our estimates percentages of sales on open account have been held constant for the entire post-war period.   We are aware of opinions freely expressed *both* to the effect that the proportion of open account

TABLE 43.—PERCENTAGES OF TOTAL SALES ON OPEN ACCOUNTS

Commodities	Percentage
Foods	25
Women's Clothing	45
Millinery	10
Fur Goods	50
Knit Goods	45
Men's Clothing, Hats, Furnishings	20
Boots and Shoes	20
All Other Clothing	30
Gasoline and Oil	15
Auto Tires, Parts, etc.	40
Automobiles	5
House Furnishings	40
Electrical Appliances	40
Household Supplies	35
Crockery and China	50
Stoves	50
Musical Instruments	5
Jewelry	45
Drugs and Toilet Goods	10
Books and Stationery	60
All Others	20

sales has risen sharply and also to the exact contrary; but we can find no evidence in the reports of the *National Retail Credit Survey*, covering several recent years, or in any other reliable source that either opinion has a solid base.

The usually accepted judgment is that the average term of payment of open accounts with retailers runs from 70 to 80 days; and this judgment is confirmed by the *National Retail Credit Survey*.[6]   We have, therefore, considered 20% of the annual purchases on open accounts to be outstanding at the end of the year.

[5] See Table 7A in the *United States Summary* of the 1930 Census of Retail Distribution.

[6] The average time of payment appears to have been considerably longer in 1933 and 1934, but not during the period covered in the present study.

TABLE 44.—A SUMMARY OF SHORT-TERM CONSUMERS' DEBTS OUTSTANDING AT END OF EACH YEAR

(In millions of dollars; decreases in italics)

	1919	1920	1921	1922	1923	1924	1925	1926	1927	1928	1929	1930	1931
1. Installment Paper	1,119	1,408	1,050	1,333	1,698	1,824	1,954	1,919	1,886	2,028	2,222	1,696	1,170
2. Mercantile Open Accounts	1,884	2,028	1,762	1,908	2,126	2,177	2,243	2,305	2,341	2,418	2,490	2,177	1,749
3. Overdue Items (rents, taxes, life insurance premiums, etc.)	500	500	1,000	500	500	500	500	500	500	500	500	1,000	2,000
4. Totals of Debts Arising from Purchases	3,503	3,936	3,812	3,741	4,324	4,501	4,697	4,724	4,677	4,946	5,212	4,873	4,919
5. Small-Loan Agency Loans (by licensed agencies, pawnbrokers, personal loan departments of commercial banks, etc.)	600	600	700	700	800	800	900	1,000	1,100	1,200	1,300	1,400	1,500
6. Personal Loans (non-departmentized) by Commercial Banks	800	900	900	850	900	1,000	1,100	1,100	1,150	1,200	1,200	1,100	1,000
7. Life Insurance Policy Loans	540	570	705	760	800	880	965	1,070	1,190	1,330	1,585	1,870	2,270
8. United States Government Loans to Veterans	....	....	1	2	5	9	13	20	60	110	180	280	1,210
9. Totals of Debts Arising from Loans	1,940	2,070	2,306	2,312	2,505	2,689	2,978	3,190	3,500	3,840	4,265	4,650	5,980
10. Totals of Short-Term Consumers' Debts	5,443	6,006	6,118	6,053	6,829	7,190	7,675	7,914	8,177	8,786	9,477	9,523	10,899
11. Annual Increase or Decrease	-207	+563	+112	-65	+776	+361	+485	+239	+263	+609	+691	+46	+1,376
12. Deductions for Carrying Charges	-384	-385	-463	-432	-479	-493	-547	-594	-647	-702	-760	-842	-994
13. Net Sums Received or Repaid	-591	+178	-351	-497	+297	-132	-62	-355	-384	-93	-69	-796	+382

Line 1. Computed by applying percentages given in the text to our estimates of commodity sales.

Line 2. Computed by applying percentages given in the text to our estimates of commodity sales.

Line 3. Derived, for 1931, from Chap. XI by Franklin W. Ryan in "Internal Debts of the United States"; for 1929, from "The Personal Finance Business" by M. R. Neifeld, Harper, New York, 1933, p. 58. For other years, the 1929 amount has been accepted except for the depression years, 1921 and 1930, when it is arbitrarily doubled. A slight substantiation of the $500,000,000 figure for normal years is found in the 1922 report of the Department of Commerce on "Wealth, Public Debt and Taxation" which shows uncollected taxes as $232,000,000.

Line 4. Totals of Line 1, 2 and 3.

Line 5. Derived, for 1931 and 1929, from sources above cited; for 1925, from "Financing the Consumer" by Evans Clark, Macmillan, New York, 1930, pp. 30 and 191; for intervening years, figures based on straight-line trend. The figures for earlier years are consistent with such fragmentary data as could be found in the three sources cited, in Moulton ("Financial Organization of Society," University of Chicago Press, 1921, p. 706) and elsewhere.

Line 6. Derived, for 1931, from Ryan (*op. cit.*); for earlier years, based on 3% of the total loans of all reporting banks. This percentage is the ratio between Ryan's estimate and total loans in 1931; it may be low. Clark's opinion ("The Challenge of Consumer Credit" by Evans Clark, *American Labor Legislation Review*, Sept., 1931, p. 347) is that "only from 4% to 5% of commercial bank loans could properly be classified as consumer credit."

Line 7. Sixty per cent of policy loans, as reported in *Insurance Yearbook*, are assumed to be for consumption. The percentage is somewhat below that assigned by Cullen, as cited in "Internal Debts of the United States," p. 309.

Line 8. Ninety per cent of policy loans and adjusted service certificate loans are assumed to be for consumption (*ibid.*).

Line 9. Totals of Lines 5 through 8.

Line 10. Totals of Lines 4 and 9. These totals are considerably lower than corresponding estimates by Neifeld for 1929 ($11,800,000,000), by Clark for 1929 ($10,500,000 000) and by Ryan for 1931 ($12,900,000,000, eliminating personal loans between individuals); see references in preceding notes. The discrepancies arise largely from our new estimates of installment paper and open accounts, which are well below most previous estimates. Ryan's rough total of $22,000,-000,000 for 1929 (*op. cit.*, p. 301) apparently has no substantial basis.

Line 11. Derived from Line 10; the decrease in 1919 is based on an estimate for 1918 not shown in Table 44.

Line 12. Carrying charges on installment accounts are omitted here, as they have been included in our computations of installment debts. No carrying charges are added for open accounts. Carrying charges on other debts are based on the following percentages: overdue items, 6%; life insurance policy loans. 6%; United States government loans, 4%; small-loan agency loans, 40% (on the net end-of-year debt); non-departmentized loans by banks, 9%.

Line 13. Line 11 *minus* Line 12

COMPARISONS WITH OTHER ESTIMATES

All the foregoing calculations pertain to the censual (odd-numbered) years, these being the only years for which we have itemized estimates of commodity sales. On the basis of the interpolated totals of commodity sales, however (Table 3 of Chapter II), it is possible to work out interpolations of installment paper and open accounts outstanding at the end of inter-censual years. In this way Lines 1 and 2 of Table 44 have been filled in for all post-war years, beginning with 1919.

The results check reasonably well with other estimates. The totals of installment sales and paper for 1925, though largely based on Seligman, differ from his figures, because his allowances for new and used trucks, tractors and farm machinery have been excluded in our figuring on the ground that they are producers' goods and because his furniture estimate includes open accounts as well as installment sales. Making adjustments for these items, we find his total of installment sales to be $4,145,000,000 against our $4,064,000,000 and his installment paper outstanding to be $1,909,000,000 against our $1,954,000,000.

The Census of Distribution arrives at 34.3% of all retail sales in 1929 as the proportion sold on credit, counting both installment and open credits, whereas our corresponding figure is 37.9%. The Census, on the strength of a test run of five states, divides the foregoing 34% into 21% of open accounts and 13% of installment accounts, whereas our corresponding figures are 27 and 11%. It should be added that the Census leaves out some $1,500,000,000 (3% of retail sales) of installment obligations financed by outside finance companies which we have included. It appears, then, that the totals of the census figures and of our independent estimates are in close agreement; but there is a wide, unexplained discrepancy in the division between open and installment accounts. One possible explanation is that many credit sales could have been assigned by reporting retailers to either the open account or the installment account category.

THE GROWING LOAD OF FAMILY DEBT

The remaining figures in Table 44 are adapted from various reports and estimates cited in the notes subjoined to the table. They do not call for further explanation except the remark that some of the figures (particularly those for overdue items) are obviously guesses. The estimates for the more important forms of personal loans, however, rest on fairly substantial data. Though we do not care to vouch for the accuracy of Table 44, some general deductions are in order.

The first point to strike one, on examining the totals shown in Line 10, is the unbroken rise of consumers' debt, except for a slight check in 1922, throughout the post-war period. Some forms of debt undergo considerable fluctuations—for instance, the drastic reductions in both installment paper and open accounts from 1929 to 1931 and the sharp bulges in both overdue items and governmental loans in the same years; but these variations evidently tend to offset each other.

However, the rise in total debts is quite unequally distributed between the two major classes of debts summarized in Lines 4 and 9 of Table 44. The relationships are made plain in Chart I of Chapter II, showing short-term indebtedness per family. Note the stability of debts arising from purchases in contrast with the rapid upward sweep of debts arising from loans. The family load in 1919 was $230, of which only a little more than one-third consisted of debts arising out of loans: by 1931 it had gone up to $359, and 55% consisted of debts arising out of loans. The load had been picked up too quickly and too easily; it became a crushing burden when incomes fell.

The comparative conservatism of the average American family in taking on installment debts is well illustrated in Cover's study of personal bankruptcy cases in the Chicago district.[7] The following statement bears directly on the point.

The small number of cases owing upon installment purchases is significant and apparently is not altogether, or even largely, due to the removal of goods which were being purchased on the payment plan. Most bankrupts appeared not to have obligated themselves with this kind of debt in the 12 months preceding bankruptcy, though prior to that period their financial standing may have been impaired by such obligations. In fact, of the 384 cases analyzed, the last 100 cases, chronologically, reduced the average proportion in this category to 8 per cent from 24 per cent.

RECEIPTS OVERBALANCED BY REPAYMENTS

Line 11 of Table 44 shows the annual increase or decrease in consumers' debts outstanding. Except for the two slight decreases in 1919 and in 1922, they expanded every year and rose ominously in 1931.

Yet the net result was not a corresponding gain, even a temporary gain, in consumers' cash receipts; for carrying charges, set forth in Line 12, advanced with still greater speed. They ate up all the cash provided by fresh borrowings, and more.

Line 13 will prove something of a shock to those readers who have been led to believe that consumers' borrowings have yielded a vast augmentation of spending power. The surprising truth is that only in 3 years out of 13 have consumers received more from their borrowings than they have returned in the form of repayments and carrying charges. In the other 10 years, consumers turned back amounts running from $62,-000,000 in 1925 to nearly $800,000,000 in 1930. From the end of 1918

[7] "Business and Personal Failure and Readjustment in Chicago" by John H. Cover, University of Chicago Press, 1933, p. 76.

to the end of 1931, the short-term debt burden of consumers increased $5,200,000,000; carrying charges during the period totaled about $7,700,000,000; the excess of payments over receipts was $2,500,000,000.

These are large sums; yet $2,500,000,000 is but slightly more than one-fourth of 1% of the aggregate national outgo during those years. Plainly, the effects of borrowings on total spending power were not far from negligible. In no year did the excess of payments or receipts, as the case may be, rise to as much as 1% of consumers' outgo in that year.

Effects in Congesting Demand

The *general* effects of consumers' borrowings, then, may be put aside on the strength of these findings, as relatively inconsequential. This does not signify, however, that borrowings are wholly unimportant. Two specific effects should not be overlooked.

First is the effect on distribution of spending power. Short-term debts both for purchases and for loans appear to have been incurred chiefly by families in the lower-middle-income groups. Seligman, to be sure, expresses a contrary opinion as to installment obligations: "Inasmuch as modern installment buying affects, as we have seen, primarily the more durable and the higher-priced goods, they will naturally be purchased by consumers in the higher-income class."[8] But everyday observations and such evidence as can be found point the other way. A study of the United States Bureau of Labor Statistics in 1928 of the family budgets of 506 federal employees, with an average income of less than $2,500, showed that 41.5% were buying one or more articles on the installment plan; of these 210 families, 136 were paying for a single installment purchase, 59 for two installment purchases and 15 for three to five installment purchases.[9] Purchases by finance companies of automobile installment paper in 1928, 1929 and 1930 averaged somewhat below $600 for new cars and $300 for used cars, plainly indicating that the bulk of the financing was for low-priced cars.[10] Out of 275,311 borrowers from the Household Finance Corporation from January 1 to September 30, 1931, more than 75% came within the income brackets of $1,200 to $3,000.[11] Though the over-all effects of the debt load on consumers' spending power were relatively slight, it was doubtless relatively a more important influence on the well-being and the purchases of lower-middle-income families.

[8] *Op. cit.*, vol. 1, p. 267.

[9] Cited in "Prosperity and Consumers' Credit" by Julian Goldman, Harper, New York, 1930, pp. 119–122.

[10] *N.A.M.T. News*, issued by National Association of Finance Companies, Feb., 1931.

[11] *American Federationist*, Dec., 1931.

The second noteworthy effect is on the kinds of commodities purchased, a comment which pertains particularly to installment purchases. Installment financing has been successfully applied on a sizeable scale to only a limited group of commodities—automobiles, furniture, musical instruments and household supplies; and mainly to the lower-priced forms of these commodities. In this limited group it has been a powerful sales-building force. All these articles, because they are durable, are easily postponable purchases, which makes them peculiarly subject to the influence of easy financing.

Various guesses have been made as to the extent of this influence. Here is one of them: "Automobile manufacturers and others who venture opinions on the subject say that if automobiles were sold for cash only, the sales would amount to possibly only 35% of the present volume."[12] On the other hand, Danielian points out that "in the automobile industry the rate of increasing sales was greatest from 1900 up to the introduction of installment credit (about 1915), and the rate of increase was very low from 1920 on, when an unprecedented liberality in the extension of consumers' credit existed. Automobiles, radios, refrigerators, etc., are probably attractive enough to have forced a redirection of the cash expenditure of consumers."[13] The truth probably lies somewhere between these two opinions.

To the extent that installment financing strongly influenced the choice of commodities, normal diversification of spendings was reduced. A considerable proportion of consumers' outgo became congested within a narrow area. The condition thus created is dangerous, as we have since learned; for congestion of spendings on postponable purchases creates a hectic, unstable demand which is liable to dry up suddenly.

The American economic system, as it exists in our generation, has proved itself peculiarly vulnerable. One of its serious weaknesses, discussed elsewhere in this book, is the large proportion of durable commodities among consumers' takings. The demand for such commodities, as just remarked, is highly elastic, and their sales are subject to extreme fluctuations. The free extension of credit to consumers has pushed the sales of durable commodities higher than they would otherwise have gone. It has thereby aggravated the instability of the present-day economy and has weakened its resistance to depression.

However, I do not wish to create an exaggerated impression. The actual weight exerted by consumers' borrowings is a question of fact; and the estimates which have been given do not justify assigning to these borrowings more than a minor role either in bringing on depressions or in stimulating recovery.

[12] From an article on "The Effects of Installment Selling on Stability" by Wilbar C. Plummer, *Annals of the American Academy of Political and Social Science*," Sept., 1928.

[13] From an article on "The Theory of Consumers' Credit" by N. R. Danielian, in *American Economic Review*, Sept., 1929.

APPENDIX F

ALLOCATIONS OF CONSUMERS' TAKINGS ON BASIS OF GOVERNING CONDITIONS OF PURCHASE

Frequency of Repetition of Purchases	Primary (here defined as goods or services, the purchase of which is not directly controlled by the purchase or ownership of other goods or services)		Derived (here defined as goods or services which are required in order to obtain satisfactory use of other goods or services)	
	Takings	Percentage	Takings	Percentage
Frequently Repetitive (here defined as services which are normally continuous and as goods or services which are customarily consumed and replaced within a few weeks of purchase)	Food	90	Food	10
	Alcoholic Beverages	100	Gasoline and Oil, and Gasoline Tax	100
	Tobacco	100	Automobile Repair and Storage	20
	Street Railway Fares	100	Chauffeurs	100
	Bus Fares	100	Blacksmiths	100
	Taxicab and Hack Fares	25		
	Soap and Cleaning Preparations	100		
	Ice, Manufactured and Natural	100		
	Rentals Paid for Leased Homes	100		
	Net Rental Values of Owner-Occupied Homes	100		
	Electric, Current, Gas, Telephone	100		
	Home Services of Laborers, Launderers, Servants, Housekeepers	100		
	Laundering and Dry Cleaning	100		
	Personal Appearance—Services	80		
	Recreation—Admissions	80		
	Stationery, Printed Matter and Artists' Materials	100		
	Postage	100		
	Ferries	100		
Less Frequently Repetitive (here defined as other goods or services which are likely to be required again in less than three years)	Women's Clothing	80	Dry Goods and Notions	40
	Men's Clothing	80	Clothing Services	100
	Boots and Shoes	60	Automobile Parts and Accessories	50
	Men's Furnishings	60	Automobile Repair and Storage	80
	Millinery	40	Automobile Insurance, Licenses	100
	Fur Goods	60	House Insurance, Interest, Taxes	100
	Men's Hats and Caps	60	Communal Services for House Maintenance	100
	Dry Goods and Notions	40	Craftsmen's Services for House Upkeep	100
	Piece Goods (Cotton, Silk, Woolen)	80	Boots and Shoes[1]	20
	Knit Goods	60	Men's Furnishings[1]	60
	Gloves	60	Millinery[1]	40
	Umbrellas	60	Fur Goods[1]	20

Item	Percentage
Taxicab and Hack Fares	100
Household Supplies (except soap and cleaning preparations)	100
Coal, Wood and Ice (except Ice)	100
Flowers, Plants and Seeds	100
Sickness and Death	100
Personal Appearance—Commodities	20
Personal Appearance—Services	100
Recreation—Commodities	100
Recreation—Club Dues	100
Recreation—Hotels	100
Recreation—Railroad Fares	20
Recreation—Admissions	100
Recreation—Airways	100
Contributions	100
Fraternal Dues	100
Immigrant Remittances	100
Artists, Musicians, Lawyers, Tuition	100
Direct Taxes	100
Savings	100

Item	Percentage
Men's Hats and Caps[1]	20
Knit Goods[1]	20
Gloves[1]	20
Umbrellas[1]	20

Infrequently Repetitive (here defined as goods or services not likely to be required again in less than three years)

Item	Percentage
Automobiles	100
Motorcycles and Bicycles	100
Carriages, Wagons, Sleighs	100
House Furnishings	90
Electric Appliances (except Fixtures)	100
Musical Instruments and Radio	100
Recreation—Foreign Travel	100
Clothing Items	20

Item	Percentage
Horse-drawn Vehicle Equipment	100
Gas and Electric Fixtures	100
House Furnishings[1]	10
Automobile Parts and Accessories	50
Furniture Repairs	100
Moving	100

[1] These items are represented in the "Derived" groups, because of the large proportion of purchases made in order to carry out a planned wardrobe or ensemble. The percentages are, of course arbitrary.

NOTES ON ESTIMATES AND CONCLUSIONS IN "AMERICA'S CAPACITY TO CONSUME"[1]

The above-named publication of the Brookings Institution presents national estimates of consumption expenditures and of savings by individuals in 1929 which are roughly comparable with our estimates for that year. Following is a tabular comparison:

TABLE 45.—COMPARATIVE OUTGO ESTIMATES FOR 1929
(In billions of current dollars)

From "America's Capacity to Consume"[1]		From the present study[2]	
Total Income (Outgo)	92.9	Total Outgo...............	89.4
Food......................	19.8	Food and Soft Drinks......	19.6
Attire.....................	11.1	Attire.....................	12.1[3]
Home......................	21.5	Home Maintenance........	22.4[4]
Other Living...............	22.7	All Other Expenditures.....	26.0
Savings...................	17.8	Savings...................	9.3

[1] Derived from tables on pp. 88, 260, 261 and 265.
[2] Derived from Appendix A.
[3] Clothing *plus* 50% of laundering and all of personal appearance.
[4] 50% of laundering transferred to the "attire" group.

The two food estimates are remarkably close. The classification of items under this head is almost self-evident; records are generally clear; and a well-marked regularity of relationship exists between size of income and spendings for food. It seems probable that the error at this point has been reduced to a small percentage.

"Attire," as defined in the Brookings Institution study, includes "amounts spent for clothing, jewelry, tonsorial service and toilet articles, and for the care of clothing" (p. 67). The items we have placed under the same heading appear to correspond fairly well with the Brookings grouping. Allowing for differences of classification, the two estimates are probably not far apart.

The Brookings grouping under "Home" and ours under "Home Maintenance" seem to cover the same main items except for house-

[1] Brookings, Washington, 1934.

320

hold supplies, which are not mentioned in the Brookings definition. Again, it appears that the two estimates would be likely to approach agreement if the classifications were uniform.

The remaining two estimates, however, are not so easily reconciled. The "Other Living" and the "All Other" groups show a rather wide divergence. The Brookings estimate for "Savings" is almost twice our figure. The discrepancy at this point cannot be explained as merely a matter of classification; for this term, like "Food," is clearly defined by everyday usage.

PROCEDURE IN FORMING THE BROOKINGS ESTIMATES

In order to locate the sources of the discrepancies it is necessary to compare briefly the distinct methods used in preparing the two sets of estimates of aggregate national expenditures by consumers. Our method, as fully described in preceding appendixes, consists mainly of building up estimates from census records of output and from other records of receipts and transactions. The results are checked (in Chapter X) against family budget studies; plausible relationships appear in respect to food, clothing, and home maintenance.

The Brookings method consists of deriving national estimates from family budget studies through two main steps:

1. Expenditures of groups of families on various income levels "were plotted as functions of income," and readings from the charted plottings (after certain adjustments) were taken as estimates of average family outgo at designated income levels for six major classes of objects (pp. 254–259).

2. Aggregate national expenditures were then calculated by "applying the average amount spent by families in the various income classes . . . to the number of families in each class, as estimated in Chapter V" (p. 82). The last reference is to an estimate of distribution of the national income among families which will be discussed below.

Obviously the method is far from exact and involves a large number of unsupported judgments. It is not fairly open to criticism on that score, however, for inadequacy of data is common to all estimates of national income and expenditure. Much more serious objections arise when the fundamental procedure is examined.

ALLOCATION OF OUTGO

The weaknesses of family budget studies as a base for estimates of national outgo have been stated in Chapter I. The reasons there listed are believed to be sufficient in themselves to justify rejecting the family budget method of formulating such estimates. In addition, the Brookings procedure introduces other grave drawbacks.

1. The "limited number" (apparently less than twenty) of surveys of family expenditures found suitable are scattered through the thirteen years 1918–1930;

and they are taken as they stand without correction for price changes or for changes in habits of consumption during the period.   The last-mentioned defect, on the strength of our findings, probably affected only slightly the estimates for food and clothing; but it cannot be dismissed so easily when we come to estimates for homes, other living expenses (including transportation) and savings, all of which are strongly influenced by changing consumption habits. Even more vital is the failure to take into account sweeping alterations in price relationships, particularly those affecting rentals, automobile transportation and savings.[2]

2. The expenditures of farm families, constituting 23% of all families, are derived from only six budget studies at various times during the 1924–1930 period; and the records are accepted uncritically without plainly needed corrections for outgo of a business nature.   "The savings of farmers, in these surveys, include income reinvested in their farm properties, and the net increase in their herds of livestock" (p. 78).   One consequence is a wholly incredible showing that farm families with incomes about $4,000 save from half to two-thirds of their incomes.

3. The expenditures of families with incomes above $6,000 are apportioned on the basis of three small surveys supplemented by a "widely distributed" questionnaire (pp. 78–80, 248–249, 254–255).   Questionnaires are notoriously unreliable sources.   This particular questionnaire was sent out in 1933; it purports to yield records for the calendar year 1929.   According to the Brookings study, the families in this group, though constituting only 6% of all families, received approximately 37% of the income of all families in 1929.   These percentages may be high; but even after discounting them liberally, we still find ourselves dealing here with a large segment of the national income.   One showing from the questionnaire returns, which has an important bearing on estimates of aggregate national outgo, is that the average savings of income groups above $6,000 ranged from a low of 20% to a high of nearly 50%.   This showing is dated, be it remembered, 1929, a year characterized by big spendings in the early part and heavy stock market losses near the end.   It needs support, before it can properly be accepted, by better evidence than a few replies to a questionnaire.

4. The income of unattached individuals is apportioned by means of a series of arbitrary compromises between computations based on two widely disparate assumptions, both of which are untenable: (a) "that unattached individuals spend the same proportions of their incomes for the five major categories (food, attire, home, other living, and savings) as do families with the same amounts of income"; (b) "that unattached individuals spend the same proportions of their incomes for the five major categories as do families having the same income per capita" (pp. 85–87, 262–265).   This is indeed loose figuring from which to draw weighty conclusions:

The aggregate incomes apportioned by the procedure above sketched are:

---

[2] *Ibid.*, pp. 252–253.   In fairness, it should be observed that the authors call attention to these defects; but they deny them much significance and make no effort to correct them.

	Income (Billions of
Groups	Dollars)
1. Non-farm families with incomes below $6,000...........	41.5
2. Farm families with incomes below $6,000..............	7.0
3. Families with incomes above $6,000..................	28.5
4. Unattached individuals.............................	16.0
Total...	93.0

Of the four groups of estimates of expenditures, the first may reasonably be regarded as having a passable—though by no means a satisfying—factual basis. But the estimates for the other three groups, totaling over 55% of the whole, formed by the methods sketched above, can scarcely rank as anything better than crude guesswork.

The largest discrepancies between the Brookings estimates and our estimates of national expenditures center in two of the major categories. The following tabulation of the amounts (in billions of dollars) apportioned to the two categories in the Brookings study is enlightening.

Groups	"Other Living"	Savings
1. Non-farm families with incomes below $6,000	9.6	2.0
2. Farm families with incomes below $6,000...	1.0	1.3
3. Families with incomes above $6,000.......	8.0	11.8
4. Unattached individuals.................	4.2	2.6
Total...........................	22.8	17.7

Approximately three-fifths of the "other living" category and nearly nine-tenths of savings are found in the three groups of estimates which are derived from especially scanty and questionable sources.

It is worth while to carry this line of analysis one step farther. The number of families enjoying incomes of $20,000 or more is calculated (p. 261) to be 219,000. The only data for apportioning their outgo is supplied by 44 replies to the questionnaire above mentioned (p. 255). On this slender and exceedingly doubtful foundation is erected an estimate of savings by these families and unattached individuals in corresponding income classes totaling 9.7 billion dollars, or 55% of the grand total of savings by all families and individuals.

One cannot properly ignore, in appraising estimates of savings derived from family budget records, the strong likelihood that the item as reported is in many cases a residual; that is, it is the unaccounted-for balance after known consumptive expenditures have been set down. The Brookings study at one point recognizes this tendency: "There were withdrawals from savings by families and individuals for purposes that were considered to be unusual, and hence not reported in surveys of family income and expenditures—such, for example, as a long vacation, a trip abroad, or exceptional educational or medical expense" (p. 89). These so-called "withdrawals from savings" are all in fact consumptive expenditures improperly classified as savings.

The study also grants that: "The figures for savings are less reliable than those for the four types of living expense. This is due in part to the greater variation in savings . . . . and in part to the fact that errors in the reporting of living expenses in the original collection of data are also reflected in the figures of savings" (p. 258). Unfortunately scarcely a hint of these well-founded doubts creeps into the subsequent deductions.

DISTRIBUTION OF INCOME

The national aggregates of categories of expenditures are obtained in the Brookings study, as we have seen, by multiplying the spendings ascribed to the typical family of each income group by the number of families in the corresponding income group as shown in the distribution of income which is presented in another part of the study. In order to appraise the validity of the estimates of national expenditures, therefore, we are forced to examine the soundness of the Brookings distribution. This estimate is important in itself; for it has a direct bearing on current problems of "social justice." Our immediate concern, however, is only with the influence of the distribution of income estimate on the outgo estimate, and particularly on the Brookings figure for savings.

For the distribution of income estimate a peculiar definition of national income is adopted in the Brookings study. It includes not only realized income in the forms of wages, salaries, rents, and interest, plus imputed income on owned homes, but also capital gains from the sale of property. The last-named element is admitted to be questionable: "The distribution contains profits from the sale of property, which may or may not be considered as income, depending upon the point of view and upon the purpose for which the figures are to be used. The major portion of these profits was in the higher incomes" (p. 209).[3]

---

[3] A more extended explanation and defense of the inclusion of capital gains appears on p. 145. The authors here go so far as to grant that "the spurious nature of much of this income [i.e., profits from sale of property], even insofar as individuals are concerned, is well recognized" and that "if a choice were possible, we would be inclined to leave capital gains out of consideration." Yet they proceed to put them in on the excuse that the customary income accounts of individuals include profits from the sale of property—an assumption which seems highly improbable and in any case is irrelevant to what purports to be an estimate of distribution of national income.

This is scarcely an adequate statement of the whole truth. The inclusion of capital gains in authoritative estimates of national income, whether in this country or abroad, is certainly unusual and perhaps unprecedented. Capital gains have been generally, if not universally, treated as essentially the ephemeral results of revaluations arising out of widespread shifts in the price level of securities, real estate, and other assets. Hence, the gains of some years are offset by the losses of other years. To take them into account in one year of extravagant inflation, such as 1929, is to create a distorted picture. The degree of distortion is far from negligible. The Brookings figure for capital gains in 1929 is 6.2 billion dollars, nearly 7% of the total estimated income of 93 billion dollars.

Furthermore, it is not merely the "major portion of these profits" that is assigned to the higher incomes; more than 96% goes to incomes over $10,000 and more than 60% to incomes over $100,000 (pp. 206–208). Obviously, the effect is to raise enormously the amounts attributed to high incomes—lifting those above $10,000 from 17.5 billion dollars to 23 billion dollars, or 31%, and those above $100,000 from 6 billion dollars to 10 billion dollars, or 65%.

The distribution of income estimate begins with a calculation of the number of income recipients in each income class. The calculation takes into account non-occupational income which "in the upper brackets came . . . to a large extent from profits on the sale of securities" (p. 220). The next step is to translate distribution of individual incomes into distribution of family incomes. The crux of the problem here is to allocate to families the earnings of extra workers or other income recipients in the 8,600,000 families which obtain income from persons other than the head of the family. The problem is not new. It has been prominent in this country since the publication of Macaulay's estimate of the distribution of the national income of 1918 among income recipients; and it has been more than once attacked by competent statisticians and given up as insoluble with the data in hand.[4] Hence, the Brookings solution is quite properly to be approached with a certain degree of caution.

The solution consists in substance of calculating separately the distribution of incomes of heads of families and the distribution of supplemental incomes of families; then adding to each income group in the first distribution the average income of the corresponding group in the second distribution (pp. 223–226). Obviously the solution implies two assumptions: (a) that the ratio of supplemental incomes per family is uniform

---

[4] See "Income in the United States," Part III, by Frederick R. Macaulay, National Bureau of Economic Research, New York, 1922, p. 342: "We would have attempted its construction [i.e., the construction of distribution of income among actual biological families] had the data been adequate for such a purpose."

for different income classes (up to $15,000 in the Brookings calculation); and (b) that the sizes of suplemental incomes are roughly proportionate to the incomes of heads of families. These assumptions are unsupported and run counter to everyday observations.

It would probably be nearer the truth to assume that supplemental income recipients (chiefly women workers in shops and offices) are more frequently found in low income than in higher income families and that supplemental incomes with few exceptions cluster quite closely around a low median figure. If the suggested assumptions had been taken as a basis, a much larger number of the families statistically placed (in the Brookings estimate) in the small income groups would have been raised to middle income groups by the greater allowance for supplemental incomes. In the absence of solid ground for judgment, it is impracticable to propose an acceptable correction. Quite evidently, however, the unproved assumptions at the base of the Brookings estimate tend to nullify the effect, which would be reasonably attributed to supplemental earnings, of increasing chiefly the incomes of low income families.

Numerous other questions might well be raised in a more extended review. But for the immediate purpose it is enough to call attention to the two major distortions discussed above, namely: (a) the exaggeration of high incomes by adding to them almost all the estimated 6.2 billion dollars of capital gains, chiefly the speculative profits realized in an inflation year; (b) the undervaluation of low incomes by failing to make adequate allowance for the relatively large weight of supplemental earnings in low income families. The joint result is to warp the estimate of distribution, both of numbers of families and of their aggregate incomes, to a degree that creates a seriously distorted picture of the relative weights of income classes.

ESTIMATES OF AGGREGATE SAVINGS IN 1929

The effects on the Brookings estimate of savings—and to a smaller extent on the estimate of "other living" expenditures—are unmistakable. Counting capital gains as income automatically carries with it a considerable shifting of families from middle income to high income classes. At the same time failure to allow adequately for supplementa earnings in low income families bars their being shifted upward into the next higher income classes. The number of families to which a large ratio of savings is attributed is raised, while the number to which a small ratio is attributed is cut down. In short, extravagant figures for savings of typical families, especially those above the $6,000 level, are multiplied by an excessive number of families on the higher levels, creating a quite incredible estimate of aggregate savings. On the other hand, the estimate of savings by middle income classes may be too low.

The summary of savings by income classes (p. 95) is sufficient in itself to cause hesitation. According to the summary, in 1929 American families in the aggregate saved 20% of their incomes; non-farm families with incomes of $3,000 to $6,000 saved 14%; those in the $6,000 to $10,000 group, 24%; and those receiving from $10,000 up, 47% (ranging from 36% to 66%). Anyone who recalls vividly the spending and saving standards of 1929 can form his own opinion of the plausibility of such percentages. At the least, one is justified in seeking for stronger statistical evidence before accepting them.

TREND OF SAVINGS

On the shaky foundation of estimated savings in 1929, supplemented by some casual assumptions, the Brookings study builds an airy super-structure called "The Trend in Savings, 1900–29" (Chapter IX). The general conclusion of the chapter is: "It appears that the economic developments during the first three decades of the present century have not only increased the ease with which national savings may be made, but have in general speeded up the rate of savings" (p. 111). One of the authors of the study (Dr. Clark Warburton in footnote, p. 111) expresses the opinion that the conclusion "does not seem to me to be adequately supported by the data presented." His four criticisms, in point of fact, so completely undermine the whole chapter that only brief additional comments on the underlying assumptions are needed.

Assumed ratios of savings to incomes. It is put forward as "a self-evident proposition that, as people's incomes expand, they are in a position to save more" (p. 101). Literally speaking, this is true; but in the rest of the chapter the original proposition transforms itself into an assumption that as people's incomes expand, they actually do save more, which is a different and a highly doubtful statement. The proposition is equally self-evident that, as people's incomes expand, they are in a position to spend more—specifically, for automobiles, amusements, beauty treatments, and innumerable other items that may be more attractive than savings. In 1918–1919, for example, unusual social pressure was being applied to induce people to buy Liberty Bonds; and at that time the spending habits developed during the succeeding decade were relatively weak. To assume, as the Brookings study does, that "on the average the percentages of income saved by individuals in the different income groups were the same in 1918–19 as in 1929" is to ignore plain facts.

Assumed "increasing inequality" of distribution of income. "While the proportion of high incomes was increasing," says the Brookings study (p. 104), "there is evidence that the incomes of those at the very top were increasing still more rapidly." The evidence is not presented. The statement runs directly counter to King's conclusion as to the period 1914–1926: "It appears that there is some slight tendency toward a concentration both of numbers of persons and of income in the prosperous class having incomes in 1926 between $8,309 and

$41,543 but that there is practically no tendency towards the putting of more income into the hands of the extremely opulent sections of the community."[5] The statement is scarcely consistent, also, with the showing in the Brookings study itself (p. 158) that a rising proportion of the national production income flowed to employees. If new evidence on this important question is really available, it should be set forth. Meanwhile, the assertion of "increasing inequality" is at best no more than an unsupported hypothesis.

Assumed persistence of capital gains regarded as income. Exception has been taken above to the inclusion of capital gains in a computation of national income. Now a related, yet distinct question arises. If capital gains are to be included, surely their fluctuations ought to be taken into account in any examination of the *trends* of savings. Let it be remembered that capital gains in 1929 were very large and that more than 96% of them are ascribed in the Brookings study to incomes over $10,000, which are also the sources, according to the study, of 67% of aggregate savings by families (p. 93). The study refers to capital gains as coming "chiefly from bank credit expansion" (p. 12) and as "inflationary profits" (p. 104). Yet when it comes to appraising long-term trends of savings no allowance is made for the exceptional and temporary inflation of the boom years. The implied assumption is that capital gains constitute a persistent factor in savings, while *per contra* capital losses are unheard of. The absurdity of the assumption needs no demonstration.

The conclusion of the chapter as to the assertedly accelerating rate of savings (quoted above) rests, then, on three unwarranted, if not wholly fallacious, assumptions. The conclusion is controverted by the estimates of annual savings set forth elsewhere in this book (Appendix D).

OTHER UNFOUNDED CONCLUSIONS

"How much can we consume?" asks Chapter X of the Brookings study. One might reasonably expect as the answer a calculated, realistic evaluation of probable consumption under hypothetical, but feasible conditions. What is offered is a fanciful picture of a society in which the minimum family income is $2,500 (presumably in 1929 dollars) while the output of consumers' goods has been miraculously enlarged to the level required in order to supply the resultant increased demands. Whatever relationship exists between income and productivity—and certainly there is *some* relationship—is blandly disregarded. If it be granted as a plausible surmise that an unknown but sizable proportion of the families below the $2,500 level in 1929 remained poor because they lacked either the capacity or the willingness to do hard, effective work, then it follows that increasing their incomes would not enlarge production; on the contrary, insofar as it diminished the urge to work, it would cut down production. This statement, though

[5] "The National Income and Its Purchasing Power," p. 180.

admittedly unpopular, will be found difficult to deny. The presupposed $2,500 minimum could be attained, then, in only two ways: either by taking the necessary amount from well-to-do families, which is not provided for in the Brookings hypothesis; or by realizing gains in machine productivity well beyond those envisaged in the Brookings study, "America's Capacity to Produce." It may be said that the sole purpose of the chapter is to show in concrete terms a potential demand for a larger output than that of 1929. Even so, it seems regrettable that a more closely reasoned, realistic answer was not presented.

The regret is accentuated when we come to the "fundamental conclusions" of the study and discover that the hypothesis of a $2,500 minimum income apparently grows out of a preconception which may have influenced the entire study. Introduced without explanation is the alleged "fact that the purchasing power of the great masses of the population is quite inadequate to absorb, at the prices prevailing, the output of our productive establishment" (p. 132). If the statement refers, as it presumably does, to the period under survey in the Brookings study—that is, to a period of widespread prosperity when productive facilities, according to "America's Capacity to Produce," were as fully utilized as at any time in our recent history—it is a patent absurdity. It is amazing to find the popular delusion of inadequate purchasing power—which derives its authority mainly from incessant repetition— labeled "fact" in a scientific report. It has no factual basis whatever in the findings of the Brookings study. It is a glaring non-sequitur worth citing chiefly because it illuminates the viewpoint and motivation of the study.

The ultimate aim of the series of studies by the Brookings Institution now in progress, the authors explain, is to lead up to "a consideration of the means which may possibly be devised for bringing about such a distribution of current annual income as will promote a more efficiently functioning and developing economic organization" (p. 133). The conclusion that distribution of income is the key to a balanced, efficient economy has evidently been pre-formed. It is a conclusion that demands searching analysis before it is accepted. Statistical studies pointing toward a foregone conclusion are rightly received with more than ordinary skepticism.

SUMMARY

1. The Brookings estimates of outgo per family in various income groups rest upon a few scattered samples of family budgets which furnish insufficient data for national figures; this comment applies with especial force to the figures for savings drawn mainly from the least trustworthy samples.

2. The estimated distribution of national income among income classes is distorted by (a) the inclusion of capital gains in national income and (b) an unreasonable allocation of supplemental incomes to families; the distortion tends to magnify the groups to which very large savings are attributed, and this effect is only slightly offset by minimizing the middle income groups to which small to moderate savings are attributed.

3. The major errors in both the foregoing estimates combine to create a highly exaggerated estimate of savings.

4. The statements in the Brookings study as to the trend of savings are the products of assumptions which are certainly questionable and probably untrue.

5. Some of the general conclusions are mere assertions unsupported even by the doubtful estimates for one year set forth in the study. They do not strengthen confidence in the unbiased soundness of the study.

6. The American public has a right to expect from the Brookings Institution something better than this extraordinary tissue of groundless assumptions, twisted statistics and preconceived dogmas.

INDEX

331

Waldron, G. B., 54

Wants, as conditioning increased production, 178, 187
essential wants in industrialized countries not widely dissimilar, 158
five major defined, 90
at high-level, 188
knowledge of, needed for forecasts, 88, 101
measured by takings, 89
in relation to focal points, 107
spending power, 99
relative strength of, 96
as stabilizers, 103

War, changes in fashions and, 141
effect on takings, 80
increased acceptance of new products since, 144
uniformed men as cause of clothing decrease, 81

Warburton, Clark, 18n, 19n, 246n, 261, 262, 327

Warren, George F., 69n

Waters, Lewis W., 202n

Whitehead, Alfred N., 102, 181

Whitehead, T. N., 181n

Wholesaling, over-all gross margins, 260

Wickens, David L., 293

Winslow, Emma A., 91, 154n

Withholdings, decline in free-spendables, 95
definition, 17, 280
dispensability, 127
elasticity, 122
factors governing real worth, 67–69
forecast, 198–199
increase, post-war, 80
in inflationary or deflationary period, 68, 282–283
irregular ratio to total outgo, 26–28
low volume in 1929, 203
residual, 196
trends of, 45, 81
variability, 132

Wolman, Leo, 267

Woods, Struther & Co., 292n

Wood, E. E., 274n

Woodhouse, Charles Going, 54n

Woolen goods, allocation, 251
competition in, 138
shoddy imitations in, 143

Work, distaste for, expressed in three forms, 178

Workers, changes in prices of budget items, 70
number per family, 62
weighted budgets for, understate real wages, 74